Real-Life READING ACTIVITIES for Grades 6-12

JAMES F. SILVER

Professor Emeritus in Residence at the College of New Jersey

JOSSEY-BASS
A Wiley Imprint
www.josseybass.com

Published by Jossey-Bass
A Wiley Imprint
989 Market Street, San Francisco, CA 94103-1741   www.josseybass.com

Jossey-Bass books and products are available through most bookstores. To contact Jossey-Bass directly
call our Customer Care Department within the U.S. at 800-956-7739, outside the U.S. at 317-572-3986
or fax 317-572-4002.

Jossey-Bass also publishes its books in a variety of electronic formats. Some content that appears in
print may not be available in electronic books.

Library of Congress Cataloging-in-Publication Data
Silver, James F.
        Real life reading activities for grades 6-12 : over 200 ready-to-
    use lessons & activities to help students master practical reading
    skills / James F. Silver
        p.   cm.
        ISBN 0-13-044460-X
        1. Reading (Secondary)—United States.   2. Reading (Middle school)—
    United States.   3. Education, Secondary—Activity programs—
    United States.   4. content area reading—United States.   I. Title.
    LB1632.S49   2002
    428.4'071'2—dc21   02-12632

FIRST EDITION
PB Printing 10 9 8 7 6 5 4

DEDICATION

This book is dedicated to . . .

◆ *Edith, my wife, a teacher—one who has supported, encouraged, and advised me not only in the writing of this book, but also in all things I undertake to accomplish;*

◆ *Beverly, my daughter, a professional business person and on-going student—one whose love, devotion, and joy of life are contagious to me and all who know her;*

◆ *Pamela, my daughter, a teacher—one who is loyal, steadfast, and a model of strength, courage, and endurance for all with whom she has contact;*

◆ *Lorna Jean, my daughter, a professional writer and editor—one whose keen intelligence, exceptional insights, responsibility, and search for perfection have helped me to write this book;*

◆ *Frank, my son, a builder—one who possesses uncommon ability to take something from its very beginning and carry it through until the product of his mind and skill become a reality and a source of satisfaction and pleasure to others.*

J.F. Silver

ACKNOWLEDGMENTS

Several individuals and publishing houses have been of immeasurable help in the creation of *Real-Life Reading Activities for Grades 6–12*.

Steve Busti, a graduate of The College of New Jersey, drew most of the maps and several diagrams in the book. Steve has the ability to include detail in his maps yet keep them clear and easy to read.

David Evanetz, free-lance artist, drew most of the illustrations in the book. Artist Evanetz has the rare ability to create illustrations that are remarkable for their accuracy, appropriateness, and clarity.

Lorna Jean Elliot, who received her B.A. in English from Susquehanna University, PA, and her M.A. in English from the Bread Loaf School of English, Middlebury College, VT, edited the entire manuscript and answer key. Her ability to detect errors and to offer suggestions for correction, clarification, and improvement has been most helpful.

Mary Salerno, a graduate of The College of New Jersey School of Business, who is now a free-lance computer and desktop publishing professional, made ready the entire book, including all of the charts, graphs, tables, and diagrams. She was able to take rough sketches and descriptions and enhance them through the application of her technical skill, resourcefulness, and creativity.

Special thanks are given to Silver Burdett Ginn, Simon and Schuster Education Group, for permission to use illustrations from books published by them. The illustrations used are from the books listed below; the numbers at the end of each listing tell on which pages the illustrations appear in *Real-Life Reading Activities for Grades 6–12*.

- *Learning About Latin America*, James F. Silver, © 1967, Silver Burdett Company, page 132
- *United States Yesterday and Today*, James F. Silver, © 1968, Ginn and Company, pages 17, 126, 127, 133, 134
- *The Changing New World*, James F. Silver, © 1963, Silver Burdett Company, page 131

ABOUT THE AUTHOR

James F. Silver received his B.A. in Social Studies from Montclair University, Montclair, NJ; his M.A. in History from Boston University; his M.A. in Educational Administration from Montclair University; and his Ed.D. in Curriculum and Instruction from Pacific Western University in Los Angeles. Professor Silver also studied the psychology of reading at Temple University in Philadelphia, which led to his New Jersey state certification as a reading specialist.

Professor Silver's experience includes nine years as an elementary school teacher and principal in Morris County, New Jersey, and more than 35 years in the School of Education at The College of New Jersey, where he is now Professor Emeritus in Residence.

During his educational career, Professor Silver has written numerous teacher's manuals, geography and history skill development books, and achievement tests for Silver Burdett Company. He also wrote the two-volume *United States Yesterday and Today* for Ginn and company. He is author of *Geography Skills Activity Kit*, *World Geography Activities*, *American History Activities*, and *The American Continents*—all published by The Center for Applied Research in Education. Previous to *American History Activities*, he authored *Environmental Awareness*, published by Kendall/Hunt Company. The last five books cited above were written on the professional level for in-service teachers.

ABOUT THIS RESOURCE

Reading may be defined as the mental act of assigning meaning to symbols and then relating those symbols to arrive at a complete thought. This definition, then, goes beyond deriving meaning only from printed *words*: there are numerous other kinds of symbols that convey meaning. For example, a circled dot (◉) on a map can stand for a *city*. If the circled dot is located adjacent to a line that is the symbol for *river* (◉) we can relate the symbols and read, "The city is on a river." The circle/dot symbol could tell the approximate population of the city, according to the key of the map. Other symbols could tell us that the city is located on the north side of the river, and so on. The psychological process used in reading the map is the same process that is used when reading words.

Diagrams, charts, tables, pictures, cartoons, maps, and graphs all utilize symbols to represent meaning. A cartoon may represent the United States by such symbols as "Uncle Sam," the American flag, or the American eagle. A picture graph may utilize silhouettes as symbols for humans, animals, automobiles, and so on. A graph may utilize symbols that represent population. On charts and diagrams symbols may be found that represent a hierarchy of authority as, for example, the organization of a state or federal government.

Reading is obviously related to research. Symbols, and not only word symbols, are often used in reporting the results of research, especially in experiments in which drawings are used to show locations, sequences, quantities, and results. Those who are interested in studying scientific reports will have to recognize and interpret symbols to understand the reports.

Which came first, reading or writing? Probably writing; it is obvious that no reading could take place if there were no writing. If one's writing is to be effective, one must have command of all the ways there are to convey meaning via symbols. As an example, could American Indian petroglyphs be interpreted if archaeologists didn't have the ability to interpret symbols? And, the dots and dashes of the International Code are symbols of yet another kind that give us information.

All of the above examples show the need for a broad approach to teaching reading. Although systematic instruction is given to recognizing and interpreting printed words, consistent, planned instruction in other forms of communication in which symbols are used is often neglected. If instruction in reading and using alternative symbols is given, it is given sporadically or spontaneously as situations arise. Lack of consistent, planned instruction in nonword symbols is one reason why many students do not do well on achievement tests that test reading ability. For example, the interpretation of symbols in one form or another exists in all of the divisions of the Iowa Tests of Basic Skills—16 pages of this achievement test are concerned with reading and interpreting maps, graphs, and tables.

Suggestions for Using This Resource

Real-Life Reading Activities for Grades 6–12 is organized into seven major sections. They are:

- Section 1: Reading for Deeper Meanings (R), 26 pages
- Section 2: Reading and Vocabulary (RV), 26 pages
- Section 3: Reading Diagrams/Charts, Tables and Graphs (RD/C, RT, RG), 61 pages.
- Section 4: Reading Pictures/Cartoons and Maps (RP/C, RM), 48 pages
- Section 5: Reading and Study Skills (RSS), 20 pages
- Section 6: Reading and Its Writing Connection (RW), 26 pages
- Section 7: Reading and Research (RR), 20 pages

For purposes of easy identification, each of the pages in the book is numbered traditionally and has an abbreviated identification, as may be seen in the above listing. For example, the first page of the "Reading for Deeper Meanings" section is R–1 on page 2, the eighth page in the "Reading and Study Skills" section is RSS–8 on page 179, and so on.

Instructor's Pages

There are 74 instructor's pages in *Real-Life Reading Activities for Grades 6–12*. These pages are designed to be helpful to instructors in their teaching of particular skills. For example, page R–13, "Guidelines for Distinguishing Between Fact and Opinion," lists words and phrases that are indicators of whether the information that will follow is opinion or fact. Each of the cautionary words and phrases are exemplified in sentences. Thus, the instructor has some ready-made help to prepare students for the up-coming application page. It is important to note also that most of the instructor's pages can be adapted for use as student application pages.

Textual features that instructors may find helpful are listed:

- Extra information, explanations, and suggestions that include and go beyond activities on the student application pages

- Diagrams and other graphics that may be made into transparencies

- Additional activities to supplement those on the student application pages

- A complete answer key for all student application pages (in the Appendix)

Student Application Pages

There are 152 student application pages in *Real-Life Reading Activities for Grades 6–12*. These pages are designed to provide intense activities in a particular skill. For example, RR–11, "Basic Reference Books," lists and describes eight widely used reference books such as *The World Almanac and Book of Facts*, *Reader's Guide to Periodical Literature*, and others. The student activity consists of 14 questions that require students to decide which reference they would use to find answers to the questions. Following this student page is another page modeled on TV's JEOPARDY! game. Students use appropriate references so that they may compose a question that fits the stated facts, as, for example, "This large island (?) south of Australia is the home of some animals not found anywhere else." Question to be asked, "Where is Tasmania?"

Because skills are best taught in contextual situations, efforts have been made to include subject matter that is vital and interesting and, perhaps, supplemental to what is being studied in the regular curriculum. Hence, *Real-Life Reading Activities for Grades 6–12* contains numerous student activities that are concerned with Earth's environment. Example environment-centered page titles are listed here:

- RD/C–4: "Dangers Birds Face"
- RD/C–13: "Understanding Windbreaks"
- RP/C–6: "An Abandoned Farm: Pictorial Facts and Inferences"
- RP/C–16: "Air Pollution Situations in Cartoons"

Systematic Instruction

Earlier in this foreword, mention was made of the need for systematic instruction in basic skills. A way to provide for this would be to set aside one or two class periods a week during which skill instruction would take place. In the course of a school year of some 40 weeks, students could make significant progress in developing skills applicable to their regular courses of study. One approach would be to take a particular section, for example, "Reading and Vocabulary," and work through it. Then, after its completion the class would begin another section such as "Reading and Study Skills." Concurrent with the skill development program, as many applications as possible should be made to the regular subject matter courses. For example, in the section on study skills, the Main Idea/Detail (MI/D) study method is explained and exemplified. After completing the application pages related to the method, students could be directed to use the method on a portion of a textbook they are using. The same kind of application could be made after the students have been exposed to the application page that explains how to use—and provides practice in—mnemonic techniques that aid retention and recall of events, processes, and other kinds of information.

Table of Contents

SECTION 3: READING DIAGRAMS/CHARTS, TABLES AND GRAPHS 57

Reading Diagrams/Charts (RD/C)

SECTION 4: READING PICTURES/CARTOONS AND MAPS 121

SECTION 5: READING AND STUDY SKILLS 171

<u>Reading and Study Skills (RSS)</u>

SECTION 6: READING AND ITS WRITING CONNECTION 193

<u>Reading and Its Writing Connection (RW)</u>

NOTES

Section 1: Reading for Deeper Meanings

UNDERSTANDING EYE MOVEMENTS

Understanding how the eyes function as they move across a line of print can prove helpful to readers. Such knowledge can lead to more efficient and effective reading.

Ask your students to respond to the following true-or-false statement: "As we read across a line of print our eyes move continuously from left to right."

Don't be surprised if students answer true. However, the statement is false. Many people do not realize that their eyes make a series of stops as they move across a line. This has been proved beyond a doubt by many researchers.*

That the eyes stop several times as they attack a line of print can be seen by watching someone's eyes as the person reads. Ask someone to read a few lines. Be sure the person's head is not bowed down but is held up so that the eyes are easily seen. Not only will eye-stops (fixations) be readily observable, but also the return sweep to the beginning of the next line will be obvious. During the return sweep there will be no fixations because no reading is taking place.

There is a more scientific and accurate way of observing eye movements through the use of an eye-movement camera.* Following is an explanation of how the camera works. Refer to Figure 1 as the sequences are explained.

1. The subject is seated at a table on which the camera has been placed.

2. Reading material printed on a card is positioned in a card holder.

3. A light within the camera is focused on the reader's eyes. The light in no way interferes with the reader's vision.

4. A blank roll of film is placed in a holder.

5. When a switch is thrown the film starts rolling and the reader starts reading.

6. The light is reflected from the reader's eyes to the moving film.

7. Each time the reader makes a fixation, a vertical line is made on the film. When the reader's eyes make a side movement (interfixation) to the next portion of print, a horizontal line is made on the film.

8. At the end of the line the eyes move left, return sweep, to the beginning of the next line. The return sweep will also be recorded on the film.

9. Assume that the lines of print contain the following sentence:

"(People read)(along)(a line)(of print)(in a) (series)(of eye-stops,)(or fixations.)"

A count of the dots, each of which stands for a fixation, shows that there were 8 fixations.

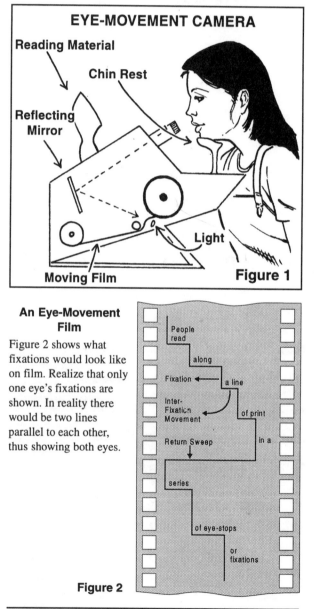

EYE-MOVEMENT CAMERA

Reading Material
Chin Rest
Reflecting Mirror
Light
Moving Film
Figure 1

An Eye-Movement Film

Figure 2 shows what fixations would look like on film. Realize that only one eye's fixations are shown. In reality there would be two lines parallel to each other, thus showing both eyes.

People read
along
Fixation — a line
Inter-Fixation Movement
of print
Return Sweep
in a
series
of eye-stops
or fixations

Figure 2

* Educational Development Laboratories (EDL) has been a pioneer in developing the eye-movement camera and in performing basic research on the mechanics of the reading act.

HELPING READERS TO BE MORE EFFICIENT AND EFFECTIVE

1. Some facts relative to eye movements and the eye-movement camera and films:

a.   The length of the vertical line on the film is an indicator of how long it took to make the fixation.

b.   The length of the horizontal line is an indicator of how much print was "taken in" during the fixation.

c.   The nature of the return sweep—straight, bowed-down, bowed-up, swooping up and down—is an indicator of the efficiency of the movement to the next line of print.

d.   A regression is a leftward movement of the eyes while reading along a line of print. A regression may go back to a previous word or several words.

Regression

2.   Comments relative to eye movements:

a.   There is not much that one can do to widen the span of recognition, that is, the amount that one can see in a fixation. This is a physical problem that has to do with limitations of the eyes.

b.   The duration of fixation can be shortened with practice. Also, the difficulty of the material being read is an important factor in duration.

c.   Regressions are among the most serious negative, yet repairable, elements of the reading act. Eye- movement studies have shown that the average sixth-grader reading grade material makes 25 regressions for every 100 words read. This means that 25% of the time is spent in regressions.*

Very often, regression is a habit formed in children's early reading experiences when binocular control, insecurity, and the inability to sight-recognize words is present. Children are taught, and rightly so, that when they do not recognize a word they should "sound it out" phonetically. This procedure is helpful to understanding, but it also has the effect of causing numerous fixations on a single word. An Educational Developmental Laboratory publication reports that the average first-grade child makes 224 fixations per 100 words.

3.   Suggestions for helping students read more efficiently and effectively:

a.   Reading that is done for a specific purpose will bring better results than reading that has no specific purpose. If students are told, for example, to read to determine the cause of the so-called "Boston Massacre"—and if they are committed to that purpose—their reading will probably bring better results in both understanding and speed.

In this regard, it is good practice for students to read the questions found after sections and at the end of chapters before reading the selection. This will result in reading for purposes. The questions and answers will make impressions, consciously and unconsciously, as students read.

b.   Train students to survey/skim a selection before thorough reading. The survey/skim might include reading topic headings, first sentences of paragraphs, and noting graphics such as pictures and diagrams. This activity develops a readiness for reading the selection in its entirety.

c.   To help break inefficient reading habits, encourage students to read materials that are relatively simple and uncomplicated. If this is done often enough and with the purpose of breaking old habits and developing new ones, students can make considerable progress.

d.   Have students read orally only after they have read the material silently. Oral reading at sight has negative impacts on smooth, silent reading. Moreover, a poor oral reader "forces" other students to read just as poorly. In effect, the readers who are following the poor oral reader are practicing the poor reader's habits.

e.   Some materials do not have to be read word-for-word. These are the times when scanning is useful. For example, scanning takes place when one runs one's eyes down a column of names in a telephone directory to find a particular name. Scanning is a single-minded search for a particular bit of information.

Provide frequent opportunities for scanning to take place. For example, on a particular page tell students to find a definition of "lava," or to find the place where the explanations of tornadoes begins, or to find how many square acres there are in a square mile.

Scanning is also very useful after one has found page references in an index. Somewhere on the page the answer to the question or the desired information is to be found.

Eye Movements and Reading: Facts and Fallacies,
Educational Developmental Laboratories, Huntington, NY, 1963.

PRACTICE IN SCANNING I

The following activity will provide an opportunity for your students to practice scanning. Be sure they understand the following procedure: 1) Keep the single objective in mind; 2) Do not attempt to read the lines in full from left to right; 3) Run eyes down the column, perhaps zig-zagging slightly, until a clue or clues indicate the single objective has been located.

Procedure: Photocopy the reading material below the line. In a one-at-a-time sequence tell the students what it is they are trying to find. After they have located the item hands should be quietly raised. Wait until the majority of hands have been raised before soliciting responses.

To Find:

1. What percent of electrical energy was produced by wind action in the United States in a recent year? (Less than 1%)

2. How many wind generators are there in California? (7,500)

To Find:

1. What is the sun's surface temperature? (11,000°F)

2. What causes plants to undergo changes that convert them to fossil fuels? (Weight)

3. Are ultraviolet rays from the sun visible? (No)

WIND ENERGY

The expression "free as the wind" is most often used to express freedom to do as one thinks is right or as one chooses, to come and go as one pleases, to choose one's life work, companions, and so on. Environmentally speaking, however, it could mean this: The wind is here to take—it's clean, it doesn't cost anything, no one is being deprived of property, and no matter how much is used the supply will never be diminished. So, more and more, we are taking this offer of "free" wind and using it to fulfill the world's ever-growing need for energy.

Wind action accounted for less than 1% of all the electricity generated in the United States in a recent year. Ninety-eight percent of that wind-generated electricity was produced by 7,500 generators in California. Wind is being used more and more each year, not only in California but all over the world.

SUN FACTS

☐ The sun is a star, one of millions of stars, and a small star at that. However, it is the star nearest to Earth. One star, Betelguese, is one million times larger.

☐ The sun is much larger than Earth—in fact, one million times larger. The sun's diameter is 865,000 miles, while Earth's is 7,921 miles.

☐ The temperature of the sun at its surface is about 11,000°F. Compare this with Earth's surface temperature, which rarely exceeds 110°F even in equatorial deserts.

☐ Millions of years ago giant ferns and other plants covered the earth. These plants stored up energy from the sun and used the energy to manufacture their own food. When the plants died they gradually sank into the ground. During the centuries this occurred thousands of times over. The tremendous weight of the decaying plants caused them to undergo changes that converted them to fossil fuels. So, when we burn coal, oil, and natural gas, we are really obtaining light, heat, and power that originally came from the sun.

☐ One day's solar energy is more than equal to the energy obtained by burning 500 million tons of coal.

☐ Ultraviolet rays from the sun are not visible, but they are very potent. It is these rays that cause suntanning and sunburn. Ultraviolet light is absorbed by plants and, in turn, enables them to make vitamin D. Without vitamin D, we would become sick and die.

Name: *Jennifer Carlson*   Date: _____

PRACTICE IN SCANNING II

The article below is written in "newspaper style." There is a major headline (large type), a subheadline (small type), and the name of the place where the story originated.

To Do:

1. Scan the article for answers to the very specific questions that follow. Remember: When scanning you should not read the whole article line-for-line.

2. Answer only one question at a time by scanning the article for the answer.

3. The questions you are to answer are not written in the order in which they are mentioned in the article.

Questions

1. What is the top speed of the electric car developed in New Jersey? _52 miles per hour_

2. About how many miles can the electric car go without a recharge? _60 miles_

3. What is one of the gases that results when gasoline or fuel oil is burned? _Carbon monoxide_

4. What is the name of the NJDEPE director who took the car for a trial spin? _Nancy Wittenburg_

5. Why might some people become impatient with the electric car at stop streets? _It does not have umph to accelerate_

ELECTRIC CARS ARE COMING

Pollution Emissions = Zero

Trenton, New Jersey

Imagine a car that has no engine, burns no gasoline, gives off no air pollutants, makes very little noise, and has practically no vibration. That's what is possible with a battery-powered automobile. What's more, there are hundreds of such vehicles now in use.

Ordinary automobiles burn gasoline or diesel fuel, and, when that happens, poisonous gases such as carbon monoxide, one of the gases that make smog, are released. The result is polluted air that can be harmful to your health.

Although progress has been made in reducing the gases given off by fuel-burning engines, it is doubtful that they will ever be perfect. So, the search is on for nonpolluting ways to power cars and trucks. The electric car may be the best solution to the problem. Car makers and state and federal governments are spending millions on researching ways to make practical, affordable battery-powered vehicles.

The New Jersey Department of Environmental Protection and Energy—NJDEPE for short—is experimenting with an electric car. You can see the car in and around the streets and roads of Trenton, N. J. You'll know the car when you see it. It's a minivan with the sign "Electric Powered" on a side panel. It probably won't be traveling in the fast lane of a highway, although it can go as fast as 52 miles an hour. You might get a little impatient if you are behind it at a stop street. The vehicle doesn't have a fast getaway.

Don't expect to hear the kind of roaring noise that ordinary vehicles make. The van's electric motor makes a soft, whining sound—something like the sound you hear coming from a refrigerator motor. As reported in *The Times* (Trenton, N. J.), Nancy Wittenberg, a director in the

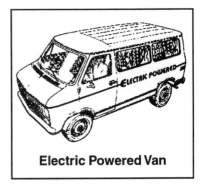

Electric Powered Van

NJDEPE, took the electric car for a spin. Afterwards she was quoted as saying, "There's no noise. It's very weird. But it's a regular van—nice, comfy seats, a radio and cassette player."

After about 60 miles on the road, the car's several batteries need recharging. No problem: just plug them into a special outlet outside your house or garage. Ms. Wittenberg spoke of the future when she said, "Someone's going to market an electric car with a long range, that's easy to recharge, and for a good price, and it's going to be successful." Let's hope she's right—we will all breathe easier.

GUIDELINES FOR PARAGRAPH TOPICS

1.   A paragraph is composed of a group of related sentences that are concerned about a particular point or topic. It is helpful to think of the topic of the paragraph as a title. As titles, topics should be stated in phrase form as compared to sentence form. If paragraphs are well written, their topics should be readily identifiable.

The following illustrates a paragraph that is concerned with one topic.

> Stamp collecting can help Americans to become more aware of and knowledgeable about their country's history. Many stamps show pictures of great historic leaders such as George Washington, Thomas Jefferson, Benjamin Franklin, Woodrow Wilson, and Dwight Eisenhower. There are many historic landmarks that are shown on stamps, including the Statue of Liberty and Mount Rushmore. Holidays receive considerable attention, for example, Independence Day and Memorial Day. Commemorative stamps give recognition to past and recent events: Olympic Games, the World War II invasion of Europe known as D-Day, and so on.

What would be a topic heading for this paragraph? Stamps would not be suitable because it is too general. The topic needs to tell what particular aspect of stamps is being discussed. On the other hand, Stamps of Historic Leaders, Landmarks, Holidays, and Commemorative Events is much too specific and detailed.

Stamps That Show Great Americans would not be a good topic for the paragraph because it singles out one aspect and does not include the other aspects. American History and Stamps is the best choice for a topic because it is short but inclusive enough to alert readers of the basic content of the paragraph.

If there is difficulty in identifying the topic of a paragraph, the fault might be that the paragraph is poorly written. Perhaps there are things mentioned in the paragraph that don't belong in the paragraph and serve to confuse the main point. Perhaps there are not enough specific details to support the topic heading.

2.   After the paragraph in the opposite column has been read and the explanations discussed, further practice in identifying paragraph topics should be helpful.

Read the paragraph below. Then ask students to consider the four suggested topics that follow it. Which of the topics is most suitable? Discuss each choice.

> In early September 1992, Hurricane Andrew struck southern Florida and the coast of the Gulf of Mexico west to Louisiana. The damage to roads, homes, businesses, communications, and agriculture has been estimated to be well over $15 billion. In terms of human misery, thousands of families were made homeless. People would have had difficulty surviving if it were not for aid from federal, state, and local governments; organizations such as the American Red Cross and the Salvation Army; and generous, caring citizens from all over the United States. Very prominent in the rendering of aid were components of the United States armed services.

Topic Choices

a.   The Red Cross to the Rescue (Not suitable: concerned with one detail)

b.   Charity Organizations, Armed Services, Government Agencies, Citizens Help Victims of Hurricane Andrew (Not suitable: too detailed)

c.   Hurricane Damages Florida (Not suitable: omits rescue operations)

d.   Aid for Hurricane Andrew Victims (Suitable: presents the two basic related elements)

Name: _Jennifer Carlson_ Date: _____

DETERMINING PARAGRAPH TOPICS

Remember that a well written paragraph is concerned with one topic. The sentences in the paragraph should all be related to the topic.

1. Read the two paragraphs that follow. Then decide which of the suggested topic choices best tells what the paragraph is about.

a. Mike was a rough-and-ready kind of athlete, one who before the school year was over had wrestled and pinned every boy in his class. He was the best runner, the best baseball player, and the one most likely to take a dare. He took karate lessons at the dojo on Windsor Street in Cornwall. He learned not only how to defend himself, but also how to give and command respect. He learned how to consider others and how to conduct himself modestly. The dojo master, Kesaka, once said of Mike, "Good boy. Concentrate. Work hard. Good feet. Smart hands."

___ Mike As an Athlete

___ Mike at the Karate Club

✓ Mike's Personal and Physical Qualities

___ Mike As a Runner, Baseball Player, and Karate Student

b. Mitzi bought a guitar at a flea market for only three dollars. When she bought it, it didn't have any strings, and four of the wind-up keys were missing. There was no way to replace the keys; they were not a standard make. So, her father carved new keys from wood. He refinished the instrument and bought new strings. The guitar was so beautiful and had such a fine sound that any professional musician would have been proud to own it.

___ Replacing Keys on a Broken Guitar

___ A Guitar with a Beautiful Sound

___ Mitzi's Guitar

✓ A Repaired Guitar for Mitzi

2. Read each of the paragraphs that follow. Then on the lines below the paragraphs write an appropriate topic for the paragraph.

a. Tom's large, wooden tool box was something he made himself. The box contained a variety of hand tools that he might need on a job. In special compartments of the box he stored a carpenter's square, a hammer, a saw, a variety of chisels and files, a wood plane, and a 24" level. From several compartments he could quickly pick up nail punches, stud finders, a sheetrock knife and extra blades, carpenter's pencils, an electric drill with drill bits, and an extension cord.

Topic: _Tom's Carpentry Box_

b. To make the school basketball team Pam knew she would have to practice very hard; she was only 5'5", and other candidates were taller and had the advantage of height. Every morning in the summer, before it became too warm, she practiced free throws from the foul line, dribbling, layups, and jump shots from every angle. After about 30 minutes of practice she jogged for three miles; she wanted to build up her wind and endurance.

Topic: _Pam's Basketball Dream_

c. Luke believed that his parents shouldn't have to give him an allowance each week. He was determined to get a job—possibly delivering newspapers—and earn his own money. If he had a job he would be able to save some money. He would be able to buy some of the things he needed: new bike, clothing, even a computer of his own. He knew his mother wanted a new toaster; he could get her one for her birthday. He had an idea for a gift for his father, too. Luke had heard him say he wished he had a battery-operated hand drill. His brother, Jesse, was constantly looking at the soccer balls in the sports shop. Luke realized he could not get all those things at once, but he could buy them one by one if he had a job.

Topic: _Luke's Job_

GUIDELINES FOR PARAGRAPH MAIN IDEAS

1. Topics tell the general nature of a paragraph, whereas main ideas explain more about the topic. Most often the main idea is stated in the first sentence of a paragraph. It's a kind of forecast of what is to come. Here is an example:

In handwriting analysis, one of the most productive indicators of personality is the cursive letter "t". A long, strong, and upward-moving crossing of the letter is indicative of enthusiasm, optimism, and enduring effort.[1] A "t" that is crossed above the stem is indicative of idealism and hopefulness, the degree of which is determined by how far above the stem the crossing is made.[2] If the crossing is made to the right of the stem we see anxiousness to "get on."[3] On the other hand, a crossing to the left of the stem is a sign of procrastination and hesitancy.[4] If the stem is crossed by a loop, a "tie," so to speak, we have an indication of persistence.[5]

1. 𝓉   2. 𝓉̄   3. 𝓀   4. 𝓉   5. 𝓉

The topic of the paragraph is The Cursive Letter "t"; the main idea is stated in the first sentence of the paragraph. Following the main idea are five examples that support it.

2. Sometimes, the main idea sentence is placed in the middle of a paragraph. Here is an example.

Lurking and peering from behind trees, weapons at readiness, were dozens of natives. They were witnessing something that was entirely new in their experience. Columbus and his men were rowing toward shore in a small "canoe" in an attempt to make the first Spanish landing in the New World. Floating behind them was a much larger canoe with white sails that, to the natives, had the appearance of clouds. As the smaller boat approached the beach, several men in strange garments jumped into the surf and guided the boat to a landing. Then, a tall, authoritative person stepped out of the boat and waded to shore as other men formed a circle around him.

---

3. The main idea of some paragraphs is stated in the last sentence. This is not unlike the procedure that research scientists follow. That is, they gather a number of facts about a particular matter, discern a pattern or relationship from the facts, and then draw a conclusion. However, unlike the scientists who arrive at their own conclusions, the writer makes the conclusion for the reader. Following is an example of a paragraph whose main idea is stated in the final sentence.

At the college of your choice you will spend thousands of dollars, hopefully make friends for a lifetime, and gain an education that will enable you to make a good living in the future. So, before you decide, visit the college, talk to faculty and administrators. Ask to sit in on some classes. Talk to students you meet in the dining halls, dormitories, and playing fields. If possible, talk to some recent graduates; ask them how they feel about their education. Are there provisions for financial aid? What about scholarships? Choosing a college is a serious matter; there are many things to consider.

---

4. The sentences in some paragraphs may all be related to a particular topic, but no main idea is stated. In such a case, it is the reader's task to discern the main idea. Following is an example of such a paragraph.

Earth's earliest people often made their homes in caves. The entrance of a cave could be blocked by branches, rocks, or animal skins. This helped keep the cave warm in winter and cool in summer. The cave offered protection from wild animals and human intruders. If the cave people were attacked they had only one entrance to defend. If the cave was in a cliff or steep hillside, the ladders that were used to climb up to the cave could be withdrawn. Also, rocks could be hurled down upon attackers who were trying to reach the cave.

No main idea is stated as such in the paragraph, but from all the evidence a topic (Caves of Early People) and a main idea (Caves of early people offered protection against the elements, animals, and human attackers) can be readily deduced.

DETERMINING MAIN IDEAS

1. It is helpful when reading a selection to be alert for the main idea of each paragraph. This is especially true when a textbook is being studied. If you remember the main idea, the details that support the main idea will be more easily recalled.

Some things to realize about main ideas:

a. They may appear at the beginning, middle, or end of a paragraph.

b. They most often will be in the form of a complete sentence. However, readers may want to state main ideas in words slightly different from those used in the paragraph.

c. Sometimes, a main idea may not be stated in a paragraph. In such a case, the reader has to think about the details in the paragraph and formulate a main idea.

2. There is no main idea sentence in the following paragraph; however, there <u>is</u> a main idea. Write what you think the main idea is on the lines following the paragraph. Also, state the <u>topic</u> of the paragraph.

> In the Great Plains in the mid 1800s there was very little wood available for building houses. So, settlers had to find some other material. The most abundant material was *sod*. Sod is thick, matted grass attached to a layer of soil. Sod, in the form of blocks, can be cut from the ground. When one block is piled upon another, a wall is formed. Make three more walls connected at the corners to form a square or rectangle, and the house, called a *soddy*, is framed and ready for the next step—a roof.

Topic: _Living in the Great Plains_

Main idea: _Sod homes were built in the Great Plains_

3. Read the following paragraph and underline the sentence that contains the main idea. Then, on the line at the end of the paragraph, state the topic of the paragraph.

> For thousands of years, *draft* horses have pulled heavy wagons and plows. *Coach* horses, not as heavy or strong as draft horses, pull

lighter vehicles such as carriages in which people ride; sometimes they are used as saddle horses. Many other kinds of horses are used for different purposes. For example, *ponies* are small horses that pull light wagons or carts; they are also popular as pets or for children to ride at carnivals and circuses. *Donkeys* are relatives of horses, but are not as large. One of their important uses is to carry loads on their backs over rough trails. Cowboys love their *quarter* horses. These swift, strong animals have the ability to turn quickly and separate a particular cow from a herd or keep a herd of cattle from separating.

Topic: _Horses and the job they do_

4. Read the two related paragraphs that follow. In each one underline the main idea sentence. Also, on the line below each paragraph state the topic of the paragraph.

> Taking minerals such as iron or copper ore from the surface of the earth is called strip mining. In strip mining operations, bulldozers and other earthmovers scrape away topsoil and vegetation to expose the desired minerals. Then giant mechanical shovels dig out the minerals and load them on trucks or railroad cars for further processing.

Topic: _The strip mining process_

> Because the earth has lost its protective covering of plants and trees it lies open to the eroding effects of rains and melting snows. The constant maneuvering of trucks and other vehicles further loosens the soil. All too frequently after the mine has been worked out, topsoil is not replaced, and grasses and trees are not replanted. Strip mining is a great contributor to soil erosion.

Topic: _Strip mining affects the earth_

COMBINING DETAILS TO REACH CONCLUSIONS

There is only one way to arrive at a valid conclusion or overall understanding: one must know facts about the issue at hand, then combine those facts in meaningful ways. The conclusion that results is greater than the sum of all the facts. Thus, in reading a paragraph or longer selection, the main idea may be derived only after the details have been read, understood, and absorbed.

To Do:

1. Read the following selections.

2. Answer the questions that follow the selections, all of which are concerned with details. If necessary, reread parts of a selection to arrive at the correct answer.

3. Examine the facts and then write the conclusion/main idea of the selection.

WIND ENERGY

The expression "free as the wind" is most often used to express freedom to do as one thinks is right or as one chooses, to come and go as one pleases, to choose one's life work, companions, and so on. Environmentally speaking, however, it could mean this: The wind is here to take—it's clean, it doesn't cost anything, no one is being deprived of property, and no matter how much is used the supply will never be diminished. So, more and more, we are taking this offer of "free" wind and using it to fulfill the world's ever-growing need for energy.

Questions

1. What are four ways that the expression "free as the wind" applies to personal choices?

a. _____

b. _____

c. _____

d. _____

2. From an environmental point of view, what are four advantages of using wind-produced energy?

a. _____

b. _____

c. _____

d. _____

3. Conclusion/main idea:

_____

_____

In California alone, from 1981 to 1997, wind-generated power grew steadily from 36,000 kilowatt hours (KWH) to more than 200,000 KWH, nearly a sixfold increase. As the world's oil resources shrink and the demand for energy increases, electricity generated by the wind will turn on more and more electric lights and run more and more washing machines, vacuum cleaners, furnaces, and thousands of other devices. Oil will eventually disappear or, at the least, become so scarce as to be very expensive. The wind, however, will always be with us.

Questions

1. How many times more wind-generated power was used in 1997 than in 1981?

_____

2. What are two reasons why wind energy will be more and more in demand?

a. _____

b. _____

3. Conclusion/main idea:

_____

_____

COMPARING ACCOUNTS OF THE SAME EVENT

Sometimes two reporters writing for two different newspapers but reporting the same event will differ on details. Also, one reporter may be sympathetic about the event, while the other reporter may be unsympathetic. And, even though the two stories may agree on details and the reporters may be trying to be honest, readers may arrive at different conclusions because of the way the stories are written. So, the reader has to be careful about whom and what to believe.

Contradictions also occur in criminal trials. Witnesses may differ in the details they offer. The result can be that the jurors may have difficulty deciding a case. The innocent may be convicted; the guilty may go free.

Following are the eyewitness accounts given by two people who were outside a bank when a robber was fleeing from the bank after a holdup.

To Do:

1. Read both accounts. Pay special attention to details.

2. Assume you are a detective investigating the robbery. Your job is to make two lists, one headed DETAILS IN AGREEMENT and the other headed DETAILS IN DISAGREEMENT. Compile your lists on the other side of this page.

Eyewitness Report

Date: June 9, 1996
Name: Susan McInverarry
Address: 17 Sunset Drive, Sparkleville, VA
Age: 59

I was walking on Bank Street when I saw a man, about 6'2" tall, come running out of the bank. He had a baseball-type hat on his head; his hair was blond. He wore blue denim trousers and a black and red jacket; it looked like a kind of checkerboard. He had tennis shoes. He had a revolver in his right hand and what looked like a bundle of money in his left hand. He looked to be about 25 years old.

He jumped into a cherry-red Chevrolet Blazer, passenger side. The driver was a redhead; he didn't have a hat. The car sped out of the parking lot—almost hit me—and made a right turn onto Harding Drive. I noted the license plate: AWE 397.

Just before the getaway car left the lot a security guard ran out of the bank. He shouted, "Stop, thief!" Then, he aimed at the car and shot one bullet at it. He missed.

About three minutes after the thieves drove off, a police car came speeding into the bank lot, but, of course, they were too late.

Signed: *Susan McInverarry*

Eyewitness Report

Date: June 9, 1996
Name: Michael Jankoski
Address: 233 William Street, Sparkleville, VA
Age: 33

I was cashing a check at the bank's drive-in window when I saw a man running out of the bank with an automatic in his right hand. I noticed that on his left hand he had a bandage that was kind of bulky. He was bareheaded. He had red hair that came down to his shoulders. He wore a black-and-red striped jacket that was open almost all the way down to his waist. He wore blue denim trousers. His shoes were the kind you might wear if you were going hiking. I could see something that looked like a bundle of money sticking out of his jacket. Maybe the bundle was stuck under his pants' belt.

He was bent over, but my guess is that he was about 5'9" and middle-aged, maybe 50 years old.

He jumped into the passenger side of a cherry-red Ford Explorer. I couldn't make out all the license plate, but I remember the first three letters; they spelled "AWE."

I got just a glimpse of the driver's face, but I did notice that he also had red hair. On his head he had a woolen hat—the kind you might wear in winter. The car turned left onto Harding Drive. Just before the car left the parking lot—it was going very fast and almost hit an old lady who was watching everything—a security guard came running out. He shouted something and then took a shot. I don't know if his bullet hit the car.

Signed: *Michael Jankoski*

Name: _____ Date: _____

RECOGNIZING CAUSE-AND-EFFECT RELATIONSHIPS I

1. After a very successful first semester in his senior year, Jack was not doing very well in the second semester. He was failing English, social studies, and science; his average in mathematics was barely passing. When his parents asked him why this was happening, he shrugged and gave vague answers. Then, one day as he was leaving home for school he handed his mother a letter that he had received at the end of the first semester. It was a letter from his local congressman telling him he was sorry but he wasn't able to gain Jack an appointment to the military academy at West Point.

Question: What was probably the cause of Jack's failing grades? _____

2. The road was deserted. No other cars, no pedestrians, no houses were in sight. Madeline's car just sat there, and Madeline sat behind the steering wheel and cried. What was she going to do? How did she get into this mess? It wasn't her fault that the car had overheated; it was her brother Mike's fault. Instead of telling her to check the water in the radiator he should have checked it himself. After all, it was his car wasn't it? Wasn't he responsible for his own car?

Question: What was the cause of the breakdown of the car? _____

Question: What was the effect of the breakdown of the car on Madeline?_____

3. During the last inning of a major league baseball game, the hitter gave the pitched ball a solid whack. The center fielder knew instantly that the ball might go over the wall into the stands for a homer. Just as the fielder leaped into the air to catch the ball, a young fan leaned over the wall and caught the ball before it reached the fielder's glove. The umpire ruled that it was a home run. The fielder argued with the umpire that his ruling wasn't fair. The umpire ruled him out of order and ejected him from the game.

   The person who caught the ball was admired by many of the fans, and he was featured on television. The loss of the game eliminated the fielder's team from the playoffs. Being eliminated from the playoffs meant a loss of thousands of dollars to the players on the losing team.

   For one of the losing team's players the loss of money meant that he would not be able to pay for his mother and father to become residents of a country retirement village. The couple would have to continue living in a rough section of the city. This resulted in a tragedy a few weeks later. An evil person knew that the couple were both handicapped. So, one night he entered their apartment through a window, tied them both with tape, and stole the few valuables and sentimental possessions they had.

Questions: What were some of the effects of the fan catching the ball?

- On the outcome of the game? _____

- On the fan who caught the ball? _____

- On the players on the losing team? _____

- On the center fielder who didn't catch the ball? _____

- On one of the losing player's plans to help his mother and father?_____

   _____

- On the mother and father? _____

   _____

Name: _____ Date: _____

RECOGNIZING CAUSE-AND-EFFECT RELATIONSHIPS II

1.   On the blank line before each EFFECT item, write the number of the CAUSE item that best completes the sentence and makes the most sense.

CAUSE	**EFFECT**
a. He studied long and hard, so . . .	___ it lost the race.
b. The airplane's nearly empty fuel tank was not checked before takeoff, so . . .	___ the roof caved.
c. The saw was dull, so . . .	___ he passed the course with an A.
d. The extra-point kick was blocked, so . . .	___ the board was not well cut.
e. The snow on the roof was more than two feet deep, so . . .	___ an emergency landing was necessary.
f. She ignored the stop sign, so . . .	___ she was frightened but unhurt.
g. The horse lost a shoe on the first lap, so . . .	___ the game finished in a tie.
h. The lost child found shelter during the storm, so . . .	___ the policeman gave her a ticket.

2.   Following are six <u>causes</u> that do not have stated effects. Think of a reasonable effect for each cause, and write it on the blank line following the cause.

a.   He gave a shout, and _____ .

b.   He ran to the bus station, but he was too late; consequently, _____ .

c.   She fell and broke her wrist, so _____ .

d.   The clock was five minutes slow, which resulted in _____

_____ .

e.   Because he pulled the baby out of the burning car, _____

_____ .

f.   The nine inches of rain that fell within 24 hours caused _____

_____ .

3.   Following are five <u>effects</u> that do not have stated causes. Think of a reasonable cause for each effect, and write it on the blank line before the effect.

CAUSE	**EFFECT**
a. _____	the house burned down.
b. _____	the battle was lost.
c. _____	the crowd cheered for him.
d. _____	all the fish in the pond died.
e. _____	she used her credit card.
f. _____	he stopped smoking.

GUIDELINES FOR DISTINGUISHING BETWEEN FACT AND OPINION

The information on this page should sharpen student awareness of opinions, facts, and inferences. One of the positive results could be their lessened susceptibility to propaganda in newspaper, television, radio advertisements, talk shows, and other propaganda vehicles.

The two pages that follow will provide practice in distinguishing between fact, opinion, and inferences.

Fact and Opinion

1. It is important to know if something read or heard is a fact or an opinion. An incorrect impression may lead to decisions with negative results. Think of a fact as something that can be proved by measurement, tests, or observation. Think of an opinion as an unproven belief or theory.

That an opinion is going to be expressed is sometimes signaled by certain words and phrases. A list of such signals, placed in contexts, may prove helpful to your students. *Note*: Even the previous sentence contains a signal of opinion with the use of the word "may."

a. <u>We have the feeling</u> that no fruit is as beneficial as oranges.

b. It <u>appeared</u> that every person in the audience thought the show was wonderful.

c. He said, "I <u>probably</u> could run the mile in four minutes if I really tried."

d. It <u>seems</u> that the referee made an error.

e. It is <u>likely</u> that the United States will win the most medals at the Olympic Games.

f. My <u>guess</u> is that there would be fewer automobile accidents if people weren't in such a hurry.

g. It is <u>most likely</u> true that the atom bomb was the most destructive invention in history.

h. The <u>theory</u> that the dinosaurs became extinct because of climatic changes makes good sense. *Note*: A theory is an unproven explanation.

2. Often, judgements are taken at face value simply because they appear in declarative sentences. Readers should be aware that what appears to be factual is really a matter of opinion. Can what appears to be a fact, because it is expressed with conviction and sincerity, be proved true? If there is any doubt, the statement should be treated as opinion.

The following statements probably could not be proved true; therefore, they should be treated as opinions.

a. Mary Jane is the prettiest girl in Central High School.

b. The most important problem facing the nation is drug abuse.

c. Boys have a greater potential for excelling in mathematics than girls do.

d. Nothing can compare with the thrill one gets from downhill skiing.

e. Bear cubs are the most lovable of all wild animals.

f. College teachers are more intelligent than high-school teachers.

g. As people become older they also become wiser.

h. You would look better if you didn't have a beard.

i. The love of money is the cause of all evil.

3. Inferences are, in one respect, similar to opinions: they are guesses. However, inferences differ from opinions in that they are based on demonstrable facts and/or past experiences; they are capable of being proved true or false.

It could be said that an inference is a higher-order opinion. As *Webster's New Collegiate Dictionary* points out, "to infer is a normal process of thought." For example, a water biologist may gather considerable data about the life cycle of salmon and infer from it that if water temperature is below a certain point salmon eggs will not hatch. Then, through additional tests and experimentation the inference could be proved or disproved. In contrast, no amount of data or testing could prove or disprove that Mary Jane is the prettiest girl in Central High School.

WORDS THAT SIGNAL OPINIONS

Sometimes, especially if we are reading swiftly, we take something we read as a fact when it is really an opinion. We may have missed a key word that foretold that an opinion was going to be expressed. The result might be that we are influenced by and respond to opinion as though it were fact. We might, for example, pass information on that could cause someone else a problem.

We can be better prepared to recognize opinions by being aware of "signal words" that tell us to accept what is printed with caution.

Following is a group of sentences that all express opinions. Circle the word or words in each sentence that signal an opinion is being expressed.

1. Apparently, he didn't follow directions or he would be here by now.

2. My guess as to the amount of damage caused by the storm is $100,000.

3. The governor made the prediction that we will soon have a law allowing people to drive if they are 15 years old.

4. The possibility is strong that he failed the driver's test because he is colorblind.

5. It is my supposition that no one will ever high-jump more than nine feet.

6. He speculated that Florida State University would be chosen to play in the Orange Bowl.

7. His hypothesis was that crickets make chirping noises when they are frightened.

8. He surmised that Hurricane Zeke would strike Bermuda early Saturday morning.

9. It is my belief that there is no life on the planet Pluto.

10. Perchance she will succeed if she studies harder.

11. Sharks have been sighted offshore, so it seems reasonable that swimming has been prohibited.

12. He conjectured that only 80% of the students will pass the course.

13. It is likely that we will run out of gas before we get there.

14. The theory is that the Spanish sailing ship was attacked because it was carrying gold and silver.

15. I don't think it was done on purpose; it probably was an unfortunate accident.

16. The man is alleged to be the person who robbed the bank.

17. There is a chance that Saturday will be a rainy day.

18. From my point-of-view the situation is hopeless.

19. My inference, based on the facts presented, is that California will have a population of more than 30 million by the year 2010.

DETERMINING IF A STATEMENT IS PROVABLE

Fact or Opinion

1. Read the following statements. If a statement is capable of being proved either true or false circle P (Provable). If a statement cannot be proved either true or false, circle NP (Not Provable).

a. The Battle of Trenton in 1776 was the most important battle of the Revolutionary War.

                                   P   NP

b. Abraham Lincoln was elected president in 1860; he was the 16th president.   P   NP

c. The best answer to question 16 in the multiple choice test is item B.   P   NP

d. No one in the race tried harder to win than Mike.   P   NP

e. The best time in the 100 yard dash was 10:08.   P   NP

f. Only 43% of the people eligible to vote exercised their right.   P   NP

g. In the future a woman will win the Boston Marathon.   P   NP

h. Of the two magazines, *Time* is definitely the best.   P   NP

i. His opinions were closer to being true than those of any of the other panelists.   P   NP

j. Country people are happier than city people.   P   NP

k. The car was going more than 75 miles per hour when it hit the telephone pole.   P   NP

l. A train ride is more pleasurable than an airplane flight.   P   NP

m. California, the third largest state, has a larger population than any other state.   P   NP

2. The story below is part of a letter that Tom, who lives in Kansas, wrote to his friend Steve.

Read the story, and underline all the sentences and phrases in which Tom is offering an opinion.

> Nobody was ever more frightened than I was when I saw the tornado approaching. It was coming from the west. I'd say that it was moving about 15 miles per hour. To me, it looked like a twirling top with clouds of dust flying off its sides. It passed over Mr. Brown's barn. A newspaper photograph showed bales of hay and milking equipment being sucked into the mouth of the tornado. I'll bet that some of Mr. Brown's chickens were flying higher than they ever had flown before.
>
> I said to myself that I'd better get out of the way of the approaching twister. I probably broke the world record for the 100-yard dash as I ran for the tornado cellar. When I reached it my Dad was holding the door open. He grabbed me and pulled me in, and not too soon, either. I could see through the peep hole that our house was being blown apart. I don't think in my whole life I'll ever feel as sad as I did then. My Dad and some friends had built an addition to our house only two weeks ago.
>
> You live in New Jersey, Steve. You'll probably never be in a tornado. I sure hope not.
>
> Your friend,
>
> Tom

FACT AND OPINION IN HISTORY

1. How does a writer of history decide what happened at a past event? One thing he does is to examine everything that has been written about the event. Such writings, or sources, would include official reports, proclamations, and articles in pamphlets and magazines. **What are four kinds of sources shown at the bottom of this page?** _____

_____

Very often, historians find that there are differences of opinion as to what actually happened at an event. Some reporters might want to make themselves out to be heroes and write in a way that would do this. Others might have strong feelings about what they saw and this would influence, or "color," what they write. Still other reporters might write about something even though they were in a poor position to see or hear what was actually going on. Perhaps some people reporting an event might have something to gain by not telling the truth. **What might be one reason why a person might deliberately lie about an event that he or she was a part of? Give an example.** _____

_____

_____

After historians study all the available accounts of an event, they must make some decisions as to what is true, partly true, and false. When historians are not sure about what happened, they use such words and phrases as "perhaps," "approximately," "We think . . . ," etc.

The story of the death of Sieur de La Salle, commonly called **La Salle**, can serve as a helpful example of the problems historians would have in writing about him.

La Salle, you may remember, was the French explorer who explored the Mississippi River. La Salle was shot by one of his own men as he started a journey following the Mississippi River north from the Gulf of Mexico. The full story of who shot him is not fully known.

2. Suppose that the imaginary picture shown above was true. Why should you be careful about accepting reports given by the following men?

a. Number 5: _____

_____

_____

b. Number 2: _____

_____

_____

c. Number 4: _____

_____

_____

d. What person would probably give the most accurate account of the shooting? _____

Explain your answer: _____

_____

3. What two words are used in this column to warn you that La Salle's death could have happened in some way other than what is shown in the picture?

_____

JUSTIFYING INFERENCES I

1.   An inference is a guess that people make when they study facts and then think, "What do these facts mean?" In other words they try to "see" beyond the facts.

> Imagine a small, single-winged airplane flying at about 5,000' above sea level. The engine suddenly stops. The plane begins to lose altitude.
>
> The pilot asks himself what has happened. He makes two inferences based on the observed facts. One is that the airplane is out of fuel; the other is that the airplane motor "blew" a cylinder. He discards the first inference because just before the engine stopped he heard a loud explosion. Even if the gas tanks were empty, he would not have heard an explosion. It must be the engine.
>
> Based on his inference, the pilot took quick action. His only chance was to find a place to land. The land below was hilly and wooded. No good. He spied a four-lane highway. There were few cars, especially in the northbound lane. He lowered the flaps to decrease speed and to descend. He brought the airplane to a safe landing.
>
> Upon inspecting the engine, the pilot noticed oil and pieces of metal. He then knew that the inference he made that the engine had blown a cylinder was true.

2.   Here are some examples of inferences made as a result of observed facts.

a.   You see and smell smoke. You infer that there is a fire.

b.   You see a broken window in your house. You notice that some boys are playing baseball near your house. You infer that a baseball broke the window. You enter the house and find a ball by the window wall. Your inference was correct.

3.   Following is a story from which several inferences may be made. Read each inference, and then tell why it might be true.

> Tom found a piece of copper pipe in the garage. He cut the pipe into three lengths: 8", 10", and 12". He made two holes near the end of each piece. Then he took lengths of nylon string used in fishing poles and threaded them through the holes in the pipes. He attached the threaded pipes to a piece of wood, about 4" square, that he had cut from a plank.

> He attached the device to the ceiling of the front porch. There was no sound. The wind began to blow, and the pipes made lovely tinkling sounds. Some notes were high and some were low. Tom's mother cocked her head and smiled when she heard the tinkling pipes.

Inferences

a.   Tom was more than five years old.

_____

_____

b.   Tom's family had an automobile or truck.

_____

_____

c.   Tom had a saw that cut metal.

_____

_____

d.   Tom had a saw that cut wood.

_____

_____

e.   Tom had a pair of scissors or a knife.

_____

_____

f.   Tom had a ruler.

_____

_____

g.   Tom had a metal-cutting drill bit.

_____

_____

h.   Someone in Tom's family was interested in fishing.

_____

_____

i.   High notes and low notes are made by different length pipes.

_____

_____

j.   Tom's mother approved of what Tom had made.

_____

_____

Name: _____ Date: _____

JUSTIFYING INFERENCES II

Mary Jane's Big Chance

Mary Jane wanted so much to win the race. It was a county meet, the most important of the season. If she won, it might be the deciding factor in her attempt to win an athletic scholarship to the state university. There was no way her family could pay her tuition without financial help. Her brother and sister, who had told her stories about college life and had helped motivate her, had both won scholarships.

As she crouched on the starting line, her body was tensed for the sound of the starter's gun. Bang! And she was off like a scared rabbit. Over the first, the second; and then the last barrier loomed ahead of her. It seemed so high! A burst of energy and she cleared it, but she stumbled slightly on landing. She recovered quickly. Then, the yellow ribbon streamed behind her as she slowed to a jog, the cheers of the crowd in her ears.

As she circled the track, she saw the university's athletic director walking toward her. He smiled, held out his hand to shake hers, congratulated her, and then said, "Spring training starts the Monday after registration."

1. None of the questions that follow is directly answered in the story. However, there are elements in the story that could help you make inferences that answer the questions.

Make your own inferences to answer the following questions. Then, briefly explain what there is in the story that led you to make the inferences. Write your inferences in the form of statements, that is, declarative sentences.

a. What kind of race is it?

Inference: _____

Explanation: _____

_____

b. In what year of high school is Mary Jane?

Inference: _____

Explanation: _____

_____

c. What is the family's financial position?

Inference: _____

Explanation: _____

_____

d. What is Mary Jane's age as compared to her brother and sister?

Inference: _____

Explanation: _____

_____

e. Who is the winner of the race?

Inference: _____

Explanation: _____

_____

f. Did Mary Jane win a scholarship?

Inference: _____

Explanation: _____

_____

2. Read the story below. Then make three inferences based on the details of the story. Write your inferences in sentence form.

As the small, single-winged airplane approached the landing strip, sirens were blowing, and a fire truck and an ambulance were standing by. The airplane was just about to touch down when a Civil Air Patrol official waved it off. The plane lifted, made a go-round, and once more tried to land. Again the pilot was waved off, but this time he ignored the signal. The airplane slid down the runway and finally came to a stop no more than ten feet from the end. The plane burst into flames, but not before the pilot was seen jumping from the cabin.

Inference: _____

_____

Inference: _____

_____

Inference: _____

_____

GUIDELINES FOR RECOGNIZING PROPAGANDA

The ability to identify an author's purpose for writing is useful because it helps make the reader less susceptible to propaganda. Authors sometimes have a particular "axe to grind"; some of the axes are positive and some are negative. An author's purpose may be to convince the reader to support an organization's goals; the reverse might also be true. Of course, whether something is positive or negative depends upon the reader's orientation or perspective.

Advertisements are loaded with persuasive techniques that may appeal to one's emotions rather than to one's good sense. Political messages, written or spoken, are meant to gain votes or support for an issue.

Even school textbooks, wittingly or unwittingly, shape children's thinking by what is—or isn't—printed. What is "left out" may be more significant than what is "put in." Adjectives, for example, are sometimes used to create impressions. There is a significant difference between calling one president "foresighted" and another, perhaps a successor, "unimaginative." Both descriptions are opinions, but young learners tend to believe that everything they read in a textbook is factual. In fact, it would be helpful to student understanding of fact and opinion and underlying purposes to take a typical textbook chapter and identify all the statements of opinion.

Studies made by The Institute for Propaganda Analysis resulted in its publication of the seven most widely used persuasive propaganda techniques. They are as follows:

1. **Band Wagon**: "Everybody is doing it, so why don't you get with it and join the crowd?" Example: "Eight out of ten doctors prescribe TRANQUILITY as the best medicine to calm your nerves." Another: "Nine out of ten people said they preferred CHOO-CHOO over any other kind of gum.'

2. **Testimonial**: A person famous in sports, acting, or some other highly visible activity is shown using a particular brand of soap, tennis racket, etc. People who admire the personality may then be influenced to buy the product she or he is touting. Example: A famous basketball player is shown making a layup.

Afterwards, he says of the shoes he's wearing, "JUMPIES give me that extra bounce I need."

3. **Transfer**: This is a situation when the love, respect, or admiration one has for a patriotic symbol or organization is transferred to something else. Example: A person seeking election might choose to give a talk with the Lincoln Memorial in the background. People may tend to transfer their respect for the memorial to the candidate.

4. **Plain Folks**: This approach to persuasion is often used by people seeking public office. The idea is to convince voters that the candidate belongs to the common people, that he understands them and their needs. Example: A news program or newspaper photograph shows a candidate talking to blue collar workers at a factory site. What is the candidate wearing? Not a coat and tie, but a blue denim shirt open at the collar.

5. **Card Stacking**: In this approach the cards are "stacked" in favor of a candidate or in opposition to an opponent or a suggested proposal. The facts and figures presented are those that support or deride a candidate or a proposal. Example: A table of figures is displayed that enumerates all the "yes" votes a congressman made that are in accord with his audience's point of view. No other votes are tabulated in the table—that is, votes that his listeners might not appreciate.

6. **Glittering Generalities**: Words or phrases are used that may not have a specific meaning but sound good. They create favorable impressions in the minds of some listeners. Example: "Americanism," "sanctity of the home," and "equality for all."

7. **Name Calling:** A label that is not complimentary is used to influence others to dislike a person or organization. Examples: "Nit Wit," "Snob," and "Big Shot."

Suggestions for Teaching

At the end of each item on the student application page, students are asked to decide what form of propaganda is being exemplified.

RECOGNIZING PROPAGANDA

1.   Each of the numbered items below is an example of one of the seven propaganda techniques. The techniques are Band Wagon, Name Calling, Transfer, Testimonial, Plain Folks, Glittering Generalities, and Card Stacking.

2.   Read each example and decide which one of the seven propaganda techniques is being exemplified. Write its name on the blank line following the example.

a.   A politician who is seeking election is shown talking to a group of farmers. He is wearing denim overalls and a straw hat. He is saying, "I understand your problems. I worked on the family farm—milking cows, cleaning the barn, and plowing the fields."

_____

b.   An advertisement on prime-time television: A man wearing a laboratory coat is saying, "Eight of every ten patients who come to my office have switched to CLEANTOOTH toothpaste."

_____

c.   Advertisement in a newspaper: Our utility vehicle, the ALLMOBILE, has twelve features that are standard equipment; on the TRAILBOUND they are all extra-cost options.

_____

d.   A well known female professional golfer is shown talking to a group of women, all golfers, at the eighteenth hole of a golf course. She says, "The only clubs I use in a tournament are SURECLUBS; they give the ball that extra lift."

_____

e.   Two candidates for United States senator are having a debate before a crowd of people in a high-school auditorium. Candidate A says, "I'm for stopping aid to all foreign countries." Candidate B says, "It's isolationists like you who are responsible for the starvation of helpless women and children all over the world."

_____

f.   A speaker is attempting to discredit an organization that is trying to raise money for people living below the poverty level: "If we left it up to the do-gooders, they would give so much money away that the country would go bankrupt."

_____

g.   A member of a political organization is standing on a flag-decorated wooden platform in a park. On the stage is a United States flag and a statue of a golden eagle. "The Star Spangled Banner," our national anthem, is being played. The candidate has a copy of the United States Constitution in his hand. He is asking the audience to vote for him.

_____

h.   A reporter is interviewing a candidate for the presidency. The interview is being held in a nicely furnished office. The candidate is saying, "If I'm elected there will be a chicken in every pot and a car in very garage and, what's more, a significant pension for everyone who retires."

_____

i.   A department store advertisement shows a long line of people patiently waiting their turn to buy a new computer program. Under the photo is a caption: THE DEMAND FOR THE NEW PROGRAM IS SO GREAT—EVERYBODY WANTS ONE—THAT WE HAVE DECIDED TO EXTEND THE SALE FOR TWO MORE DAYS. DON'T MIND THE LINES, THE WAIT IS WORTH IT.

_____

j.   A candidate for Congress included the following in a speech: "I voted for aid to the poor, greater money allotment to senior citizens living in nursing homes, 'no interest' loans to college students, more federal money to help inner city schools, high fines for those who pollute the environment, and no salary increases for congressmen and senators. My opponent? He voted for a 15% increase in income taxes for people in the lower income brackets."

_____

RECOGNIZING THE AUTHOR'S PURPOSE I

Dear Jan,

In your last letter you wrote that you are an "undeclared major" at Rocky Mountain College and that you don't feel good about that; you feel that it is aimless.

Why not concentrate on a major course of study that will prepare you for a particular profession? Then, after graduation you can apply for a specific job.

My suggestion is to take courses that would lead to certification as a teacher. Think of the benefits—a ten-month teaching year, health benefits, a pension following retirement, regular increases in salary, and opportunities to advance to become, for example, a reading specialist, a guidance counselor, or a principal. But, most of all, by teaching you are doing something worthwhile for children, for humanity. As they say, and it's true, "A teacher affects eternity." Think about it.

                                        Love,
                                        Dad

What two things is Dad trying to persuade Jan to do?

1. _____

2. _____

A hike of the entire Appalachian Trail—some 2,000 miles—is, to say the least, demanding. It takes stamina, determination, knowledge, physical strength, and courage. Yes, courage. You never know when you might encounter a bear standing in your path. And, it's not unusual to see a rattlesnake coiled on a rock outcropping. There is a risk of accidental injury, such as a twisted ankle or broken arm due to tripping over a root or stepping into a crevice covered by leaves. Nights can be scary, too. For example, you could wake up to screeching animal cries or movements in the woods—movements that you can't see but you can hear. A sudden storm could send a flood of water your way, or a lightning bolt could shatter a tree, causing it to crash down on your head.

The author's purpose in writing this article is _____

_____

To the Editor:

The Tuesday edition of *The Chronicle* carried an editorial expressing the opinion that it would be wrong to have all-year-round schools. With all due respect, I disagree.

Studies have shown that children lose a significant amount of knowledge and skills over the summer months. Consequently, at the start of the new school year, teachers find it necessary to do a great amount of reviewing. Unfortunately, some children do not read even one book in the nine- or ten-week vacation. The break in the continuity of learning to read can be disastrous for young children.

Children, especially those in the inner city, may have nothing constructive to do during the summer. This often results in negative activities such as hanging out on street corners until late in the evening and searching for some kind of excitement. Children in the suburbs may be able to go on trips to the seashore or spend vacations in summer camps, but for economically deprived families this is not a possibility. Such children would be better off in school, where a planned program would allow not only for studies, but also recreational opportunities.

                                        Respectfully yours,
                                        Joseph Tomasino

Mr. Tomasino wrote this letter in an attempt to convince readers that _____

_____

RECOGNIZING THE AUTHOR'S PURPOSE II

1. Authors sometimes try to convince readers to react favorably or unfavorably to an event, a person, a group, or an issue by using words that are emotionally charged. Here is an example: *The gentle, innocent, and trusting old lady didn't realize that the salesperson with the false smile was trying to persuade her to buy a toaster that had been discontinued and no longer carried a guarantee.* The words that the author uses to help you be sympathetic to the old lady are *gentle, innocent,* and *trusting.* The words he uses to cause you to dislike the salesperson are *false smile.*

In the paragraph that follows, underline the words or phrases that are designed to create a favorable impression of "Susan."

> Susan was modest and not forward or aggressive in any way. Without being asked she would graciously do such things as set the table for dinner, remove clothes from the dryer, or do the ironing for the entire family. She was cheerful and had a ready smile for everybody. She was generous with her time and possessions. She often helped her younger sister with homework and willingly spent money she earned as a baby-sitter to buy toys for her four-year-old brother.

2. Other devices used to persuade readers are to describe something in completely negative ways and to offer arguments that are almost impossible to deny.

In the following paragraph, what arguments does the author use to discourage people from smoking? The author makes at least seven points. Briefly list the points on the lines following the paragraphs.

> When you think about smoking you have to wonder why anybody would do it. It's a disgusting habit. Smokers have the smell of tobacco smoke on their breath and clothing. Nicotine eventually stains the smoker's fingers yellow. That's just the outside of a smoker. What about the inside where the smoker's lungs become covered with smoke soot that may eventually lead to cancer or emphysema. And, yellow nicotine stains on the smoker's teeth are not pretty to look at.
>
> And, lest we forget, tobacco smoke can seriously affect people who don't smoke. Once smoke is inhaled and then puffed out of the smoker's mouth into the air, the pollution is almost as bad for the innocent nonsmoker as it is for the smoker. It's kind of sad to think that a little child, sincerely loved by the smoking mom and dad, may be seriously injured by being in a smoke-filled house 24 hours a day. And, another thing: It has been proved beyond a doubt that the smoke inhaled by a pregnant woman can seriously harm her unborn child.

Arguments Against Smoking

a. _____

b. _____

c. _____

d. _____

e. _____

f. _____

g. _____

3. Imagine that you wanted to persuade a friend to take a course with a particular teacher, a teacher that you believed would be helpful to her/him. Make a list of favorable words or phrases about the teacher that you could include in a conversation with the person you want to help.

a. _____

b. _____

c. _____

d. _____

e. _____

f. _____

g. _____

RECOGNIZING THE AUTHOR'S PURPOSE IN POETRY I

Wild Things

Why take an animal that was born to be free
And stick it in a cage or tie it to a tree—
An animal that was made to run or jump or swim,
To burrow in a hole, or perch upon a limb?

If you give it lots of time, and think it through and through,
Would you want that to happen to a friend—or even you?
Imagine being taken and placed on exhibition,
To be stared at and laughed at in a 6-by-8 partition—

Pacing up and down, removed from friends and home,
Longing for a field or forest, a place where you can roam;
Forced to swim in circles inside a glass bowl
Or run around a treadmill and never reach a goal.

There's something not quite right, there's something that is wrong,
With putting birds inside a cage, where they may never sing a song,
With taking Arctic polar bears from their frigid north domain
And imprisoning them in tropic zoos—never to slide on ice again.

So—think about it long and hard before you decide to buy
A rabbit that was made to run or a bird that was meant to fly.

JFS

People often write poems to persuade readers to do—or not do—something. The thoughts they express and the language they use are designed to appeal not only to readers' reasoning, but also to their emotions. The poem printed above is such a poem.

1. The idea of being decent to one another is sometimes put this way: "Do unto others what you would want done to you." Quote the line in the poem that expresses the same basic idea. _____

_____

2. Quote the line from the third verse that expresses what you might feel like and do if your were a prisoner in jail. _____

_____

3. Quote the two lines that could apply to fish and small animals such as hamsters. _____

_____

_____

4. What climate contrast is the author making between the natural home of a polar bear and the one in a zoo?

_____

5. Complete the following two lines with your own examples:

So think about it long and hard upon entering a store

To buy a/an _____ that was meant to crawl or a/an _____ that was meant to soar.

RECOGNIZING THE AUTHOR'S PURPOSE IN POETRY II

The first three poems below are examples of haiku. Haiku has four major characteristics.

1. A brief title

2. Subjects: Nature and the seasons

3. Three lines: 1st line, 5 syllables; 2nd line, 7 syllables; 3rd line, 5 syllables

4. Rhyming: Not necessary; rarely used

Haiku is often written to give a message to readers; that is, the author has a purpose. It sometimes takes deep thinking to determine the purpose. And, different readers may see different purposes.

To Do:

1. Try to determine the author's purposes in the following haikus. Write your ideas on the lines that follow each poem.

Earth

Earth, so very old—
Flowers, trees, rocks, sky, water—
Strong, yet so fragile.

Purpose: _____

_____

_____

_____

Redwood Tree

Tall, strong, but tender,
On Earth a thousand seasons,
Blunt the axe that strikes.

Purpose: _____

_____

_____

_____

Eagle

Soaring, climbing high,
Wind under your spreading wings—
Stay safe, stay aloft.

Purpose: _____

_____

_____

_____

2. The poem that follows was written for a book on the environment. It was in a section of the book that was about the importance of conservation.

Read the poem, and then write what you think was in the author's mind.

Animals

Whales, dolphins, and manatees,
Lions, tigers, chimpanzees,
Chipmunks, rabbits, elephants, too—
Are part of Earth, just like you!

_____

_____

_____

_____

3. Write a haiku for which you have a purpose in mind. Environmental topics lend themselves well to purposes. Some topics: whales, dolphins, tigers, hawks, elephants, soil, trees, flowers, water, air, etc.

Before writing your poem on the lines below, work out the details on another piece of paper. When you are finished, share your poem with others and see if they understand its purpose.

Title: _____

_____

_____

READING FOR THOROUGH COMPREHENSION I

Mike, a rough-and-ready kind of boy, and Jonathan, who was just the opposite, were the best of friends. Jonathan had a severe heart condition that prohibited him from engaging in any kind of strenuous activity. The story that follows is part of a longer story called "On Being Friends."* As the episode below opens, Mike and Jonathan are taking a shortcut through the woods on their way home from school.

1 Jonathan and Mike broke out of the woods, and there was the pond—frozen over. Mike became excited and said that he hoped to be able to go skating the next day, which was Saturday. He said to Jonathan, "I'm going to test the ice to see if it's okay for skating."

2 Jonathan didn't think that was a good idea. He said, "No, Mike. Don't do that. The police will test the ice, and they'll put a sign up if it's safe to skate."

3 "I'm going to test it anyway." Mike replied. "I won't go far." Then he picked up a slender branch about eight feet long and handed it to Jonathan. "Here, Jon, you hold this branch on one end, and I'll hold the other end. If the ice cracks or breaks, you can pull me in." Then, seeing the doubt on Jonathan's face, he continued, "It's going to be okay, Jon. I won't be out there more than a few feet."

4 Jonathan still had misgivings, but Mike seemed sure of himself, so Jon didn't protest anymore. He just warned Mike to be careful and not to let go of the branch.

5 Mike stepped gingerly onto the ice. "See," he said. "It's solid." Then he ventured the length of the branch, one step at a time. Suddenly, the ice cracked. Mike screamed, and down he went into the icy water, over his head. Then be bobbed up. Jonathan was almost pulled onto the ice when Mike went down, but somehow he managed to stay on shore and hold on to the branch.

6 Mike was trying desperately to get back on the ice, but although he tried again and again he couldn't make it. He was rapidly becoming cold and numb; he couldn't survive much longer.

7 Jonathan kept tugging on the branch, but to no avail. Finally, Mike's stiffened hands gave up the branch. He shouted, "Jon! Go for help. I can't get out! I can't get out!"

8 Jonathan didn't know what to do. The nearest house was about half of a mile away. He knew he couldn't run that far, and he had the awful feeling that Mike would slip under the ice and never be found if he left. He decided that there was only one thing to do—try to save Mike himself. He picked up a rock somewhat smaller than a soccer ball. He was going to break a path through the ice to Mike; then Mike could swim and walk out.

The next step was when Jonathan showed his true intelligence. Instead of pounding the ice start-

9 ing from the shore, he laid himself on the ice and wriggled out to the edge of the ice that surrounded Mike. He did it that way because he knew that if he started from the shore and worked outward he would be in frigid water. He also knew that he wouldn't be able to stand that—his heart would give up.

10 After he reached the open water by Mike he laboriously lifted the rock over his head and pounded it on the ice. Crunch, a piece of the ice broke off. Then, he wriggled a little backward toward the shore. Crunch, another piece. Wriggle. Crunch, another piece. With each piece Mike moved a little closer to the shore. Jonathan was becoming exhausted; he didn't have much wind or strength left, but he did have determination. Wriggle, crunch, and still another piece broke off.

11 Mike was now up to his waist because the bank of the pond sloped upward, and he was able to help Jonathan. He took the rock from his friend and began breaking the ice with all his strength. Suddenly, the ice gave way and Jonathan was in the water. But now Mike could walk out because there was an open path to the shore. He pulled Jonathan with him until both lay exhausted and gasping on the beach. Jonathan was all but done in.

12 Mike knew they couldn't stay on the shore. Jonathan would die if Mike didn't fetch help. Then, Mike showed his real mettle. He took off his coat, laid it on the ground, and dragged Jonathan until he was lying on the coat. Then he used the coat as a sled to pull Jonathan over the snow-covered ground.

13 After prodigious effort Mike hauled his friend within a quarter mile of the nearest house. He didn't have the strength to pull anymore. So he told Jonathan to stay there, that he was going to run to the nearest house and get help.

14 Mike covered the distance to the house in Olympic-record time. He pounded on the door, roused the people, and told them the problem. Mike and the man of the house ran to where Jon was lying. Meanwhile, the man's wife called the emergency squad. The man, a strapping fellow, picked Jonathan up and ran for the house. Mike, with the welcome siren of the emergency vehicle in his ears, trailed behind. When they reached the house, the man's wife was waiting with blankets in her arms.

*Adapted from *On Becoming a Teacher: Tales of Tears and Laughter*, James F. Silver.

© 1998 by John Wiley & Sons, Inc.

READING FOR THOROUGH COMPREHENSION II

The questions that follow review some of the reading skills you practiced in this section. The questions are divided into several categories.

Details and Facts

1. On what day did the incident reported in the story occur? _____

2. Why were the boys going through the woods? _____

3. What was Mike's purpose in going out on the ice? _____

_____

4. What two things did Jonathan tell Mike to do before Mike went out on the ice? _____ and _____

5. Was the water deeper than Mike was tall? _____ Explain your answer. _____

_____

6. Why did Mike let go of the branch? _____

_____

7. What is one reason Jonathan didn't run to the nearest house for help? _____

_____

8. Underline the two sentences that explain why Jonathan started to break the ice from Mike to the shore rather than from the shore to Mike.

9. Why was Mike able to swim and walk out of the lake? _____

_____

10. What did Mike use to drag/pull Jonathan over the snow? _____

_____

11. How far was Mike from the nearest house when he stopped dragging Mike? _____

_____

12. What two things did the woman of the house do to help? _____ and _____

Main Ideas

Each of the main ideas stated below is related to one of the numbered paragraphs. On the line before each main idea write the number of the paragraph with which it is most closely related.

____ Jonathan warns Mike not to go out on the ice.

____ Mike falls into the lake.

____ Jonathan plans to save Mike.

____ Jonathan falls into the icy water.

____ Mike decides to seek help.

Vocabulary

What is the meaning of the underlined words as used in the sentences?

a. Paragraph 10: **laboriously**

____with ease   ____with great effort

____without strain

b. Paragraph 5: **gingerly**

____heavily   ____awkwardly   ____carefully

c. Paragraph 13: **prodigious**

____minor   ____extraordinary   ____minimum

Figurative Speech

What sentence in paragraph 14 is exaggeration?

_____

_____

_____

_____

Inferences

1. Write one inference about Mike's personality.

2. Write one inference about the relationship between Mike and Jonathan.

3. Write one inference about the wife of the man who rescued Jonathan.

Note: Write your inferences on the reverse side of this page.

NOTES

Section 2: Reading and Vocabulary

Reading and Vocabulary (RV)

RV–1	Guidelines for Prefixes and Suffixes (Instructor)
RV–2	Practice in Prefixes and Suffixes I
RV–3	Practice in Prefixes and Suffixes II
RV–4	Guidelines for Root Words (Instructor)
RV–5	Practice in Root Words
RV–6	Guidelines for Glossaries (Instructor)
RV–7	Determining Word Meanings from Glossaries
RV–8	Grouping Words with Similar Meanings
RV–9	Dictionaries and Context as Word-Meaning Helps (Instructor)
RV–10	Determining the Meanings of Unknown Words
RV–11	Using Context Clues to Determine Meanings of Words
RV–12	Synonym Crossword Puzzle
RV–13	Antonym Crossword Puzzle
RV–14	Guidelines for Figurative Language (Instructor)
RV–15	Practice in Figurative Language
RV–16	Stimulate Imaginations with Similes and Metaphors (Instructor)
RV–17	Creating Similes and Metaphors
RV–18	Guidelines for Analogies (Instructor)
RV–19	Completing Analogies I
RV–20	Completing Analogies II
RV–21	A "Synonymous Titles" Puzzle
RV–22	Understanding Compound Words
RV–23	Recognizing Homophones
RV–24	Homophone Crossword Puzzle
RV–25	Understanding and Using Homographs
RV–26	Some Experiences with Foreign Expressions

GUIDELINES FOR PREFIXES AND SUFFIXES

Knowledge of prefixes and suffixes has the effect of widening one's vocabulary. They are much like basic tools that have multiple uses as, for example, a boy-scout knife that can be used as a can opener, a screwdriver, an awl, and other ways. Likewise, prefixes and suffixes can be added to base words to create new words.

Prefixes

1. What is a prefix?

A prefix is a part of a word, always at the beginning, that modifies the part of the word that comes after it.

2. How are prefixes useful?

If one knows the meaning and applications of a prefix one can decipher the meaning of a strange or unknown word, especially if the unfamiliar word is encountered in a contextual situation. For example, the prefix mono means one or only. So, one who talks in a monotone, as a robot, does not vary volume or expression when speaking. Following are some other applications of mono as a prefix:

- **monocle**: a single eyeglass
- **monocular**: using only one eye
- **monolith**: single great stone, as Georgia's Stone Mountain
- **monomaniac**: a person obsessed with one main idea, theory, or objective
- **monosyllable**: a word that has only one syllable
- **monotheism**: a belief that there is only one God

A prefix that has the opposite meaning of mono is poly. Poly is an especially helpful prefix because it has many applications. *Webster's New Collegiate Dictionary* lists more than 125 words that begin with poly. Following are some examples:

- **polyandry**: the practice in some cultures of women having more than one husband
- **polychromatic**: having a variety of colors, as a rainbow
- **polyglot**: having a mixture of languages, as a polyglot nation
- **polytheism**: a belief that there is more than one god, as in ancient Greece

3. In some cases the prefix is separated from the root word by a hyphen. The separation is designed to avoid confusion. Following are some examples:

- **re-covered** the pillow (re- again)
- **pro-American** (pro- for)
- **pre-Colombian** (pre- before)
- **post-Middle Ages** (post- after)
- **co-worker** (co- with)
- **anti-hero** (anti- against, opposite)

Suffixes

1. Suffixes appear at the ends of words and serve the same purposes as prefixes; that is, they modify the meaning of the part of the word that precedes them.

Following are some examples:

- **able** (also ible): capable of, full of, fit for, as **lovable**, a person who has endearing qualities; or **knowledgeable**, one who is full of learning; or **flexible**, something that can be moved or changed
- **hood**: state of being, as **adulthood**, state of a person who has reached full maturity; or **priesthood**, state of one who has qualified to be a priest
- **ist**: one who performs in a particular profession, as, for example, **dentist**; or one who works with or studies living things, as, for example, **biologist**

2. Some words contain both prefixes and suffixes. Following are some examples: (The prefixes and suffixes are underlined.)

- **transportable**: capable of being moved
- **impossible**: cannot be done
- **unavailable**: cannot be had
- **incredible**: cannot be believed
- **exporter**: one who sends things out of the country

PRACTICE IN PREFIXES AND SUFFIXES I

Prefixes and suffixes can give root words new meanings. For example, the word <u>developed</u> takes on a new meaning when we put the prefix <u>un</u> (which means not) in front of it so that the word becomes <u>undeveloped</u>. Undeveloped means not completed or not changed.

The word <u>American</u> takes another meaning when we add the suffix <u>ize</u> and make the word <u>Americanize</u>. To Americanize someone is to help someone of a different culture assimilate American culture.

Following is a list of some of the most common prefixes and suffixes with meanings and examples.

Prefixes

Prefix	Meaning	Examples
anti	against, opposite	*Uncle Tom's Cabin* is an <u>anti</u>slavery novel.
bi	two	To <u>bi</u>sect a square is to cut it in half.
circum	to go around	Magellan was the first to <u>circum</u>navigate the world.
dis	deprive, exclude	We will <u>dis</u>miss the class in time for the game.
ex	out of, from, outside	Your bad behavior means we will have to <u>ex</u>clude you. / We <u>ex</u>port corn to Europe.
im, in, non, un	not, the absence of	The story was <u>un</u>believable. / The account of the event was <u>in</u>accurate.
inter	between, among	In the group there was an <u>inter</u>change of ideas.
mis	wrong, incorrect	Please do not <u>mis</u>understand what I am saying.
mono	one, only	A person giving a <u>mono</u>logue about one subject is sometimes <u>mono</u>tonous.
poly, multi	many	A <u>poly</u>hedron has two or more sides. / People from many countries made the group <u>multi</u>ethnic.
post	after, later	A <u>post</u>script, which follows the main part of a letter, is an afterthought.
pre	before, early	She took a <u>pre</u>test as part of her <u>pre</u>paration.
sub	under, below	A <u>sub</u>way helps keep traffic off the streets above it.
super	best, great	He made a <u>super</u>human effort in the last 20 yards and helped his team win the game.

Suffixes

Suffix	Meaning	Examples
able, ible	capable, fit for	Fruit is perish<u>able</u>. / It was imposs<u>ible</u> to cross the canyon.
ate	act on, change	The doctor will oper<u>ate</u> to mend the broken leg.
ify	become, make, cause	Caves terr<u>ify</u> some people. / He did not qual<u>ify</u> for the scholarship.
graph	written, recorded	The petro<u>graph</u> was carved in the granite wall.
ic	form of, consisting of	A person who is insane is sometimes called a luna<u>tic</u>.
ion	process, condition	Irrigat<u>ion</u> uses much water, but plants die without it.
ist	one who does something	Her constant piano practicing made her an excellent pian<u>ist</u>.
ism	a belief	Rac<u>ism</u> can do nothing but hurt innocent people.
ite	a part of something, follower	As a Jersey<u>ite</u>, he was proud of the part his state played in the Revolutionary War.
ity	quality, state of being	He showed his hostil<u>ity</u> by refusing to cooperate.
ize	change, alter, treat as	Some people idol<u>ize</u> movie stars. / Try not to critic<u>ize</u>; look for the good.
less	without	Her singing and acting were fault<u>less</u>.
ory	a place of or for	The observat<u>ory</u> was high on a mountain, where the air was clear.
ous	full of something	It was a marvel<u>ous</u> exhibition of art.

PRACTICE IN PREFIXES AND SUFFIXES II

Prefixes

Add an appropriate prefix to the following root words.

1. One day we shall _____plore the planets.
2. I _____approve of your smoking.
3. Space is scarce on a _____marine.
4. Some day there will be _____planetary travel.
5. With only one eye, you have what is known as _____cular vision.
6. Read carefully or you might _____interpret the message.
7. The _____market had a special sale on frozen food.
8. Don't _____pone until tomorrow what you can do today.
9. I want to _____view the film before I show it to my class.
10. It is _____gracious to accept a gift and not thank the giver.
11. You are all required to write _____weekly reports.
12. Norma uses a _____stick pan when she fries eggs.
13. The demonstration was an _____war protest.
14. The geometric figure was a _____gon.

Suffixes

Add an appropriate suffix to the following root words.

1. He has the agil_____ of a monkey.
2. If you simon_____ your car, it will have a bright shine.
3. Her voice on the telephone was so frant___ I could tell that she was very frightened.
4. His auto_____ was difficult to read.
5. Prisoners were often treated in a heart_____ manner.
6. He swore an unending enm_____ against those who attacked his country.
7. The laborat_____ was filled with the odor of chemicals.
8. He gave the student a favor_____ recommendation.
9. He tried to obliter_____ all traces of the mess he had made.
10. He managed to amass a fabul_____ fortune in the shipping business.
11. Some mushrooms are not ed_____; they are poison_____.
12. Isolation_____ means that we will not have anything to do with other countries.
13. It is through perspirat_____ that the human body cools itself.

It is probable that you frequently use words that contain prefixes and suffixes. Recall some of those words and list them below. The words you list probably contain prefixes and suffixes that are on your photocopy page, or some of them may not be on the list. In either case, underline the prefixes or suffixes in your words.

Prefixes

_____ _____

_____ _____

_____ _____

_____ _____

_____ _____

Suffixes

_____ _____

_____ _____

_____ _____

_____ _____

_____ _____

GUIDELINES FOR ROOT WORDS

Many of the words we use originated with the ancient Greeks and Romans. In most cases such words are no longer written in their original form; we have adapted them to our use. For example, from the Latin (Roman) word *spectare* (to look at) many English words have been derived: spectator (one who looks), spectacles (eye glasses we look through), spectroscope (an instrument used for a closer look), and at least 20 other words. What this example shows, then, is that if we are familiar with Greek and Latin words, we may be able to decipher the meaning of a strange word, especially if we encounter the word in a contextual setting such as a complete sentence or paragraph.

The following sentence uses the word *porter*, a word that might be unknown to some young readers: The *porter* carried the tourist's bags to her room. *Porter* derives from the Latin word *portare* (to carry); a porter is one who carries things. There is an obvious relationship between *portare* and *porter*. So, with a little associative thought, the meaning of *portare*, as used in the sentence, can be derived.

Suggested Instructional Procedure

Following are lists of selected Greek and Roman words. The lists may be photocopied and distributed to students for use with the accompanying student application page.

Latin

English Verbs	Latin Equivalent
to believe	credare
to carry	portare
to hear	audire
to judge	judicare
to lead	ducere
to look at	spectare
to say	dicere
to turn	volvere
to write	scribere

English Nouns	Latin Equivalent
doctor	medicus
feast	festum
future	futurus
great	magnus
hand	manus
head, chief	caput
middle	medius
oil	oleum
people	populous
rock	petra
shade	umbra
water	aqua
year	annus

Greek

English Words	Greek Spelling	English Spelling
ancient	archaios	archaeo
belief	ismos	ism
book(s)	biblion	biblio
city	polis	polis
earth, ground	geo	geo
fear	phobos	phobe
god	theos	theo
humans, man	anthropos	anthropo
knowledge, wisdom	sophia	sophy
life (related to)	bios	bio
loving, liking	philos	phila
many, much	polys	poly
on top, high	akros	acro
one, alone	monos	mono
people	demos	demos
rule, government	kratos	cracy
self	autos	auto
study	legein	logy
writing, listing	graphein	graph

PRACTICE IN ROOT WORDS

In the following sentences some English words are used that were developed from Greek and Roman words. You may have never seen or heard the words, but by consulting the lists of Greek and Latin words you will be able to decipher their meanings and significantly add to your vocabulary.

1. On the blank line in each item write what you think is the meaning of the underlined word.

a. She has a phobia about flying in an airplane.

_____

b. A great amount of petroleum is needed to keep America's automobiles rolling. _____

c. A country that is a democracy gives great power to the people. _____

d. She said she was going to college to study geology. _____

e. He doesn't read very much; I think he is a bibliophobe. _____

f. Benjamin Franklin's autobiography is interesting. _____

g. The gears on the old automobile had to be operated manually. _____

h. The excavators found many things of archaeological value. _____

i. The television show had a futuristic theme.

_____

j. The earth revolves around the sun; it takes one year. _____

k. The parade takes place annually on Memorial Day. _____

l. The conductor of the orchestra bowed to the audience when they applauded. _____

m. The crowd was so noisy that the speaker's voice was barely audible. _____

n. He decided to devote his life to theology.

_____

2. What would it mean if a person was said to be:

a. polytheistic? _____

_____

_____

b. a philosopher? _____

_____

_____

c. an acrophobe? _____

_____

_____

d. an archaeologist? _____

_____

_____

3. Write two words that end with ism.

a. _____

b. _____

4. Think of one English word that is related to or probably came from the Latin word for:

a. shade _____

b. doctor _____

c. middle _____

d. people _____

e. to write _____

f. to hear _____

g. to believe _____

5. Think of one English word that is related to or probably came from the Greek word for:

a. one _____

b. earth _____

c. many _____

d. belief _____

e. life _____

f. city _____

GUIDELINES FOR GLOSSARIES

Glossaries

A glossary is a collection of special or unusual words, terms, and phrases and their explanations used in a particular book. The expressions are listed in alphabetical order and are defined. Glossaries appear in an appendix of a book, generally immediately after the main text.

Glossaries are useful for several reasons:

1. They are convenient. The quickly and easily located strange or new expressions make it unnecessary to use a dictionary. Some students place a paper tab or clip on the page where a glossary begins and, thus, save time when an explanation of an expression is needed.

2. Some words have multiple meanings. If a dictionary is used it may be necessary to select a meaning that satisfies a need from a number of offered meanings. When using a dictionary some inexperienced readers may decide on a meaning that is not really compatible with the context where the expression appears. However, in a glossary the definitions offered have direct and specific application to the subject being studied.

3. Some glossaries tell both the page and column where glossary words first appear.

4. Some glossaries offer information as to how unusual words are pronounced and syllabicated.

5. A glossary may be thought of as being a list of the key words or phrases of a subject. It has been said that if one knows the vocabulary of a subject, one knows the subject. If the words in a glossary are studied and learned, it is probable that the student's understanding of the subject—and test scores—will be greater.

Note: The following page offers students an opportunity to become familiar with glossaries.

Procedure

1. Distribute photocopies of the following page.

2. Read the explanation of glossaries at the bottom of this page. Supplement with information from the information at the top of this page.

3. Give your students some practice in using a dictionary's pronunciation guide using words from the Glossary on the following page (adobe, spermaceti, travois).

4. Direct students to complete the activity on their photocopied pages.

Directions

The partial glossary on your photocopy page contains expressions (words, terms, phrases, etc.) that might appear in a typical American history textbook. Notice that you are told where in the textbook the expression is first used. For example, p. 114, col. 1 means that the expression was first used on page 114 in the first column. The glossary explanation helps you understand the expression as it was used in the book.

DETERMINING WORD MEANINGS FROM GLOSSARIES

Glossary

(1) **adobe**, p. 26, col. 2: Dried mud or clay poured into molds and allowed to harden and then used as building blocks

(2) **Emancipation Proclamation**, p. 260, col. 2: An announcement by the U.S. government that slaves in the Confederacy were to be free

(3) **forty-niners**, p. 220, col. 2: People who journeyed to California in 1849 seeking gold

(4) **fur fair**, 108, col. 2: An annual event held in Quebec where French traders and Indians met to carry on trade and to enjoy food and games

(5) **Mercator map**, p. 17: A flat map on which lines of longitude are straight north and south rather than curved toward the poles

(6) **parallels**, p. 13, col. 2: East-west map lines parallel to the equator

(7) **Pennsylvania Dutch**, p. 129, col. 1: German-speaking people who settled in what is now southeastern Pennsylvania

(8) **polls**, p. 175, col. 1: A designated place in a community where people go to vote

(9) **sod house** (picture caption), p. 198: A house with outside walls made of square or rectangular blocks of sod grass and turf; sometimes referred to as "soddies"

(10) **spermaceti**, p. 152, col. 1: A waxy solid obtained from whale oil; used for candles, cosmetics, ointments

(11) **travois**, p. 142, col. 1: Two trailing poles harnessed to dogs; used by Indians for transporting loads

(12) **windbreak**, p. 190, col. 2: A line of trees that slows and blocks winds, thus preventing soil erosion and dust storms

© 1998 by John Wiley & Sons, Inc.

The sentences below are typical of those found in an American history book. Read the sentences and notice the italicized words. Then find the explanation of the words in the glossary and write the appropriate number on the line in front of the sentence.

— In spite of many hardships, the *forty-niners* crossed the country in search of their fortunes.

— Many slaves in the Confederacy could hardly believe the words of the *Emancipation Proclamation.*

— In general, it is much colder on the 70th *parallel* north of the equator than on the 20th north *parallel.*

— *Poll* workers are carefully chosen; they must ensure that voting is properly conducted.

— *Pennsylvania Dutch* is a way of speaking in which German words and English words are used in the same sentence.

— Wood and stone are scarce on the Great Plains, so settlers made *sod houses*, or "soddies" as they were sometimes called.

— At the *fur fair* the Indians traded their furs for knives, hatchets, guns, and ammunition.

— The Southwest Indians built *adobe* houses, sometimes three or four stories high and connected, as in today's condominiums.

— As a result of extensive planting of *windbreaks*, thousands of tons of topsoil have been prevented from blowing away.

— When you read a *Mercator map*, realize that places in the far northern and southern parts of the world are shown much larger than they really are.

— It was easy to tell when a group of Indians had passed by, the *travois* left two evenly spaced lines in the earth.

— Colonial settlers were very dependent upon whales to furnish the *spermaceti* needed to make candles.

Name: _____   Date: _____

GROUPING WORDS WITH SIMILAR MEANINGS

This is a vocabulary/categorization activity. It has been designed to help you to broaden your verbal concepts and your vocabulary. Also, you will better realize that in writing it is possible to use a variety of words having the same basic meaning but having slight differences, or "shades," of meaning.

Your task is to list words from the word list that are related to the word at the head of each column. All the words you place under a particular heading should make sense as substitutes for the underlined words in the sentence.

| leading (adj.) as used in, "He was the leading negotiator in arranging the treaty." | riot (noun) as in, "The National Guard was called to break up the riot." | announce (verb) as used in, "We will announce the law throughout the country." | bold (adj.) as used in, "Paul Revere was a bold patriot in the American Revolution." | honest (adj.) as used in, "Abe Lincoln was known to be an honest person." |

advertise	publish	truthful	free from trickery	disturbance
reliable	daring	heroic	courageous	make known
uproar	declare	foremost	dauntless	brawl
fearless	valiant	unafraid	head	give notice of
most important	chief	sincere	proclaim	trustworthy
quarrel	outbreak	principal	major	strife
first	commotion	broadcast	circulate	decent
main	honorable	fair	mutiny	brave

leading	riot	announce	bold	honest

DICTIONARIES AND CONTEXT AS WORD-MEANING HELPS

Often, a reader recognizes a word and has previously learned meanings to attach to it. Unfortunately, sometimes none of the meanings are what the author intended to convey. And, sometimes the reader can attach no meaning to an encountered word. These situations can lead to misunderstandings and mistakes.

For example, the three-letter word <u>run</u> seems simple enough; however, it has literally scores of meanings that are dependent upon how it is used. <u>Run</u> can be a noun (the dog run) or a verb (See Dick run!). Then, to complicate the meanings of run even more, there are numerous spinoffs of the word. *Webster's New Collegiate Dictionary* lists more than 50 run words such as <u>runaway</u> (overwhelming victory) and <u>run over</u> (extending beyond allotted time).

Ask your students to visualize the following situations as though they didn't know the meaning of the expression.

- "The train ran down the track." (Does the train have legs?)

- "She ran the office most efficiently." (Is there a track in the office?)

- "The lady ran up a very high bill at the clothing store." (She must be very tired.)

- "I don't need this runaround any more." (A portable exercise machine?)

- "He ran down his opponent's character. (Must be some kind of ladder or ramp.)

What to do in a situation where a familiar word is used in an unfamiliar way or where one encounters an entirely new word? The obvious answer is to check in a dictionary, but, before doing that, the reader should consider the context surrounding the word. Otherwise, the dictionary search may be frustrating.

The context may give the reader enough clues to attack the multiple meanings that may be offered in the dictionary. Is the word acting as a verb? A noun? An adjective? Is there a part of the word that is familiar, for example, the prefix <u>pseudo</u> (false), the suffix <u>phile</u> (love), or the root <u>volvere</u> (to turn)? Then, if the reader does look in the dictionary, it may verify what the reader thinks is the meaning, or the dictionary may suggest a meaning that fits the context. Or, maybe, a search in the dictionary will not prove necessary because the reader's analyzation solved the mystery. However, in any case, context should be considered.

Suggestions for Teaching

1. The following page offers practice opportunities for learners to discern the meanings of words by using context clues and/or dictionaries.

2. If there are not enough dictionaries in the class for every student, use this lesson as an opportunity for cooperative learning/sharing, which could add to the total learning experience.

3. After the activity has been completed it would be helpful to discuss each item and discover the "mind-workings" that led to the students' answers.

"The train ran down the track."

DETERMINING THE MEANINGS OF UNKNOWN WORDS

1.　Visitors to Alaska are amazed to see glaciers <u>calve</u>. Large chunks of ice break off, crash into the water, sink deep, rise, and then float away.

___ melt

___ separate

___ explode

2.　The <u>aborigines</u> of Australia were very surprised to see the first European explorers, who wore strange clothes and carried "sticks" that made loud noises.

___ kangaroos

___ first English settlers

___ native people

3.　The <u>archipelago</u> was first discovered by European explorers. It took three days to sail around it. Almost immediately after sight of land was lost, another palm-lined shore was sighted.

___ an island

___ group of islands

___ a continent

___ a peninsula

4.　The <u>cairn</u> could not have happened by accident; the human touch was there even though some of the stones were off to the side.

___ a jumble of rocks

___ an even pile of stones

5.　Most of the trees were <u>coniferous</u>. Pine cones were all over the forest floor. Occasionally an oak tree was seen, but they were few and far between.

___ trees with needles

___ trees with broad leaves

6.　The <u>drumlin</u> left by the retreating glacier was perfect for skiing. The slope at the south end was quite steep; the slope at the north end was more gradual.

___ oval hill shaped like a half egg with its flat side on the ground

___ a plateau that has steep sides

___ a mountain peak

7.　When hiking in the Alps Mountains one must be careful of <u>crevasses</u>. Usually they are not wide and not easily seen. It can be a very long way down to the bottom, very cold, and others may not hear your cries for help.

___ a deep crack in the surface of ice

___ a hole in an ice-covered lake

___ a volcano crater

8.　The <u>geologist</u> said, "The glaciers had the effect of scraping the surface of the earth and then carrying what they had scraped, such as soil and large rocks, for long distances."

___ a scientist who studies the countries of the world and how humans use natural resources to live.

___ a scientist who studies how wind, water, heat, and cold affect the earth; the layers of the earth; earthquakes, volcanoes, and so on.

9.　Some rivers flow rapidly, others flow slowly. When viewed from the air, a river that <u>meanders</u> gives the appearance of a great snake winding its way across the land.

___ flows around curves

___ tumbles over falls and rapids

___ flows only part of the year

___ flows through very mountainous land

10. If you are in the mountains and it is warm and it starts to <u>mizzle</u>, you had better put on a raincoat, or you will get soaking wet.

___ sleet

___ snow

___ hail

___ lightly rain within a cloud

USING CONTEXT CLUES TO DETERMINE MEANINGS OF WORDS

To complete the activity on the previous page it was necessary to choose a meaning for a strange word from two or more choices. In this activity no clues are given except those that are expressed or implied in the context of the short paragraphs.

To Do:

Write a synonym and a definition for each of the italicized words in the following selections.

1. It is not enough to know a subject to teach it effectively. A teacher must be knowledgeable in the *methodology* of instruction. How a lesson is taught is at least as important as what is taught.

Synonym:_____ Definition: _____

_____

2. There is something good to be said about the *heterogeneous* grouping of students in a class. A mixture of students with different ethnic, racial, economic, and cultural backgrounds is more akin to a democracy than a *homogeneous* grouping of students with similar backgrounds, traits, and social characteristics.

Synonym:_____ Definition: _____

_____

Synonym:_____ Definition: _____

_____

3. Many grievances between individuals, groups, and public and private organizations could be settled *amicably* if there were more *ombudsmen*. They could bring disputing parties together to talk things over and settle differences in peaceful ways, without hiring attorneys and going to court.

Synonym:_____ Definition: _____

_____

Synonym:_____ Definition: _____

_____

4. Persons who are thinking about purchasing large pieces of land find it useful to *perambulate* the boundaries before buying. By walking boundaries they may discover some undesirable features, for example, places where waste products were illegally dumped.

Synonym:_____ Definition: _____

_____

5. Deer ticks are *minuscule*, but the disease they can transmit can be very serious. They are not much larger than the period at the end of this sentence, so they are often undetected as they burrow their way into their victim's skin. The result of their burrowing can be an infection that causes Lyme disease.

Synonym:_____ Definition: _____

_____

6. Graduating from college with the term *summa cum laude* on your degree is a very special recognition. You must have worked very hard to be included in the highest-scoring portion of your class.

Synonym:_____ Definition: _____

_____

© 1998 by John Wiley & Sons, Inc.

Name: _____ **Date:** _____

SYNONYM CROSSWORD PUZZLE

1. This activity will help you increase your vocabulary by introducing words that may not be in your everyday usage.

2. To complete the Synonym Crossword Puzzle, think of synonyms for the words in the ACROSS and DOWN listings. You can find synonyms by looking in a thesaurus or a dictionary.

3. All the words that are to be printed in the puzzle are listed in alphabetical order at the bottom of the page.

SYNONYM CROSSWORD PUZZLE

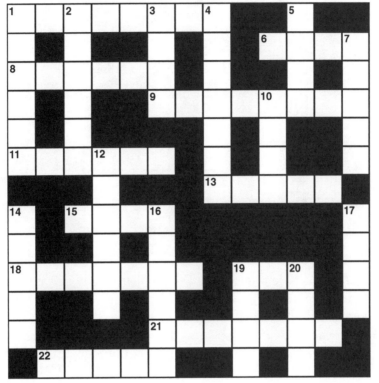

ACROSS

1. RESIGN, QUIT
6. STAB, PIERCE
8. ERASE, ELIMINATE
9. PASS THROUGH
11. OPINION, HYPOTHESIS
13. PRAISE, COMMEND
15. TOP, PEAK
18. INTRODUCTION, BEGINNING
19. MODERN, UP-TO-DATE
21. BLAME, CRITICIZE
22. FIRST

DOWN

1. KIDNAP, CARRY OFF
2. FLOOD, OVERFLOW
3. HELP, AID
4. INCREASE, EXPAND
5. FASTEN, SECURE
7. OPPONENT, FOE
10. SEND FORTH, DISCHARGE
12. HIDDEN, SECRET
14. LUKEWARM, MILD
16. SUFFER, PUT UP WITH
17. TRUDGE, TRAVEL SLOWLY
19. MARKET
20. GO UNDER

SYNONYM LIST

ABDICATE	DELETE	ENDURE	GORE	OCCULT	REPROVE
ABDUCT	DELUGE	ENEMY	MART	PLOD	TEPID
ABET	DIVE	ENLARGE	MOD	PRELUDE	THEORY
ACME	EMIT	EXTOL	MOOR	PRIME	TRAVERSE

Name: _____ **Date:** _____

ANTONYM CROSSWORD PUZZLE

1. The crossword puzzle on this page is an ANTONYM CROSSWORD PUZZLE. Antonyms, you will remember, are opposite words. For example the opposite of **up** is **down**; the opposite of **near** is **far**, and so on. As in the synonym puzzle, a dictionary or a thesaurus can be helpful.

2. All the words that are to be printed in the puzzle are listed in alphabetical order at the bottom of this page.

3. As you will note, the first ACROSS antonym has already been printed in the puzzle to help you get started. UNSCRUPULOUS is an antonym for, a word that contrasts the meaning of, HONEST.

© 1998 by John Wiley & Sons, Inc.

ACROSS

1. HONEST
5. AMATEUR
8. INNER
10. REMAIN THE SAME
11. INCAPABLE
13. RECEIVED
14. EXHALE
17. ALLOW
20. STOP
21. INEFFICIENT
22. WRITTEN
23. PERSUADE, COAX

DOWN

2. UNCOOPERATIVE
3. ACTIVE
4. FANCY
6. YES
7. FEEBLE
9. FEARFUL, COWARDLY
12. CALM
15. LIGHTWEIGHT
16. HAVE
18. WHISPER
19. APPROVE

ANTONYM AND CONTRASTING WORD LIST

ABLE	EFFICIENT	HEFTY	ORAL	PROFESSIONAL	UNSCRUPULOUS
BAN	FORCE	INHALE	OUTER	ROAR	VARY
BRAVE	FRANTIC	LACK	PASSIVE	ROBUST	VETO
COOPERATIVE	GO	NAY	PLAIN	SENT	

GUIDELINES FOR FIGURATIVE LANGUAGE

Students should become familiar with figures of speech and learn to recognize and interpret them when they are used in poetry or prose. This is especially important for readers who are inclined to assign literal meanings to what they read or hear. Some readers take printed and spoken words as rigid expressions that are not to be extended. They are utterly lost by figurative language such as, "His eyes were glued to the blackboard." They are liable to misinterpret or not completely understand what they are reading. Also, from an appreciation point-of-view they don't experience the humor or irony of what is being expressed.

Following are the most common forms of figurative language, each accompanied by a definition and examples.

1. **Simile**: Two or more things are compared with **as** or **like** stating the relationship between the items. Note that for a simile to be meaningful it is necessary for the reader/hearer to know about both items in the comparison. Consider, for example, "Sparks and ashes spurted out of the chimney like an erupting volcano." This simile would have little meaning to one who had never experienced a spurting chimney or an erupting volcano.

Examples
- His movements were as stiff and mechanical as a robot's.
- When she sang her voice was as clear and resonant as a bell.

2. **Metaphor**: A comparison that suggests a likeness between two objects. However, a metaphor differs from a simile; it does not use **as** or **like**. A metaphor does not say something is **like** something; rather it asserts one thing **is** the other thing.

Examples
- In his anger he was a hurricane blowing down everything that was in his path.
- When she danced she was a butterfly flitting from flower to flower.

3. **Oxymoron**: An expression that is self-contradicting. It contains words that are the opposite of each other. Oxymorons are sometimes used purposefully for effect and emphasis; sometimes they are inadvertent.

Examples
- It was a quiet riot.
- She softly shouted.

4. **Hyperbole**: An excessive description of a person, place, thing, or event intended to impress by exaggeration. Often, hyperbole is used in humorous ways such as, "I pushed her on the swing until my arms fell off."

Examples
- His yell was so loud that it made a statue hold its ears.
- At one meal he eats enough to feed an army.

5. **Personification**: Something not human, animate or inanimate, is characterized as having human qualities. Whether an animal, such as a dog, possesses the ability to appreciate humor is moot. Nevertheless, a dog whose mouth curls up is sometimes said to be "laughing."

Examples
- As the raging flood swept down the valley, it swallowed house after house.
- The stubborn car refused to start even after jumper cables were used.

6. **Unnecessary Words**: (Redundancies) An expression, usually two words in succession, in which the first or second word is not needed because the second word cannot be qualified. In effect, the two words are redundant, and redundancies are sometimes used for emphasis.

Examples
- The car came to a full stop. (Stop cannot be qualified. Either something is at a standstill or it is moving.)
- It is a complete total. (A total already implies completeness.)

Suggestions for Teaching

1. After explaining and exemplifying the figures of speech above, have students work out the activity on the following page. *Note*: Instructors may want to photocopy this page for distribution.

2. Some of the figures of speech created by students may not be understood by other students. In such cases have the originators explain the reasoning behind their examples.

Name: _____ **Date:** _____

PRACTICE IN FIGURATIVE LANGUAGE

Figurative language can be expressed in a number of ways. Six of the most frequently used forms are as follows:

- Simile
- Metaphor
- Oxymoron
- Hyperbole
- Personification
- Unnecessary Words (Redundancy)

1. Decide which figure of speech is used in each of the sentences below. Then, write your choice on the blank line that follows each sentence.

a. The couch groaned in protest as the heavy man sat on it. _____

b. The conversation was brilliantly boring. ____

_____

c. He was a charging bull when he broke through the line and made the extra point. _____

d. Just before I fell asleep I heard the sad whistle of the passing train. _____

e. He was as nimble as a squirrel when he walked across the tightrope. _____

f. She was so angry sparks came out of her eyes and mouth. _____

g. Whenever he speaks the building shakes.

_____

h. There was an overwhelming lack of response from the audience. _____

i. It seemed as though all the automobiles in New Jersey were on Interstate 95 at the same time. ___

_____

j. Give me only the true facts. _____

k. He was a roadblock that the committee couldn't get around despite two hours of discussion. _____

_____

l. The car's motor purred like a kitten. _____

_____

2. You can improve your compositions through the use of figurative language. For practice make up one example of each of the four types listed below.

Hyperbole: _____

_____

_____

_____

Simile: _____

_____

_____

_____

Metaphor: _____

_____

_____

_____

Personification: _____

_____

_____

_____

3. Two other types of figurative language are **Oxymoron** and **Unnecessary Words**. These two types do not represent "proper" usage; however, it is interesting and useful to recognize them when you meet them in your reading and even in your own writing. To demonstrate that you really understand them, write an example of each in the spaces provided below. *Note*: They are not easy to compose, so this activity represents a real challenge.

Oxymoron: _____

_____

_____

_____

Unnecessary Words: _____

_____

_____

_____

STIMULATE IMAGINATIONS WITH SIMILES AND METAPHORS

Soup can be nourishing, yet uninteresting to the diner. However, if a few spices are mixed into that soup the result can be delightful eating. Likewise, writing—fiction or nonfiction—can be informative but dull and boring. Without colorful words and expressions there is the possibility that the reader may doze off in the middle of a page.

Comparisons made by similes and metaphors are as helpful to writing as spices are to soup. An apt comparison can bring a smile to a reader's face or, perhaps, contribute insights that might otherwise not come. "She was as nervous as a mouse nibbling the cat's food" does more to stimulate one's imagination than a simple "She was nervous."

Some similes and metaphors, however, have been overworked to the point where they have lost their power to stimulate the imagination—"smooth as glass" and "clumsy as an elephant" are but two examples.

Suggestions for Teaching

1. Be sure that students know the definitions of similes and metaphors. Both are comparisons; however, only a simile employs *like* or *as* as a link between the things being compared. A metaphor makes a comparison by directly applying a name or action to something with which the reader or listener is familiar; consequently, a metaphor is much more direct than a simile.

Example

Simile: "She was as methodical in her typing as a woodpecker tapping a tree trunk."

Metaphor: "When she typed, she was a woodpecker tapping a tree trunk."

2. Write the adjective <u>strong</u> on the chalkboard. Then, encourage students to "brainstorm" <u>strong</u> by offering suggestions as to how the adjective may be used in comparisons.

Ask: To what can strong be applied?

Suggestions:

☐ oxen
☐ bulls
☐ Atlas
☐ Hercules
☐ iron rods
☐ concrete
☐ gravity

☐ oak tree
☐ steel cable
☐ team of horses
☐ vise
☐ hurricane
☐ ocean tides
☐ linked chain

3. After a list of things related to <u>strong</u> has been compiled, students may suggest full similes and metaphors.

Example

<u>Similes</u>: His grip was as strong as a vise.

or

His arms were strong like woven cables.

<u>Metaphors</u>: She was an oak tree standing straight and tall as the crowd pushed past her.

or

His arms were linked chains holding his friend who had slipped off the scaffold.

4. Follow up explanations and examples by assigning the facing student application page. This activity may offer a suitable opportunity for two or more students to work cooperatively.

5. After the work period students may share their creative efforts with their classmates.

Note: It may be that students who are talented in art can draw cartoon-like representations of their similes and metaphors. The results could make an interesting and attractive bulletin board.

Here is a description of a cartoon metaphor in which a man's arms are likened to "linked chains." A worker is shown on a scaffold. He is holding on to another worker who has fallen off the scaffold. The arms of the worker who is holding his coworker are shown as chains with fingers on their ends. Beneath the cartoon is a caption, "His arms were linked chains holding his friend who had slipped off the scaffold."

CREATING SIMILES AND METAPHORS

As a student you have read many books, viewed motion pictures and videos, and experienced many things. The result is that your mind has stored thousands of images that can be used to create original comparisons in the forms of similes and metaphors. The only thing that is necessary is to "mine" your brain for the memories that are deposited there.

To Do:

1. On this page is a list of words that you can use to make comparisons. Think of things that are related to the words. Write them in the spaces provided. Try to list two words for each listed adjective, and try to be as original and creative as possible.

Example: The word is *fast*. What things go fast?

* racing cars
* cheetahs
* race horses
* race cars
* light

* satellites
* house flies
* lightning
* sounds
* electricity

a. **Word**: slow

(1) _____

(2) _____

b. **Word**: quiet

(1) _____

(2) _____

c. **Word**: noisy

(1) _____

(2) _____

d. **Word**: blue

(1) _____

(2) _____

e. **Word**: beautiful

(1) _____

(2) _____

f. **Word**: big

(1) _____

(2) _____

g. **Word**: small

(1) _____

(2) _____

h. **Word**: smooth

(1) _____

(2) _____

2. Write two *similies* in which you use two of the words you have written in a–h on this page. Write complete sentences.

a. _____

_____

_____

b. _____

_____

_____

3. Write two *metaphors* in which you use two of the words you have written in a–h on this page. Write complete sentences.

a. _____

_____

_____

_____

b. _____

_____

_____

_____

GUIDELINES FOR ANALOGIES

Webster's New Collegiate Dictionary defines **analogy** as, "Resemblance in some particulars between things otherwise unlike." The dictionary entry that follows defines **analogy test** as, "A reasoning test that requires the person tested to supply the missing term in a proportion (as **darkness** in the proportion day: light :: night : darkness).* This is an example of a *characteristic* analogy: **day** is characterized by **light**, as **night** is characterized by **darkness**. Thus, the "resemblance in some particulars" requirement is fulfilled.

The "resemblance in some parts" requirement may be fulfilled in other ways. For example, the *antonym* analogy **powerful : weak :: strong : helpless** implies an opposite relationship between the two words in the first part of the analogy. The analogy is completed by two more opposites. In completing analogies it is of first importance to discern the relationship on the left side, and then apply that relationship to the right side.

Parts analogies are concerned with the relationship between the "whole" and the "part." For example, **trigger : gun :: switch : ligh**t. Trigger is the part of a gun that begins the firing sequence, and switch begins the lighting sequence.

Persons analogies associate prominent personalities to major causes, endeavors, organizations, or occupations. This kind of analogy may be useful in teaching history. Consider, for example, Clara Barton : beginning of the American Red Cross :: Woodrow Wilson : ___. Let's assume that students cannot complete the analogy. First, the left side states that Clara Barton started something. So, the right side of the analogy may be completed by telling what Woodrow Wilson was important in starting. A little research in encyclopedias or American history textbooks will reveal Wilson's part in the formation of the League of Nations after World War I.

There is the possibility that Wilson was the originator of other worthy organizations. If a valid and different choice is made to complete the analogy, it still would be a proper comparison/relationship.

An important word used in the definition of **analogy test** is **proportion**. This word indicates that the left and right side of the analogy should be balanced. In one sense, analogies are the word equivalents of equations, as in mathematics. Of course, mathematical equations are always exact, whereas word analogies may not be. Nevertheless, the basic idea of balance is helpful in understanding them. Incidentally, *mathematics* analogies are useful in teaching number relationships as, for example, 64 : 8 :: 81 : 9.

One positive result of completing and creating analogies is that they are helpful in developing vocabulary as in the case of synonyms and antonyms. Also, they require inferential thinking. The left side of an analogy is stated as a fact. What inference may be made from that fact as to how the right side should be completed? Finally, students must use context clues, an important reading skill, and reasoning skills to complete the analogy.

Suggestions for Teaching

1. Use the information on this page to help students understand analogies. Present and explain the suggested analogies.

2. Further illustrate basic types of analogies, as follows.

- **Characteristics**: velvet : soft :: sandpaper : rough
- **Antonyms**: war : peace :: chaos : order
- **Parts**: faucet : sink :: wheels : wagon
- **Persons**: Lincoln : Emancipation Proclamation :: Monroe : Monroe Doctrine
- **Mathematics**: 14 : 28 :: 18 : 36
- **Geography**: Massachusetts : Northeast States :: Georgia : Southeast States

3. Photocopy and distribute the two following application pages.

---

* The symbol : stands for <u>is to</u>, and the symbol :: stands for <u>as</u>.

Name: _____   Date: _____

COMPLETING ANALOGIES I

In these first twelve analogies only one of the three suggested endings is correct. Circle the word that you think best completes the analogy.*

1. **bridge : river :: overpass :** channel   road   lake

2. **ocean : fiord :: land :** isthmus   strait   peninsula

3. **longitude : prime meridian :: latitude :** equinox   eclipse   equator

4. **arid : climate :: freezing :** dew point   temperature   windchill

5. **ocean : fishing bank :: land :** valley   plain   plateau

6. **delta : river mouth :: terminal moraine :** glacier   crevasse   water

7. **mineral : geology :: animal :** biology   geography   zoology

8. **water : ice :: lava :** steam   rock   crystals

9. **islet : island :: brook :** rivulet   creek   river

10. **import : taking in :: export :** selling off   sending out   buying up

11. **coniferous tree : needles :: deciduous trees :** bark   branches   leaves

12. **river : rapids :: roads :** asphalt   curves   bumps

In the next set of analogies it will be up to you to complete them with your own words. Write you choices on the blank lines at the end of each incomplete analogy.

13. **terrace : shelf :: plateau :** _____

14. **Rome : Italy :: Paris :** _____

15. **sunrise : east :: sunset :** _____

16. **northeast : southwest :: northwest :** _____

17. **revolution of the earth around the sun : year :: rotation of the earth on its axis :** _____

18. **potato : Idaho :: orange :** _____

19. **telephone directory : phone numbers :: atlas :** _____

Make up two analogies of your own. They may be on any subject you choose.

20. _____

_____

21. _____

_____

* The symbol : stands for <u>is to</u>, and the symbol :: stands for <u>as</u>

COMPLETING ANALOGIES II

1. mattress : bed :: cushion : _____

2. general : sergeant :: principal : _____

3. wing : bird :: fin : _____

4. 3 : 21 :: 6 : _____

5. fancy : simple :: generous : _____

6. peddles : bicycle :: propeller :_____

7. hoot : owl :: caw : _____

8. Madrid : Spain :: Athens : _____

9. rudder : ship :: steering wheel : _____

10. addition : subtraction :: multiplication : _____

11. stem : plant :: trunk : _____

12. clean : dirty :: fresh : _____

13. New Jersey : Delaware River :: Georgia : _____

14. Thomas Edison : electric light bulb :: Eli Whitney : _____

15. present : absent :: complete : _____

The following incomplete analogies require an appropriate word in the first part of the right side.

16. a magnifying glass : a small object :: _____ : far distant object

17. fireplace : chimney :: muffler : _____

18. North Dakota : South Dakota :: _____ : South Carolina

19. On the line below make one **antonym** analogy.

_____

20. On the line below make one **geography** analogy.

_____

21. On the line below make one **whole to part** analogy.

_____

* The symbol : stands for <u>is to</u>, and the symbol :: stands for <u>as</u>.

Name: _____ Date: _____

A "SYNONYMOUS TITLES" PUZZLE

The reworded song titles in the first column will challenge your vocabulary and your ability to derive meanings from contextual situations. If you are "stumped" by one of the reworded titles, look for help in the list of real titles at the bottom of the page. Write the correct titles in the second column.

REWORDED SONG TITLES	ACTUAL SONG TITLES
1. Heavenly Object Scattered over a Streamer	--
2. Oh Country That Is Most Comely	--
3. Abode That Is Best Described by the Word "Sugar"	--
4. To Me You Are the Light That Radiates from the Bright Orb in the Sky	--
5. The Covering of My Brain Is Constantly Experiencing Precipitation	--
6. Rodent Trio with Blinkered Eyes	--
7. Repeatedly Rotate, Repeatedly Rotate, Repeatedly Rotate the Ship	--
8. May the Supreme Being Beatify This Nation of 48 Contiguous States and 2 Noncontiguous States	--
9. All Day I Have Labored to Keep the Trains Operating	--
10. The Place Where H_2O Flows over the Paddles	--
11. An Ancient Scot Once Possessed an Agricultural Site	--
12. Minuscule Celestial Object, Continue Making Flickering Lights	--
13. It Could Be Anywhere Above the Multi-colored Arc in the Sky	--

Somewhere in the list that follows are the real titles of the songs: Down by the Old Mill Stream . . . Somewhere over the Rainbow . . . Old MacDonald Had a Farm . . . I've Been Working on the Railroad . . . Row, Row, Row Your Boat . . . Three Blind Mice . . . Star-Spangled Banner . . . God Bless America . . . Raindrops Keep Falling on My Head . . . You Are My Sunshine . . . Twinkle, Twinkle Little Star . . . America the Beautiful. . . Home Sweet Home

UNDERSTANDING COMPOUND WORDS

1.   Compound words are words in which two words have been combined; either word could stand alone. For example, football combines foot and ball. Likewise, toothpick combines tooth and pick. What two words make up each of the following compound words?

a.   dishwasher: _____ and _____

b.   crossbow: _____ and _____

c.   necktie: _____ and _____

d.   blueberry: _____ and _____

e.   blowtorch: _____ and _____

f.   cookware: _____ and _____

g.   entryway: _____ and _____

2.   Each item that follows contains the beginning word of a compound word. From the list at the bottom of this column, select a word that makes a useful combination, and write the complete compound word on the blank line. Any word that is properly compounded can be found in a comprehensive dictionary such as *Webster's Intercollegiate Dictionary*.

a.   cheese: _____

b.   drive: _____

c.   eye: _____

d.   top: _____

e.   trail: _____

f.   trap: _____

g.   view: _____

h.   light: _____

i.   nurse: _____

j.   over: _____

k.   butter: _____

l.   head: _____

fly	door	night	way
master	blazer	soil	house
point	glass	cake	maid

3.   There are other words, called hyphenated words, that are a kind of compound word. The main difference between the two is that the two or more words in a hyphenated word are separated by a hyphen (-). Here are two examples of hyphenated words: trigger-happy and two-faced. A trigger-happy person is someone who is easily excited and quick to argue. A two-faced person is someone who is false, not trustworthy. *Webster's New Collegiate Dictionary* lists more than 30 hyphenated words in which the first word is two.

It would be very difficult to memorize the words that are separated by hyphens and those that are not. The best place to find out is in a good dictionary.

Following are some compound words with wide spaces between the letters. Use a dictionary to determine which should have hyphens. If a hyphen is required, place it between the two. If no hyphen is required leave the word as it is printed.

a.   r o w b o a t   d.   d o o r k n o b

b.   p a p e r w o r k   e.   c r o s s w o r d

c.   l o w l e v e l   f.   d r y c l e a n

4.   Most compound words are easily understood, as, for example, baseball. However, some require the reader to stop and think. Study the following compound words as they are used in sentences. Then, write what you think they mean.

a.   The pilot met a crosswind as she landed the airplane. _____

_____

b.   He was a closemouthed person; he hardly ever offered an opinion. _____

_____

c.   She said, "Don't be such a crybaby when you don't get your own way." _____

_____

d.   "Why are you fence-sitting? Make up your mind!" _____

_____

© 1998 by John Wiley & Sons, Inc.

RECOGNIZING HOMOPHONES

Some people in the United States who come from countries where English is not spoken are confused by homophones, two or more words that have the same sound but have different spellings and meanings. Here is an example:

- The <u>bear</u> was catching salmon in the stream.
- A rug was installed over the <u>bare</u> floor.

Here is a short list of common homophones accompanied by brief definitions. Realize that the examples below may have additional definitions.

1. grate: an opening in a sink, drain, etc.
   great: very good, large
2. fir: a kind of tree
   fur: the hairy covering of an animal
3. steak: a slice of beef
   stake: a length of wood or metal
4. coarse: rough
   course: path or trail
5. fowl: birds, especially chickens, etc.
   foul: dirty, bad smelling
6. peak: the top
   peek: a quick look or glance
7. sight: something that is seen
   site: a place
8. two: a numeral between one and three
   too: also, excessively
9. deer: a four-legged animal
   dear: expensive
10. horse: a four-legged animal
    hoarse: gruff, harsh
11. right: correct
    rite: a ceremony
12. break: to injure, hurt, crack
    brake: to come to a halt
13. wring: to squeeze
    ring: a circled enclosure
14. pier: a dock for tying boats
    peer: someone who is equal to you in one or more ways
15. rap: a sharp knock
    wrap: a covering

To Do:

1. Which of the homophones in parentheses in the following sentences should be used so that the sentence makes sense? Cross out the incorrect word. The meaning of the whole sentence will help you make decisions.

a. The (stake, steak) that held the tent was pulled out by the wind.
b. The decaying dead animal gave off a (foul, fowl) odor.
c. It was (too, two) heavy for one person to lift.
d. The (grate, great) in the basement was too clogged for water to drain.
e. Don't use (coarse, course) sandpaper if you want a smooth finish on wood.
f. The Christmas (wrap, rap) had holly leaves and berries printed on its edges.
g. My (peers, piers) all did very well on the achievement test.
h. You should put a (brake, break) on your spending habits.
i. The initiation (rite, right) was short, but meaningful.
j. The (site, sight) chosen for the camp was in a great forest.
k. A (fir, fur) tree has needles rather than broad leaves.
l. I thought that ten dollars was (deer, dear) for a bushel of apples.
m. I couldn't help but take a (peak, peek) at the presents in the closet.
n. He was so (horse, hoarse) that we couldn't understand what he was saying.
o. The children held hands and formed a large (wring, ring) in the middle of the yard.

2. Rewrite the following sentences using correct same-sounding words (homophones) in place of the underlined words.

a. A <u>plane</u> is a flat area with <u>sum</u> hills <u>hear</u> and <u>their</u>, <u>butt</u> the hills are <u>knot</u> very high. _____

_____

_____

b. When <u>yew</u> are at the <u>beech</u> <u>inn</u> the summer, be careful that <u>ewe</u> <u>due</u> <u>knot</u> get <u>to</u> much <u>son</u>. _____

_____

_____

c. <u>Wee</u> <u>maid</u> a wrong <u>tern</u> on the <u>rode</u>, <u>sew</u> <u>wee</u> were <u>won</u> <u>our</u> late and <u>mist</u> the <u>plain</u>. _____

_____

_____

HOMOPHONE CROSSWORD PUZZLE

Each of the words listed in ACROSS and DOWN has a homophone that can be printed in the puzzle. For example, 1 DOWN is listed as SEA. Its homophone, SEE, is already printed in the puzzle.

Number 3 ACROSS is WEIGH. What is a three-letter homophone for WEIGH? When you think you have the answer, print the word in the puzzle and continue.

DOWN

1. SEA
2. KNEW
4. ADD
5. EWE
6. NO
9. FOR
10. TWO
12. ATE
13. PEER
14. WRAP
15. SUM
16. NONE
17. PEEK
18. SIGHT
19. TEA
20. KNOT
22. SEW

ACROSS

1. SUN
3. WEIGH
7. DOUGH
8. ONE
11. HOLE
13. PORE
15. SENT
18. STEAK
21. HOARSE

UNDERSTANDING AND USING HOMOGRAPHS

As you have learned, homophones are words that have the same sound or pronunciation but different meanings. Two, to, and too are examples of homophones. See and sea, and knot and not are also homophones.

A homograph, on the other hand, is two or more words that have the same spelling but different pronunciations and different meanings. For example:

a. The wind is blowing hard today.

b. Please be sure not to wind the clock too tight.

In example *a* the vowel "i" has a short, or hard sound; in example *b* the vowel "i" has a long, or soft sound.

To Do:

Each sentence below contains a homograph that is underlined. On the line beneath each sentence write another sentence that uses the underlined word in a different way and with a different sound.

1. The dove in the tree made a soft cooing sound.

_____

2. A tear dropped from her eye when she heard the sad news.

_____

3. He will present an award to the winner of the race.

_____

4. The wound in the soldier's arm quickly healed.

_____

5. A region with less than ten inches of rain a year is called a desert.

_____

6. The teacher read a part of the book every day.

_____

7. He worked hard to perfect his batting skills.

_____

8. After his piano performance he made a bow to the audience.

_____

9. A live coal started the fire in the forest.

_____

10. An acorn is a minute seed—so very small—yet it grows to be a great tree.

_____

11. At the museum a guide will conduct you on a tour.

_____

SOME EXPERIENCES WITH FOREIGN EXPRESSIONS

Often, when one is reading, foreign expressions are met. The writer of the material has assumed the reader knows and understands the expression. Sometimes the assumption is correct—and sometimes not.

Following is a list of some of the more common foreign expressions accompanied by brief explanations. The origin of the word or phrase is given: F (French), I (Italian), G (German), L (Latin), S (Spanish). If you want to know how to pronounce a phrase, consult a good dictionary, such as *Webster's New Collegiate Dictionary*.

- **Amor vincit omnia.** (L): Love conquers all.

- **arivederci** (I): until we meet again

- **au contraire** (F): contrary, opposite

- **Bon jour.** (F): Good morning.

- **Bon soir.** F: Good evening.

- **Buenos dias.** (S): Good day.

- **e pluribus unum** (L): Out of many—one; (used on United States seal and coins)

- **Guten tag.** (G): Good day.

- **Hasta la vista.** (S): Until I see you again.

- **Ici on parle francais.** (F): French is spoken here.

- **pro patria** (L): for one's country

- **Respondez sil vous plait.** (F): Please respond. (as to a letter or invitation)

- **Requiescat in pace.** (L): Rest in peace. (as found on tombstones or in services for the dead)

- **se defendendo** (L): action taken in defense of one's self

- **semper fidelis** (L): always faithful (Marine Corps motto)

- **Tempus fugit.** (L): Time goes quickly by.

- **Tout de suite!** (F): Do it immediately!

- **Veni, vidi, vici** (L): I came, I saw, I conquered.

- **Wie gehts?** (G) How are things going?

To Do:

Each of the following sentences contains foreign expressions. Write the meaning of the expression on the blank line that follows it.

1. The final words of the minister at the grave site were, **"Requiescat in pace."** _____
_____

2. My French grandmother said, **"Tout de suite!"**
_____

3. My friend said, **"Guten tag!"** _____
_____
Then he added, **"Wie gehts?"** _____
_____

4. When you are having fun with your friends, **tempus fugit**. _____

5. I don't know much Spanish, but I understood what she meant when she said, **"Hasta la vista."**
_____
So, I replied, **"Arivederci."** _____

6. As I entered the store, the clerk said, **"Buenos dias."** _____

7. My friend ended his letter with **"Semper fidelis."** _____

8. She mailed 25 invitations to the party. At the bottom of each invitation were the words **"Respondez sil vous plait."** _____
_____

9. I was walking on a street in New York and saw the words **"Ici on parle francias"**_____
_____ printed on a poster in the window of a store.

10. My friend had a puzzled look on his face when he read **"e pluribus unum"** _____
_____ on the Great Seal of the United States.

11. Across the top of the patriotic banner were these words printed in large gold letters: **Pro Patria.**
_____

NOTES

Section 3: Reading Diagrams/Charts, Tables and Graphs

Reading Diagrams/Charts (RD/C)

RD/C–1   Guidelines for Diagrams and Charts (Instructor)

RD/C–2   Polluted Air

RD/C–3   Solar Water Heaters

RD/C–4   Annotating a Cross Section

RD/C–5   Sequences in the Water Cycle I (Instructor)

RD/C–6   Sequences in the Water Cycle II

RD/C–7   Air Has Weight

RD/C–8   Understanding Whales

RD/C–9   The Earth's Atmosphere

RD/C–10   Sources of Water

RD/C–11   Protecting Soil I (Instructor)

RD/C–12   Protecting Soil II

RD/C–13   Understanding Windbreaks

RD/C–14   Dangers Birds Face

RD/C–15   How Country People Get Rid of Household Wastes I

RD/C–16   How Country People Get Rid of Household Wastes II

RD/C–17   Understanding Watersheds and River Flow I (Instructor)

RD/C–18   Understanding Watersheds and River Flow II

RD/C–19   Using a Form to Record a Demonstration (Instructor)

RD/C–20   Science Demonstration Observation Form

RD/C–21   Your Environmental Beliefs

Reading Tables (RT)

RT–1   Guidelines for Tables (Instructor)

RT–2   Reading a Year Calendar

RT–3   Reading a Membership/Unit Table

GUIDELINES FOR DIAGRAMS AND CHARTS

Because diagrams and charts are widely used in science and social studies textbooks, and also in the media, it would be helpful to student development to have some concentrated experiences with them.

• Diagrams and charts, much like illustrations, are helpful in clarifying sequences. The reader is led, step-by-step, to a final understanding, conclusion, or solution. What might take dozens of sentences to explain can be reduced to a few phrases accompanied by simple drawings.

• Some diagrams are not sequential; they are static. The item illustrated may be surrounded by clusters of descriptive words with arrows pointing to the details described. If only words were used to describe the item, some readers would get "lost" and never gain a clear picture of what is described.

• In most situations readers are exposed to diagrams and charts created by someone else. What does it take to make such graphics? The answer is research, followed by thought, followed by imagination, followed by organization. So, it might not be too far wrong to say that those who gain the most from diagrams and charts are those who create them.

• It would be helpful to student development, then, to place students in positions where they are the creators of graphics. When they write essays and term papers a requirement might be that they include at least one chart and/or diagram.

• Assume, for example, that the class is studying settlement of the Great Plains of the United States. What might be an appropriate diagram for a student to include in a related paper? Why not a drawing of a Conestoga wagon surrounded by clusters of descriptions and information—the average length, uses of the canvas after the trek is over, why the wooden sides were made watertight and deep, and so on?

Suggestions for Teaching

1. As an introduction to a mini-unit on reading, interpreting, and making diagrams and charts, present and discuss the information above.

2. Follow the instructions on the panel below. Point out the advantages of using the diagram on the facing page to present information rather than using a 13-paragraph article with no illustrations.

This page can be the basis for an oral presentation to your students, or it can be photocopied and distributed along with the facing page. If you make an oral presentation, it would be helpful to make a transparency of the facing page. As you present the information, your students can write the phrases below in the boxes on the facing page.

POLLUTED AIR IS EXPENSIVE

Polluted air . . .

✓ kills trees and plants (1)

✓ rots leather products (2)

✓ damages glass (3)

✓ corrodes train rails (4)

✓ defaces buildings (5)

✓ causes lung disease (6)

✓ ruins car paint (7)

✓ turns paper brittle (8)

✓ destroys wire insulation (9)

✓ tarnishes silverware (10)

✓ causes car accidents (11)

✓ cuts down on sunlight (12)

✓ irritates eyes, throats (13)

POLLUTED AIR

Challenge Problems

1. Why might polluted air cause lung disease?

_____

_____

_____

2. One of the signs in the illustration above reads, "defaces buildings." When buildings are defaced by pollution they should be cleaned; otherwise, the erosion of the stone will continue.

Suppose a building were 200' wide and 300' tall. Suppose that it costs $.10 a square foot to clean the building.

How much would it cost to clean one side?

_____ All four sides? _____

3. Complete the sentences below with one of the phrases that appears above.

a. Polluted air _____
by covering leaves with harmful chemicals.

b. Polluted air _____ ;
this exposes bare wires that may start fires.

c. Polluted air _____ ,
which could cause important books and papers to be damaged.

d. Polluted air _____ ,
which can result in train wrecks.

e. Polluted air _____ ,
which could result in rust and the need to repaint.

SOLAR WATER HEATERS

Solar water heaters can help homeowners save money; cut down on the use of oil, coal, and natural gas; and help decrease the amount of pollution emitted into the air. After completing the following activity you will have a good understanding of how solar heaters work. You should realize, of course, that there are many different kinds of solar heaters, but most work on the same principles as the one on this page.

1. Label **Figure 1** below as indicated:

    A Heat Collector   D Solar Storage Tank

    B Water Supply   E Regular Water Heater

    C Water Pump   F Shower

2. The solar collector on the roof of the house has been enlarged in **Figure 2**. There are some important parts that should be labeled as indicated:

    a Glass Cover

    b Tubing

    c Heat Absorber

    d Insulation

    e Weatherproof Box

3. Following is an explanation of how the solar water heater works:

• The heat collector (A) collects heat from the sun through the glass cover (a).

• Beneath the cover, a heat absorber (c) absorbs the heat and passes it to the tubing (b), which holds nonfreezing liquid.

• The liquid carries the heat to a solar storage tank (D) and warms the water in the tank. Pipes distribute the warm water to outlets in the house such as the shower (F).

If there are several days when the sun doesn't shine, the regular water heater (E) can be turned on. The solar storage tank, however, is usually large enough to hold at least one day's supply of warm water.

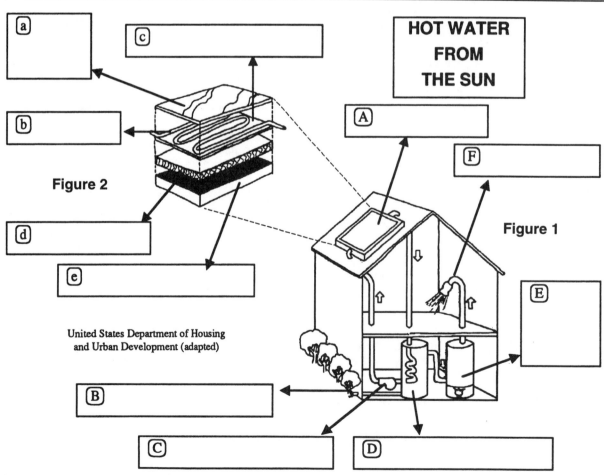

Figure 2

HOT WATER FROM THE SUN

Figure 1

United States Department of Housing and Urban Development (adapted)

ANNOTATING A CROSS SECTION

People may be more in danger of air pollutants inside the home than outside. For example, asbestos fibers, which are dangerous air pollutants, might be in a house for years. Occupants would be exposed to them every day. Outside in the open air a person might only occasionally breathe in fibers that are so damaging to the lungs.

The cross section below tells where pollution may be found in a typical home. Of course, not all homes have these hazards, but almost any home has some of them.

Study the diagram; then, on the lines outside the diagram write the names of the potential sources of pollution that are illustrated.

The pollutant sources are as follows:

① Kerosene heater
② Rug
③ Fireplace
④ Mothballs
⑤ Dry cleaning (recent)
⑥ Air conditioner
⑦ Curtains
⑧ Foam cushions

⑨ Cigarettes
⑩ Plywood cabinets
⑪ Refrigerator
⑫ Gas stove
⑬ Radon gas
⑭ Styrofoam insulation
⑮ Asbestos pipe wrapping
⑯ Heater

⑰ a. Disinfectants
  b. Insecticides
  c. Cleaners
  d. Solvents
  e. Aerosols
  f. Glues
⑱ Exhaust (carbon monoxide)
⑲ Gasoline (mower & can)

1: _____
2: _____
3: _____
6: _____
7: _____
8: _____

4: _____
5: _____
9: _____
10: _____
11: _____
12: _____
17: a _____
  b _____
  c _____
  d _____
  e _____
  f _____

13: _____
14: _____
15: _____
16: _____
18: _____
19: _____

Source: United States Environmental Protection Agency (adapted)

SEQUENCES IN THE WATER CYCLE I

Reading may be defined as gaining information from symbolic representations of real and unreal things. Thus, deriving information from printed words, maps, graphs, pictures, charts, and diagrams is "reading." Learners should have specific instruction about and practice with all of these forms of reading. Each form may utilize its own symbols; however, most forms use a variety of symbolic representations, including words, to convey messages.

Reading and Interpreting Diagrams

Diagrams can convey a wide variety of information, and, as a result, they utilize a wide variety of symbols. Diagrams are especially adaptable for showing sequences. The suggestions that follow will help students learn how to read and interpret a diagram of the water cycle, which is, essentially, a sequential process.

Suggestions for Teaching the Water Cycle

1. Make a transparency of the facing page for yourself, and make photocopies for your students.

2. As outlined below, present the general process for the water cycle, or hydrologic cycle as it is sometimes called, to your students.

> Water is in constant movement from the earth, in the form of a gas or vapor, to the atmosphere. After reaching the atmosphere the water vapor cools. When it cools it condenses into water droplets. These droplets fall to the earth in the form of rain, snow, sleet, or hail. Some of the water may seep into the earth and be stored, and some will return to the ocean via rivers and streams.

As you explain the general process, have your students *number the large arrowheads in the diagram*. Start with the ocean as ▲**1** (already numbered) and proceed through the cycle with ▲**2**, ▲**3**, ▲**4**, and ▲**5**.

▲**1**. Evaporation takes place on both water and land. Almost all objects, including humans, give off moisture, which rises into the atmosphere in the form of vapor.

Have your students identify the various sources of moisture, as follows, on the diagram:

1. Animals (perspiration, wastes)

2. Snow (evaporation)

3. Orchards (evaporation)

4. Tractors (exhaust, soil disturbance)

5. Trees (evaporation)

6. Swamps (evaporation)

7. Lakes (evaporation)

8. Airplanes (exhaust)

9. Boats (exhaust, spray)

10. Oceans (evaporation)

▲**2**. As vapor cools and condenses into droplets, it gathers together as clouds. Then, as a cold front advances with accompanying winds, the clouds are pushed over the land or perhaps over the oceans.

In the diagram have your students print *wind* on some of the horizontal lines pointing toward land.

▲**3**. When droplets reach a certain weight, they fall as precipitation. To better show this, have your students complete the phrases in the clouds as follows:

♦ Cloud B—Vapor forming into *clouds*.

♦ Cloud A—Water forming into *droplets*.

▲**4**. Some precipitation soaks into the ground and is stored. This stored water may come to the surface through natural flow, as in springs and artesian wells. Dug or drilled wells may also be used to reach the water.

Have your students draw small droplets ($^0_0{}^0_0{}^0$) throughout the water storage area.

▲**5**. Your students can make their diagrams more attractive and interesting by coloring them, e.g., coloring all the water blue.

Name: _____ **Date:** _____

SEQUENCES IN THE WATER CYCLE II

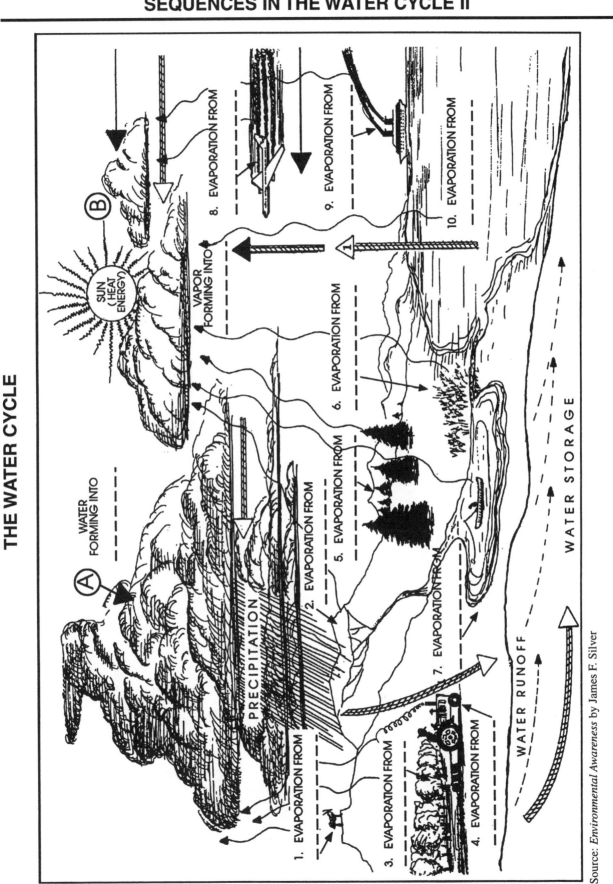

THE WATER CYCLE

A WATER FORMING INTO

B VAPOR FORMING INTO

SUN (HEAT ENERGY)

PRECIPITATION

1. EVAPORATION FROM
2. EVAPORATION FROM
3. EVAPORATION FROM
4. EVAPORATION FROM
5. EVAPORATION FROM
6. EVAPORATION FROM
7. EVAPORATION FROM
8. EVAPORATION FROM
9. EVAPORATION FROM
10. EVAPORATION FROM

WATER RUNOFF

WATER STORAGE

Source: *Environmental Awareness* by James F. Silver

Name: _____ Date: _____

AIR HAS WEIGHT

1. You have probably noticed that when air is blown into rubber rafts or automobile tires they become heavier. This is because air has weight. Tiny bits of dust, pollen from plants, gases, and other things give air its weight. All these things are called *particulates*.

At sea level, a column of air pressing on one square inch of sand and stretching far into the atmosphere weighs almost 15 pounds. (See the diagram.)

At the seashore (sea level), how many pounds of air are pressing on a towel that is 20" × 20", or 400 square inches?

Answer: Approximately 6,000 pounds!

The problem was solved by multiplying the number of square inches (400) by 15 lbs. (the weight of air).

a. At sea level, what is the weight of air on a towel that is 20" × 30", or 600 square inches?

_____ lbs.

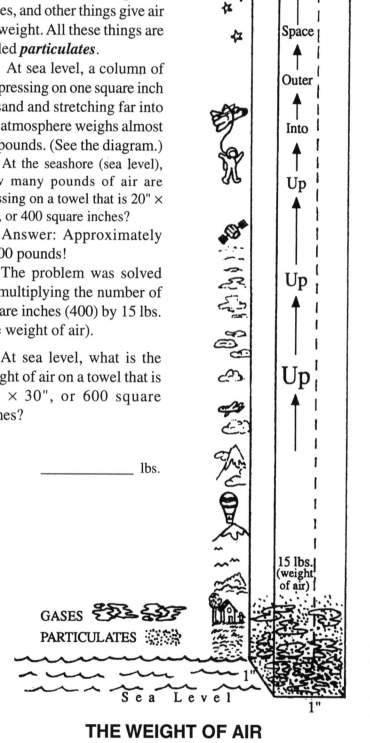

THE WEIGHT OF AIR

b. At sea level, what is the weight of air on a paper napkin that is 10"× 8"?

_____ lbs.

2. Air presses on objects on all sides. A cube has six sides. Suppose you suspended a cube whose sides were all 1 square inch. What would be the total amount of air pressing on the cube?

Answer: 90 lbs. (6 sq. in. × 15 lbs.)

Suppose you suspended a cube that was 5 square inches on each side. What would be the total weight of air pressing on the cube?

_____ lbs.

3. The force of gravity pulls things toward the earth; so, there are more particulates near the earth's surface than high in the atmosphere. You can show this on the "Weight of Air" diagram by drawing lots (LOTS!) of dots (for particulates) and shapes (for gases) at the bottom of the column. As you go up the column, make fewer and fewer particulates and gases. Finally, there should be only blank space at the top of the column.

UNDERSTANDING WHALES

Following are some interesting facts about whales:

• Whales are not fish; they are mammals. They are thought to be among the most intelligent of mammals. As mammals, the young are born alive and feed on their mother's milk.

• When whales surface, they blow air out of their lungs and then take in more air. In a matter of seconds the largest whales breathe in as much as 500 gallons of air. Some whales can stay under water for half an hour or more.

• Whales, depending on the type, can range from 4 feet in length to 100 feet and can weigh from 50 pounds to 100 tons.

• Historically, what was obtained from whales that made them so commercially desirable and almost led to their extinction in some cases?

  ✓ Whalebones for fishing rods, buggy whips, corsets, etc.

  ✓ Oil for lamps

  ✓ Food for humans, pets

  ✓ Oil for margarine, soaps, lubricants

Diagram of a Typical Baleen (no teeth) Whale

On the diagram print the names of the parts as indicated below:

A: FLUKES (These "tails" move whales forward with an up-and-down motion.)

B: DORSAL FIN (This helps to keep whales steady in the water, a kind of keel as in a sail boat.)

C: FLIPPERS (These help whales "steer" and keep balance.)

D: BLOWHOLES (Whales inhale and exhale air through these holes. Some whales have two holes; some have only one.)

E: BALEEN (These are comb-like bones in the whale's mouth. They are used to obtain food. Huge quantities of water enter the whale's mouth and are squeezed out. Plankton and small fish remain behind the baleen and are then swallowed.)

F: PLEATS (These are folds similar in appearance to an accordion's. They expand when a whale takes in food and water.)

G: EYES (There are eyes on both sides of the whale's head for front and side vision.)

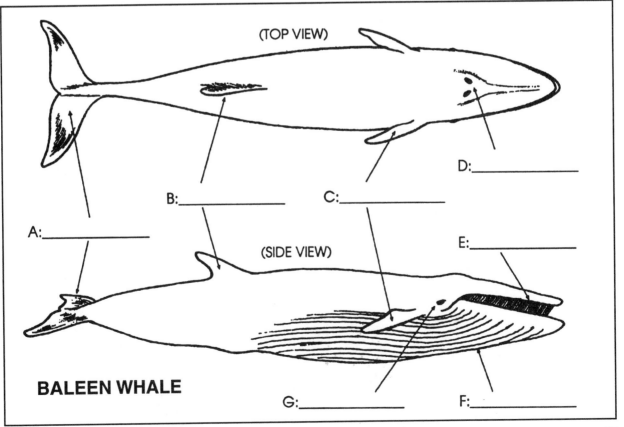

(TOP VIEW)

(SIDE VIEW)

A: _____

B: _____

C: _____

D: _____

E: _____

F: _____

G: _____

BALEEN WHALE

Name: _____   **Date:** _____

THE EARTH'S ATMOSPHERE

Air Is a Mixture of Gases

1. Air is made up of a number of gases:
    - ✓ Nitrogen: 78%
    - ✓ Oxygen: 21%
    - ✓ Other Gases: 1%

2. The circle graph to the right shows the gases that make up air. Make the segments stand out by shading them, as follows:

    Nitrogen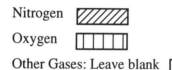

    Oxygen   [| | | | |]

    Other Gases: Leave blank   [   ]

3. Notice the footnote at the bottom of the page. It tells the names of the gases that make up the "Other Gases" segment shown in the circle graph. On the lines below "Other Gases" in the graph, write the names of the gases.

4. Make a title for the graph and write it on the title line.

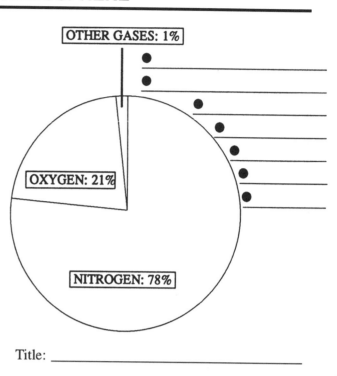

Title: _____

_____

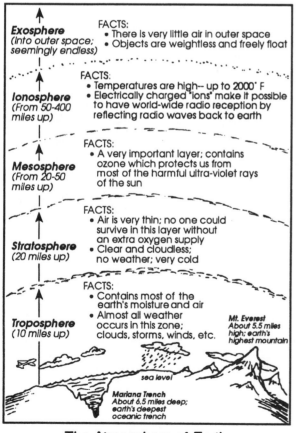

The Atmosphere of Earth

The Atmosphere of Earth

1. Name the layer of the atmosphere

a. closest to Earth: _____

b. farthest from Earth: _____

c. containing the least air: _____

d. containing the most air: _____

e. with a special kind of oxygen that protects us from the sun: _____

f. where objects float free: _____

g. where most of Earth's weather occurs: _____

h. helpful to radio transmission and reception:

_____

2. How high does Mt. Everest extend into the troposphere?

_____ miles

3. How deep is the Mariana Trench?

_____ miles

* Other Gases: Argon, Helium, Neon, Krypton, Hydrogen, Ozone, Methane

SOURCES OF WATER

1. The diagram below shows five ways of obtaining water from underground sources. The blank boxes show the location of the five ways. Label each of the boxes as indicated below:

- ☐1 **Pump** (The well is dug by a drill. An electric motor pumps the water to the surface.)
- ☐2 **Dipping Well** (The well is dug by hand and walled with stone. The water is cranked to the surface in buckets.)
- ☐3 **Artesian Well** (The well hole is dug by a drill, and the water flows to the surface naturally.)
- ☐4 **Spring** (The water flows naturally through openings in the earth's surface.)
- ☐5 **Windmill** (The well hole is dug by a drill. The wind supplies the power to pump the water to the surface.)

2. The earth is composed of several layers of material—soil, rocks, gravel, etc. The diagram shows the various layers. Most well water is in the layer labeled with "Ds." The material in the layer is porous and holds water as a sponge would. To better show the layer, make small circles (°₀°₀°₀°) throughout the layer.

3. The layer labeled with "Cs" is mostly clay. Unless there is a hole or crack in it, it keeps the water in the porous layer (D) from rising. Draw this symbol (/ / / / /) throughout the layer.

4. The layer labeled with "Bs" is subsoil. This layer contains some water, but not enough for a good well. The water might also be impure. Draw this symbol (÷ ÷ ÷ ÷) in the layer.

5. The layer labeled with "As" is topsoil and is good for growing crops. Draw this symbol (| | | | |) in the layer.

6. The layer with labeled "Es" is solid rock. Show this layer with this symbol (# # # #).

7. You can make your diagram more interesting and attractive as follows:

- ☐ Color the sun, buildings, land, and trees.
- ☐ Color each layer differently using reds, browns, etc. Color lightly.
- ☐ Color the small pools of water at the bases of the wells blue.

© 1998 by John Wiley & Sons, Inc.

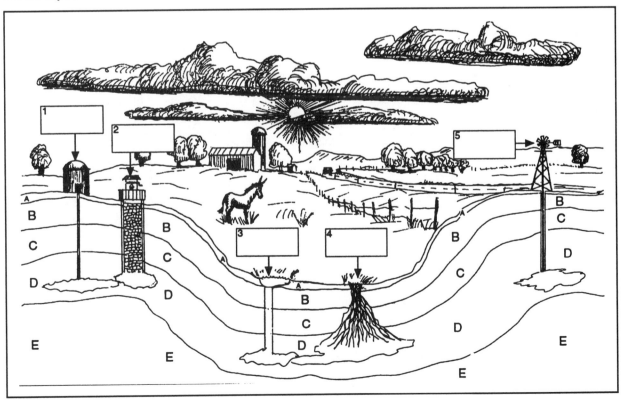

PROTECTING SOIL I

Suggestions for Teaching

1.   Photocopy and distribute the facing page, and make a transparency for your own use.

2.   With the help of the transparency, convey the information under each of the headings below. Direct students to annotate their photocopies as you annotate the transparency.

3.   Alternative: Cut off the top portion of this page, photocopy the remainder of the page. Have students read the information and complete the diagrams.

Contour Farming

Contour farming is plowing, planting, cultivating, and harvesting *across* the slope of land rather than down the slope. Contour *strip cropping* is the practice of alternating rows of crops such as corn with rows of crops such as clover.

There are several advantages to contour farming. Contours hold water long enough for much of it to soak into the ground. Another advantage is that the speed at which the water runs downhill is reduced because the lower ridge of the contour acts as a kind of dam, thus enabling the center of the contour to act as a catch basin. The slower the water moves, the less soil it can cut away and carry.

Activity for cross section 1:

Have your students label *Contour* at A, *Contour Ridge* at B, *Basin* at C, *Strip Crops* at D.

Activity for picture 1:

Have your students label *Contours* at A, *Strip Crops* at B.

Terracing

Terracing is much like contouring, but on a much larger scale. Its purpose is to make it possible to farm on a steep slope and to conserve water and soil.

In terracing, a series of "steps" is cut into a hillside. The level steps allow for level plowing. Sometimes the steps may be narrow, and at other times quite wide, perhaps ten feet or more. Also, the steps are not always the same width; the width of the steps depends on the changes of pitch in the slope.

Activity for cross section 2:

Have your students label *Terrace* at A, *Steps* at B, *Ridges* at C, *Floor* at D, *Crops* at E.

Activity for picture 2:

Have your students label *Terrace* at A, *Steps* at B, *Ridge* at C, *Floor* at D, *Crops* at E.

Willow Planting

As water flows in a stream, especially after a heavy rain, it wears away the stream's banks through "cutting" action. The roots of willow trees, which are tough and stringy, can lace together and help reduce the power of the water to cut. The network of roots holds the soil firm. Willow plantings are especially useful where streams curve because it is at curved places where the cutting action of streams is greatest.

Activity for diagram 3:

Have your students label *Stream* at A and draw arrows in the stream pointing toward the bottom left of the diagram. The arrows show the direction of flow.

Because running water cuts away the outside banks of streams, a row of willow trees should be drawn on the curves at B and C.

Activity for picture 3:

Have your students show the direction of flow of the stream by drawing arrows in the stream pointing to the top right of the picture.

Label *Willow Trees* at A.

Note: To make the diagram and picture in 3 more identifiable and colorful, carefully color the streams blue and the trees green.

Name: _____ **Date:** _____

PROTECTING SOIL II

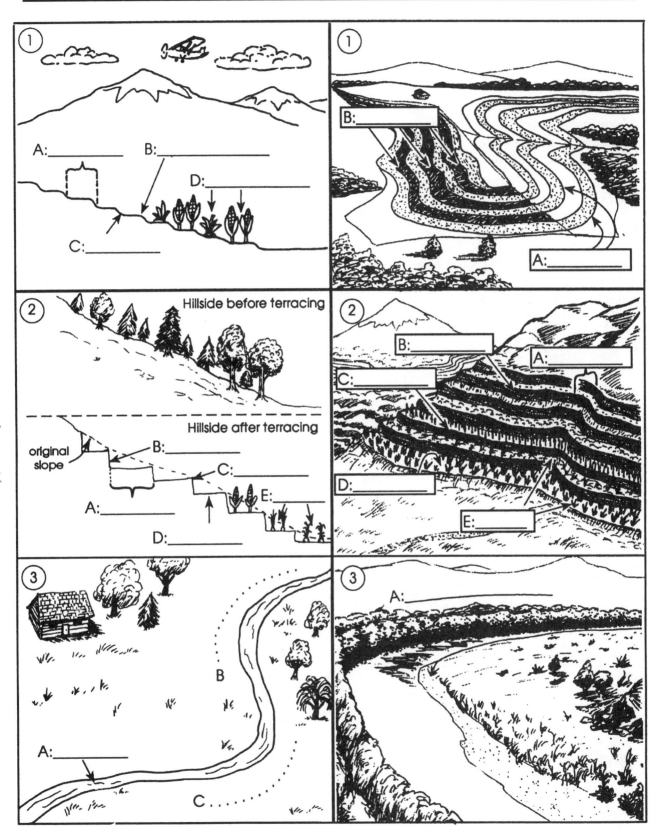

①

A: _____ B: _____

D: _____

C: _____

② Hillside before terracing

Hillside after terracing

original slope

B: _____

C: _____

A: _____

E: _____

D: _____

③

A: _____

B

C . . . .

①

B: _____

A: _____

②

B: _____

A: _____

C: _____

D: _____

E: _____

③

A: _____

UNDERSTANDING WINDBREAKS

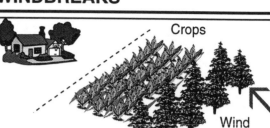

WINDBREAK
Figure 2

Each year thousands upon thousands of tons of topsoil are picked up by winds and carried away. Gradually, the thickness of the topsoil decreases. The result of this is smaller crops—each year a little bit less. In a period of only ten or twenty years, topsoil on a farm can become so thin that even weeds have a hard time growing. Crops become so poor that farmers must abandon their farms; it is no longer possible to make a decent living.

The undesirable results of wind erosion are not limited to smaller crops. Windblown soil may fill irrigation and drainage ditches and pile up along fence rows and on roads. Blowing soil may even create highway driving hazards by limiting vision. The loose soil may eventually be carried to streams and rivers, where it fills channels and is eventually deposited at the mouths of streams.

Wind erosion can be controlled in several ways, one of the most effective being *windbreaks*. Windbreaks are simply rows of trees that are positioned to break the force of winds. They are always planted perpendicular to the prevailing winds of a region. (**Figures 1 and 2**)

Once windbreaks are well established, they protect fields all year. But, for the protection to continue into winter, the trees should be of the evergreen type—spruce, pine, hemlock—because these trees have needles the entire year. Trees that lose their leaves, such as oak and maple, would not be very effective in breaking the force of winter winds.

To Do:

1. In the information in the first column, underline the sentence that:
   a. tells how blowing soil is a safety hazard for drivers
   b. offers a definition of windbreaks
2. What is the result of loss of topsoil to farmers?

_____

3. In Figure 1 the wind is sweeping across a field and over the trees. What is the wind's speed as it crosses the field? _____m.p.h. What is its speed 370' after the windbreak? _____m.p.h.

   What is the speed of the wind at ground level before it meets the trees? _____ m.p.h. What is its speed immediately after it has passed through the trees? _____ m.p.h.

4. Usually, several lines of trees make up a windbreaking system. Draw several trees on the dashed line in Figure 2 to show a second windbreak.

Figure 1

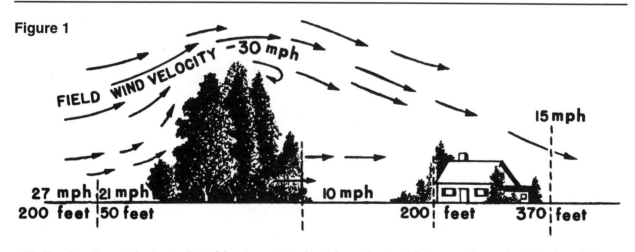

Windbreaks reduce wind currents: Part of the air current is diverted over the top of the trees and part of it filters through the trees. Farmstead, livestock, and wildlife windbreaks should be relatively dense and wide to give maximum protection close to the trees. Field, orchard, and garden-type windbreaks need not be so wide and dense.

Source: Adapted from a pamphlet of the United States Department of Agriculture, Soil Conservation Service.

Name: _____ Date: _____

DANGERS BIRDS FACE

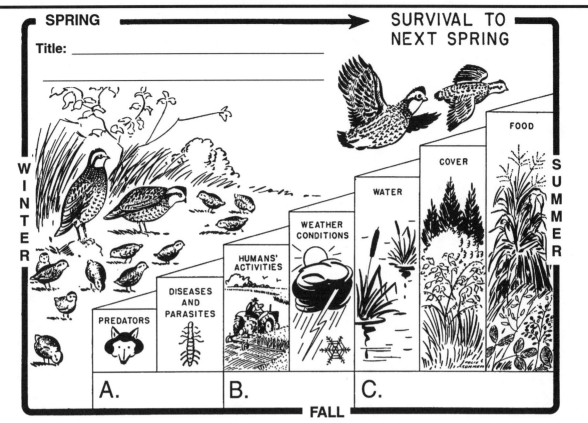

1. Print the following title on the lines at the top of the chart: A BIRD'S LIFE ISN'T EASY—MANY DANGERS EXIST

2. Notice the three main divisions of the chart. These divisions show *dangers* that birds face. Carefully print the following in the chart:
A. ANIMALS
B. HUMANS, CLIMATE
C. HABITAT

3. List some animals, including other birds, that might kill birds for food.

a. _____   c. _____

b. _____   d. _____

4. What are two human activities that are harmful to birds?

a. _____

b. _____

5. What are some weather conditions that are threats to birds?

a. Severe _____

b. Severe _____

6. Three possible dangers within bird's habitat (living area) are:

a. lack of _____

b. lack of _____

c. lack of _____

7. Write two reasons why lack of cover (absence of trees, bushes, grass, etc.) is dangerous to birds.

a. _____

b. _____

8. Winter and early spring are the most difficult times of the year for nonmigrating birds. List two things humans can do to help such birds survive.

a. _____

b. _____

9. Imagine that the large bird in the chart is giving some advice to the three chicks in front of her. What might she be saying? (Use the reverse side of this page for your answer.)

Source: Adapted from *Making Land Produce Useful Wildlife*, U.S. Dept. of Agriculture.

HOW COUNTRY PEOPLE GET RID OF HOUSEHOLD WASTES I

There are many houses in the United States that are not connected to city sewer lines. So, each house must have its own sewage disposal plant. The most common private system for the treatment of household wastes is the septic tank.

Description of a Septic Tank

A septic tank is an airtight and watertight tank usually made of concrete. The tanks vary in size, depending on how large a family they are designed to serve. A family of six would require a tank that could hold about 600 gallons of liquid. Such a tank would be about four feet deep, three feet wide, and seven feet long.

1. In **Diagram 1** of a septic tank label the following:

Ⓐ Inlet pipe

Ⓑ Ground level

Ⓒ Concrete slabs

Ⓓ Outlet pipe

Ⓔ Concrete

Ⓕ Sand/gravel

Placement of a Septic Tank

The septic tank is placed in the ground, usually from 20 to 40 feet from the house. The top of the tank should be buried about 12 inches below the surface. The tank should never be less than 100 feet from a well. Also, the tank should never drain in the direction of a well. The well could become polluted.

2. What are two things to consider when deciding where to place a septic tank?

a. _____

_____

_____

b. _____

_____

_____

How a Septic Tank Works

Wastes from the house flow through pipes into the septic tank. In the tank, bacteria help reduce the waste solids and organisms to a liquid state.

Not all of the solids that enter the tank are reduced to liquid. Some solids settle to the bottom of the tank as sludge. Over a period of time the sludge builds up and must be pumped out.

3. In **Diagram 1** label the following:

Ⓖ Liquid level

Ⓗ Bacteria

Ⓘ Sludge

4. In **Diagram 2** of a septic system label the following:

Ⓐ House sewer line

Ⓑ Septic tank

Ⓒ Drainage/waste pipes

5. What two things happen to the solid wastes that enter the tank?

a. _____

_____

_____

b. _____

_____

_____

Where the Liquid Goes

As more wastes enter the septic tank the liquids that are there flow through the outlet pipe into leaching fields.

6. In **Diagram 2** label the following:

Ⓓ Leaching field

The best leaching fields consist of porous materials such as sand and gravel. The liquids drain from the pipes through small holes. Sometimes openings are purposely left between the pipe sections so that the liquid may drain into the field.

Some of the liquid evaporates into the air. There is also a natural cleansing of the liquid as it filters through layers of sand and gravel.

7. Circle the two sentences that tell how the liquids get from the pipes into the earth.

HOW COUNTRY PEOPLE GET RID OF HOUSEHOLD WASTES II

8. What two things happen to the liquids in the leaching field?

a. _____

_____

b. _____

_____

    As you have read, the liquids that flow from septic tanks are by no means pure. It takes time for nature to convert the liquids back to pure water.

Therefore, a septic system should not be leached too close to a stream or lake. There will be great danger that the liquids will enter the water before the purifying process has been completed.

9. Why is it dangerous to locate a septic system too close to a stream?

_____

_____

_____

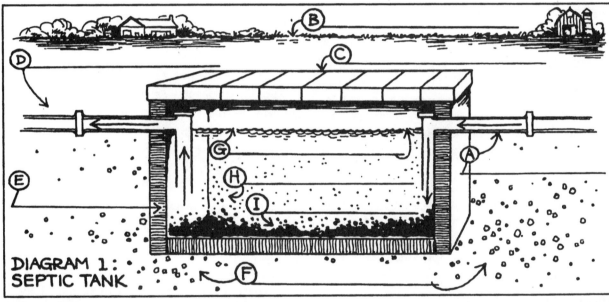

DIAGRAM 1:
SEPTIC TANK

DIAGRAM 2:
SEPTIC SYSTEM

UNDERSTANDING WATERSHEDS AND RIVER FLOW I

Suggestions for Teaching

1. Photocopy the diagram on the facing page, and, if desirable, make a transparency for overhead projection.

2. Read and/or explain the brief definition of a watershed that follows. Also, present the vocabulary of watersheds.

3. Lead your students through the activities outlined below, and, as you do, annotate the transparency.

Watersheds

Large rivers collect water from smaller streams. These streams, in turn, collect water from even smaller streams. All the water collected eventually empties into bodies of water such as lakes, bays, and gulfs. The area drained by the streams is called a drainage basin, or *watershed*.

The area drained by the Mississippi River is a wonderful example of a watershed. The precipitation that falls between the Appalachian Mountains and the Rocky Mountains collects in rivers such as the Ohio River on the east and the Arkansas River on the west. All the water eventually empties into the Gulf of Mexico.

As in the example of the Mississippi Watershed, watersheds are surrounded by high land. A watershed generally takes its name from the main river. In the diagram on the opposite page, the Big Elk River is the main conduit or "pipeline," so that is why the watershed bears its name.

Watershed Vocabulary

a. **Source**: Where a stream begins. The beginning could be small rivulets, a spring, a pond, or a lake.

b. **Mouth**: Where a stream ends as it enters another stream, a lake, or part of an ocean such as a bay or gulf.

c. **Tributary**: A small stream that enters a larger stream.

d. **Watershed**: The area drained by a number of streams.

e. **Downstream**: The direction in which a stream flows. Whether a stream flows north, east, west, or south, it must flow downstream. The Nile River, for example, flows north from high interior land to the Mediterranean Sea.

f. **Upstream**: One is going upstream when one is going against the flow, or current.

Activities

1. Print **S** for **source** at the beginnings of all the streams in the watershed.

2. Print **M** for **mouth** at all stream endings.

3. Connect all the dashes to better show the boundaries of the Big Elk River Watershed. Name all the tributaries in the watershed.

a. _____   d. _____

b. _____   e. _____

c. _____   f. _____

4. Draw arrows next to each of the labeled streams to show the direction of river flow.

5. Show rows of wheat in the area bound by the road in the southwest corner of the diagram. Show the wheat plants with the symbol for wheat in the key.

6. Show forests in the area south of Goose Creek, east of the road, and west of the highlands. Refer to the key for the symbol for trees.

7. Show marshland (wetland) in the area north of the Big Elk River, east of the Otter River, west of the Indian River, and south of the highlands. Refer to the key for the marshland symbol.

8. Label the highway Big Elk Boulevard.

9. Color all the waters of the watershed and Dolphin Bay light blue.

Questions

1. How does the road get through the mountains in the northeastern part of the watershed?

_____

2. What do you notice about the sources of all the rivers and streams; that is, where do they all start?

_____

_____

3. In what general direction does each of the following rivers flow?

a. Snake River: _____

b. Wolf River: _____

c. Goose Creek: _____

d. Indian River: _____

e. Otter River: _____

UNDERSTANDING WATERSHEDS AND RIVER FLOW II

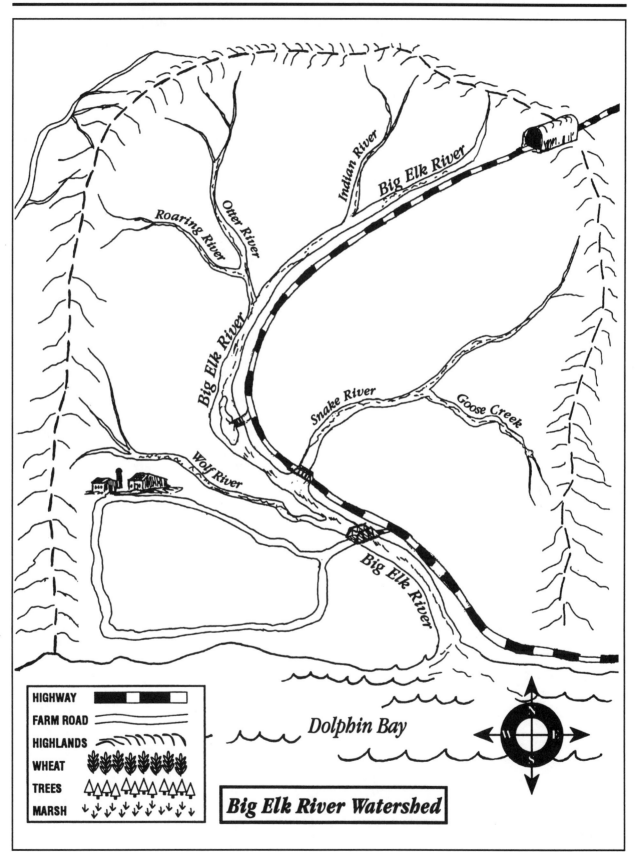

HIGHWAY

FARM ROAD

HIGHLANDS

WHEAT

TREES

MARSH

Big Elk River Watershed

Dolphin Bay

USING A FORM TO RECORD A DEMONSTRATION

This activity will provide an opportunity for students to learn from an instructor-conducted demonstration. The diagrams at the bottom of the page can be made into a transparencies to be projected at the end of each demonstration. Students may copy the diagrams on the reverse of the "Science Demonstration Observation Form (SDOF) that follows.

The lesson is written in "lesson plan" form to facilitate the demonstration.*

1. Objectives

Subject matter: Air has weight and under certain conditions has the capacity to crush objects.

Skills: a. Making diagrams
b. Recording information

2. Introduction

Pose the question: "Suppose that for some reason you wanted to crush this can. What are some ways it could be done?" (Accept all suggestions.) "Do you think it might be possible to crush it with air?"

3. Development

a. *Demonstrate the weight property of air through the use of a yardstick with identical large balloons tied at each end.* (**Figure 1**)

☐ Tie the uninflated balloons to the ends of the yardstick. *Note*: Use large balloons.

☐ Suspend the yardstick by string so that it is balanced.

☐ *Ask*: "If I blow up one of the balloons and not the other, which end of the yardstick will rise?" (The

end with the empty balloon will rise. The balloon at the opposite end is heavier due to the weight of air in it.) *Note*: Explain the elevation/air pressure diagram on the right of Figure 1.

b. *Demonstrate the weight property of air by crushing a can.* (**Figure 2**)

☐ Obtain a gallon can with screw-type cap, a hot plate, a tablespoon of water, and paper towels. *Caution*: Be sure the interior of the can is completely clean of any liquid it might have held, and be sure to remove all paper (labels, etc.) from the outside of the can.

☐ Remove the cap from the can and pour the water into the can.

☐ Place the can on the hot plate.

☐ After all the air (in the form of vapor) has been driven from the can, quickly replace the cap on the can. *Caution*: Use the paper towels as insulation when touching or picking up the can.

☐ Remove the can from the heat and allow it to cool.

☐ *To observe*: The can will crush.

☐ *Explanation*: The air pressure on the outside of the can is greater than the air pressure within the can; therefore, the can crushes.

☐ *Extension question*: What was the total weight of the air on the can? (Find the area in square inches of all six sides of the can, then multiply by 15, the weight of air at sea level).

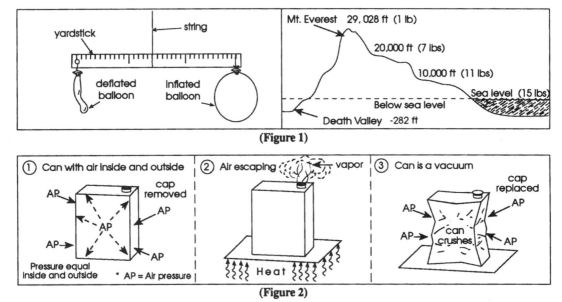

(Figure 1)

(Figure 2)

* The plan and the *Demonstration Observation Form* is meant to be used for the "crushed can" demonstration. However, the form may also be used in the "yardstick/balloon" demonstration.

SCIENCE DEMONSTRATION OBSERVATION FORM

1. Topic: _____

2. Title: _____

    _____

3. Problem: _____

    _____

    _____

    _____

    _____

    _____

4. Equipment and Materials:

    _____

    _____

    _____

    _____

    _____

    _____

5. Steps in Demonstration:

    a. _____

    _____

    b. _____

    _____

    c. _____

    _____

    d. _____

    _____

    e. _____

    _____

    f. _____

    _____

6. Observations:

    a. _____

    b. _____

    c. _____

    d. _____

    e. _____

    f. _____

    g. _____

    h. _____

7. Explanation:

    _____

    _____

    _____

    _____

    _____

    _____

8. Notes and Questions:

    _____

    _____

    _____

    _____

    _____

    _____

    _____

    _____

    _____

9. Drawings & Diagrams (Use reverse side.)

YOUR ENVIRONMENTAL BELIEFS

Design your personal environmental coat of arms with symbols, words, and phrases that tell what you stand for and what you believe.

The blank shield below contains five parts. Follow the directions below for each part:

1. Draw a symbol of the part of the environment about which you care most. For example, if you believe that saving forests is most important you might draw a tree.

2. Think of a motto that has to do with the environment. Your motto might even be suitable for a bumper sticker. Example: "No forests—No oxygen."

3. Design an illustration or symbol of something that you personally are going to try to do something about. Example: You might want to join or start a group that adopts a portion of road to keep free of litter.

4. Think of two or three brief phrases that complete this sentence: For the future I would want . . . Example: More wild life protection.

5. Compose a Haiku that expresses your feelings about the environment. Remember, a Haiku does not have to rhyme, and it has three lines: 5 syllables in the first line, 7 syllables in the second line, and 5 syllables in the third line. Here is an example:

The world is lovely—
Water, earth, the sky above—
For all to enjoy.

Decorate your shield in some way, perhaps by coloring or by drawing a border around it. You might want to share your coat of arms and the meaning of the symbols with your classmates.

GUIDELINES FOR TABLES

Elements of Tables

1. Titles of tables should be carefully noted. For example, many table titles will have the date of the information contained in the table. Dates are important because an out-of-date table may contain information that is not relevant to the current research investigation.

2. Footnotes are important. Often, they point out limitations or exceptions to the data contained in the table.

3. Most tables are designed so that the reader must coordinate the vertical (column) and horizontal (row) to locate the cell that contains the desired information.

4. The source of information should be noted. Users should be skeptical about information in a table that does not indicate sources.

5. Students need to recognize that serious mistakes can be made when reading tables if quantitative designations are misunderstood. If there is no qualifying information in a title, row or column headings, or footnotes, the information presented should be taken with reservations.

Example:

Bales of Cotton Produced (1996)	
State	Amount
X	937

Read as 937 Bales

If there is a designation such as 000's or thousands, three zeroes should be added to the figure in the table.

Example:

Bales of Cotton Produced (1996) (in 000's)	
State	Amount
Y	937

Read as 937,000 bales

If somewhere on the table there is a designation such as millions, six zeroes should be added to the figures in the table.

Example:

Bales of Cotton Produced (1996) (in millions)	
State	Amount
Z	937

Read as 937,000,000 bales

Students should also be aware of other quantitative notes. For example, in the cotton bales examples, there is a possibility of a note telling the reader that a bale of cotton weighs 480 pounds. Such a figure conveys a more complete understanding of the quantity of cotton produced.

6. Students should be aware of some reliable, easily available references that contain statistics that are, in most cases, in table form.

The Statistical Abstract of the United States is published annually by the United States Department of Commerce. It can be found in most libraries, or it can be purchased from the Superintendent of Documents, United States Government Printing Office, Washington, DC 20402. A typical edition will contain some 1,400 tables on population, energy, agriculture, forests and fisheries, transportation, and 26 other major topics.

The World Almanac and Book of Facts, and *Information Please Almanac* both contain scores of tables about United States and world affairs. They may be purchased in book stores and other retail outlets such as pharmacies and newsstands. These two almanacs are possibly the best single-volume reference books available. Coverage ranges from listings of all four-year and two-year colleges (name, enrollment, location, etc.) to a listing of every country in the world (name, population, area, capital, etc.).

The "Yearbooks" of many encyclopedias such as the *Encyclopedia Britannica* contain up-to-date statistical information on a large variety of domestic and foreign topics. Their very complete indexes are helpful in locating information quickly, and the books use tables extensively for presenting information.

Name: _____ Date: _____

READING A YEAR CALENDAR

1997

JANUARY	FEBRUARY	MARCH	APRIL
S M T W T F S	S M T W T F S	S M T W T F S	S M T W T F S
1 2 3 4	1	1	1 2 3 4 5
5 6 7 8 9 10 11	2 3 4 5 6 7 8	2 3 4 5 6 7 8	6 7 8 9 10 11 12
12 13 14 15 16 17 18	9 10 11 12 13 14 15	9 10 11 12 13 14 15	13 14 15 16 17 18 19
19 20 21 22 23 24 25	16 17 18 19 20 21 22	16 17 18 19 20 21 22	20 21 22 23 24 25 26
26 27 28 29 30 31	23 24 25 26 27 28	23 24 25 26 27 28 29	27 28 29 30
		30 31	

MAY	JUNE	JULY	AUGUST
S M T W T F S	S M T W T F S	S M T W T F S	S M T W T F S
1 2 3	1 2 3 4 5 6 7	1 2 3 4 5	1 2
4 5 6 7 8 9 10	8 9 10 11 12 13 14	6 7 8 9 10 11 12	3 4 5 6 7 8 9
11 12 13 14 15 16 17	15 16 17 18 19 20 21	13 14 15 16 17 18 19	10 11 12 13 14 15 16
18 19 20 21 22 23 24	22 23 24 25 26 27 28	20 21 22 23 24 25 26	17 18 19 20 21 22 23
25 26 27 28 29 30 31	29 30	27 28 29 30 31	24 25 26 27 28 29 30
			31

SEPTEMBER	OCTOBER	NOVEMBER	DECEMBER
S M T W T F S	S M T W T F S	S M T W T F S	S M T W T F S
1 2 3 4 5 6	1 2 3 4	1	1 2 3 4 5 6
7 8 9 10 11 12 13	5 6 7 8 9 10 11	2 3 4 5 6 7 8	7 8 9 10 11 12 13
14 15 16 17 18 19 20	12 13 14 15 16 17 18	9 10 11 12 13 14 15	14 15 16 17 18 19 20
21 22 23 24 25 26 27	19 20 21 22 23 24 25	16 17 18 19 20 21 22	21 22 23 24 25 26 27
28 29 30	26 27 28 29 30 31	23 24 25 26 27 28 29	28 29 30 31
		30	

Reading a Calendar for Dates

A calendar for a particular month is a kind of table. The graphic above shows that in a year there are 12 tables. Monthly calendars change from year to year.

To read a calendar it is necessary to read across for the days of the week and down for the dates on which the days fall. The date revealed is the cell where the day column and the date row intersect. A study of a year calendar can reveal interesting information.

To Do:

1. What are the dates of all the Fridays in March 1997? _____

2. In which month of 1997 does the first day of the month fall on Sunday? _____

3. Imagine that you have meetings to attend and that the meetings are held the third Tuesday of each month. What are the dates of the meetings for 1997?

Jan. _____   May _____   Sept. _____

Feb. _____   June _____   Oct. _____

Mar. _____   July _____   Nov. _____

Apr. _____   Aug. _____   Dec. _____

4. On the calendar draw a circle around the dates for the following holidays in the year shown.

a. Martin Luther King, Jr.: January 20
b. Memorial Day: May 26
c. Flag Day: June 14
d. United Nations Day: Oct. 24
e. Mother's Day: 2nd Sunday in May
f. Veteran's Day: November 11
g. Father's Day: 3rd Sunday in June

5. What is the date:

a. three weeks from July 3? _____

b. four weeks from August 1? _____

c. three weeks from October 9? _____

6. How many months have only 30 days? _____

7. How many months have 31 days? _____

READING A MEMBERSHIP/UNIT TABLE

The table on this page has been copied from the *Statistical Abstract of the United States, 1995*. The *Statistical Abstract*, as it is called, is published by the United States government. It contains information in table form on hundreds of topics. It is one of the most reliable sources of information you could use.

One thing you should realize about the *Statistical Abstract* is that the statistics are sometimes from one to three years older than the date of the Abstract's publication. This is because it sometimes takes three or four years to gather the statistics. For example, the statistics about scouting on this page were the latest available at the time of publication of this book.

No.424. Boy Scouts and Girl Scouts—Membership and Units: 1970 to 1993

[In thousands. Boy Scouts as of Dec. 31; Girl Scouts as of Sept.30. Includes Puerto Rico and outlying areas]

ITEM	1970	1975	1980	1985	1987	1988	1989	1990	1991	1992	1993
BOY SCOUTS OF AMERICA											
Membership...	6,287	5,318	4,318	4,845	5,347	5,364	5,356	5,448	5,319	5,338	5,355
Boys	4,683	3,933	3,207	3,755	4,180	4,228	4,247	4,293	4,150	4,150	4,165
Adults	1,604	1,385	1,110	1,090	1,168	1,136	1,109	1,155	1,168	1,188	1,190
Total units (packs, troops, posts, groups).	157	150	129	134	131	131	130	130	128	128	129
GIRL SCOUTS OF THE U.S.A.											
Membership...	3,922	3,234	2,784	2,802	2,947	3,052	3,166	3,269	3,383	3,510	3,440
Girls..	3,248	2,723	2,250	2,172	2,274	2,345	2,415	2,480	2,561	2,647	2,613
Adults	674	511	534	630	673	707	751	788	822	863	827
Total units (troops, groups)	164	159	154	166	180	189	196	202	210	219	221

Source: Boy Scouts of America. National Council. Irving, TX, *Annual Report,* and Girl Scouts of the United States of America, New York, NY, *Annual Report*

1. Notice that in the title notes are the words "in thousands." This tells you that you should add three zeroes (thousand) after each figure in the table. So, in 1970 there were 6,287,000 boy scouts—not 6,287 as you might think if you didn't add thousands to the printed figures.

a.   How many boy scouts were there in 1993?* _____

b.   How many girl scouts were there in 1993?* _____

2.   In what year were there fewer boy scouts than in any other year?* _____

3.   In what year were there more girl scouts than in any other year?* _____

4.   How many adults were involved in the boy scouts in 1993? _____

5.   How many adults were involved in the girl scouts in 1993? _____

6.   How many fewer boy scout units were there in 1993 than in 1970? _____

7.   Has the number of girl scout units increased over the years from 1980 to 1993? _____

8.   What was the average number of boy scouts per unit in 1993?* _____ (rounded to tenths)

9.   What was the average number of girl scouts per unit in 1993?* _____ (rounded to tenths)

10. Where is the National Council of the Boy Scouts located? _____

11. Where is the National Council for Girl Scouts located? _____

* Not including adults

TWO WAYS TO LIST THE SAME INFORMATION

No.1191. World Crude Oil Production: 1980 to 1993*
[In thousands of barrels]

COUNTRY	1980	1985	1988	1989	1990	1991	1992	1993
Total [1]	**59,599**	**53,981**	**58,662**	**59,773**	**60,471**	**60,105**	**60,255**	**60,070**
Algeria	1,106	1,037	1,040	1,095	1,175	1,230	1,217	1,190
Kuwait	1,656	1,023	1,492	1,783	1,175	190	1,029	1,872
Libya	1,787	1,059	1,175	1,150	1,375	1,483	1,483	1,377
Saudi Arabia	9,900	3,388	5,086	5,064	6,410	8,115	8,438	8,198
United Arab Emirates	1,709	1,193	1,565	1,860	2,117	2,386	2,325	2,241
Indonesia	1,577	1,325	1,342	1,409	1,462	1,592	1,566	1,507
Iran	1,662	2,250	2,240	2,810	3,088	3,312	3,429	3,650
Nigeria	2,055	1,495	1,450	1,716	1,810	1,892	1,982	2,050
Venezuela	2,168	1,677	1,903	1,907	2,137	2,375	2,334	2,377
Canada	1,435	1,471	1,616	1,560	1,553	1,548	1,598	1,678
Mexico	1,936	2,745	2,512	2,520	2.553	2,680	2,668	2,671
United Kingdom	1,622	2,530	2,232	1,802	1,820	1,797	1,825	1,909
United States	8,597	8,971	8,140	7,613	7,355	7,417	7,171	6,847
China	2,114	2,505	2,730	2.757	2,774	2,835	2,838	2,911
U.S.S.R. (former)	11,706	11,585	11,978	11,625	10,880	9,887	8,388	7,297

[1] Includes countries not shown separately.
Source: U.S. Energy Information Administration, *Monthly Energy Review.*

1. The table above contains the latest available information on the production of crude oil. Crude oil is oil just as it comes from the ground. After crude oil is transported to refineries, it is made into dozens of products such as gasoline and motor oil.

Notice the footnote in the table. It tells you that the countries listed in the table are not the only oil-producing countries. Dozens of other countries produce oil, but they don't produce enough to be listed among the 15 highest producers. The figures in bold type at the top of each column tell the total amount of oil produced in the world in a particular year.

When you read the amounts of oil produced, remember that the subtitle reads "in thousands of barrels." So, the total amount of oil produced in 1993 was not 60,070 barrels, it was 60,070,000 barrels.

2. The table lists the oil-producing countries in alphabetical order. Another way of organizing the table is to list the countries from the highest producer to the lowest producer.

In the uncompleted table below list the countries in order of production for 1993. Then, as a challenge, add the total amount of oil produced by the 15 countries in 1993.

FIFTEEN LEADING OIL PRODUCERS–1993*			
Country	**Barrels of Oil (000's)**	**Country**	**Barrels of Oil (000's)**
Saudi Arabia	8,198		
		Total	
	Total	Total of two columns	

*Source of the table: *Statistical Abstract of the United States.*

READING A BUS SCHEDULE

1.   A bus or train schedule is a kind of table that is used frequently by many people, especially those who are commuters or frequent travelers. With a little practice, these schedules are easy to learn how to read.

To find the times that transportation vehicles will depart from designated locations it is necessary to scan the column under a station heading. For example, the "TO SUSSEX" schedule below shows that a bus will be leaving from the Hill and Oak Street station, Neptune, at 6:40 a.m. (Find the time circled in the first column of the schedule.) If a commuter should miss the 6:40 bus, the schedule tells that another bus will be departing at 7:40 a.m.

By reading across from the 6:40 a.m. cell it can be seen that the 6:40 Neptune bus will arrive at the Sussex Station, Devon and Pine Streets, at 9:10 a.m.—circled in the last column of the schedule.

2.   Practice reading a transportation schedule by finding the answers to the following questions.

a.   At what time does the last bus leave the Neptune Station at Hill and Oak Streets? _____ p.m. At what time does it arrive at the Sussex Station at Devon and Pine Streets? _____ p.m. How long is the bus ride between these two places? _____

b.   At what time does the last bus leave the S. Cape Station? _____ p.m. How long does it take for the bus to reach the Sussex Station? _____ minutes

c.   How many daily bus departures are there from the S. Cape Station? _____ How many minutes' "wait" is there between the last and next-to-last departures at the S. Cape Station? _____ minutes

d.   Suppose that you got on a bus at the Neptune Station at 3:40 p.m. Would that bus take you to the Sussex Station? _____ Yes _____ No

Briefly explain your answer. _____

_____
_____
_____
_____
_____
_____
_____
_____

TO SUSSEX Weekdays				
NEPTUNE	AVALON	N. CAPE	S. CAPE	SUSSEX
(Hill & Oak)	(Shore & Cod)	(Maple & Dix)	(Hope & Ash)	(Devon & Pine)
A.M.	A.M.	A.M.	A.M.	A.M.
6:40	7:00	7:35	8:50	9:10
7:40	8:00	8:35	—	10:10
8:40	9:00	10:35	10:50	11:10
9:40	10:00	11:35	11:50	P.M.
10:40	11:00	P.M.	P.M.	12:10
11:40	12:00	12:35	12:50	1:10
P.M.	P.M.	1:35	1:50	2:10
12:40	1:00	2:35	2:50	3:10
1:40	2:00	3:35	3:50	4:10
2:40	3:00	—	4:50	5:10
3:40	4:00	4:35	—	—
4:40	5:00	5:35	6:50	7:10
5:40	6:00	6:35	7:50	8:10

READING A ROAD MILEAGE TABLE

Miles Between Cities

1. What is the distance in road miles from

a. Boston to Atlanta? _____ miles

b. Chicago to Denver? _____ miles

c. Boston to Seattle? _____ miles

d. New Orleans to Indianapolis? _____ miles

e. Atlanta to Chicago? _____ miles

f. Dallas to Salt Lake City? _____ miles

2. What is the distance in road miles from

a. San Francisco to Seattle to Chicago?

_____ miles

b. New Orleans to Atlanta to Boston?

_____ miles

c. New York to Denver to San Francisco?

_____ miles

3. Check the shorter road trip.

_____ Dallas to Boston

_____ Dallas to Seattle

4. Assume you could average 20 miles per gallon of gasoline and that the average price of gasoline is $1.25 per gallon. What would it cost to drive from New Orleans to Atlanta?

$ _____

5. Notice the lines on the map that connect the five cities. On the lines write the road distances between the cities.

ROAD MILEAGE TABLE

Cities →

	Atlanta	Boston	Chicago	Denver	Indianapolis	New Orleans	Salt Lake City	Seattle	Washington, D.C.
Atlanta	—	1037	674	1398	493	480	1878	2618	608
Boston	1037	—	963	1949	906	1507	2343	2976	429
Chicago	674	963	—	996	181	912	1390	2013	671
Dallas	795	1748	917	781	865	496	1242	2078	1319
Denver	1398	1949	996	—	1058	1273	504	1307	1616
New Orleans	480	1507	912	1273	796	—	1738	2574	1078
New York	841	206	802	1771	713	1311	2182	2815	233
San Francisco	2496	3045	2142	1235	2256	2246	752	808	2799
Washington, D.C.	608	429	671	1616	558	1078	2047	2684	—

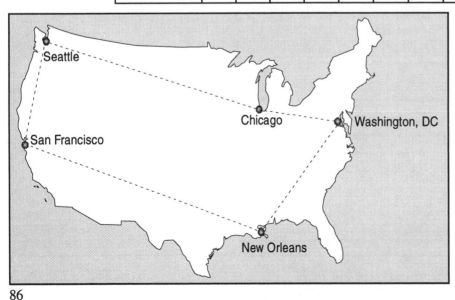

Note: The lines between cities are drawn straight; however, it should be realized that there are many twists and turns and ups and downs in the roads. That is why airline distances are shorter than road distances are. Airplanes can fly straight from city to city.

Name: _____ **Date:** _____

TRANSFERRING INFORMATION FROM A TABLE TO A MAP

The temperatures and sky predictions recorded below are typical for a day in early June in the United States.

City	High	Low	Sky	City	High	Low	Sky
Anchorage, AK	57°	47°	Rain	New Orleans, LA	86°	65°	Sunny
Atlanta, GA	78°	64°	Rain	New York, NY	85°	70°	Cloudy
Dallas, TX	86°	59°	Cloudy	Pierre, SD	90°	68°	Sunny
Denver, CO	88°	56°	Cloudy	St. Louis, MO	68°	59°	Sun and Clouds
Helena, MT	89°	74°	Sunny	San Francisco, CA	71°	54°	Cloudy
Miami, FL	90°	77°	Sunny	Seattle, WA	67°	49°	Cloudy
Minneapolis, MN	80°	55°	Sunny				

Sky Key: Sunny ☀ Cloudy ☁ Sun and Clouds ⛅ Rain 🌧 **Note:** *All temperatures are Fahrenheit.*

To Do:

1. All of the cities shown in the table are labeled on the map. In the box by the name of each city note the predicted high and low temperatures and draw a symbol that tells the kind of day the city is predicted to experience.

2. Which city is expected to have the highest temperature?

___ Miami   ___ Denver

___ Anchorage   ___ Helena

3. Which city is expected to have the greatest change in temperature? _____

How many degrees' change? _____

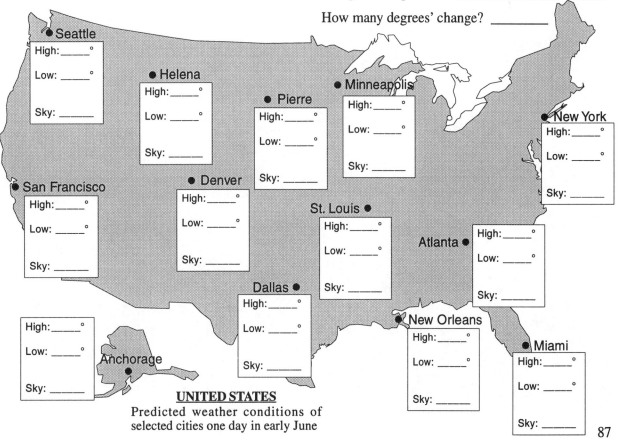

UNITED STATES
Predicted weather conditions of selected cities one day in early June

Name: _____ Date: _____

COMPLETING A TABLE OF "ANIMAL WORKERS"

The cartoon-like illustration at the bottom of the page is interesting because it shows how certain animals and natural features do "work." All things are interrelated on earth—air, soil, water, animals, natural resources—and everything that happens affects humans in some way. If even one animal or plant is lost, the lifecycle in which we all participate is disturbed in some way, however slight that may be.

See how many animals and natural features you can identify in the illustration. List them and make a short note that tells what is happening.

Number	Animal or Natural Feature	Work	Number	Animal or Natural Feature	Work
1			8		
2			9		
3			10		
4			11		
5			12		
6			13		
7			14		

Adapted from a United States Department of Agriculture Soil Conservation Service publication "Making Land Produce Useful Wildlife."

READING A TABLE THAT SHOWS CONTRASTS

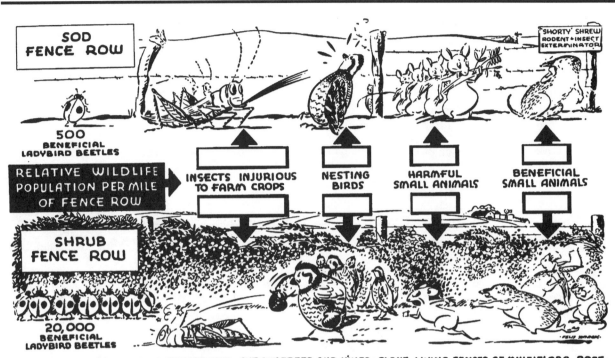

·LET SHRUBS GROW IN YOUR FENCEROWS · CUT OUT TREES AND VINES · PLANT LIVING FENCES OF MULTIFLORA ROSE·

Adapted from a United States Department of Agriculture Soil Conservation Service publication, "Making Land Produce Useful Wildlife."

Suggestions for Teaching

1. Make a transparency of the table at the top of the page. *Note*: You may want to make photocopies for students.

2. Point out that the table contrasts two kinds of fence rows: *Sod Fence Row* and *Shrub Fence Row*.

3. Ask: What might be some of the advantages of the shrub fence row? (Requires no wire, no nails, and no lumber; requires no expenditure of money; materials will not rot or rust or need to be replaced; no trimming or pruning; can serve as a low windbreak; can shut out unpleasant views; discourages trespassers; and, of course, prevents cattle from wandering.)

4. Ask: Why is the shrub fence row more helpful to wildlife than a sod fence row? (Provides cover and protection, food in the form of berries and insects, and safe nesting places.)

5. Present the statistics that follow and print them in the blank spaces in the table. (As on the table, the top numbers relate to the sod fence row, and the bottom numbers relate to the shrub fence row.)

79,000	1.5	84	8
INSECTS INJURIOUS TO FARM CROPS	NESTING BIRDS	HARMFUL SMALL ANIMALS	BENEFICIAL SMALL ANIMALS
54,000	21	21	28

6. Help your students understand both the facts and the relationships among the facts. For example, in the mile of shrub fence row there are fewer insects than there are in a mile of sod fence row (54,000 vs. 79,000). Why is this so? This is so because the mile of shrub fence row fosters 21 nesting birds, who feed on insects. A mile of sod fence row, on the other hand, fosters only 1.5 nesting birds, so the insects are less threatened.

7. Be sure to point out the humorous aspects of the illustration; e.g., the nesting bird with boxing gloves is giving a knockout blow to the crop-eating grasshopper. In the sod row segment, the grasshopper is arrogantly defying the nesting bird.

RECORDING INFORMATION INTO A TABLE

1.   There are numerous sources of energy. Each has advantages and disadvantages. Through information and prompting-type questions and critical thinking, including making inferences, your students may be able to discover most of the advantages and disadvantages.

2.   **Procedure**

a.   Make enlarged photocopies of the chart below, omitting information in the "Advantages" and "Disadvantages" columns. Also, make a transparency for your own use.

b.   Mention a potential source of energy such as *fossil fuels*. Have your students "brainstorm" advantages and disadvantages. Add information of your own, and record on the chart. Encourage students to keep their notes brief.

Sources of Energy: Advantages and Disadvantages		
Source of Energy	**Advantages**	**Disadvantages**
Fossil Fuels (oil, coal, natural gas) *Note:* Kinetic energy occurs when potential energy is put into motion. Example: Gasoline in a tank is *potential* energy; when it is ignited in a carburetor and the resultant explosions move pistons, it is *kinetic* energy.	• Quickly converts to kinetic energy to heat homes, run engines, etc. • Provides thousand of jobs in drilling, refining, transporting, etc.	• Not renewable • Pollutes air • About one half of what we use must be imported, which creates dependency on other nations • Expensive • Must be stored
Uranium (atomic energy; others of the 109 elements could be used, but uranium atoms are easiest to split)	• Heat quickly results from the splitting of the atoms; thus, can rapidly convert water into steam to turn turbines to create electricity, etc. • Does not pollute the atmosphere • Helps to conserve fossil fuels, which can then be converted into non-burning products such as lubricating oil	• Scarcity of uranium • Accidents can result in radiation that can be devastating to humans and the entire environment • Difficult to dispose of atomic waste; elaborate precautions are necessary • Expensive to build, safeguard, and maintain nuclear plants
Solar (heat and light from the sun)	• Does not pollute the atmosphere • Inexpensive once installations have been made • Easily used to provide power for small devices such as solar-powered calculators • Unlimited supply • No waste disposal problems	• Collection in large amounts requires extensive construction expenditures and acreage • Difficult to obtain when cloudy or night • Difficult to store • Latitudinal position precludes extensive use in far northern or southern locations
Water (falling water used to generate electricity or to turn water wheels as in mills)	• Does not pollute the atmosphere • No waste disposal problems • Inexpensive once all construction is completed, including dams, etc. • Renewable (water supply constantly replenished) • No waste • Lakes created by dams can be used for recreation	• Not available in many world locations • Dams must be built and maintained • Possibility of drought to interrupt water supply • Possibility of heavy rains to create flooding behind dams • Intermittent flow of water downstream can have adverse effects on the ecology of the region • Sedimentation build-up behind dams must be removed
Wind	• Does not pollute the atmosphere • No waste disposal problems • Renewable • Inexpensive once installations are made	• Wind may not be constant • High installation expense: considerable acreage needed to make "wind farm"

READING A WINDCHILL TABLE

Very often an announcer on television or radio will say something like this: "The temperature is 40°F, but the **windchill** is 22°F, so you had better bundle up this morning."

People pay attention to the windchill temperature, but there are many who do not understand how it is determined. The information on this page will help you to know; then, you can explain it to others.

The Windchill Effect

Your skin, normally at a temperature of 91.1°F, loses heat quickly when there is wind blowing on it. The stronger the wind, the greater the cooling effect. This is not unlike the cooling a hand fan provides in the summer.

The table below is based on a study by United States Army research teams on the effect of wind on human skin surface in Antarctica and other places. A single number—called the *windchill index*—relays the combined effect of wind and temperature. A 30 mile-per-hour (mph) wind at a temperature of 10°F, for example, can cause the same heat loss from exposed skin as a real temperature of -33°F with no wind.

© 1998 by John Wiley & Sons, Inc.

To Do:

1. What is the windchill effect for wind speed and thermometer readings of:

Wind Speed	Temperature	Windchill
10 mph	30°F	
20 mph	10°F	
20 mph	-20°F	
30 mph	50°F	
Calm	-40°F	
40 mph	-40°F	

2. Imagine that you know the windchill effect and the temperature. What would be the wind speed for the following?

Wind Speed	Temperature	Windchill
	40°F	28°F
	30°F	11°F
	-10°F	-63°F
	0°F	-45°F

Wind Speed	Windchill Index for Thermometer Reading of—									
	50°F	40°F	30°F	20°F	10°F	0°F	–10°F	–20°F	–30°F	–40°F
Calm......................	50	40	30	20	10	0	–10	–20	–30	–40
5 mph	48	37	27	16	7	–6	–15	–26	–35	–47
10 mph	40	28	16	2	–9	–22	–31	–45	–58	–70
15 mph	36	22	11	–6	–18	–33	–45	–60	–70	–85
20 mph	32	18	3	–9	–24	–40	–52	–68	–81	–96
25 mph	30	16	0	–15	–29	–45	–58	–75	–89	–104
30 mph	28	13	–2	–18	–33	–49	–63	–78	–94	–109
35 mph	27	11	–4	–20	–35	–52	–67	–83	–98	–113
40 mph	26	10	–6	–22	–36	–54	–69	–87	–101	–116

Source: Adapted from a publication of the United States Department of Agriculture, Soil Conservation Service.

Name: _____ Date: _____

WORKING WITH LARGE POPULATION NUMBERS

There are relationships between population growth and the environment. It appears that as the world's population increases so do environmental issues and problems. Increased population brings about the following:

• Greater use of transportation vehicles—cars, buses, trucks, etc.—and a subsequent increase in harmful emissions

• Greater need for food, which, in turn, brings about deforestation, drainage of wetlands, and increased use of marginal lands because more land is needed for cultivation

• Greater need for paper, books, newspaper, wrapping, packaging, etc., which results in more deforestation since wood is the chief source of paper and cardboard

• Greater need for homes, factories, and roads, which means disturbing habitats of wild animals and birds and the subsequent loss of species through deforestation

1. The table at the bottom of this column contains information about the growth in population of the entire world from 1950 to the year 2000 (estimated).

a. How many more people will there be in the year 2000 than there were in 1950?

_____ million

b. What was the increase in the number of people in the world in the ten-year spans listed below?

1950–1960: _____ million

1960–1970: _____ million

1970–1980: _____ million

1980–1990: _____ million

Year	World Population*
1950	2,500,000,000
1960	3,000,000,000
1970	3,700,000,000
1980	4,400,000,000
1990	5,300,000,000
2000	6,300,000,000**
* Rounded to nearest 100,000,000 ** Projected	

2. The table below lists the world's most populous nations and their populations as of 1995.

| World's Most Populous Nations ||
Country	Population (1995) (to nearest million)
Brazil	161,000,000
China	1,203,000,000
India	937,000,000
Indonesia	204,000,000
Japan	126,000,000
Russia	150,000,000
U.S.A	264,000,000

a. Reorganize the information in the table above: in the blank table below, list the countries in order by the size of their populations. China should be listed first.

| World's Most Populous Nations ||
Country	Population (1995) (to nearest million)

b. How many more people live in China than in the U.S.A.? _____

c. Is the combined population of the U.S.A. and India greater than the population of China?

____ Yes ____ No

d. How many more people live in the U.S.A. than in Russia? _____

e. What is the total population of the seven listed countries? _____

Name: _____ **Date:** _____

HOW MUCH WATER GOES DOWN THE DRAIN?

The table on the right can serve as a guide that tells how much water is used in several household activities. Of course, some people use less water for the activities, and some use more.

In most places in the United States water is so readily available that people may not have a real understanding of how much they use. This activity will help you realize how much water a family of <u>four</u> may use.

Home Water Usage	
Activity	**Amount of Water Used**
Shower	6 gallons per minute each person
Toilet flush	5 gallons per flush each person
Washing machine	30 gallons per load
Dishwasher	15 gallons per load
Brushing teeth, washing hands	4 gallons per day each person

1. How much water for taking showers would a family of <u>four</u> use in a week?

____1____ × _____ × ____5____ × _____ × _____ equals _____ gallons

# of showers per person each day	# of gallons used per minute	# of minutes in shower	# of people using shower	# of days in week

2. Suppose each member of a family of <u>four</u> flushes a toilet four times, each day. How many gallons of water would be used for flushing in a week?

_____ × _____ × _____ × _____ equals _____ gallons

# of flushes per person each day	# of gallons used per flush	# of people flushing	# of days in week

3. This family loads soiled dishes in a dishwasher during the day; then, in the evening, they wash all the dishes. How much water would be used for washing dishes in a week?

_____ × _____ × _____ equals _____ gallons

# of dishwashings each day	# of gallons used per washing	# of days in week

4. Each day of the week one load of laundry is washed in the washing machine.

_____ × _____ × _____ equals _____ gallons

# of washes per day	# of gallons per wash	# of days in week

5. Brushing teeth and washing hands is also a daily task for each of the <u>four</u> family members.

_____ × _____ × _____ × _____ equals _____ gallons

# of brushings, hand washings per day per person	# of gallons per person	# of people	# of days in week

6. What is the total number of gallons of water used each week for the five water-use activities described in questions 1–5?.. week total _____ gallons

7. What is the total number of gallons of water used each year for the five activities? (52 weeks per year)
.... year total _____ gallons

SPACE-SHUTTLE FLIGHTS

The table below is from the *Statistical Abstract of the United States*, published by the United States Government. The *Statistical Abstract*, as it is called, contains hundreds of tables on hundreds of different topics.

No. 1004. Space Shuttle Flights—Summary: 1981 to November 1994

FLIGHT NUMBER	Date	Mission/ Orbiter name	Days duration	FLIGHT NUMBER	Date	Mission/ Orbiter name	Days duration
1	4/12/81	Columbia	2	36	2/28/90	Atlantis	5
4	6/27/81	Columbia	7	31	4/24/90	Discovery	6
2	11/12/81	Columbia	2	41	10/6/90	Discovery	4
3	3/22/82	Columbia	8	38	11/15/90	Atlantis	4
5	11/11/82	Columbia	5	35	12/2/90	Columbia	9
6	4/4/83	Challenger	5	39	4/28/91	Discovery	8
7	6/18/83	Challenger	6	37	4/5/91	Atlantis	6
8	8/30/83	Challenger	6	40	6/5/91	Columbia	9
9	11/28/83	Columbia	10	43	8/2/91	Atlantis	9
10	2/3/84	Challenger	8	44	11/24/91	Atlantis	7
11	4/6/84	Challenger	7	42	1/22/92	Discovery	8
12	8/30/84	Discovery	6	45	3/24/92	Atlantis	8
13	10/5/84	Challenger	8	49	5/7/92	Endeavour	8
14	11/8/84	Discovery	8	50	6/25/92	Columbia	13
15	1/24/85	Discovery	3	46	7/31/92	Atlantis	7
16	4/12/85	Discovery	7	47	9/12/92	Endeavour	7
17	4/29/85	Challenger	7	52	10/22/92	Columbia	9
18	6/17/85	Discovery	7	53	12/2/92	Discovery	7
19	7/29/85	Challenger	8	54	1/13/93	Endeavour	6
20	8/27/85	Discovery	7	56	4/8/93	Discovery	9
21	10/3/85	Atlantis	4	55	4/26/93	Columbia	10
22	10/30/85	Challenger	7	57	6/21/93	Endeavour	10
23	11/26/85	Atlantis	7	51	9/12/93	Discovery	10
24	1/12/86	Columbia	6	58	10/18/93	Columbia	14
25	1/28/86	Challenger*	–	61	12/2/93	Endeavour	11
26	9/29/88	Discovery	4	60	2/3/94	Discovery	8
27	12/2/88	Atlantis	4	62	3/4/94	Columbia	14
29	3/13/89	Discovery	5	59	4/9/94	Endeavour	11
30	5/4/89	Atlantis	4	65	7/8/94	Columbia	14
28	8/8/89	Columbia	5	64	9/9/94	Discovery	10
34	10/18/89	Atlantis	5	68	9/30/94	Endeavour	11
33	11/22/89	Discovery	5	66	11/3/94	Atlantis	10
32	1/9/90	Columbia	10				

* Exploded 73 seconds after take-off. To be considered a flight, however short.

Source: U S National Aeronautics and Space Administration, *Payload Flight Assignments NASA Mixed Fleets*, January 1992, and "Space Shuttle Flights as of November 1994"

© 1998 by John Wiley & Sons, Inc.

To Do:

Study the table and answer the following questions.

1. What was the date of the first shuttle flight?

_____

2. In what year did the greatest number of shuttle flights take place? _____

3. In what month of the year did most of the shuttle flights take place?

Name of month: _____

Number of flights: _____

4. Complete the table below with information from the table above.

Space-Shuttle Flights: Number of Flights in Space	
Shuttle Flight Name	**Number of Flights**
Atlantis	
Challenger	
Columbia	
Discovery	
Endeavour	

COUNTING CALORIES

Many people are concerned about their weight. One of the most important considerations in weight control has to do with calorie intake. In general, the more calories consumed the more weight gained; the fewer calories consumed the more weight lost.

CALORIES VALUE OF SELECTED FOODS

Food	Measure	Calories
Dairy Products		
Milk, whole	1 cup	150
Milk, skim	1 cup	85
Cheese, Swiss	1 oz.	95
Ice cream, hardened	1 cup	270
Eggs		
Fried, in margarine	1	90
Hard boiled	1	75
Scrambled, in margarine, milk added	1	100
Fats and Oils		
Butter, salted	1 tbsp.	100
Mayonnaise	1 tbsp.	100
Fish, Meat, Poultry		
Tuna, canned in oil	3 oz.	165
Bacon, fried, broiled	3 slices	110
Beef, ground	3 oz.	245

Food	Measure	Calories
Hot dog, pork	1	145
Turkey, roasted	1 cup	240
Fruits		
Apple, 2 3/4" dia.	1	80
Banana	1	105
Orange, 2 5/8" dia.	1	60
Grain Products		
Bagel, plain	1	200
Bread, white, enriched	1 slice	65
Oatmeal	1 cup	145
Corn flakes, added sugar	1 oz.	110
Brownie, with nuts	1	100
Cracker, graham, 2 1/2" square	1	30
Pie, pecan 1/6 of a pie	1	575
Legumes, Nuts, Seeds		
Beans, black	1 cup	225
Peanut butter	1 tbsp.	95

Food	Measure	Calories
Peanuts, roasted in oil, salted	1 cup	840
Sugars and Sweets		
Candy, caramel	1 oz.	115
Candy, milk chocolate	1 oz.	145
Honey	1 tbsp.	65
Popsicle, 3 oz.	1	70
Sugar, white	1 tbsp.	45
Vegetables		
Broccoli	1 spear	50
Carrots, raw	1	30
Peas	1 cup	125
Potato chips	10	105
Tomatoes, raw	1	25
Miscellaneous		
Cola beverage	12 oz.	160
Catsup	1 tbsp.	15
Soup, tomato, with milk	1 cup	160
Soup, chicken noodle	1 cup	75

1. One day Mary kept a careful record of the amount and calorie count of the food she ate. Use the table to determine how many calories she consumed.

Breakfast	Measure	Calories
Orange	1	
Milk, whole	1 cup	
Oatmeal	1 cup	
Total calories		

Lunch	Measure	Calories
Swiss cheese	2 oz.	
Bread, white	2 slices	
Mayonnaise	1 tbsp.	
Potato chips	20	
Cola	12 oz.	
Brownie	1	
Total calories		

Supper	Measure	Calories
Beef, ground	6 oz.	
Broccoli	3 spears	
Milk, whole	1 cup	
Bread, white	2 slices	
Butter, salted	2 tbsp.	
Pie, pecan	1 piece	
Total calories		
Total calories for the day		

2. Mary weighed herself and became concerned about her weight. She decided to reduce her calorie intake. Following is what she ate on her first day of dieting.

Breakfast	Measure	Calories
Orange	1	
Milk, skim	1 cup	
Corn flakes/sugar	2 oz.	
Total calories		

Lunch	Measure	Calories
Tuna, canned in oil	3 oz.	
Bread, white	2 slices	
Potato chips	10	
Milk, skim	1 cup	
Crackers, graham	2	
Total calories		

Supper	Measure	Calories
Turkey, roasted	1 cup	
Carrot, raw	2	
Tomatoes	2	
Soup, chicken noodle	2 cups	
Ice cream, hardened	1 cup	
Total calories		
Total calories for the day		

How many fewer calories did she consume on the second day? _____

AN ARRAY OF CATTLE BRANDS

Cattle from one ranch sometimes mix with cattle from another ranch. So, when cattle are "rounded up" there has to be a way to tell which ranch owns which cattle. To solve the problem, cattle are branded. That is, a symbol, or brand, that represents a particular ranch is pressed into the hides of cattle.

1. Match the brand names listed below with the brands shown at the top of the page. Write the letter of the brand in the box in the corner of each brand.

A   FIVE TRIANGLES
B. JOGGER IN SQUARE
C. OARLESS BOAT
D. FLYING KITE
E. O-DIAMOND-O
F. BIG DIPPER AND NORTH STAR
G. LIGHTNING IN BUBBLE
H. DIAGONALS IN SQUARES

I.   BAR BELL X
J.   POLES ON RAILROAD
K. CRISS-CROSS-CREW
L. JACK IN BOX
M. SPRUCE WITH HALO
N. ROCKING CHAIRS
O. CIRCLES IN CIRCLES
P. FIVE IN CUBE

2. In the space below draw your own brand symbol, and give it a brief name.

Name: _____

_____

COMPLETING A MAP AND TABLE OF SEA DISTANCES

From New York to:	Sea Distance in Miles	Hours of Sea Travel at an Average Speed of 30 Miles Per Hour
1. Helsinki, Finland	4,257	141.9 hrs.
2. Oslo, Norway	3,644	
3. Glasgow, Scotland	3,210	
4. Southampton, England	3,169	
5. Cherbourgh, France	3,134	
6. Barcelona, Spain	3,714	
7. Athens*, Greece *Actual port is Piraeus	4,688	

To Do:

The table lists the water distances from New York to seven European cities.

1. The numbers next to the names of the cities in the table are also shown on the map. Label the cities on the map.

2. Assume that a ship is sailing at an average speed of 30 miles per hour. How many hours would it take to sail to each city? Write your answers in the spaces in the table. Take your division only one place beyond the decimal; do not round.

Example: New York to
Helsinki

```
       141.9
30 )4257.0
     30
     125
     120
      57
      30
     270
     270
       0
```

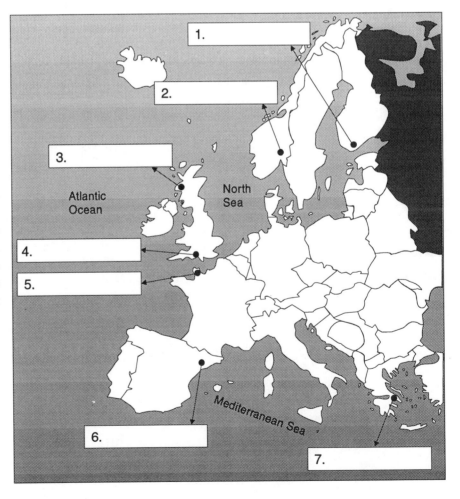

A "TIME" TABLE OF VARIOUS UNITED STATES CITIES

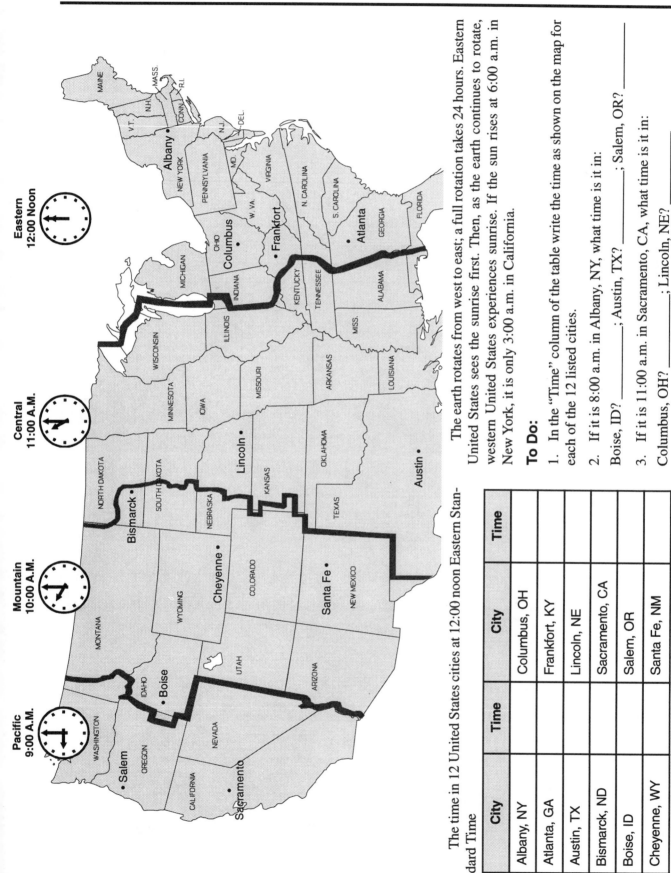

The time in 12 United States cities at 12:00 noon Eastern Standard Time

The earth rotates from west to east; a full rotation takes 24 hours. Eastern United States sees the sunrise first. Then, as the earth continues to rotate, western United States experiences sunrise. If the sun rises at 6:00 a.m. in New York, it is only 3:00 a.m. in California.

To Do:

1. In the "Time" column of the table write the time as shown on the map for each of the 12 listed cities.

2. If it is 8:00 a.m. in Albany, NY, what time is it in: Boise, ID? _____ ; Austin, TX? _____ ; Salem, OR? _____

3. If it is 11:00 a.m. in Sacramento, CA, what time is it in: Columbus, OH? _____ ; Lincoln, NE? _____

City	Time	City	Time
Albany, NY		Columbus, OH	
Atlanta, GA		Frankfort, KY	
Austin, TX		Lincoln, NE	
Bismarck, ND		Sacramento, CA	
Boise, ID		Salem, OR	
Cheyenne, WY		Santa Fe, NM	

COMPARING THE YEARLY SALARIES OF MEN AND WOMEN

No.728. Average Earnings of Year-Round, Full-Time Workers: 1994

[In dollars. For persons 25 years old and over as of March 1994]

AGE AND SEX	All workers	Less than 9th grade	HIGH SCHOOL		COLLEGE		
			9th to 12th grade (no diploma)	High school graduate (includes equivalency)	Some college (no degree)	Associate degree	Bachelor's degree or more
Male, total	**41,118**	**20,461**	**24,377**	**31,081**	**35,639**	**38,944**	**61,008**
25 to 34 years old	30,715	17,622	20,594	26,363	29,922	31,400	40,403
35 to 44 years old	43,058	17,576	24,089	31,452	36,298	40,198	65,358
45 to 54 years old	49,187	24,421	26,745	35,975	40,787	44,682	70,546
55 to 64 years old	47,044	23,855	30,380	35,373	41,595	47,127	73,318
65 years old and over	40,229	17,326	21,596	28,433	29,880	(B)	71,964
Female, total	**27,162**	**13,349**	**16,188**	**21,383**	**24,787**	**26,903**	**39,271**
25 to 34 years old	24,273	12,220	14,364	19,581	22,023	24,068	32,507
35 to 44 years old	29,189	14,153	15,416	21,321	25,976	28,855	43,954
45 to 54 years old	29,424	14,297	17,530	23,217	27,131	28,297	43,480
55 to 64 years old	24,816	12,541	18,351	21,770	24,327	27,726	37,134
65 years old and over	22,869	(B)	(B)	22,457	20,128	(B)	32,805

B Base figure too small to meet statistical standards for reliability of derived figure.

The information in the table above is from the *Statistical Abstract of the United States*—a very reliable source of information available in most libraries.

Study the table carefully before you answer the questions below. You will see that there are noticeable differences in yearly earnings between men and women, even if they have the same amount of education. Also note the differences in earnings that come about as the result of differences in education.

1. What is the difference in average yearly pay between all males with less than a 9th-grade education and:

a. all who graduated from high school?

$ _____

b. all who graduated with a bachelor's (college) degree or more?

$ _____

2. What is the difference in average yearly pay between those females with less than a 9th-grade education and:

a. those females who graduated from high school?

$ _____

b. those females who graduated with a bachelor's (college) degree or more?

$ _____

3. How much less in average yearly salary does the female high school graduate earn than the male high school graduate?

$ _____

4. A male college graduate with a bachelor's degree averages how much more money a year than a female with the same education?

$ _____

5. Circle the words in parentheses that correctly complete the following sentences.

a. In general, women with the same level of education as men earn (less, the same, more) money than men do.

b. In general, yearly earnings of both men and women increase as they grow older, but the table indicates that earnings can begin to decrease when people are as young as (35–44, 45–54).

Name: _____ Date: _____

DESIGNING A TABLE

Assume that you are an editor for a book such as the *World Almanac and Book of Facts* or the *Statistical Abstract of the United States*. It is your job to gather facts and then arrange them into a table that will be published.

Your assignment is to make a table of facts about public high school graduation rates. The facts you receive (next column) tell what percent (%) of the students who entered high school in 1990 graduated in 1994. For example: Maine, 74%, which means 74 of every 100 students who entered Maine high schools in 1990 graduated in 1994. This also means that 26% did not graduate in four years. The table you are assigned to make is concerned with the section of the United States known as the Northeast.

To Do:

1. The table below has been ruled so that you can list the states in alphabetical order.

2. Write headings at the top of the columns. What does each column show?

3. These are the states and their percent of graduates: Maine, 74.0%; New Hampshire, 78.3%; Vermont, 84.6%; Massachusetts, 78.0%; Connecticut, 78.9%; Rhode Island, 73.4%; New York, 64.5%; New Jersey, 85.3%; Pennsylvania, 78.9%; Delaware, 66.5%; Maryland, 74.7%; West Virginia, 78.0%; Virginia, 72.4%.

STUDENTS IN THE NORTHEASTERN UNITED STATES
WHO ENTERED HIGH SCHOOL IN 1990 AND GRADUATED IN 1994

Column Headings

Note: Data is from the *World Almanac & Book of Facts*, 1997.

GUIDELINES FOR PICTURE GRAPHS

There are four basic kinds of graphs your students should know: picture, bar, line, and area. A typical area graph can be in the form of a circle or a single bar, each containing segments that total 100%.

The first consideration in teaching about graphs is how to read and interpret them. The second consideration, which is significantly more difficult, is how to construct graphs from data. This page and the two that follow are concerned about reading and making picture graphs.

Picture Graphs

There are two essential characteristics of picture graphs:

• Quantities of things are represented by symbols. Each whole symbol represents a whole quantity. Partial symbols represent a portion of a whole quantity. For example, a half symbol represents one half of the quantity.

• Each graph should have a title that expresses the main idea of the graph. Each graph should have a key that tells how many things are represented by each symbol. The vertical and horizontal columns should have headings.

Notes

1. A picture graph resembles a bar graph in that in both kinds of graphs the length of the lines may be compared. For example, one line of symbols may be twice as long as another line; this clearly indicates a twice-as-great relationship.

2. Symbols used in picture graphs, especially for beginning graph readers (2nd, 3rd, 4th grades) should be very explicit. If a graph is to represent the number of children who have brown, blue, green, or hazel eyes, the symbol used in the graph should leave no doubt that eyes are being compared.

3. In the primary grades, symbols should have a one-to-one relationship; that is, one apple symbol should represent one apple. However, as the children's arithmetic skills increase, one symbol can come to represent two or more of a particular item.

4. Children should first learn to read a graph for basic facts: How many apples were brought to school on Monday? On Tuesday? And so on. What was the total number of apples for the week? Comparisons can be made: How many more apples were brought in on Monday than on Tuesday?

Next, inferences may be made. What might be the reason why there were more apples brought in on Monday and Tuesday than on Thursday and Friday? How many apples do you think will be brought to school next week? (predicting)

5. In the primary grades, the first picture graphs should apply to real things in the children's lives. Example: "How many of you were born in January? February? Let's make a picture graph that shows the months of the year and how many of you were born in each month."

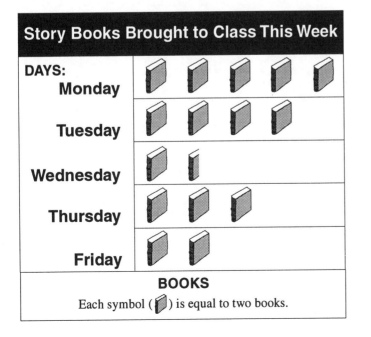

Story Books Brought to Class This Week

DAYS:	
Monday	📘 📘 📘 📘 📘
Tuesday	📘 📘 📘 📘
Wednesday	📘 📘
Thursday	📘 📘 📘
Friday	📘 📘

BOOKS

Each symbol (📘) is equal to two books.

The picture graph at the left is typical of the level of difficulty that most second- or third-grade children could easily learn to read.

The picture graphs on the following page vary from easy to more difficult.

READING PICTURE GRAPHS

1. Six students went fishing on a boat that was called *Nancy Ann*. The boat left from Manasquan Inlet in New Jersey. The boys teased the girls and said that the most fish would be caught by the boys.

   The fishing was very good that day. Many different kinds of fish were caught. The picture graph that follows tells the names of the fish and the total number of fish caught by everyone on the boat.

**THE KIND AND NUMBER OF FISH
CAUGHT ON A ONE-DAY FISHING TRIP**

KINDS OF FISH					
Cod	🐟	🐟	🐟	🐟	🐟
Flounder	🐟	🐟	🐟	🐟	🐟
Fluke	🐟	🐟	🐟	🐟	🐟
Halibut	🐟	🐟	🐟	🐟	
Porgy	🐟	🐟	🐟	🐟	🐟
Sea Bass	🐟	🐟	🐟	🐟	

NUMBER OF FISH CAUGHT
Each symbol (🐟) equals four fish

a.   How many porgy were caught? _____

b.   How many more fluke were caught than flounder? _____

c.   All together, how many fish were caught?
_____

d.   The fish are listed in alphabetical order. What other way could the fish have been listed?
_____

2.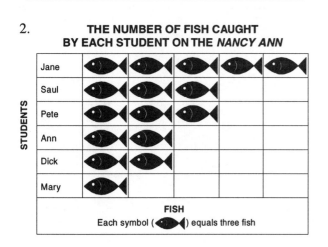

**THE NUMBER OF FISH CAUGHT
BY EACH STUDENT ON THE *NANCY ANN***

a.   How many fish did Jane catch? _____

b.   How many more fish did Saul catch than Mary?
_____

c.   Did Jane catch more fish than the other two girls combined? _____

d.   How many fish were caught by the boys?
_____ By the girls? _____

3. Bill earned $0.50 (fifty cents) a week for each customer he served on his paper route. When he started he had 30 customers. He wanted to increase the number of customers so he could buy a racing bike. So, he worked hard at getting new customers. His campaign was very successful. The picture graph below shows the gains he made in the six-month period from April through September.

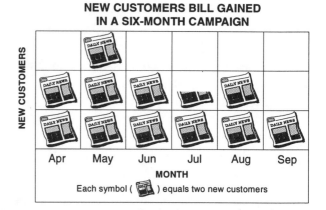

**NEW CUSTOMERS BILL GAINED
IN A SIX-MONTH CAMPAIGN**

MONTH
Each symbol (📰) equals two new customers

a.   In what month did Bill gain the most customers? _____ How many? _____

b.   What was the total number of customers Bill gained in the six-month period from April through September? _____

c.   What was the total number of customers Bill served—including the old customers? _____

d.   At the end of September how much was Bill earning each week? _____

MAKING PICTURE GRAPHS

Steve Improves His Basketball Skills

Steve decided that in the fall he was going to try out for his school's basketball team. He thought he would have a better chance of making the team if he practiced during the summer. Every day he practiced free throws from the foul line, layups, and dribbling. Every two weeks he tested his free throw progress by seeing how many shots out of 20 he could sink from the foul line.

Following is the record Steve kept. On June 20: 10; July 4: 12; July 18: 14; August 1: 14; August 15: 15; August 29: 16.

As you can see, it's difficult to read the figures as they are listed above. A picture graph would make the record easier to read and more interesting to look at. You can make a picture graph that shows the same figures. Here's how to proceed.

1. Make a title for your graph and write it on the lines provided.

2. Design a symbol, such as a basketball, to show the figures. Draw it on the key line below the graph.

3. Use 2 as the value of each symbol, and write it on the key line below the graph.

4. Under the heading **DATES** list the dates Steve tested his skill.

5. In the spaces in the graph draw the number of symbols that represents each date's score.

Title: _____

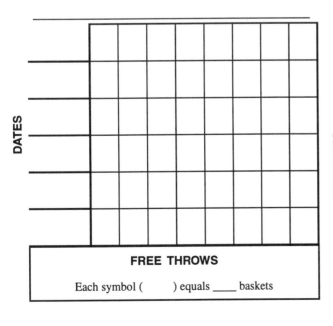

Winter Olympic Games

The 1998 Winter Olympic Games are to be held in Japan. What countries will win the most gold, silver, and bronze medals? Only time will tell. Meantime, it will be interesting to know which countries were the top eight winners in 1994. Following are the figures in alphabetical order according to country.

Country	Medals Won	Country	Medals Won
Austria	9	Norway	26
Canada	13	Russia	23
Germany	24	Switzerland	9
Italy	20	United States	13

You can arrange the medal winner information in another way in a picture graph. Place the highest winner first, the next highest winner second, and so on. When you make your graph below be sure to:

a. Write a title that tells the main idea of the graph.

b. Assign a value of 4 medals to each symbol.

c. Use this symbol: ⊕. It can be easily divided into four parts. For example, ▽ represents 2 medals; ⊕ represents 3 medals, and so on.

d. List the eight winning countries under the heading **COUNTRIES**.

e. In the spaces in the graph draw the correct number of symbols for each country.

Title: _____

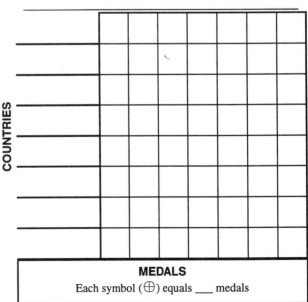

© 1998 by John Wiley & Sons, Inc.

GUIDELINES FOR BAR GRAPHS

The Essentials of Bar Graphs

1. Bar graphs consist of two or more bars positioned on a grid. The bars may show comparisons of the same item, or the bars may compare different items.

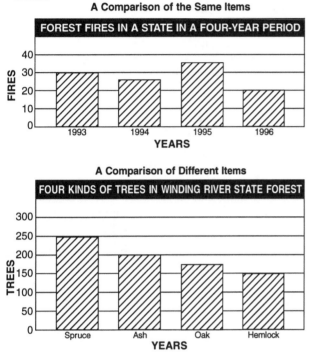

Notice in the examples above that each graph has two axes—vertical and horizontal. One axis indicates quantities; the other axis indicates names, dates, etc., of things being compared. Each axis has a heading.

2. Bars may be placed horizontally or vertically on the grid.

3. The quantity axis should be divided into equal units of measurement. There should be no fewer than five and no more than ten enumerated units. Numbers placed on the quantity axis should end evenly. The highest quantity to be graphed should be no more than the highest unit of measurement on the quantity axis.

Assume, for example, that in a household the money spent annually on various items is as follows: rent, $4,800; food, $3,600; heat, $2,000; utilities, $1,500; clothing, $1,000.

The greatest amount of money spent on one item is $4,800; therefore, the quantity axis on a graph of these household expenses should have an upper limit of $5,000. $5,000 may be divided into five measurement units of $1,000. The items for which the money was spent can be identified on the horizontal axis.

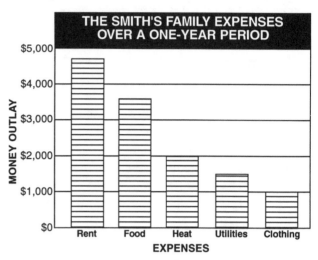

4. The quantity axis should start at zero. If not, the bars will not be proportional.

5. The graph should have a title that leaves no doubt as to what is being compared. Time, place and other factors should be as explicit as possible.

6. To avoid amounts on the quantity axis with more than four digits—such as 10,000, or 300,000, or 7,000,000—quantities may be shown with one, two, or three digits. However, there should be an explanatory note on the graph as in the example below:

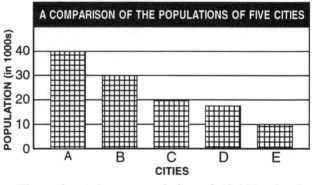

Thus, city A has a population of 40,000; city B, 30,000; city C, 20,000; city D, 18,000; city E, 10,000.

READING BAR GRAPHS

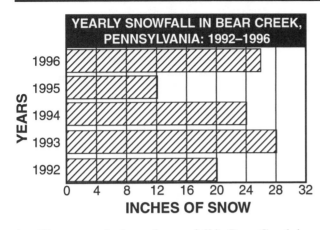

YEARLY SNOWFALL IN BEAR CREEK, PENNSYLVANIA: 1992–1996

(bar graph with YEARS on vertical axis: 1992, 1993, 1994, 1995, 1996; INCHES OF SNOW on horizontal axis: 0, 4, 8, 12, 16, 20, 24, 28, 32)

1. How many inches of snow fell in Bear Creek in 1993? _____in.   In 1996? _____in.

2. In what year was the amount of snow that fell twice as much as in 1995? _____

3. Which of the following best tells how much snow fell in the five-year period shown on the graph?
____88 in.   ____96 in.   ____110 in.   ____120 in.

4. If you put 10 inches of snow in a pail and melted it, you would find about 1" of water in the bottom of the pail. How many inches of water would the snow of 1992 have made? _____ in.

5. Deer are dependent upon vegetation, especially brush, for food. In the winter of what year would they probably have had the most difficulty finding something to eat? _____

The bar graph below compares the number of people living in the six most populous states in the United States, as reported in the *1996 World Almanac and Book of Facts.*

Notice that, under the heading POPULATION, "in 1,000,000s" is enclosed by parentheses. This tells you that you must add 6 zeroes to each measurement on the vertical axis (column). So, if a state had a bar that reached the 20 on the vertical axis, you would read its population as 20,000,000, or 20 million.

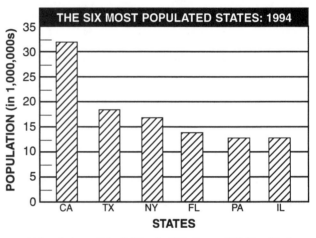

THE SIX MOST POPULATED STATES: 1994

(bar graph with POPULATION (in 1,000,000s) on vertical axis: 0, 5, 10, 15, 20, 25, 30, 35; STATES on horizontal axis: CA, TX, NY, FL, PA, IL)

*Abbreviations: CA, California; TX, Texas; NY, New York; FL, Florida; PA, Pennsylvania; IL, Illinois

6. Approximately how many million people lived in California in 1994?
____25   ____32   ____26   ____40

7. About how many fewer million people lived in Texas than in California in 1994?
____9   ____14   ____16   ____18

8. About how many more million people lived in Texas than in Florida in 1994?
____4   ____7   ____9   ____11

9. How did the combined populations of Pennsylvania and Florida compare with the population of California?
____More   ____Less   ____About the same

10. What is the approximate total population, in millions, of the six states shown on the graph?
____72   ____80   ____94   ____107

MAKING A BAR GRAPH

Many people in the world are concerned that certain animals will disappear from the earth if we do not make efforts to save them. Those animals that are in danger of being lost forever are called *endangered species*. Here is a partial list of the world's endangered animals as reported in the *1996 World Almanac and Book of Facts*.

Classes of Animals	Number of Endangered Species	Example
Mammals	307	Florida panther
Birds	253	Peregrine falcon
Reptiles	79	American alligator
Amphibians	15	Wyoming toad
Fish	79	Chinook salmon
Insects	24	Lotus blue butterfly

The first two columns of information in the table can be shown in another way—a bar graph. The fol-lowing suggestions will help you complete the in-complete graph below.

1. Think of a title that tells what the graph will show. Write the title in the blank space above the graph.

2. At the side of the vertical axis (column) find *Number of Endangered Species*.

3. Enumerate (number) the lines on the vertical axis as follows: 40, 80, 120, 160, 200, 240, 280, 320.

4. On the horizontal axis print the names of the classes of animals, going from the one with the most endangered species to the one with the least endan-gered species. Mammals is already printed to help you get started.

5. For each class, draw a bar that shows how many species are endangered. The first bar (mammals) is already drawn to show you how your bars should look.

6. After you have completed the graph, think of four questions you could ask about what the graph shows. Write your questions and answers on the back of this page.

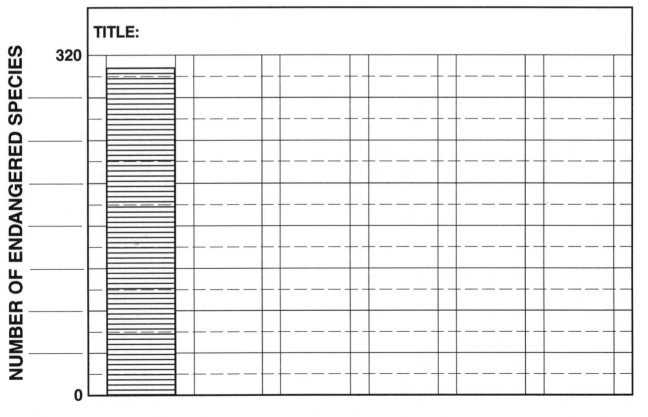

MORE GRAPH GUIDELINES

1. Sometimes, a single bar is used to show proportions or percentages of things. The entire bar represents 100%; the segments occupy space in the bar proportionate to their percent or fraction of the whole. The example that follows shows how a single bar may be divided into a number of segments.

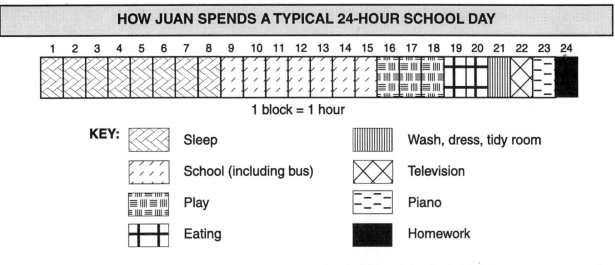

2. Frequently, all of the bars in a multibar graph are subdivided. If each bar is divided into two segments, for example, the reality is that two graphs are shown on the same grid. All of the elements shown in a particular bar use the same units of measurement found in the quantity axis.

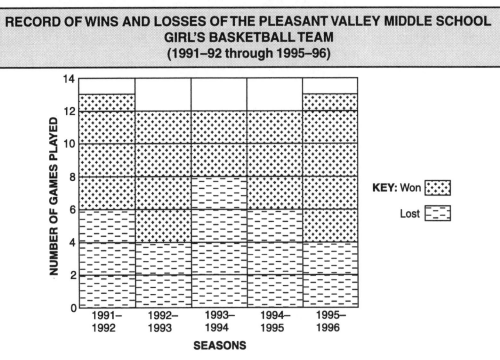

Suggested Procedure

Make a transparency of the bar graphs illustrated above; project, explain, and ask questions about each graph.

Some suggested questions about the single-bar graph: (1) How many hours does Juan sleep? <u>8</u> (2) Which of the following fractions tells how much of each day Juan spends playing: 1/3, 1/4, 1/6, <u>1/8</u>?

Some suggested questions about the multibar graph: (1) How many games were won in the 1991–1992 season? <u>7</u> How many lost? <u>6</u> (2) Over the five-season period, how many games were won? <u>34</u> How many lost? <u>28</u>

INTERPRETING A SINGLE-BAR GRAPH

> **PERCENT OF LAND IN NORTH AMERICA OCCUPIED BY CANADA, UNITED STATES, MEXICO, AND CENTRAL AMERICA**

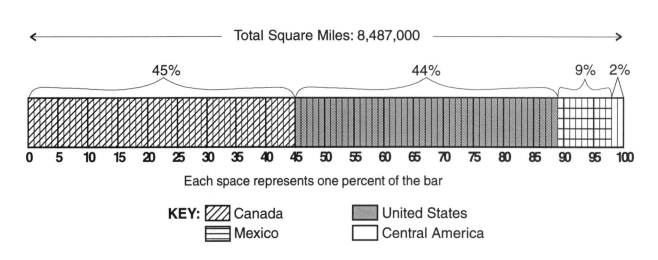

Total Square Miles: 8,487,000

45%   44%   9% 2%

0 5 10 15 20 25 30 35 40 45 50 55 60 65 70 75 80 85 90 95 100

Each space represents one percent of the bar

KEY: Canada   United States

Mexico   Central America

Reading a Single-Bar Graph

The graph above shows the combined areas of Canada, the United States, Mexico, and Central America. Central America consists of Guatemala, Belize, Honduras, Costa Rica, Nicaragua, El Salvador, and Panama. Each division of the bar equals 1%; the entire bar equals 100%.

1. What percent of the entire area represented by the bar do each of the following occupy:

Country or Region	Percent of the Total
Canada	_____ %
United States	_____ %
Mexico	_____ %
Central America	_____ %

2.a. According to the bar and the figures you have written in the table (above), how many times larger is the United States than Central America? Hint: This is a division problem. Divide 44% (United States) by 2% (Central America).

_____

b. Use the same procedure suggested in 2a.: How many times larger is the United States than Central America and Mexico combined?

_____

Challenge Question

How many square miles of the entire area does Canada occupy? Hint: This is a multiplication problem. In setting up the problem, be sure to convert Canada's 45% to a decimal (.45). Also, use the information stated above the graph.

Work Space:

GUIDELINES FOR LINE GRAPHS

1. Line graphs are useful in portraying trends over periods of time. A glance gives the casual reader an immediate impression of the overall movement of stocks, growth or decline of club membership, changes in temperature, and myriad other things. More careful study of the lines and their placements on the grid reveals reasonably accurate details.

2. The same information shown on a line graph would probably be more difficult to comprehend if it were written in a paragraph. To show the truth of this statement, you may want to have your students take a set of statistics portrayed in a line graph and then read or write the graph's information in a narrative paragraph. The clarity of the line graph will become readily apparent to the students.

3. As in all graphs there should be a title, headings on both the horizontal and vertical axes, units of measurement that start at zero and are limited to no more than ten major divisions, and a key that identifies the lines if more than one line appears on the graph.

4. One caution should be observed when reading or making line graphs: the grid must be composed of squares. If the cells are rectangular, they will convey the wrong impressions. A grid composed of rectangles that are vertically arranged conveys the impression of a steep climb or decline; if the rectangles are horizontally arranged the impression gained is just the opposite. Propagandists use rectangles in line graphs to suit their particular purpose, although some graph plotters inadvertently use rectangles. The examples that follow are all plotted correctly, but only Figure 3 utilizes squares within squares and, thus, makes no attempt to lead the reader to unreliable conclusions.

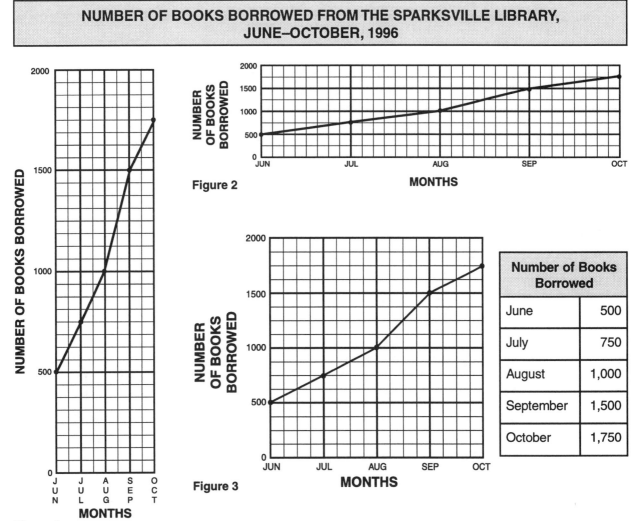

NUMBER OF BOOKS BORROWED FROM THE SPARKSVILLE LIBRARY, JUNE–OCTOBER, 1996

Figure 1

Figure 2

Figure 3

Number of Books Borrowed	
June	500
July	750
August	1,000
September	1,500
October	1,750

Name: _____ **Date:** _____

COMPLETING A "TIME LINE" BAR GRAPH

A "time line" is a kind of single-bar graph on which dates are placed at regular intervals. The total amount of time the line shows might be, for example, 600 years. If such a line were 6" long, it could be divided into six major segments, each 1" long and representing 100 years. Each segment could be further divided. Following is an example of a time line that covers 600 years. Four events have been located on the line.

At a glance, one can see that it was about 115 years after Columbus landed that Jamestown was settled. One can also easily see that there was approximately 400 years between the landing of Columbus and the Spanish-American War. Of course, the dates of the events are printed, if you desire exactness.

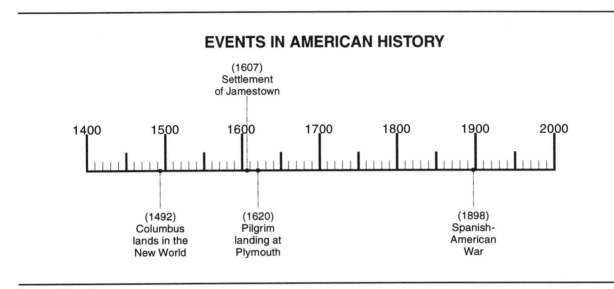

EVENTS IN AMERICAN HISTORY

The time line below can be completed by placing on it the events listed below. Refer to the example above to see how you should record each event. Note that if two events are close together, one event can be recorded below the line, and the other can be recorded above the line.

UNITED STATES WARS*

1775: Revolutionary War	1898: Spanish-American War	1950: Korean War
1812: War of 1812	1917: World War I	1964: Vietnam War
1846: Mexican War	1941: World War II	1991: Persian Gulf War
1861: Civil War		

* Dates represent the beginning of the wars.

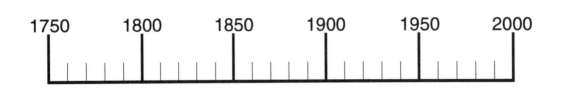

INTERPRETING AND COMPLETING LINE GRAPHS

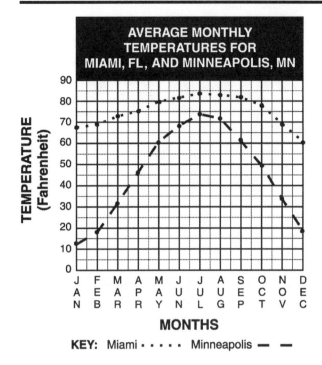

**AVERAGE MONTHLY
TEMPERATURES FOR
MIAMI, FL, AND MINNEAPOLIS, MN**

TEMPERATURE (Fahrenheit)

MONTHS

KEY: Miami · · · · · Minneapolis — —

1. Which city had a lesser change in average temperature throughout the year?

_____ Miami   _____ Minneapolis

2. Approximately how many degrees of average temperature change are there in Minneapolis from January to July?

_____38°   _____45°   _____62°   _____77°

3. In what two consecutive months is there very little change in the average temperature of Miami?

_____ and _____

4. What is the approximate difference in degrees between the highest average temperatures of Miami and Minneapolis?

_____5°   _____9°   _____13°

5. What is the approximate difference in degrees between the lowest average temperatures of Miami and Minneapolis in January?

_____40°   _____55°   _____65°

6. In what months of the year is the average temperature in Minneapolis less than 35°?

_____, _____, _____,

_____, _____

The following figures tell how much money Susan saved each year over a nine-year period, from 1988 through 1996:

1988: $25	1991: $40	1994: $70
1989: $35	1992: $50	1995: $80
1990: $50	1993: $60	1996: $95

Your task is to show the figures on the partially completed line graph in the next column.

1. Make a title for the graph. What do the figures show?

2. Divide the vertical axis into units of measurement. Since the greatest amount of money she saved in any year was less than $100, the units can be marked off in amounts of $10. Starting with zero write the rest of the numbers on the lines on the left side of the graph.

3. Write the years below the vertical axis. The first year she started saving, 1988, is already printed.

4. On each of the year columns, place a dot that shows how much Susan saved.

5. Connect the dots with straight lines.

6. Write four questions that can be answered by referring to the graph. Also, provide answers. Write your questions and answers on the back of this page.

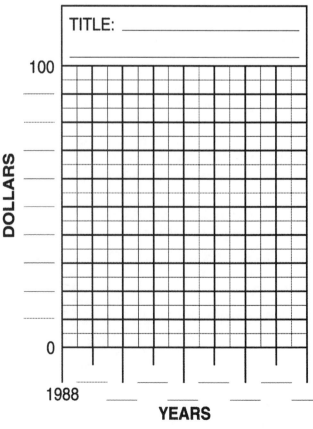

TITLE: _____

_____

DOLLARS

100

0

1988

YEARS

GUIDELINES FOR CIRCLE AND SQUARE GRAPHS

Circle Graphs

Circle graphs are easy to read, but relatively difficult to prepare. Your students will increase their understanding of circle graphs if, via a transparency, you lead them through the steps below.

Students should realize that the total of all the elements shown within the circle equals 100% and that each element is a percent of the whole.

Problem: Use a circle graph to show how much wheat the United States exports compared to the total amount exported by nine other leading wheat-exporting countries.

To Do:

1. Facts: The wheat exports of the 10 leading wheat-exporting countries, including the United States, is 106,000,000 metric tons.* Of this total the United States exports 37,000,000 metric tons.

2. 37,000,000 is approximately 35% of the total ($37,000,000 \div 106,000,000 \approx 35\%$).

3. Every circle is composed of 360°. What is 35% of 360°? Answer: 126° ($.35 \times 360° = 126°$).

4. Draw a circle with a compass. Draw a radius from the center of the circle to the top of the circle. (Figure 1)

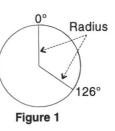

Figure 1

5. Lay the straight edge of a protractor along the radius, and measure 126°. Make a mark on the circle's circumference, and draw a second radius. The segment produced represents the United States' part of the total. The remainder of the circle represents the other nine nations' wheat exports.

6. Label the segments and provide a title. (Figure 2)

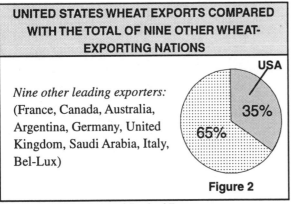

UNITED STATES WHEAT EXPORTS COMPARED WITH THE TOTAL OF NINE OTHER WHEAT-EXPORTING NATIONS

Nine other leading exporters: (France, Canada, Australia, Argentina, Germany, United Kingdom, Saudi Arabia, Italy, Bel-Lux)

USA 35%

65%

Figure 2

*1996 World Almanac and Book of Facts

Square Graphs

The enclosed area of a circle graph represents the total, or 100%, of the elements shown on the graph. The same is true of the enclosed area of a single-bar graph. Still another area graph is a large square divided into 100 squares, each square equaling 1%. This kind of graph is very useful. Elements of the graph may be compared at a glance or simply by counting the blocks representing each element.

The graph below is a typical square graph. It would be helpful to show and explain the graph via transparency. The title, key, and percent of each element should all be discussed.

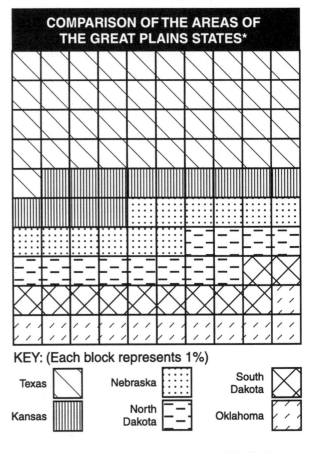

COMPARISON OF THE AREAS OF THE GREAT PLAINS STATES*

KEY: (Each block represents 1%)

Texas   Nebraska   South Dakota

Kansas   North Dakota   Oklahoma

*Areas of the Plain States, as reported in the *1996 World Almanac and Book of Facts*, are as follows, in square miles:

Texas:	268,601
Kansas:	82,282
Nebraska:	77,358
South Dakota:	77,121
North Dakota:	70,704
Oklahoma:	69,903
Total Area:	645,969 sq. mi.

INTERPRETING CIRCLE AND SQUARE GRAPHS

Circle Graph

When the circle graph at the bottom of this column is completed it will tell a sad story. The graph is a record of the number of times oil was spilled into United States rivers, lakes, and oceans in a recent year.

Oil does more than make water unfit for drinking or swimming. Fish die because their gills become oil-clogged; this prevents them from getting oxygen from the water. Birds suffer too. Their feathers become matted and stick together so that they can't fly, and, as a result, they die. Shorelines become covered with thick, gooey oil. This not only stops people from bathing, but also kills water life such as crabs and clams.

To Do:

1. Write the title on the lines above the graph: OIL SPILL INCIDENTS IN AND AROUND UNITED STATES WATERS IN A RECENT YEAR.

2. Study the graph; then, list the three main sources of oil spills.

a. _____

b. _____

c. _____

3. The graph will tell more if we also include the number of gallons spilled. In the parentheses by each label carefully print the following:

Land Spills: 912,108 gal.

Freighters, etc.   400,296 gal.

Tank ships and tank barges: 191,458 gal.

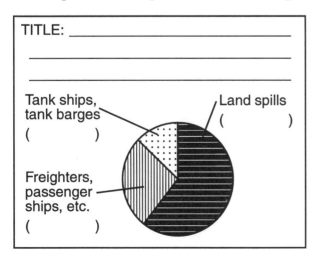

Square Graph

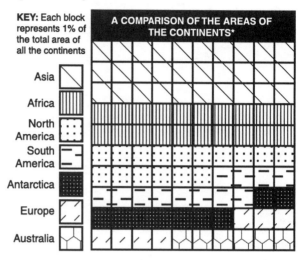

1. The square graph represents the total (100%) area, which is 57,900,000 square miles, of the seven continents. What percent of the total does each continent occupy? To find the answers, consult the key in the graph, then count the squares for each continent. Remember that each square represents 1% of the total area.

Continent	%	Continent	%
Africa		Europe	
Antarctica		North America	
Asia		South America	
Australia			

2. Approximately how many times larger is Asia than Australia? ____ 3   ____ 5   ____ 8

3. Approximately how many times larger is Africa than Europe? ____ 2   ____ 3   ____ 4

Challenge Questions

Approximately how many square miles of the earth does Asia occupy? Hint: Multiply .30 (30%) × 57,900,000.

Asia occupies_____ square miles.

Now, following the same procedure, determine approximately how many square miles North America occupies.

North America occupies_____ square miles.

Data from 1996 World Almanac and Book of Facts.

A CIRCLE GRAPH SHOWING IMMIGRATION

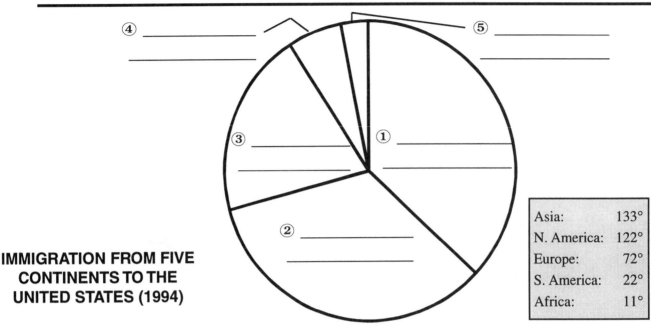

IMMIGRATION FROM FIVE CONTINENTS TO THE UNITED STATES (1994)

Asia:	133°
N. America:	122°
Europe:	72°
S. America:	22°
Africa:	11°

The motto on the Great Seal of the United States is "E Pluribus Unum." This is a Latin phrase that means "Out of Many—One." That is, the millions of people who have come to the United States from other nations have become one people.

The circle graph shows how true that motto is. The graph shows **only one year** of immigration, 1994. It should be realized that the United States has been welcoming immigrants for hundreds of years.

To Do:

1. Complete the labeling of the graph, as follows:

① ASIA   ④ SOUTH AMERICA
② NORTH AMERICA   ⑤ AFRICA
③ EUROPE

2. Below each continent's name on the graph, print one of the following figures, which represent the number of people who came to the United States from five continents in 1994.

• Asia: 293,000   • South America: 47,000
• North America: 272,000   • Africa: 27,000
• Europe: 161,000

3. How many immigrants came to the United States in 1994? _____

4. Decide whether the following statements are true (T) or false (F) according to all the information on this page, including footnotes.

a. Europe, South America, and Africa combined contributed more immigrants than Asia did.

                                             T   F

b. Asia contributed more than six times more immigrants than South America did.   **T   F**

c. North America and South America combined contributed more immigrants than Asia did.

                                             T   F

d. Central America is included in the immigrant figures for South America.   **T   F**

e. There were no immigrants to the United States from Australia or New Zealand.   **T   F**

f. The immigrants from Russia are included in the total immigrants from Asia.   **T   F**

Notes

1. Australia and New Zealand are not represented on the graph because only 4,000 (approximately) of their people migrated to the United States in 1994; the graph is too small to show that amount.

2. Central America and the countries of the Caribbean region are included in North America.

3. Russia, and the other countries that were established from the former Union of Soviet Socialist Republics (Soviet Union, USSR) are included in Europe.

© 1998 by John Wiley & Sons, Inc.

VOLCANOES—NATURAL SOURCES OF POLLUTION I

There are more than 500 active volcanoes in the world. On any given day ten or more of them are erupting. Their eruptions add substantially to the pollution of the atmosphere. Unlike pollution brought about by human activities (transportation, manufacturing, etc.), which can be controlled, it is impossible to control volcanoes. Pollution caused by volcanoes is part of nature's way of bringing about balance among plant and animal life and other elements of the earth such as land and water. It is human contribution to pollution that upsets the balance.

A notable recent volcanic eruption occurred in June 1991 in the Philippine Islands when Pinatubo erupted. Vast amounts of sulfuric acid gas were blown into the atmosphere. The immediate effect was a measurable cooling of the earth so great that the warming of the earth from the Greenhouse Effect was slowed down. It was predicted that the sulfuric acid gas would dissipate in a few years; then, the carbon dioxide gas also spewed out by Pinatubo (and other volcanoes) coupled with earth-borne carbon dioxide emissions would accelerate earth's warming.

Along with the enormous impact on the atmosphere, what were some of the other results of the Pinatubo eruptions?

- *National Geographic* (December 1992) reported that two cubic miles of ash were blown out of the volcano, enough to bury the District of Columbia up to 150 feet.

- Clark Air Base, a United States Air Force location only ten miles from Pinatubo, was covered with ash and has since been abandoned.

- Subic Naval Base, another United States installation, was also covered with ash, thus forcing the evacuation of United States personnel and dependents.

- 200,000 Filipinos were evacuated from their homes; whole villages were covered with ash; and thousands of acres of vegetation were destroyed.

- More than 900 people were killed.

- Rocks the size of grapefruit fell from the sky and punched holes in roofs, cars, etc.

- A positive consequence: Over a period of years the volcanic ash will significantly fertilize hundreds of square miles in the vicinity of the volcano.

After you have presented the preceding information, your students may, under your direction, complete the facing page.

1.   Complete the bar graph, "Notable Volcanic Eruptions" as follows:

a.   Write the title in the space provided.

b.   Write this heading at the side of the vertical axis: Deaths

c.   Starting at the bottom of the vertical axis, number the lines, as follows: 0; 5,000; 10,000; 15,000; 20,000; 25,000; 30,000; 35,000.

d.   Write this heading on the horizontal axis: Place and Year of Eruption

e.   Label each space on the horizontal axis, as follows: Numbers in ( ) indicate deaths.

- Krakatau, Indonesia, 1863 (35,000)
- Mt. Pelee, Martinique, 1902 (30,000)
- Nevado del Ruiz, Colombia, 1985 (23,000)
- Mt. Etna, Sicily, 1669 (20,000)
- Mt. Vesuvius, Italy, 79 A.D. (16,000)

f.   Complete the graph by filling in each bar with diagonal lines.

2.   Labeling the diagram of a typical volcano will help your students better understand its workings. As they label, you can explain each part by using the information below.

A: **Magma Pool**: Molten rock, called magma, collect in pools below the earth's surface. As the magma gets hotter, steam and other gases expand and break through weaknesses in the earth's crust.

B: **Lava**: When the magma emerges above the earth's surface and hardens, it is called lava.

C: **Conduit**: Fissures ("pipes") allow the magma to escape.

D: **Crater**: Hollow interior of a volcano

E: **Cone**: As the lava flows over the top of the crater some of it cools and hardens to form a cone and increase the height of the volcano.

F: **Emissions**: **Lava, Steam, Ashes, Dust**: As the molten lava flows it covers everything in its path; eventually, it hardens.

Name: _____ Date: _____

VOLCANOES—NATURAL SOURCES OF POLLUTION II

Title: _____
_____

Volcano___				
Place___				
Date___				

_____

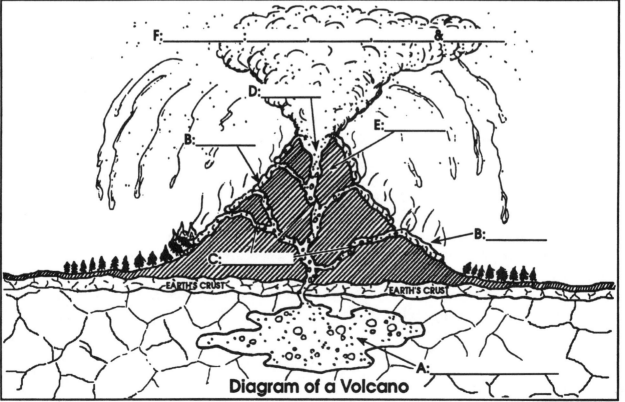

F:_____ &

D:_____

B:_____

E:_____

B:_____

EARTH'S CRUST   EARTH'S CRUST

A:_____

Diagram of a Volcano

BAR GRAPH OF RECREATIONAL ACTIVITIES

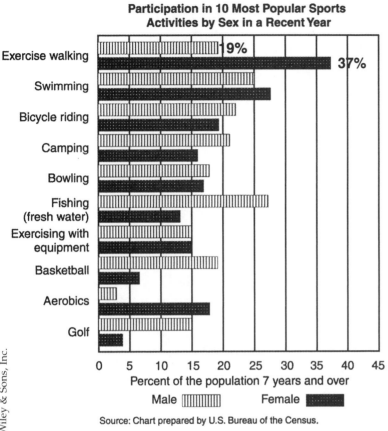

Participation in 10 Most Popular Sports Activities by Sex in a Recent Year

Exercise walking — 19% / 37%
Swimming
Bicycle riding
Camping
Bowling
Fishing (fresh water)
Exercising with equipment
Basketball
Aerobics
Golf

0 5 10 15 20 25 30 35 40 45
Percent of the population 7 years and over

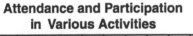

Male [||||||]   Female [███]

Source: Chart prepared by U.S. Bureau of the Census.

© 1998 by John Wiley & Sons, Inc.

The bars in the *Participation in 10 Most Popular Sports Activities* graph represent percent. For example, the bars representing exercise walking show that 19%, or 19 of every 100 males, and 37% of females participate in the activity. Notice that the population on which the graph is based is "7 years and older."

To Do:

1. At the end of each bar write the percent that the bar represents. The first activity, exercise walking, has been completed to help you get started.

2. In which activity is the difference between participating men and women the greatest? _____
_____

3. In which three activities are women more active than men? _____
_____
_____

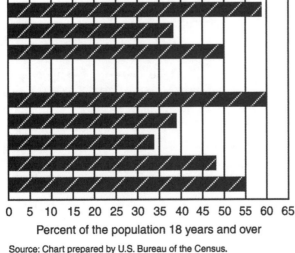

Attendance and Participation in Various Activities

Attendance of
Movies
Sports events
Amusement parks
Participation in
Exercise
Playing sports
Outdoor activities
Home improvement
Gardening

0 5 10 15 20 25 30 35 40 45 50 55 60 65
Percent of the population 18 years and over

Source: Chart prepared by U.S. Bureau of the Census.

The *Attendance and Participation in Various Activities* graph is divided into two parts: *Attendance of* and *Participation in*. Notice that this graph also uses percent as a measurement.

1. What age level is included in the graph? _____

2. As in the activity above, at the end of each bar write the percent it represents.

3. What activity is most popular as shown in the Attendance part of the graph?
_____

4. What activity is most popular as shown in the Participation part of the graph?
_____

What activity is least popular?
_____

117

LINE GRAPH OF MOTOR VEHICLE PRODUCTION

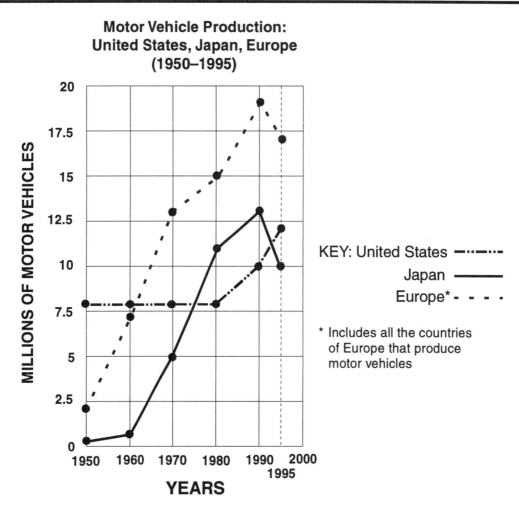

Motor Vehicle Production:
United States, Japan, Europe
(1950–1995)

KEY: United States ––·––··––
      Japan —————
      Europe* – – – –

* Includes all the countries
  of Europe that produce
  motor vehicles

1. For how many years was United States production of motor vehicles about the same?

_____ 10 years   _____ 30 years

_____ 20 years   _____ 40 years

2. In what year did United States production reach approximately 12 million motor vehicles?

_____ 1960   _____ 1980

_____ 1970   _____ 1995

3. In what two years did Japan's production exceed United States production?

_____ 1970   _____ 1990

_____ 1980   _____ 1995

4. What region/country showed the only increase in 1995?

_____ Europe   _____ Japan

_____ United States

5. Approximately how many motor vehicles did the United States and Japan combined produce in 1995?

_____ 17 million   _____ 31 million

_____ 22 million   _____ 39 million

6. The total number of vehicles produced in the world in 1995 was 50,000,000. Of that 50,000,000 the United States produced 12,000,000.

What percent listed below best tells how much of the total was produced by the United States.

_____ 10%   _____ 24%

_____ 16%   _____ 36%

Work: $\dfrac{12,000,000}{50,000,000}$ or $\dfrac{12}{50}$ or $50\overline{)12}$

MAKING A CIRCLE GRAPH I

The information below is designed to help you lead your students through the process of making a circle graph. Circle graphs may be the easiest to read, but they are the most difficult to make because a knowledge of geometry is necessary.

Note: The directions in italics in the explanation below are probably within the expertise of most students using this book. It will be to their advantage to do as much of the process as possible.

Make a Circle Graph

1. To make a circle graph it is necessary to know the total of all the parts of the graph.
Have your students compute the number of square miles in the combined five Great Lakes. The total (94,450) should be printed at the bottom of the second column in the table on the next page.

2. The next step in making a circle graph is to determine what percent (%) each part (each lake) is of the whole. To perform this operation the following formula is applied; here it is applied to Lake Superior.

Percent = the part (31,700) divided by the whole (94,450), or:

$$\frac{31,700}{94,450} \quad \text{or} \quad 94,450\,\overline{)31,700}$$

When the division is completed, we find Lake Superior occupies 33.6% of the total area of the Great Lakes (rounded to the nearest tenth).
The third column of the table has been completed.

3. The next step in making our circle graph is to determine how many degrees of the 360° circle each lake should occupy.
Procedure: Multiply each percent (in the table's third column) × 360°. Example: Lake Superior occupies 33.6% of the total Great Lakes area, or 121° of the circle (rounded to the nearest whole).
Have your students compute the number of degrees of the circle each lake should occupy and print their findings in the fourth column.

4. The next step in the procedure is to use a protractor to mark off the segment each lake occupies. To do this draw a line from the center of the circle to the top of the circle. (Figure 1)

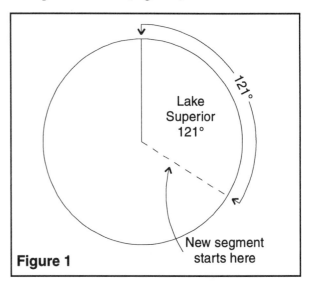

Figure 1

Then use a protractor to measure the 121° segment that represents Lake Superior. Do the same for the segments that the other four lakes occupy. Note that each new segment starts from the line that marks the end of the previous segment.

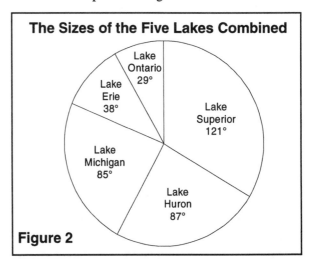

Figure 2

5. Students should give the graph an appropriate title, and they should label the segments.

MAKING A CIRCLE GRAPH II

The Great Lakes are a great asset to the United States. Fishing, recreation, water supply, and water power are four of the ways they are useful. Perhaps the most important benefit of the lakes is that they provide a waterway for ships from the Atlantic Ocean to sail far within the interior of the United States and also, of course, Canada.

The total area taken up by all the lakes is larger than any of the states except Alaska, Texas, Arizona, California, Colorado, Montana, Nevada, New Mexico, Oregon, and Wyoming. Lake Superior, for example, is more than four times larger than New Jersey.

To Do:

1. The table below tells the size of each lake. Add the numbers in the second column to determine the total number of square miles the lakes occupy.

Areas of the Five Great Lakes			
Lake	Area in Sq. Mi.	Percent of Total Area	Number of Degrees
Superior	31,700	33.6	121°
Huron	23,000	24.3*	
Michigan	22,300	23.6	
Erie	9,910	10.5	
Ontario	7,540	8.0	
Total		100.0	

* This figure has been rounded down to 24.3 rather than rounded up to 24.4 in the interest of the percents totaling 100%.

2. The third column in the table tells what percent each lake is of the total area of the lakes. The percents given were determined by dividing the area of each lake by the total area of the lakes.

3. The fourth column in the table is incomplete. To determine how many degrees each lake would be allocated in the circle graph, multiply the percent shown in the table (for each lake) times 360°. For example, Lake Superior's share of the circle is .336 × 360°, or 120.96°. The answer should be rounded to the nearest degree, 121°.

Complete the column in the manner explained in the Lake Superior example. Be sure to round to the nearest degree. Write your answers in the table.

4. The circle graph below shows each lake's segment of the circle. In the segments and outside the graph, print the name of the lake the segment represents and the number of square miles taken up by the lake.

5. Compose an appropriate title for the graph, and print it on the lines above the graph. Think: What does the graph show?

_____

Title: _____

_____

_____

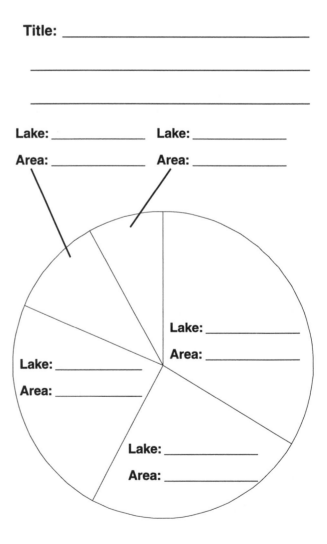

Lake: _____   Lake: _____
Area: _____   Area: _____

Lake: _____
Area: _____

Lake: _____
Area: _____

Lake: _____
Area: _____

Section 4: Reading Pictures/Cartoons and Maps

GUIDELINES FOR READING PICTURES I

Words can be used to describe things, but it takes many words to develop images that are not within a learner's life experiences. For example, even a very good description of a glacier would leave many fifth graders, especially those who have not experienced snow or ice, with an incomplete visual impression of one of nature's most spectacular formations. How can children who have never traveled more than a few miles from their Great Plains homes comprehend a tropical rain forest or ocean waves if only words are used?

Children may incorrectly visualize a person, place, or thing described with words alone. Zoe A. Thralls cogently expresses this opinion in her book *The Teaching of Geography*: "As one reads, words must be translated into mental images. Each child's mental images will differ. Furthermore, the mental image of the idea may be entirely erroneous. . . . If the word *rhea* is mentioned, no image results unless someone has seen such a bird or a picture of it. If you try to describe it, each child will build a mental image only partially correct, depending upon background and ability. An authentic and clear picture quickly gives the correct image that will be common to the class . . ."

Written descriptions attempt to convey reality through the utilization of printed symbols, that is, words, numerals, and abbreviations such as the dollar sign ($), the ampersand (&), and plus (+). *Chair* is a symbol for an elevated platform supported by one or more legs, but one such word symbol by itself is limited in meaning. It is only when symbols are connected in sequence that the meaning the writer is trying to express is conveyed. After the reader synthesizes the symbols into sentences, and the sentences into paragraphs, a main idea can be established.

Every picture has at least one main idea. The details in the picture support the main idea. There is, however, one major difference in how the reader derives main ideas from paragraphs as compared to pictures. With a glance at a picture it is possible to capture an essential message (main idea); then, by examining the picture supporting details are uncovered. On the other hand, as has been mentioned earlier, the main idea of a paragraph is developed by sequentially integrating the thoughts expressed in the sentences.

When reading a paragraph the eyes move saccadically from left to right across a line of the page; then, upon reaching the end of the line they make a return sweep to the next line, and so on. The eyes make stops called *fixations* as they move across the lines. It is during the stops that the eyes focus on a portion of print. In reading pictures, fixations are also made but in a more random manner. In one fixation it is difficult to read all the details in a picture, just as it is impossible to read all the details of a paragraph in one fixation.

Techniques for Reading Pictures

Pictures may be read for facts/details and for inferences.

Facts/details: One of the purposes for reading pictures for details is to establish a data base from which main ideas and inferences are made. There are a number of ways to establish the data base. For example, the instructor could say to the class, "Here is a picture of a riverside town; in fact, it's called Riverside. The picture can tell us many things about the river, the town, the factory, and the land surrounding the town. (See illustration, page 124.) I would like each of you to study the picture for the details it shows. For example there are two boats on the river. Make a list of details on your scratch pads; later we will make a class list on the board."

The children then go to work. After three or four minutes, the instructor asks for contributions. Every student is expected to make at least one contribution. Be careful not to accept inferences, because one of your objectives is to help the children distinguish between fact and opinion (inferences). Making inferences from the data will be a follow-up activity. Encourage simple expressions of details; discourage complete sentences. Some of the details in the picture are:

- sailboat
- marina
- rock wall along river bank
- church
- factory
- water tower
- cultivated fields
- mountains
- buildings
- picnic area

The children will uncover an astonishing amount of detail, much more than a typical textbook would include in its narrative. Soon the children become

GUIDELINES FOR READING PICTURES II

so observant that they will see minor details in a major detail, for example, a steeple on the roof of the church or a television antenna on top of one of the buildings. This is a positive sign—the children are becoming more observant.

Another important outcome of such a picture-reading activity is that, because the children are making frequent, active, and intense responses to the picture, a mental image of the scene will be imprinted in their minds. Still another desirable outcome is that, because the instructor doesn't tell the students anything, because he or she is the facilitator of the lesson, the skills developed while observing the still picture can be applied directly to an actual field situation.

The activity described above—examining a picture for the details it contains—can be varied in a number of ways. For example, students can be instructed to note a detail in the picture and then formulate a question to ask of other students. Here is an example: "Look at the road and the river bank below it. What is used to help people go to and from the river bank?" One of the advantages to this approach is that a language arts component—formulating questions—is included. Another positive result is that students are communicating with students, rather than communicating mainly with instructors.

Here is another technique that will place your students in the position of being keen observers. Compose a list that includes items that are not in the picture as well as items that are in the picture. The students are to examine the picture and cross out all the items on the list that are not present. For example, in the Riverside picture one of the cross-out items on the list might be "smoke."

MAKING INFERENCES FROM PICTURES

Inferences

When reading words the first task of the reader is to comprehend what is being stated. What is the selection saying? What are the stated facts and details? The second task of the reader is to go beyond the facts. What is being implied? What are some predictions that can be made from the facts? This two-step process is also directly applicable to reading pictures. Sir Joshua Reynolds described this process well when he wrote:

> "Invention, strictly speaking, is little more than a new combination of those images that have been previously gathered and deposited in the memory. Nothing can be made of nothing; and they who have laid up no materials can produce no combinations."

An inference is an opinion that one forms after discovering one or more details of an event, situation, picture, or depiction, and then relating the details in such ways that new combinations result. Students should realize that after formulation of an inference, testing—in the form of research, experimentation, or resort to authority—may prove the inference (opinion) to be a fact or, perhaps, not a fact. Your explaining that it is "all right" to be mistaken should encourage students to make inferences; it helps eliminate the fear of being wrong.

In the foregoing suggested activities for establishing facts in a picture, a number of observations were made. Now the class is ready to think about the facts and make inferences. To stimulate student thinking, the instructor can ask questions that allow for inferencing. Some suggested questions relative to the picture of Riverside follow:

a. What purpose is served by the wall on the outside curve of the river? (It will retard erosion of the river bank as the river flows past.)

b. Why is there no smoke coming from the factory smokestacks? (There are at least three possibilities: (1) The factory was not operating at the time the picture was drawn—perhaps it was Sunday or a holiday. (2) The factory is operating, but it has installed smoke abatement devices. (3) The smokestacks are no longer needed because some other form of energy, possibly electric or nuclear, has eliminated the need for smokestacks.)

c. What season of the year is most likely represented in the picture? Probably summer, although it could be late spring or early fall. Otherwise, it would be unlikely that a person would be water skiing. Also, the people in the right foreground are wearing lightweight clothing.

An analysis of the inference questions suggested above reveals significant geographical and environmental relationships. If the picture was examined for details alone, it is doubtful that the relationships brought out by the questions would have been explored by most of the children.

Three questions that can be asked of many pictures, especially those used in teaching geography and history follow:

a. What does this picture tell about the natural environment of humans or animals?

b. What does this picture tell about the ways that humans and animals have adapted to the natural environment?

c. What does this picture tell you about human activities?

These questions are specific and challenging, and they lead naturally into isolating detail and encouraging inferences.

> A cliche often expressed is that "a picture tells more than a thousand words." This is true if, and only if, the viewer is willing to take the time and thought necessary to analyze the picture. Some people are not willing to do that, so, although they may get the main idea, they cannot substantiate their generalization because they lack the detail necessary to support or defend it.

JAMESTOWN, 1607: PICTORIAL FACTS AND INFERENCES

1. The picture shows how people lived in Jamestown, the first permanent English colony in North America, or, as it was called, the New World.

    On each numbered line below briefly tell what each numbered person in the picture is doing.

① _____

② _____

③ _____

④ _____

⑤ _____

⑥ _____

⑦ _____

⑧ _____

⑨ _____

⑩ _____

⑪ _____

⑫ _____

2. Some important details to notice and explain:

a. Jamestown was walled for protection from attacks. Why are the upright logs of the stockade pointed?

_____

_____

b. What material is being applied to the roof of the house? _____

_____

c. What kind of weapon is on the mound next to the stockade? _____

_____

d. Where did the woman carrying the pail probably get the water? _____

_____

e. The number ④ person is carrying a weapon in his right hand. What is your guess as to what it is?

_____

_____

_____

A COLONIAL HOME: PICTORIAL FACTS AND INFERENCES

1. The picture shows what the inside of a typical colonial home might have looked like. Write at the end of each line—outside the picture—the letter of the phrase or word from the list below that best describes that object.

a. Split-log bench

b. Iron pots

c. Straight-backed chair

d. Candle, for light

e. Oven, for baking

f. Gun

g. Homemade broom

h. High-backed bench

i. Bellows to make fire burn brighter

j. Powder horn

k. Homemade table

l. Pewter dishes, made of tin and lead

m. Butter churn

n. Ladder to loft

o. Bible, found in most colonial homes

p. Trencher, wooden eating plate

2. Answer the following questions on the reverse side of this page. The questions will challenge your thinking ability. Don't be afraid to be wrong; write what you think.

a. Try to think of a reason why the boy is climbing the ladder.

b. Find the long, hanging object on the left side of the fireplace. It is a *bed-warming pan*. On cold nights it was used to warm beds in the loft. How could the bed-warming pan warm a bed? *Hint*: Notice it has a lid with holes punched through.

c. To *churn* means to stir a liquid. Study the butter churn; then try to describe how it might churn cream into butter.

d. The more air (oxygen) a fire gets, the more fiercely it will burn. In what way would the bellows shown in the picture contribute oxygen to a fire?

AN ABANDONED FARM: PICTORIAL FACTS AND INFERENCES

1. In the 1930s there was a long period of time when there was very little rainfall in the region shown on the inset map in the picture. The region was known as the "Dust Bowl."

ACCORDING TO THE MAP WHAT STATES WERE PART OF THE DUST BOWL?

_____ _____ _____

_____ _____

2. In the Dust Bowl winds picked up particles of soil and filled the air with dust. People placed masks over their mouths and noses to prevent dust from filling their lungs. Dust piled up along fence rows, houses, and barns. The winds even blew dust through key holes, window cracks, and doors.

CIRCLE THE SENTENCE THAT BEST DESCRIBES THE PICTURE.

3. Farmers could no longer make a living; they abandoned their farms and moved away.

WHAT DETAILS IN THE PICTURE HELP YOU TO KNOW THE FARM WAS ABANDONED?

_____

_____

4. THINK OF A TITLE FOR THE SCENE AND WRITE IT ON THE BLANK LINE IN THE PICTURE.

5. Notice the trail in the picture leading either to or from the barn.

IMAGINE THE TRAIL WAS MADE BY THE FARMER WHO WAS LOOKING AT THE SCENE FOR THE LAST TIME. WRITE A PARAGRAPH OR TWO THAT MIGHT TELL WHAT WAS ON HIS MIND. WHAT MIGHT BE HIS REGRETS? FOND MEMORIES?

_____

_____

_____

_____

_____

_____

_____

_____

_____

_____

_____

Name: _____ Date: _____

SOURCES OF AIR POLLUTION: PICTURES WITH A SPECIFIC MAIN IDEA

1. *Transportation*: Motor vehicles, including airplanes, are the greatest air polluters. All states now have laws that require vehicles to have devices that reduce the amount of deadly gases entering the air.

1. What three sources of pollution are shown in the picture? _____

_____, and _____

2. What ground vehicles other than those shown in the picture also contribute pollution?

_____, _____ , _____

3. How are states trying to reduce air pollution from transportation? _____

_____

2. *Power Plants and Factories*: Most of these industries burn coal or oil. They put more than 100 million tons of pollutants into the air every year. This amounts to about 800 pounds for every person in the United States.

1. Add to the picture by showing smoke and particles coming from the smoke stacks.

2. According to the caption what fuels are used in many power plants and factories?

_____

3.a. Add to the picture by showing drain pipes discharging waste from the two buildings.

b. What effect would waste have on the river's plant and animal life? _____

_____

3. *Spraying*: When spraying is done to kill insects, to paint buildings, or to destroy mosquito larvae in swamps, some of the particles and gases escape into the air.

1. What three kinds of spraying are mentioned in the caption? _____,

_____, and _____

2. What harmful effect might the spray have on the fruit on the trees? _____

What harmful effect might the spray have on the men doing the spraying? _____

3. What else in the picture is contributing to polluting the air? _____

4. *Dust*: An immeasurable amount of dust from quarries, building roads, plowing, and other activities enters the atmosphere. Sometimes the dust is carried over the earth's surface for hundreds and thousands of miles.

1. According to the caption, in what three ways does dust enter the atmosphere? _____,

_____, and _____

2. What might be one way to reduce dust from quarries? _____

_____

_____

_____

FOUR PICTURES, EACH WITH A SPECIAL MEANING

Examine each picture; then state facts that are shown in the picture. Following that, make at least one inference based on the facts. Briefly explain what led you to make the inference. An example is given to help you get started.

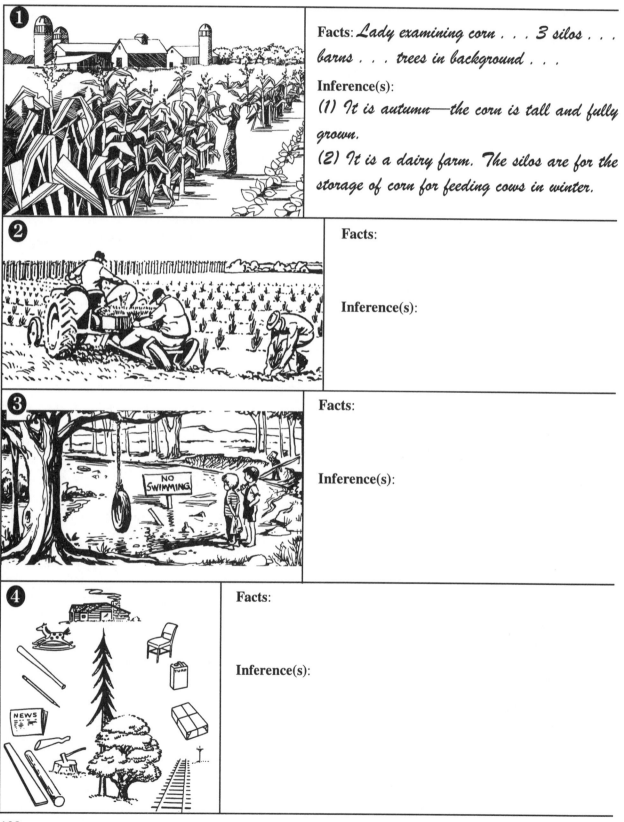

Facts: *Lady examining corn . . . 3 silos . . . barns . . . trees in background . . .*

Inference(s):

(1) It is autumn—the corn is tall and fully grown.

(2) It is a dairy farm. The silos are for the storage of corn for feeding cows in winter.

②

Facts:

Inference(s):

③

Facts:

Inference(s):

④

Facts:

Inference(s):

Name: _____ Date: _____

A FRONTIER HOME AND STORE: PICTORIAL FACTS
AND INFERENCES

It is possible to learn as much from a picture as from a written account. However, it is necessary to search a picture systematically in much the same way you would read a paragraph carefully.

To Do:

1. List details from the picture above under each of the headings below.

a. Cabin: _____

_____

_____

b. Person working in the garden: _____

_____

_____

_____

c. Person fishing: _____

_____

_____

_____

d. Person walking toward the house: _____

_____

e. Other details: _____

_____

2. Write a sentence that tells the main idea of the

picture. _____

_____

1. How many items for sale can you identify in the drawing? List each item under the proper heading below.

Household Equipment	Farm Tools	Food, Clothing, etc.

2. Write a sentence that tells what each of the following may be thinking.

Merchant: _____

_____

Shopper: _____

_____

Child: _____

_____

A PICTORIAL REPRESENTATION OF LIFE IN SPAIN'S LATIN AMERICAN COLONIES

Soon after Spain gained control of most of the area now called Latin America, the Spaniards forced the native people to work for them. The man on the horse is a Spanish supervisor.

1. List the kinds of farming activities shown in the illustration.

a. _____

b. _____

c. _____

d. _____

2. What would be your guess as to what is in the pots the young boy is handling?

_____

3. Draw a circle around the worker sharpening a scythe (cutting tool).

4. Not including the pottery, there are a number of objects shown in the picture that the Spaniards introduced into the New World—iron tools, wheels, plow, and carts. They also introduced the two kinds of animals shown:

_____ and _____

5. How can you tell from the picture that the supervisor is prepared for an attack or rebellion?

_____

_____

6. Imagine that you are describing the appearance of the supervisor. Observe closely; then, list four details you would include in your description. One example is given to help you get started.

heavy beard _____ _____

_____ _____

_____

7. Imagine that the two men in the upper left of the picture are talking while working. Write a paragraph that expresses the feelings and thoughts they might have about their Spanish conquerors and the supervisor.

_____

_____

_____

_____

_____

_____

_____

_____

_____

_____

_____

_____

A PICTURE STORY OF MAGELLAN'S VOYAGE

1. The pictures tell, in sequence, the story of Magellan's trip around the world. Each sentence below is related to one of the pictures. On the line in front of each sentence write the number of the picture that best describes it.

___ On August 10, 1519, Magellan's fleet sailed from Seville, Spain.

___ When King Manuel of Portugal heard that Magellan was sailing for Spain, he tried to have him killed.

___ Magellan put down a mutiny; then, on a beach on the east coast of South America he tried the mutineers and punished them.

___ Months after leaving South America, Magellan reached the Philippine Islands, where he became involved in local wars. Magellan was killed in a battle there.

___ Magellan searched for a way to sail around South America. He found a water passage that led to the Pacific Ocean.

___ Magellan asked King Manuel of Portugal to sponsor a voyage around the world; however, Manuel refused.

___ After leaving Spain, Magellan sailed southwest toward South America.

___ After a three years' voyage, only one ship returned to Spain. It was the first ship to sail around the world.

___ Magellan then went to King Charles of Spain, who agreed to help him. Soon, Magellan was supervising the loading of his ships.

2. Illustration 8 shows how Magellan met his death. Imagine that you were an eyewitness and that you were asked to tell how he died. Include as many details as possible. *Hint*: The small boat with some of his men is moving toward the ship. What do you think is the significance of that? (Write your account on the reverse of this page.)

Name: _____ Date: _____

A PICTURE COMPARISON OF TWO INDIAN TRIBES

Indians of the Pacific Northwest   Indians of the Southwest

The Indians of the Pacific Northwest (Washington, Oregon) and the Indians of the Southwest (New Mexico, Arizona) lived in different climates. As the pictures show, this resulted in different ways of living.

If a statement in the first column tells about the Pacific Northwest (PNW) Indians, put a (✓) in the column headed PNW. If the statement tells about the Southwest (SW) Indians, check the column headed SW. (The statements are based on facts and inferences.) Then answer the questions in the second column.

Statement	PNW	SW
1. They used fishbones for needles.		
2. They used their homes as forts.		
3. They lived in a region of plentiful rainfall.		
4. They may never have seen a canoe.		
5. Nuts and berries were a part of their diet.		
6. Their water was stored in clay pots.		
7. Furs were an important item in trade.		
8. They grew cotton or raised sheep.		
9. Their homes seldom burned down.		

1. Notice the cigar-shaped pole sticking out of the hole in the Southwest Indians picture. What was its use? _____

2. In the Southwest Indians picture, what is the woman who is kneeling at the base of the house doing? _____
_____

3. In the Pacific Northwest Indians picture, what might be the reason why a canoe is lying on racks?
_____

4. What is probably being carried by the person who is walking away from the beached boat in the Pacific Northwest Indians picture?_____

5. In case of enemy attack, what are two things the Indians of the Southwest could do to protect themselves?_____
_____

TEXTBOOK PICTURES

Following are some suggestions for making effective use of textbook pictures.

1. Make captions for all the pictures in a chapter. Have the children match the captions with the pictures. Here is an example: Assume a typical Rhine River scene. Caption: It is almost impossible to grow crops on the steep banks of the Rhine River, so something must be done to level the land. Steps called *terraces* are carved into the sides of the banks; then crops are planted on the level steps.

An effective alternative to the teacher writing the captions, one that has the additional advantage of bringing a language arts element into the lesson, is to have the children compose their own captions for pictures. This activity would most likely be carried out as the class is reading and discussing the text. Undoubtedly, the illustrations in a chapter are related to the narrative, so students should be able to include what they have learned in the captions they write.

2. One innovative instructor, who understood that children enjoy puzzles and games, used the following learning center activity to motivate her class to study the pictures in a chapter. She cut out at least one detail from each picture in a chapter. Then she assembled the cutouts on a page, which she then photocopied. Her directions to the children were for them to search the chapter, find the picture from which each cutout came, and note the page number. The abbreviated chart that follows shows how she set up the activity:

Detail	Picture Page Number
Four athletes are marching in an Olympic Games parade. Each athlete is carrying a flag.	

After the children located each picture, they were to answer a question related to the detail. This activity placed the children in a research mode. The answers to the questions could sometimes be found in the textbook narrative, but, most often, the searchers had to resort to other books such as encyclopedias and almanacs. *Note:* The question that was asked relative to the Olympic Games picture was this: What four countries are represented by the flags the athletes are carrying?

The teacher cut out the details from pictures in an old, tattered textbook that was the same edition that her class was using. From one picture she snipped out the highest peak of a range of mountains; from another picture she cut out a particular cow from a herd of cows (What kind of cow is this?), and so on.

The picture of Charles Lindbergh and the airplane he flew across the Atlantic Ocean to France is an example of the procedure explained in number 2 above.

Assume that the children have already matched the cutout detail you provided with the appropriate picture. Their task now is to answer a question about the detail: What is the name of the airplane Charles Lindbergh flew across the Atlantic Ocean to France? (Spirit of St. Louis)

Their research should center around finding information about the topic *Lindbergh*. Encyclopedia articles, *The World Almanac*, and other books should be consulted.

It should be noted that the importance of this activity is not the name of Lindbergh's airplane but the "journey" students take to find the answer: first, **observing** for detail; second, **researching** to find the answer to a specific question.

Charles Lindbergh and the airplane he flew in the first-time-ever solo flight across the Atlantic Ocean, May 21, 1927

PICTURES FROM MULTIPLE SOURCES

The activity that follows is designed to illustrate how picture reading can be carried out by using multiple books. The activity could be part of a learning center or it could be worked on by the entire class. The example below probably will not be acceptable in your class because it assumes that students will be studying the subject matter of the activity and would have access to the specific instructional materials mentioned. However, the techniques are applicable to almost any subject; also, instructors will no doubt find additional ways to exploit pictures that are available.

A PICTURE OF THE NETHERLANDS

Directions to Students

You are to do this work on your own. Do not reveal your answers to your friends. We will all have an opportunity to share our ideas later.

Sometimes someone will be using the book you want. If this happens, work on another question; the questions are not made in any particular order.

1. Underline the title that best fits the picture on page 64 of *Old World Lands*.

    • An Ideal Vacation Land

    • A Great Ocean Port

    • A Marina for Small Boats

2. Examine the picture on page 51, top, of *Our Big World*. Write a sentence that describes each of the following things.

    • the house roofs: _____

    _____

    • the fields: _____

    _____

    • the canal: _____

    _____

3. Study the pictures in chapter 4 of *Our Big World*. What seems to be the most common building material? _____ Think of a reason why this material is used so much. _____

    _____

4. You probably have noticed that the roofs of the houses are very steep. Why might the Dutch make them so steep? _____

    _____

5. The picture on page 29 of the May 15 issue of *National Geographic* shows three ways that the Dutch people use their dikes. What are the three ways?

    a. _____

    b. _____

c. _____

6. Below are some true/false statements about the pictures on pages 221, 222, and 224 of volume N of the *World Book*. Underline the statements that are true.

    • Traffic on canals is controlled by signs.

    • Animals are used to tow the canal barges.

    • The Dutch use snow plows in the winter.

    • It is not necessary for canal boat operators to be concerned about the height of their boats.

    • Sight-seeing tours are conducted on Amsterdam's canals.

    • Automobiles are driven on the same side of the road as they are in the United States.

    • Windmills are no longer used in the Netherlands.

7. Find the Dutch calendar picture for the month of January. What is the main idea of the picture? State it in a sentence. _____

    _____

8. Find the Dutch calendar picture for June. After reading the caption and studying the picture, state three facts about tulip fields and tulip culture as an industry.

    a. _____

    b. _____

    c. _____

9. Find the chapter on the Netherlands in *At Home Around the World*. From the pictures you see of children, what would you say is an important means of transportation for them? _____

    Study the picture of the children in the classroom in school. What are two things about the room and the children that are different from your classroom?

    a. _____

    b. _____

INTERPRETING CARTOONS

Observe young people with newspapers. To what part of the paper will they first turn? It will probably not be the editorial page, letters-to-the-editor, or obituaries. Most likely it will be the strip comics such as "Hagar the Horrible" or single scene cartoons such as "Far Side."

However, editorial page cartoons, many of which are graphic and bizarre, will also attract younger readers. But, political cartoons are not really "funny." They are a form of propaganda and their intention is to influence the viewer's thinking. Therefore, it is important to understand the techniques used by cartoonists, lest the viewer be swayed to adopt an unexamined point-of-view. The very intent of political cartoons is to show only one side of an issue.

There are several types of cartoons, including commercial and gag; however, this page and the following two pages will concentrate on editorial-type cartoons. Such cartoons are designed to shape public opinion for or against a political candidate and/or significant current issues such as affirmative action, smoking, drug abuse, welfare, and so on.

Some of the techniques used by cartoonists to attract attention and to influence thinking follow.

1. **Caricature and Exaggeration**: Prominent persons may have their physical features enlarged or diminished. A person who is inclined to be chubby may be shown as extremely chubby, a protruding jaw may be made to look truly prognathous, a larger-than-average nose may become bulbous, protruding eyes may appear to be popping out of a head, prominent canine teeth may appear as fangs, and a receding chin may become almost nonexistent. Caricatures are often designed to make the one caricatured appear ridiculous or ludicrous. On the other hand, clever cartoonists can draw physical features in such ways that persons are made to look appealing, brave, sympathetic, determined, and so on.

Symbolism: Well known symbols are often used in cartoons: Uncle Sam in a stovepipe hat, the Democrat's donkey, and the Republican's elephant are familiar to many newspaper readers. During World War II, the Nazi swastika was often used by cartoonists because it was associated with imprisonment, brutality, conquest, and murder. More recently, and on a positive note, cartoonists who are concerned about national and world hunger and who want to arouse positive feelings toward helping starv-ing populations portray the symbolic hollow-eyed, emaciated child with a caption, perhaps, "This could be your child."

Suggestions for Teaching

1. The cartoon below was designed to help students see the negative side of random hunting and to empathize with the hunted, in this case a bird.

2. Make the cartoon into a transparency and project it onto a screen.

3. Ask:

a. What symbol is used to show that the bird is dead. (Halo)

b. How has the cartoonist exaggerated the startled reaction of the young hunter? (Wide eyes, open mouth, ears turned outward)

c. How are the bird and young man contrasted? (The bird is very small compared to the young man; thus, sympathy is given to the bird and the young man is seen as a bully.)

d. What might the bird be saying to the young man? (Example: "Do you think it was fair for a big person with a gun to attack a little bird? or "You not only killed me, but also caused my baby birds to die for lack of food.")

AIR POLLUTION SITUATIONS IN CARTOONS

1.   Describe the look on the statue's face.

_____

_____

2.   What thing in the cartoon is designed to arouse patriotism?

_____

3.   Suppose the statue could talk. What do you think it would say about its condition? Write what you think it is saying in the cartoon's balloon.

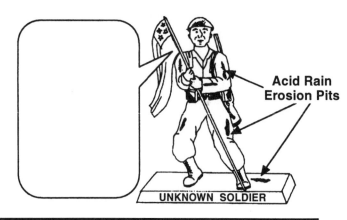

1.   The woman hanging the wash lives in a low-income area. Think of a way the cartoonist shows this.

_____

_____

_____

2.   Consider the entire scene. What might the woman be saying? Write your thoughts in the cartoon's balloon.

The cartoonist is trying to show a contradiction between what the person is doing and what he is saying. What is the contradiction?

_____

_____

_____

_____

_____

1.   What are the children trying to tell the man?

_____

_____

2.   On the lines below write a brief caption for the cartoon.

_____

_____

INTERPRETING AND CREATING CARTOONS

The two cartoons show air pollution situations. It will be up to you to write the captions. First determine what each cartoon shows. Second, jot down your captions on a piece of paper. Third, rewrite your captions until you are satisfied. Finally, print your captions in the bubbles.

In the space below make your own cartoon about air pollution. Don't forget to compose a suitable caption. Share your cartoon with your classmates. Make a preliminary sketch on another sheet of paper; then draw your final version here.

A SOIL EROSION CARTOON

The cartoon below was designed by an artist in the service of the United States Department of Agriculture, Soil Conservation Service (SCS). One of the primary purposes of the SCS is to help farmers understand that improper plowing techniques are significant causes of erosion.

Suggestions for Teaching

1. Show the cartoon via transparency.

2. Have students point out and try to explain some of the details of the cartoon.
- Downward direction of the furrows
- Magnified rain drops
- Malignant, determined expressions on the faces of the raindrops
- The systematic carrying away of soil in wheelbarrows

3. Ask:
- What is the main idea of the cartoon? (Soil that is plowed downward on a slope will wash away.)
- What will eventually happen to the slope if downward plowing continues? (Deep gullies will form.)
- What is the best way to plow a slope to prevent erosion? (Plow across the slope; this interrupts the flow of water and its power to erode and provides time for the water to sink into the soil.)
- What is the implication of the caption of the cartoon? (Farmer Brown soon will not be able to make a living on his farm.)

Name: _____ **Date:** _____

A WATER POLLUTION CARTOON

© 1998 by John Wiley & Sons, Inc.

The Environmental Protection Agency (EPA) published this cartoon in one of its pamphlets. It carries a message for both young and old.

To Do:

1. In two or three sentences tell how the pond became polluted.

_____

_____

_____

_____

_____

_____

_____

_____

2. Write what you think the reactions of the children shown in the drawing are.

_____

_____

_____

_____

_____

_____

_____

3. Notice that there are no fish to be seen; that's because they are all dead. What might one of those fish say if it could come back to life and talk?

_____

_____

_____

_____

_____

_____

_____

A CARTOON THAT DELIVERS A MESSAGE

The cartoon above has much meaning if it is carefully studied. The questions that follow will help you understand the message the cartoonist is trying to convey.

1. What five places are mentioned in the newspaper headlines and television?

_____ _____ _____

_____ _____

2. What is the student reading that shows his lack of interest in studying?

_____

3. In what way is what the student is thinking contradicted by the headlines in the papers?

_____

_____

4. How does what the television is showing indicate that geography is related not only to past events, but also to present-day events?

_____

5. Express in one sentence the main idea of the cartoon.

_____

_____

_____

6. Notice the little bird in the lower right corner of the cartoon. Some cartoonists use such characters as a means of adding special remarks.

Imagine the bird is speaking. What might he be saying to the student regarding the student's negative attitude?

_____

_____

_____

_____

_____

LIST OF MAP UNDERSTANDING AND SKILLS

There are literally dozens of component skills that make up the ability to read and interpret maps. The list that follows is designed for students who have had prior map instruction. Following the listing, suggestions are made for teaching various map components, and student application pages are included that may be photocopied and distributed. After students have had experience with and gained skill in particular map reading components, instructors should make an effort to incorporate the skills in teaching social studies elements of the school curriculum.

Map Understanding and Skills

I. Symbols

A. To realize that symbols on maps represent real and imaginary objects
B. To visualize physical and political symbols
C. To recognize standard physical and political symbols such as blue for water, various kinds of dot-dash lines for political boundaries, markers that locate communities, etc.
D. To use the legend or key of a map as an aid in recognizing symbols

II. Direction

A. To recognize and interpret cardinal and intermediate directions such as north, north-west, west central, etc.
B. To understand the use of up and down with respect to river flow, as related to altitude, and as directions from and to the center of the earth
C. To determine direction as indicated by parallels and meridians
D. To use a compass as a direction finder
E. To understand the difference between magnetic north and polar north
F. To determine direction of flow, sources, and mouths of rivers

III. Location

A. To locate places in terms of hemispheres
B. To locate places through the use of a map index
C. To locate places through the use of parallels and meridians
D. To locate places through the use of distance and direction
E. To follow routes of travel
F. To make sketch maps to show location and direction

IV. Distance and Scale

A. To determine distances through the use of a scale of miles
B. To determine distances through the use of parallels and meridians
C. To determine distances on road maps through the use of the distance-between-points system
D. To determine distances between points as shown in Great Circle routes
E. To translate distance into time between places
F. To understand that land distance and air distance between points may vary
G. To understand that maps of the same area can be portrayed by different scales

V. Coloring, Shading, and Dotting (CSD) on Maps

A. To read and interpret CSD as a means of expressing elevation
B. To read and interpret CSD as a means of showing particular factors such as political divisions, population, precipitation, industrial activities, etc.

VI. Grids

A. To understand and use map nomenclature, including such terms as North Pole, Western Hemisphere, Prime Meridian, Tropic of Cancer, etc.
B. To understand and interpret the numbering system used on maps and globes
C. To understand that lines of longitude extend from pole-to-pole for 180°E and 180°W, that lines of longitude are not parallel
D. To understand that lines of latitude circle the globe in an east-west direction and vary in length depending upon distance from the Equator
E. To understand earth-sun relations as they affect seasons
F. To understand time zones as related to longitude and the spin of the earth

VII. Projections, Special Maps

A. To recognize various map projections, and to realize their advantages and disadvantages
B. To read and interpret topographical maps, especially the reading of contour lines as representations of elevation and shape of the land
C. To read and interpret historical maps
D. To read and compare pattern maps that show such elements as precipitation, population, mineral locations, etc.
E. To read and interpret road maps

VIII. Map Interpretation and Analysis

A. To relate symbols within one map or among maps so as to infer patterns of living, reasons for locations of cities, railroads, etc.
B. To arrange information gained from maps into another form as in tables and graphs; to arrange on maps information gained from various sources

CARDINAL AND INTERMEDIATE DIRECTIONS I

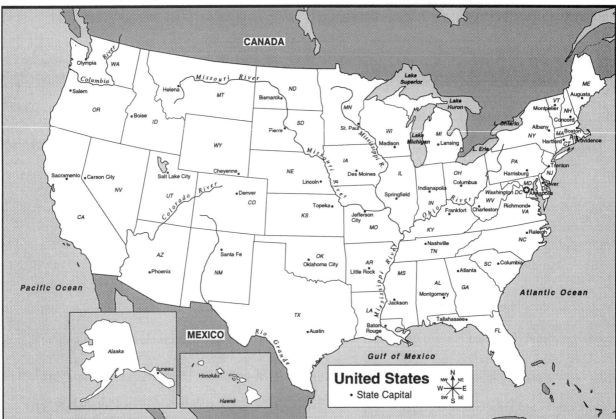

The activities that follow will help you to read and express map directions.

1. The diagram shows the eight basic directions of a compass. Notice that on the map the same diagram is reproduced with the exception that abbreviations are used in place of full words.

North (N)
Northwest (NW)
Northeast (NE)
West (W)
East (E)
Southwest (SW)
Southeast (SE)
South (S)

2. Sometimes directions such as *north central* or *west central* are used. These expressions locate places more exactly. For example, Carson City, Nevada, can be said to be in the western part of Nevada; however, since the city is approximately midway between Nevada's north and south, *west central* is more exact than plain west.

3. If a city is located in the center of a state, the direction *central* is used. Thus, Columbia, North Carolina, is in *central* North Carolina.

4. Locate each of the places listed in the next column. Use one of the directional words explained above.

5. In what part of the United States is each of the following states?

a. Washington (WA): _____

b. Minnesota (MN): _____

c. Georgia (GA): _____

d. Arizona (AZ): _____

e. Louisiana (LA): _____

f. Maine (ME): _____

g. Kansas (KS): _____

6. In what part of the state is each of the following capitals?

a. Cheyenne, WY: _____

b. Jefferson City, MO: _____

c. Pierre, SD: _____

d. Juneau, AK: _____

e. Albany, NY: _____

f. Madison, WI: _____

g. Salem, OR: _____

h. Topeka, KS: _____

CARDINAL AND INTERMEDIATE DIRECTIONS II

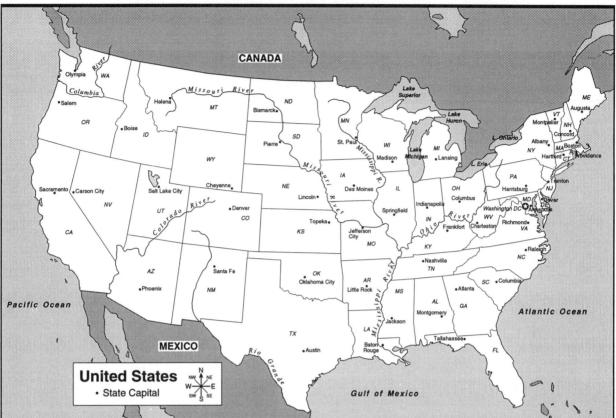

© 1998 by John Wiley & Sons, Inc.

Determining Direction

1. What direction is it to:

a. Cheyenne (WY) from Helena (MT)?

____SE   ____N   ____NW   ____W

b. Oklahoma City (OK) from Austin (TX)?

____S   ____SW   ____N   ____SE

c. Nashville (TN) from Raleigh (NC)?

____E   ____NE   ____SE   ____W

d. Topeka (KS) from Des Moines (IA)?

____W   ____NE   ____SW   ____SE

e. Denver (CO) from Phoenix (AZ)?

____W   ____NE   ____NW   ____SW

f. Bismarck (ND) from Helena (MT)?

____NE   ____NW   ____E   ____W

2. On the map, draw lines as follows:

a. From Austin (TX) *northwest* to the closest capital of another state.

b. From Sacramento (CA) *north* to the closest capital.

c. From Raleigh (NC) *north* to the closest capital; then from that capital *west* to the nearest capital.

3. What Great Lake is northwest of Lake Huron?

4. Decide whether the following statements are true or false.

a. The Columbia River first flows generally south and then flows generally west to the Pacific Ocean.

____True ____False

b. In general, the Ohio River flows in a southwest direction before it joins the Mississippi River.

____True ____False

c. If you were flying northwest from Austin (TX) to Olympia (WA), you would fly over a part of Montana.

____True ____False

DIRECTIONS AND RIVER FLOW

"Up" and "Down" as Directions

Frequently, when people are speaking or writing casually, *up* is used as a direction for *north*, and *down* is used as a direction for *south*. However, geographically speaking, *up* is away from the center of the earth into space; and *down* is from space to the center of the earth. The literal interpretation of "Let's go down to Florida for our vacation" is that Florida is located somewhere in the center of the earth.

Up and down may be correctly used in reference to river flow. For example, "We sailed up the river" means "We sailed against the flow of the river." Rivers flow from their high elevation *sources* to their lower elevation *mouths* (downhill). The *mouth* of a river is the place where it enters another river, a lake, or a large body of water such as an ocean, a sea, a bay, or a gulf.

The problem is, however, that some young geographers who incorrectly equate up with *north* cannot conceive of a river as flowing north. They think that rivers must originate high on a map (north) and flow down the map, toward the south. Thus, they may think, for example, that the Nile River flows from the Mediterranean Sea to the interior of Africa. Of course, the opposite is true.

Suggestions for Teaching

1. Make a transparency and/or photocopies of the map below.

2. Direct students to identify the source of each river with an S and the mouth of each with an M.

3. Direct students to draw an arrow along each river that points in the direction that the river flows.

4. Ask questions such as the following: In what direction do each of the following rivers flow?

- Jog River (E)
- Jump River (NW)
- Skip River (SW)
- Toe River (S)
- Tic River (SW) or (S)
- Fog River (N)

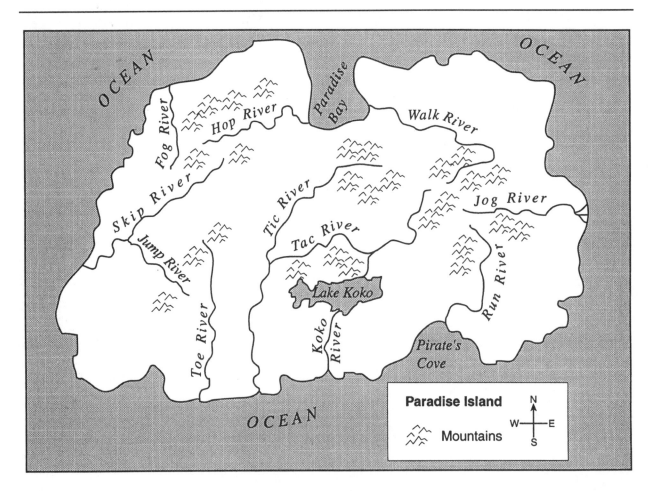

ROUTES OF TRAVEL

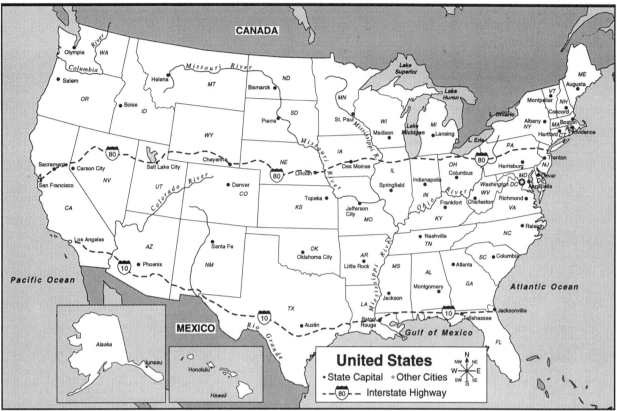

Interstate Highways 80 & 10

1. If you took 80 west from New Jersey to San Francisco, California, through which states would you pass? List the states in the order in which you would meet them, and use the abbreviations.

(1) _____   (5) _____   (9) _____

(2) _____   (6) _____   (10) _____

(3) _____   (7) _____   (11) _____

(4) _____   (8) _____

2. Through which state capitals does 80 pass? In the list that follows write the names of the states and their capitals.

State	Capital	State	Capital

3. As you drive through Utah on 80 what state is south of you? _____

4. Route 10 is another interstate highway. What city is at its eastern end? _____ at its western end? _____

5. Through what state capitals does 10 pass? _____ and _____

6. Through how many states does 10 pass? ___

7. What river would you have to cross if you took 10 through New Mexico? _____ _____

8. What river is crossed by both 80 and 10? _____ _____

9. As you drive through Louisiana on 10 what state is north of you? _____

147

PATTERN MAPS I

Farms in Ten States

Farms in 1994– no parentheses
Farms in 1984– in parentheses ( )
Note: Each number should be read as thousands

THE TEN STATES WITH THE MOST FARMS IN 1984 (000'S)			
State	**No. of farms**	**State**	**No. of farms**
Texas (TX)	194	Tennessee (TN)	95
Missouri (MO)	116	Ohio (OH)	90
Iowa (IA)	113	Wisconsin (WI)	86
Kentucky (KY)	101	California (CA)	82
Minnesota (MN)	97	Oklahoma (OK)	73

1. The *map* tells how many farms there were in each of the ten leading farm states in 1994.

2. The *table* tells how many farms there were in the same ten states in 1984.

3. The numbers in both the map and the table should be read as thousands; *89* is actually *89,000,* and *101* is *101,000,* and so on.

4. Notice that in each of the ten states on the map there is a set of blank parentheses beneath the 1994

figure. Within the parentheses write the number from the table that tells how many farms there were in each state in 1984.

5. Now study the map and answer the following questions. Write your answers on the other side of this page.

a. What state had the greatest number of farms in 1994? How many farms did this state gain from 1984 to 1994?

b. How many states lost farms since 1984? What was the total loss of farms in these states in the 10-year period?

6. The pattern of the ten largest farm states would be more evident if those states were shaded. So, lightly shade all the states that are among the first ten.

7. Nine of the largest farm states have connecting borders. What are the nine states?

8. Which section of the country—east, central, or west—has the greatest number of states with the greatest number of farms?

PATTERN MAPS II

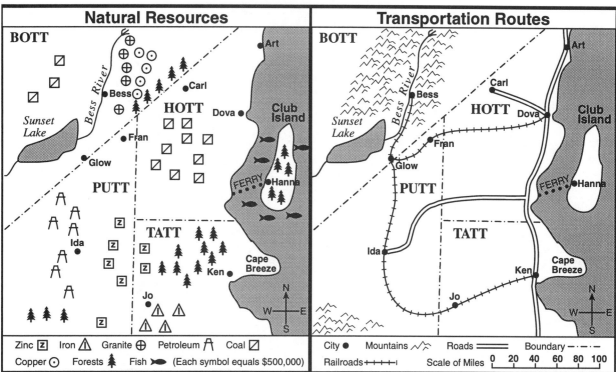

Natural Resources	Transportation Routes

Zinc ☑ Iron △ Granite ⊕ Petroleum ⋔ Coal ☑
Copper ⊙ Forests ♣ Fish ➤ (Each symbol equals $500,000)

City ● Mountains ∧∧ Roads ══ Boundary —·—
Railroads ┼┼┼ Scale of Miles 0 20 40 60 80 100

Draw a circle around the letter or letters before the best answer to each question that follows.

1. What two minerals are most likely shipped from the railroad station at Bess?

a. copper   b. coal   c. granite   d. zinc

2. Which one of the listed cities would most likely be a seaport for shipping petroleum?

a. Dova   b. Ken   c. Art   d. Hanna

3. What is the most valuable natural resource in the state of Putt?

a. petroleum   b. copper
c. zinc   d. forests

4. What is the total value of *all* the *minerals* in Tatt?

a. $2,000,000   b. $3,000,000
c. $4,000,000   d. $5,000,000

5. What *two* products are most likely shipped on ferries from Club Island to the mainland?

a. fish   b. granite   c. lumber   d. copper

6. If you were looking for work as a lumberjack which state would probably have the greatest number of opportunities?

a. Tatt   b. Hott   c. Putt   d. Bott

7. If you were traveling on the railroad from Glow to Bess what *three* things would you most likely see if you looked to the west?

a. mountains   b. river
c. forests   d. a lake

8. How much would it cost to send 700 tons of iron ore from Jo to Ken by rail at the rate of $.10 per mile per ton?

a. $6,600   b. $4,800
c. $5,600   d. $7,600

9. Which one of the listed cities would be most likely to have a ski resort?

a. Ida   b. Carl
c. Bess   d. Glow

10. The town of Art is not very prosperous or busy. What two statements best explain why this is so.

a. It's on the seacoast.

b. There are few natural resources near it.

c. It's not connected to other cities by rail.

11. Of all the resources shown on the map, which has the greatest total value?

a. iron   b. forests
c. coal   d. fish

GUIDELINES FOR LATITUDE

Things to Know About Lines of Latitude*

1. Figure 1 of the globe shows lines of latitude north and south of the Equator. For convenience of measuring and clarity, most maps number lines every 10 degrees. If the lines ran across the map at every 5 degrees, for example, the globe or map would be too cluttered. If the lines were drawn and numbered at every 20 degrees, the lines would be too far apart for accurate measurement between the lines.

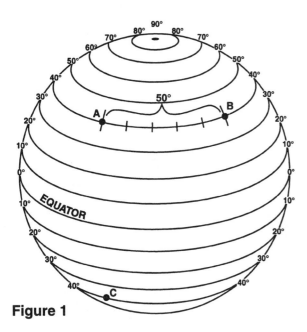

Figure 1

2. Lines of latitude are also called parallels. This is because every line of latitude is parallel to every other line of latitude.

3. One reason why lines of latitude are useful is that they help locate places on Earth. If we say a place is located on 40°N, we know that the place is somewhere on that line, but we don't know where it is on the line. Longitude lines will tell exactly where the place is on the 40°N line.

4. A place is either north or south of the Equator, unless it is exactly on the Equator. Because the numbering system is the same north and south of the Equator, it is necessary to indicate N for north, S for south. Place A is 40°N of the Equator (Figure 1); place C is 40°S of the Equator.

5. Latitude is also helpful in understanding the climate of places on Earth. In general, as one proceeds north or south of the Equator, the climate becomes colder.

It should be noted that latitude is not the only factor in determining climate, especially temperature. Altitude of a place is a critical factor: a place located on the Equator with an altitude of 15,000' would be much colder than a place on the Equator at sea level. Proximity to large bodies of water and ocean currents also affect the climate of a place. Still another factor affecting climate is the tilt of the earth at a constant 23½° as it revolves around the sun.

6. Latitude lines circle the earth, but the lines have different lengths. As the circles approach the poles they become shorter. The table that follows tells the length of the various lines and how many miles long a degree is on each.

APPROXIMATE NUMBER OF MILES IN ONE DEGREE ALONG CERTAIN LINES OF LATITUDE			
Latitude	Miles in 1 Degree	Latitude	Miles in 1 Degree
Equator	70	50°N or S	45
10°N or S	69	60°N or S	35
20°N or S	65	70°N or S	24
30°N or S	60	80°N or S	12
40°N or S	53		

How were the figures in the table determined?

a. Every circle is made up of 360°.

b. If we divide the length of any line of latitude by 360°, the resulting answer tells how many miles there are in a degree on that line. Example: The 40°N parallel and the 40°S parallel are approximately 19,000 miles long. When this figure is divided by 360 (degrees), the answer is 53 (miles).

c. Thus, it is easy to measure distances on a line of latitude. Figure 1 shows that there are 50° between place A and place B.** So, place A is 50 (degrees) × 53 (miles) from place B, or 2,650 miles.

---

*   Suggestions: It would be instructive to explain the information on this page before students work on the following application pages. A transparency of Figure 1 would be a helpful visual aid during presentation.

** To avoid confusion, full lines of longitude have been omitted purposely from Figure 1, but such degrees are determined by lines of longitude.

LATITUDE AND DISTANCE

Locating Places on Lines of Latitude

The globe in Figure 1 does not show all the lines of latitude south of the Equator. This is because it is impossible to show the entire face of a globe in one illustration. So, the globe is "tipped" toward you so you can see all of the northern hemisphere including the North Pole (90°N).

1. What is the latitude of each of the places listed in the table? Remember that you have to tell whether the place is north (N) or south (S) of the Equator. For example, place A is 70°N (Figure 1).

Place	Latitude	Place	Latitude
B		E	
C		F	
D		G	

2. If a place is located between lines of latitude it is necessary to make a reasonable guess as to what its latitude is. In the example that follows, place Z should be read as 45°N because it is halfway between 40°N and 50°N.

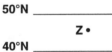

50°N _____

Z •

40°N _____

What is the latitude of each of the places listed in the table that follows?

Place	Latitude	Place	Latitude
H		K	
I		L	
J		M	

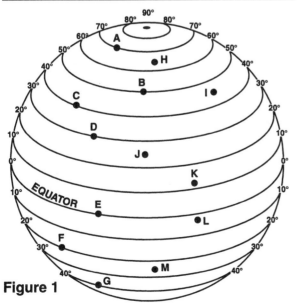

Figure 1

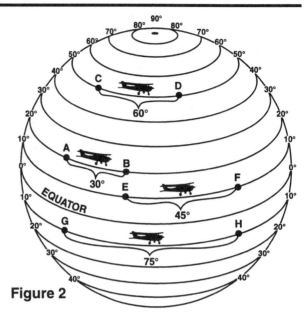

Figure 2

Determining Distance on Lines of Latitude

Imagine that you are an airplane pilot. You want to fly on the 20°N line of latitude from place A to place B (See Figure 2). You'll want to know the distance in miles between the two places because you need to know how much fuel to carry.

You consult the table that follows, and the table tells you that 1 degree along the 20°N or 20°S line of latitude is equal to 65 miles. The globe tells you that the distance in degrees from A to B is 30. If you multiply 30° × 65 miles, you find that it is 1,950 miles from A to B.

DISTANCES ON LINES OF LATITUDE			
Line of Latitude	Miles in 1°	Line of Latitude	Miles in 1°
0°	70	50°	45
10°	69	60°	35
20°	65	70°	24
30°	60	80°	12
40°	53		

Find the answers to the following distance problems. The number of degrees between places is shown on the globe in Figure 2. The number of miles for one degree is shown in the table. To solve each problem multiply degrees × miles in one degree.

1. C to D? _____ miles

2. E to F? _____ miles

3. G to H? _____ miles

151

GUIDELINES FOR LONGITUDE

Things to Know About Lines of Longitude

1. Figure 1 shows lines of longitude east and west of the Prime Meridian (0° longitude). Some maps number the lines of longitude, also called meridians, every 10°; other maps number the lines every 15°.

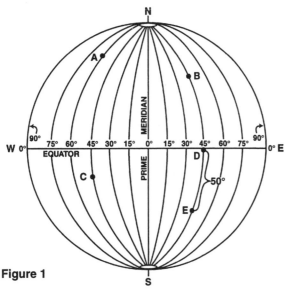

Figure 1

2. Lines of longitude extend from pole to pole, that is, 180°. The lines continue to the opposite pole, but take different numbers. In the case of the 0° line, the line becomes 180°. Lines of longitude are drawn 180° to the east and 180° to the west.

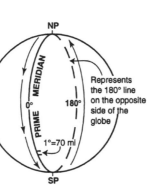

Figure 2

3. The 0° line in connection with the 180° line divides the world into two halves, or hemispheres. From 0° to 180° east is the Eastern Hemisphere; 0° to 180° west is the Western Hemisphere.

4. Unlike lines of latitude, lines of longitude are not parallel. They are furthest apart at the equator, and they converge at the poles.

5. One reason lines of longitude are useful is that they help locate places on Earth. If we say a place is located on the 75°E line, we know the place is some-where on the line, but we don't know where. When longitude is used in conjunction with latitude the exact location of the place can be determined. Thus, place A in figure 1 is on the 60°W line, place B is on the 45°E line, and place C is on the 45°W line.

6. The 0° line of longitude and its continuation, 180°, extend completely around the earth for approximately 25,000 miles. When we divide 25,000 by 360 (degrees) we find that 1 degree of distance is approximately 70 miles. The figure of 70 miles per degree applies to all lines of longitude, for they all extend around the earth for 25,000 miles. (Figure 2)

The distance from D to E as shown in Figure 1 is 50°. To translate this distance into miles, multiply 50° × 70 (miles), or 3,500 miles.

7. Longitude is the primary device for measuring time. This is because the earth rotates on its axis at a rate of 15° per hour. It takes 24 hours for the rotation to be complete.

Figure 3 shows the Prime Meridian as the starting point for measuring time. When it is 12:00 noon on the Prime Meridian, it is 1:00 p.m. on the 15°E line, 2 p.m. on the 30°E line, and so on. However, on the west side of the Prime Meridian it is 11:00 a.m. on the 15°W, 10:00 a.m. on the 30°W line, and so on. The time at New York City, which is located on 75°W, is 7:00 a.m., and it is 12:00 noon in London (Prime Meridian, 0°), a 5-hour difference.

TELLING TIME WITH LONGITUDE

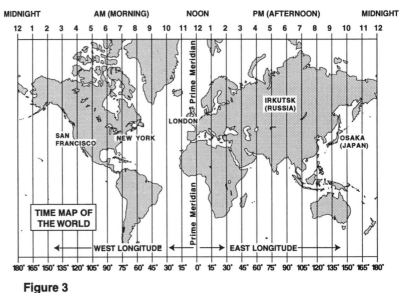

Figure 3

LONGITUDE AND DISTANCE

Locations on Lines of Longitude

1. Finding a place on a line of longitude is simple if you remember a few rules.

a. The Prime Meridian, 0° longitude, is the starting point for all longitude measurements.

b. All places located on lines of longitude should have E (for east) or W (for west) at the end of the reading. The only exception is if a place is on the 0° line; London is an example.

If you don't designate E or W, no one will know to which line you are referring because there are two lines with the same number.

c. If a place is between two lines, estimate where the place is. For example, place H (Figure 1) is approximately halfway between 30°E and 45°E. A reasonable estimate puts the place at approximately 38°E or 37°E.

2. Complete the table below with readings from the globe at Figure 1.

Place	Longitude	Place	Longitude
C		G	
D		I	
E		J	
F		K	

Distances on Lines of Longitude

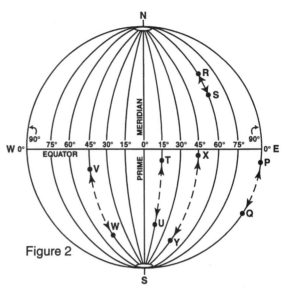

Figure 2

Determining distances on lines of longitude is not as complicated as finding distance on lines of latitude. On a line of longitude the miles in one degree of distance are always the same. This is because all lines of longitude are the same length, that is about 25,000 miles. If we divide 25,000 by 360°, we find that each degree (rounded) is approximately 70 miles.

Figure 2 shows, and it is listed in the table, that place P is 20° from place Q. So the distance between the two places is approximately 1,400 miles (20° × 70 miles = 1,400 miles).

Complete the table of distances below. Notice that the second column in the table tells you the number of degrees between each of the pairs of places.

Places	Degrees of Distance	Miles of Distance
P to Q	20°	
R to S	10°	
T to U	30°	
V to W	40°	
X to Y	50°	

Figure 1

MAPPING A HURRICANE

Hurricanes

Tropical storms such as hurricanes are "tracked" by weather experts called *meteorologists*. From the information received from satellites far above the earth and other sources, meteorologists know where hurricanes begin and the routes they travel. Tracking helps the weather people predict where hurricanes will go. People who might be in the hurricane's path can then be warned; they will be prepared for the high winds, high seas, and heavy rains that accompany a hurricane.

Meteorologists show the track of a particular hurricane by noting on a map its changing latitude and longitude. You can do the same thing by tracking an imaginary hurricane we will call "Betty."

SOUTHEAST UNITED STATES AND THE WEST INDIES

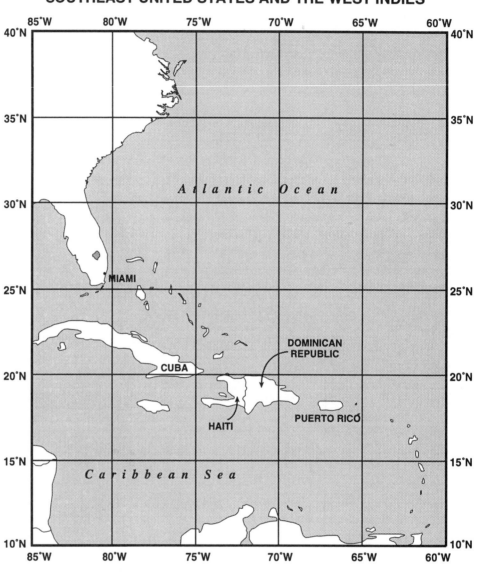

© 1998 by John Wiley & Sons, Inc.

Procedure

1. Notice that the map shows the islands of the West Indies and the southeastern coast of the United States. This region was chosen for this activity because most hurricanes that affect the United States begin there.

2. Print a small x at all the latitude and longitude locations listed below, all on Betty's route.

15°N–60°W (Where Hurricane Betty began)

18°N–65°W

20°N–67°W

25°N–70°W

26°N–81°W

30°N–78°W

35°N–75°W (Where it blew itself out over the ocean)

3. To show the track of Hurricane Betty, connect all the x's with straight lines.

4. What major island was closest to the path of Hurricane Betty? _____

5. What major city in southeast United States was in the path of Hurricane Betty? _____

Name: _____ Date: _____

LOCATIONS AND TIME ON A MERCATOR MAP I

Latitude and Longitude Locations

The best kind of maps to use for locating places through the use of latitude and longitude are Mercator maps. A Mercator world map is shown on the facing page.

One of the advantages of Mercator maps is that they make it easier to read and find locations that are between lines of latitude and longitude. Another advantage is that, unlike a globe, a Mercator map can show all the world's oceans, continents, and islands at once.

The most serious disadvantage of Mercator maps is that as you proceed north or south of the equator, places are shown larger than they actually are in comparison to places near or on the equator. Also, the shapes of land masses and distances are distorted. Greenland, for example, is shown as being larger than South America. Actually, South America is more than ten times larger than Greenland.

Why does such distortion come about? There are several reasons, but the most important one is that on a Mercator map the lines of longitude are straight north to south instead of coming together at the poles, as seen on a globe. Because the lines are shown as not coming together, the outlines of places are "stretched" to reach from vertical line to vertical line. Then, in an attempt to decrease the distortion, the distance between lines of latitude are increased as the far north and far south are approached.

The thing to remember is that no flat map of a round world is perfect. Each kind of map has its advantages and disadvantages. So, the best protection against incorrect impressions of places, shapes, and distances is to know the map you are using and what it can and cannot show.

Combining Latitude and Longitude

1. You already know how to find and read lines of latitude and longitude. In this activity you will have another opportunity to combine the two skills.

Find place A on the map. You can see that it is on 60°N latitude and 60°W longitude. The proper way to write the location of A is 60°N–60°W. Now, using the same approach, determine the latitude and longitude of the following places.

B: _____

C: _____

D: _____

E: _____

F: _____

G: _____

2. Print the following letters on the map at their locations.

 M: 30°N–15°W
 N: 60°N–120°W
 O: 60°N–105°W
 P: 40°S–105°W
 Q: 35°S–90°E
 R: 10°S–175°E

Determining Distance on Mercator Maps

How far is B from J? You will recall that on a line of longitude one degree equals 70 miles. How many degrees are there between B and J? Count, and you find that there are 100 degrees. So, 100° × 70 miles = 7,000 miles between B and J.

1. How far is it from C to G? _____ miles

2. On the 30°S line of latitude, 1° equals 60 miles.

How far is it from F to G? _____ miles

Telling Time on the Mercator Map

Remember that the earth turns 15° east every hour. So, if it is 12:00 noon on the Prime Meridian (0°), it is 11:00 a.m. on the 15°W line of longitude and 1:00 p.m. on the 15°E line. The west side of the 0° line is always behind the time on the 0° line; the east side is always ahead.

If it is 12:00 noon on the 0° line of longitude, what time is it on the following lines?

30°W: _____

45°E: _____

150°W: _____

Name: _____ Date: _____

LOCATIONS AND TIME ON A MERCATOR MAP II

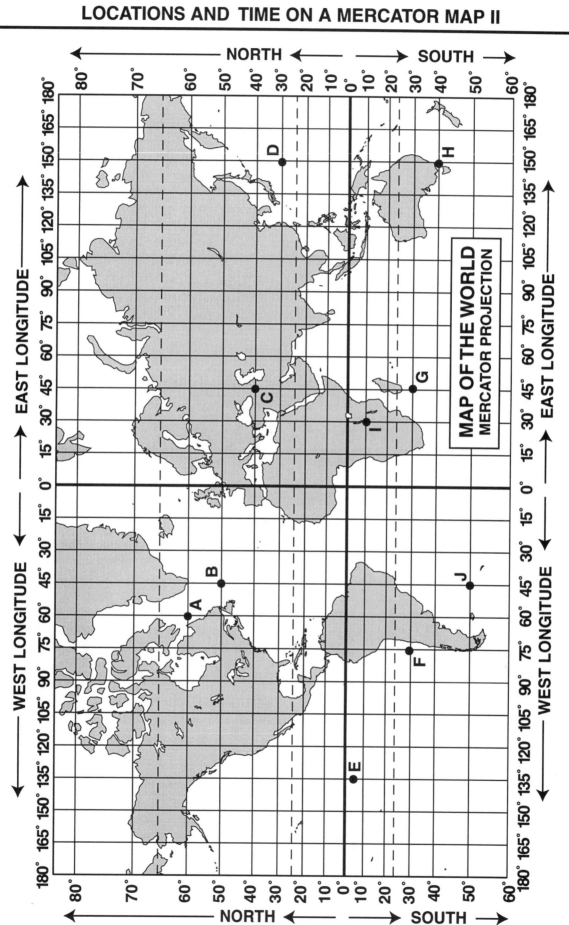

MAP OF THE WORLD
MERCATOR PROJECTION

© 1998 by John Wiley & Sons, Inc.

MAP INDEXES AND ROAD DISTANCES I

Locating Places on Maps

In some respects knowing how to use a map index is one of the most practical and useful map reading skills. Those who have occasion to use road maps—vacationers, traveling salespersons, package delivery companies—are among the most frequent users of map indexes. And, it's easy to understand why. California, for example, contains almost 1,100 communities, large and small, as listed in *The American Map Corporation United States Road Atlas*. One could spend a significant amount of time scanning the map of California, spread over two pages in the Atlas, for the town of Ysabel, and still not find it. Yet, using the map index to localize the community as being in section V–13, page 21, narrows the search so that the town is easily found.

Most road maps—national, state, local—have an index of communities somewhere on the map. All the communities are arranged in alphabetical order and followed by the letter and number of the quadrant in which they are located.

Correspondingly, the map is divided into squares, called quadrants. In the map margin, letters are listed vertically and numerals are listed horizontally so that each quadrant has an identifying letter and numeral.

In the sample grid below, Tomahawk is in quadrant B–2, and Frisco is located in quadrant C–3.

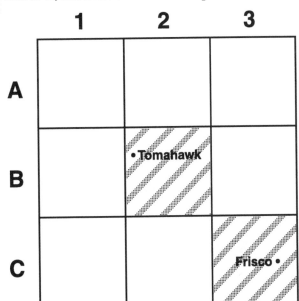

Sometimes quadrants on maps are defined by lines of latitude and lines of longitude rather than by letters and numerals. Following is an example.

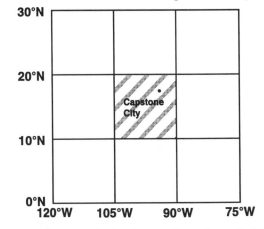

Capstone City is in the quadrant bounded by 10°N–20°N and 90°W–105°W.

Measuring Distances Between Points on a Road Map

There are two basic ways to determine distances on road maps: 1) through the use of a scale of miles and 2) through the use of distances between points printed on the map. With regard to road distances, the second mentioned method is the most reliable. This is because the scale-of-miles system tells the shortest straight-line distance between two points. This method does not take into consideration the twists and turns and the ups and downs that are parts of most roads. Another disadvantage of the scale-of-miles approach is that it is inconvenient and awkward to measure by scale while driving or riding in a vehicle.

The legend of most road maps contains a diagram and note that tells how to use the distance-between-points method. A number on a line between dots or road junctions tells how far it is from one point to another. The following example is typical of most road maps.

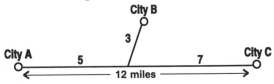

The activity on the facing page will help students develop skill in finding locations and determining distances on road maps.

Name: _____ **Date:** _____

MAP INDEXES AND ROAD DISTANCES II

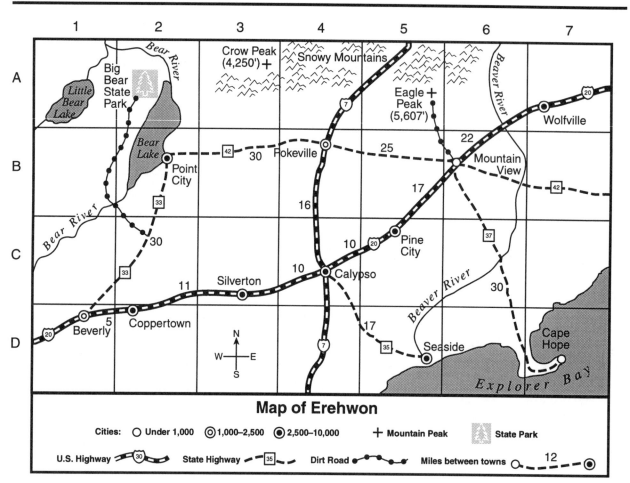

Map of Erehwon

Cities: ○ Under 1,000 ◎ 1,000–2,500 ● 2,500–10,000 + Mountain Peak 🌲 State Park

U.S. Highway ⟨30⟩ State Highway -⟨35⟩- Dirt Road ●●●● Miles between towns ○- - -12- - -◉

---

1. Complete the table below. Beverly has been done to help you get started.

Town	Quadrant	Population
Beverly	D1	1,000–2,500
Calypso		
Cape Hope		
Coppertown		
Mountain View		
Pine City		
Point City		
Pokeville		
Seaside		
Silverton		
Wolfville		

2. What is the distance in miles from

a. Wolfville to Mountain View? _____ miles

b. Pokeville to Seaside? _____ miles

c. Beverly to Point City? _____ miles

d. Beverly to Coppertown to Silverton to Calypso to Pokeville? _____ miles

3. What kind of road would one have to take to drive from ☐33 to Big Bear State Park? _____

4. How many feet higher is Eagle Peak than Crow Peak? _____ feet

5. What two roads connect Wolfville and Point City most directly? _____

MEASURING ALTITUDE I

In measuring altitude the level of the sea is used as the starting point. A place is either at, above, or below sea level. It should be realized, however, that sea level is, as the *Dictionary of Geography** points out, "The level that the surface of the sea would assume if uninfluenced by tides, wave, or swell." For practical purposes a simpler way of defining sea level is that it is the average level between high and low tides.

Students sometimes ask, "If some places are below sea level, why aren't they covered by water?" The answer is that, of course, the ocean floor is covered by water, sometimes thousands of feet deep. However, places on land that are below sea level are kept from being water-covered because higher land—acting as dams—surrounds the area and prevents the water from flooding in. Death Valley, California, is 282' below sea level, but mountains such as the Sierra Nevada Range stop sea water from flowing into the valley.

Point out that airplane pilots are concerned not only about altitude above sea level, but also about how high they are above the land over which they are flying. If they rely on sea level altitude they may crash into mountains they cannot see because of darkness, clouds, or fog. An airplane may be flying at 10,000' above sea level, but the top of an unseen mountain might have an elevation that is higher.

Colors and Hatching Tell Elevation Ranges

On maps, various colors are sometimes used to show elevation. Blue represents sea level, red is indicative of very high elevations, green for lower elevations, and so on. Often, shades of a particular color, such as dark blue for deep ocean depths and light blue for shallow waters, as on a continental shelf, are used. The key to a color map will list specific elevation ranges for specific colors.

Sometimes hatchings of various kinds are used. Hatchings are easier to read than colors are for those students who may be colorblind.

Students should realize that a particular color or hatching shows an entire range of elevations. So, within a range of 2,000' to 4,000', one place may be at 2,200' elevation and another place may be at 3,900'. Also, within a color range there may be a deep canyon or a high peak that is actually outside

of the color range; however, the place may be so small in proportion to the entire map that its true color/elevation may not be able to be shown.

Suggestions for Teaching

1. Photocopy and distribute the following two student application pages. You may also want to make transparencies of the pages if you decide to use them as a basis for presentation-type lessons.

2. Explain to your students that the purpose of the pages is to help them better understand the concept and details of measuring altitude.

3. One way to help students visualize elevations is to make a model consisting of several blocks of wood of different sizes and colors placed on top of each other. Print various ascending elevation ranges on the blocks starting on the bottom blue block, which represents sea level. Then, have students observe the blocks from the side and by looking down on the blocks. This will help them understand how the three-dimensional model can be drawn on the board as two-dimensional. Figure 1 shows the wooden model; Figure 2 shows the board drawing.

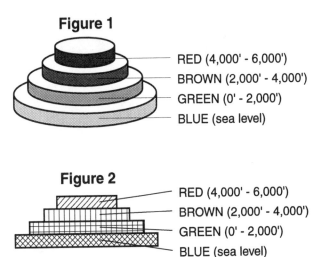

Figure 1

RED (4,000' - 6,000')
BROWN (2,000' - 4,000')
GREEN (0' - 2,000')
BLUE (sea level)

Figure 2

RED (4,000' - 6,000')
BROWN (2,000' - 4,000')
GREEN (0' - 2,000')
BLUE (sea level)

Note: Hatching as in Figure 2, may be substituted for color.

---

* Moore, W.G., *The Penguin Dictionary of Geography*, 1984.

MEASURING ALTITUDE II

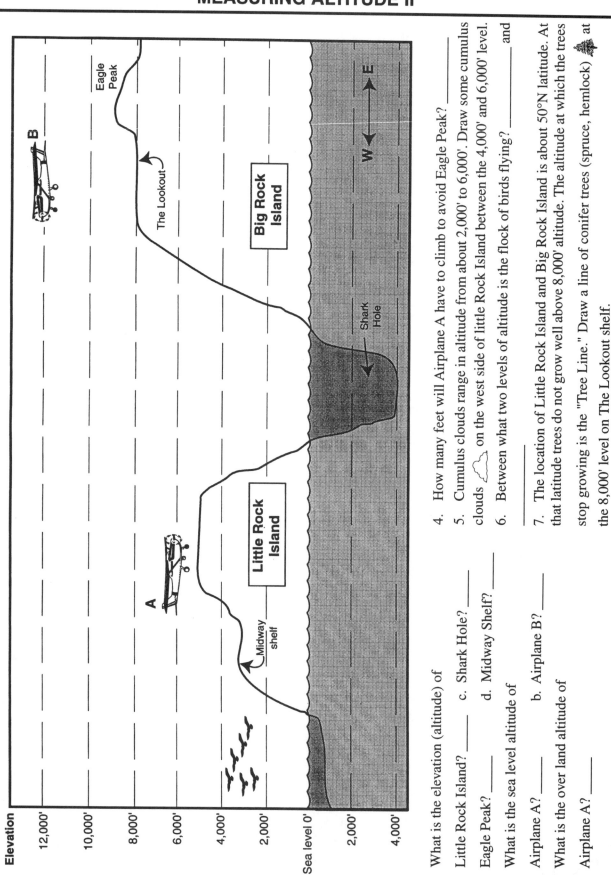

1. What is the elevation (altitude) of

a. Little Rock Island? _____   c. Shark Hole? _____

b. Eagle Peak? _____   d. Midway Shelf? _____

2. What is the sea level altitude of

a. Airplane A? _____   b. Airplane B? _____

3. What is the over land altitude of

Airplane A? _____

4. How many feet will Airplane A have to climb to avoid Eagle Peak? _____

5. Cumulus clouds range in altitude from about 2,000' to 6,000'. Draw some cumulus clouds ☁ on the west side of little Rock Island between the 4,000' and 6,000' level.

6. Between what two levels of altitude is the flock of birds flying? _____ and _____

7. The location of Little Rock Island and Big Rock Island is about 50°N latitude. At that latitude trees do not grow well above 8,000' altitude. The altitude at which the trees stop growing is the "Tree Line." Draw a line of conifer trees (spruce, hemlock) 🌲 at the 8,000' level on The Lookout shelf.

Name: _____ Date: _____

ELEVATIONS SHOWN BY NUMERALS AND COLOR

1. In what range of elevation (altitude) is:

CUTT? _____' to _____' PUTT? _____' to _____'

BUTT? _____' to _____' RUTT? _____' to _____'

2. In what range of elevation are the sources of each of the following rivers?

Deer? _____' to _____' Bear _____' to _____'

Moose? _____' to _____' Fox _____' to _____'

3. Why would it be difficult to land a boat on the north shore of Big Clipp Island? _____

_____

_____

4. Which one of these two rivers—Fox River, Deer River—is probably the faster flowing river? _____

Explain your answer: _____

_____

_____

5. Draw an X at the part of the shore of Little Clipp Island that is steeper than any other part of the island's shoreline.

6. Lightly color the land on Big Clipp Island according to the numbers on the map and the key to the map.

7. Color Great Ocean a light blue.

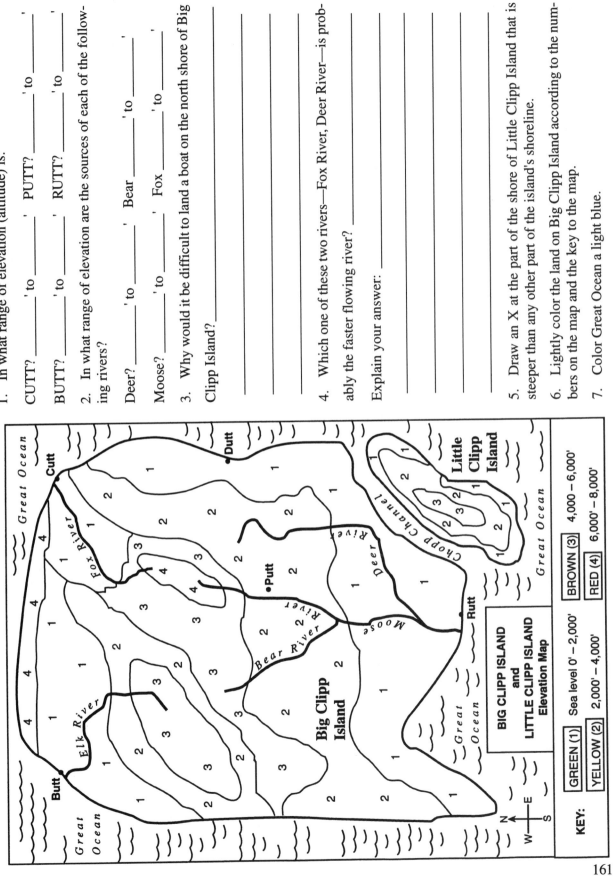

KEY: GREEN (1) Sea level 0' – 2,000'   BROWN (3) 4,000 – 6,000'
YELLOW (2) 2,000' – 4,000'   RED (4) 6,000' – 8,000'

BIG CLIPP ISLAND
and
LITTLE CLIPP ISLAND
Elevation Map

161

TOPOGRAPHICAL MAPS AND ELEVATION

Contour Lines Tell Elevation

1. Provide photocopies of this page for students and a transparency for the instructor.

2. Ask students to imagine that they are in a helicopter looking down on Dolphin Island (Figure 1). Point out that the lines they see on the map are imaginary, that they are called contour lines, and that the purpose of contour lines is to help map readers know the elevation of land.

3. Every point on a contour line is the same level above the sea; if people could walk along a contour line they would never go up or down; they would always be at the same level. Point A on the map is at sea level. Point B is on a line that has 50' printed on it. This means that point B is 50' above sea level; point C is also 50' above sea level. Points D and E are on the 100' line. Notice point F: it is not on a line; it is above the 150' line. Since there is no 200' line we know that F is somewhere between 150' and 199' above the level of the sea. So, it can be concluded that none of the land in Dolphin Island is more than 199' high.

4. If Dolphin Island were sliced from east to west, as a layer cake might be sliced, one would have a cross section of the island, as depicted in Figure 2. Notice that the island is very steep on the west side and that the slope on the east side is more gentle.

5. Look at Figure 1 again. Notice that on the west slope the lines are close together. Contour lines that are close together indicate steepness, and lines that are father apart indicate a gradual slope. So, Figures 1 and 2 show the same things about slope, but in different ways.

6. Point out line VW and line XY in Figure 1. In the 25 miles covered by line VW, the land rises 150'. But in the 25 miles covered by line XY, the land climbs only 50'. This helps explain why the contour lines in the western part of the island are close together as compared to the lines in the eastern part.

7. Maps that show contour lines are called topographical maps. The key to a topographical map tells you the contour interval. In Figure 1, the contour interval is 50'. This means that there is a 50' interval between the heavy lines.

8. On large topographical maps heavy lines are marked with numbers that tell the elevation of the land. Lighter lines are drawn between the heavy lines to indicate rises in elevation of 20'. In the diagram below, for example, place A is at an elevation of 120' and B is at 60'.

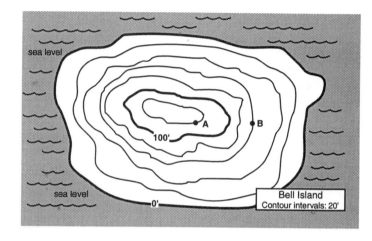

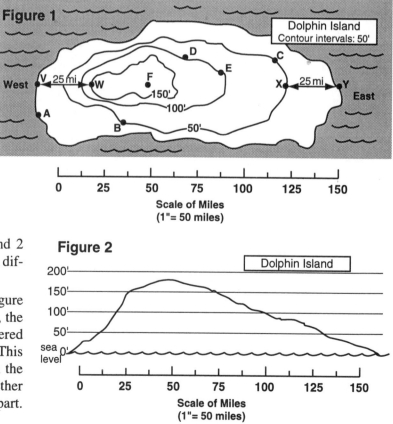

UNITED STATES GOVERNMENT TOPOGRAPHICAL MAPS

The topographical map on this page is from a larger map: PENNINGTON, NJ–PA. The map is an official map of the U.S. Geological Survey, an agency of the U.S. government.

Topographical maps are not the usual kind of map; students may not know how to read and interpret them. It would be advisable to make a transparency of the map and photocopies for students. Then, as you ask the questions on this page, students may search for the answers, or you may want students to work out answers on their own and then use the transparency for verification and further applications.

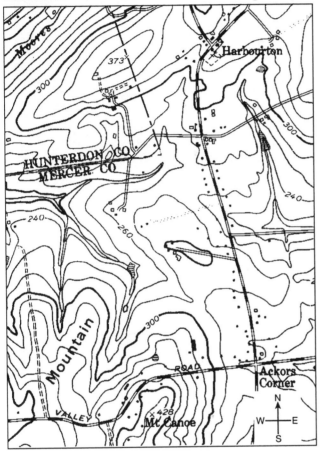

TYPOGRAPHIC MAP SYMBOLS

Hard surface, heavy duty road, four or more lanes ....
Hard surface, heavy duty road, two or three lanes ....
Hard surface, medium duty road, four or more lanes ....
Hard surface, medium duty road, two or three lanes ....
Improved light duty road ....
Unimproved dirt road—Trail ....
Dual highway, dividing strip 25 feet or less ....
Dual highway, dividing strip exceeding 25 feet ....
Road under construction ....

Buildings (dwelling, place of employment, etc.) ....
School—Church—Cemeteries .... Cem
Buildings (barn, warehouse, etc.) ....

0 .... ½ 1

1 MILE

1. React to the following statements as being either true (T) or false (F).

   a. Mt. Canoe is the highest point on the map.

   　　　　　　　　　　　　　　T　　　F

   b. There is a school on the road from Ackors Corner to Harbourton.　　　　　　T　　　F

   c. There is no cemetery in Harbourton.　T　　F

   d. On the northeast corner of Ackors Corner there is a house but no barn.　　　　T　　　F

   e. The house just northeast of the D in VALLEY ROAD is less than 300' above sea level.　T　　F

   f. There are houses on each of the four corners at Ackors Corner.　　　　　　　T　　　F

   g. The distance from Ackors corner to Harbourton is more than 1½ miles.　　　　T　　　F

2. What is the approximate distance in a straight line from the southwest corner of the map to the northwest corner?

   _____1 mile　_____1¾ miles　_____2½ miles

3. Why would it be difficult for a large, heavy truck to use the road just west of the V in VALLEY ROAD?

   _____

   _____

   _____

   _____

   _____

   _____

   _____

READING A TOPOGRAPHICAL MAP

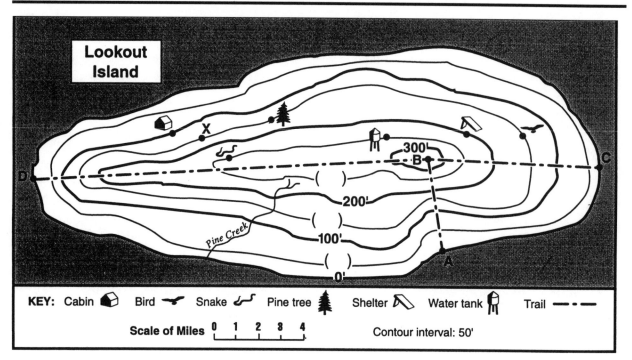

1. The heavy contour lines on the map are all labeled, but the lighter contour lines are not. The key to the map tells you that the contour interval is 50'.

In the ( ) on the light contour lines write the elevations they show.

2. At what elevation are each of the following objects. Each object's location is shown by the dot close to it.

Object	Elevation	Object	Elevation
Pine tree		Bird	
Snake		Cabin	
Water tank		Shelter	

3. Which would be the steepest walk along the trail to the top of the mountain.

_____ A to B   _____ C to B

4. About how many miles is the trail from D to B?

_____ 10 miles   _____ 17 miles   _____ 20 miles

5. About how many miles is the entire trail from A to B to C?

_____ 5 miles   _____ 7 miles   _____ 11 miles

6. Which of the following best tells the elevation of B?

_____ Between 250' and 299'
_____ Between 300' and 349'
_____ Between 350' and 399'

7. At approximately what elevation is the source or beginning of Pine Creek? _____

8. If you were at X on the map would you be able to see the cabin if there were no trees to spoil your view? _____ Yes _____ No

Explain your answer on the lines below.

_____

_____

_____

_____

Name: _____ **Date:** _____

READING POLAR MAPS I

Imagine that you are in outer space directly over the north pole. When you look toward Earth you see it much like it is shown on the polar map below, except, of course, you would not see lines of latitude or longitude. You have probably noticed that polar maps give an entirely different view of the world than do Mercator maps. Both kinds of maps have their special uses. After completing this activity your understanding of polar maps should be much more complete.

Note that a small Mercator map is shown on the following page so that you can make comparisons between it and the polar map.

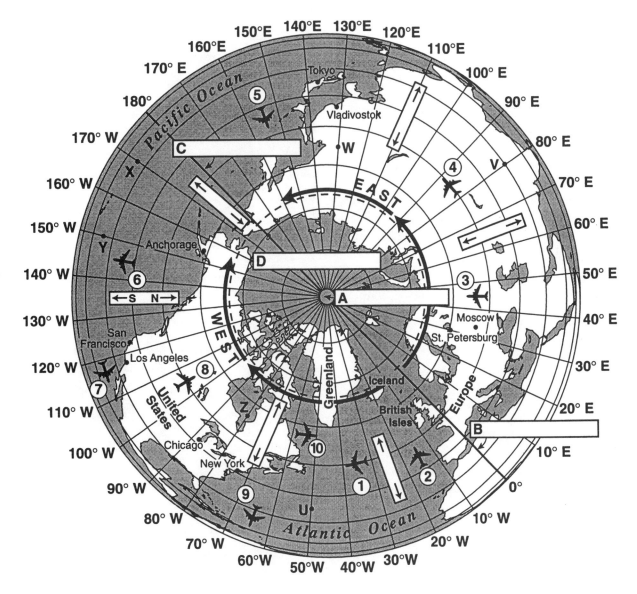

READING POLAR MAPS II

To Do:

1. On the polar map label the following:

A North Pole   **C** 180° longitude

B Prime Meridian   **D** Arctic Ocean

2. From the North Pole all directions are *south*; all directions are *north* from the south pole.

On the polar map notice the blank spaces with pointed arrows at both ends. On each end that points to the south pole print S for South. On each end that points to the north pole print N for North.

Note: This should prove to you that north may not always be at the top of a map. On a north polar map, north is at the center of the map. On a south polar map, south is at the center of the map.

3. The circles on the polar map are lines of latitude. From the Prime Meridian (0°), you may go 180° east (to the right), or 180° west (to the left). Together, 180° east and 180° west make a complete circle of 360°.

If an airplane flew west from the Prime Meridian it would make a complete circle when it reached the place where it started—the Prime Meridian. The same is true if the airplane flew eastward.

Notice the airplane silhouettes on the map. Each is numbered. In the table below, check the direction each airplane is flying.

1 __ East   __ West   6 __ North __ South

2 __ North __ South   7 __ East   __ West

3 __ North __ South   8 __ North __ South

4 __ East   __ West   9 __ North __ South

5 __ North __ South   10 __ East   __ West

4. The Mercator map in the next column shows a straight line between New York and Moscow. However, that line gives an incorrect impression of the route that an airplane would fly.

For a more accurate understanding of where an airplane would fly between the two cities, use a polar map. On the polar map draw a straight line between New York and Moscow. This line, called a *great circle route* is shorter by hundreds of miles than the route depicted on the Mercator map.

Over what two islands does the great circle route take the airplane?

_____ and _____

5. On the polar map show the great circle route between each of the following cities. Draw a straight line from one to the other.
- Chicago and Vladivostok
- Anchorage and St. Petersburg

6. Notice that all the lines of longitude are numbered starting from the Prime Meridian, or 0° longitude. They proceed as 10°E, 20°E, and so on. Likewise west longitude is also marked off in degrees numbered 10°W, 20°W, and so on.

Tell the line of longitude of each of the following letters. Be sure to designate east (E) or west (W).

Letter	Longitude	Letter	Longitude
U		X	
V		Y	
W		Z	

7. Letter U on the polar map is 55° from the North Pole. Since each degree on a line of longitude is approximately 70 miles, how many miles is it from U to the North Pole?

_____ miles

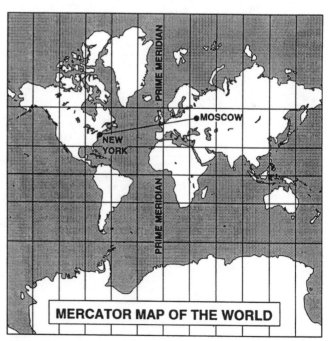

MERCATOR MAP OF THE WORLD

UNDERSTANDING GLOBE MAPS

The map below is designed to give a picture of Earth as it would appear if you were looking at a globe. In some ways, it is more accurate than a Mercator map. A Mercator map shows the lines of longitude as straight up-and-down, not coming together at the poles. The result is that, on such maps, the northern and southern parts of the world appear much larger than they really are.

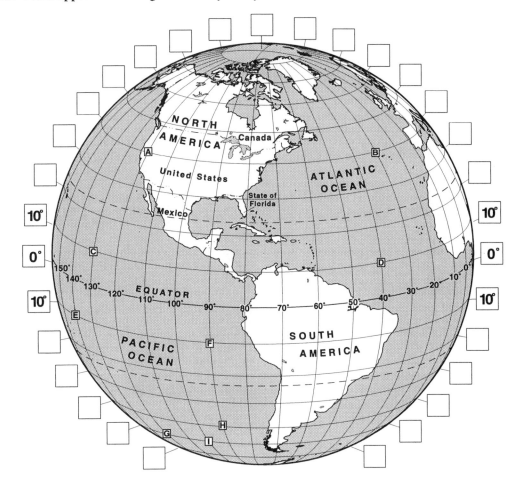

To Do:

1. On the globe map the lines of longitude are already numbered; all the lines shown are west longitude.

The map would be more meaningful if the lines of latitude were also numbered. Starting at the equator write the numbers of the lines of latitude in the boxes. The equator, 10°N, and 10°S have already been numbered to get you started.

2. Label the dashed line south of the equator as Tropic of Capricorn (23½°S). Label the dashed line north of the equator as Tropic of Cancer (23½°N).

3. It is easier to read latitude and longitude on a Mercator map than on a globe map because the lines of latitude and longitude are straight on a Mercator map. Locations between the curved lines of the globe are difficult to determine; however, where latitude and longitude lines cross on a globe map reading locations is simple and accurate.

4. On the globe map find the letters listed below. Write their latitudes and longitudes in the spaces provided. All the longitudes on this map are west.

A: _____   D: _____   G: _____

B: _____   E: _____   H: _____

C: _____   F: _____   I: _____

5. Between what two lines of longitude does most of Florida lie? _____

6. What best describes South America's direction form North America?

_____South   _____Southeast   _____Southwest

MAGNETIC NORTH AND TRUE NORTH

The information on this page is important to students' understanding of the world in which they live, especially as pertaining to geography and geography skills. The knowledge may be best conveyed by means of transparency illustrations and explanations.

If opportunity and location permit, it would be helpful, and enjoyable, to walk to a nearby park and engage students in an orienteering activity. For very explicit help on how to conduct such an activity, seek out a sporting goods or boy-scout outfitting store for compasses and information. Or, write to:

Silva, Inc.
Highway 19
La Porte, Indiana 46350

True north, or the north pole, is where the lines of longitude converge; likewise, true south is where the lines of longitude in the southern hemisphere converge at the south pole. Earth rotates on its axis, which is an imaginary line running through the earth from pole to pole.

What some people do not realize is that the magnetic compass needle is not attracted to true north. In the northern hemisphere the magnetic needle on a compass is attracted to magnetic north. And where is magnetic north? Although its exact position varies from year to year, it is approximately 1,000 miles south of the north pole near northern Canada's Prince of Wales Island. The magnetic field is some seventy miles below the surface of the earth. The southern hemisphere's magnetic field is near Sydney, Australia, which is some 1,700 miles from the south pole.

Therefore, a line drawn from a point in the United States to the north pole and another line drawn from the same point to the magnetic pole would not coincide. An angle would be created by the divergence of the two lines. The angle is known by various names, all meaning the same thing: magnetic declination, magnetic variation, and, in aviation, angle of deviation.

Magnetic declination is seldom the same from place to place because it depends upon a location's position relative to the pole and magnetic north. The map diagram shows the declination for a location in Maine and a location in California. The dashed line shows that both a line of longitude and a magnetic line pass through both magnetic north and polar north. If you are on that longitude/magnetic line there is no declination. If you are east of the line, the declination is west; if you are west of the line, the declination is east.

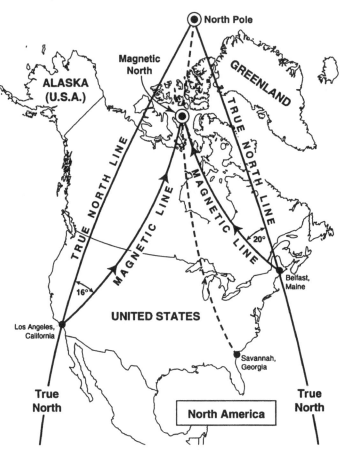

Why is knowledge of magnetic declination important? One reason is that if you determine a compass direction from a longitudinal map and then set your compass accordingly you will not reach your destination. For example, assume your destination is one mile away and the declination is 15°, but you do not add (or subtract) the declination. You would end up one-quarter of a mile off your target. If the distance to your target was longer, say ten miles, you would constantly be moving away from your target for as much as two-and-one-half miles. This is why pilots must consider declination before they leave the take-off strip for some place perhaps 200 miles away. The saying is, "Ignore declination and, perhaps, pay for it with your life."

SEASONS OF THE YEAR

A) Title:_____   B) Title:_____

_____

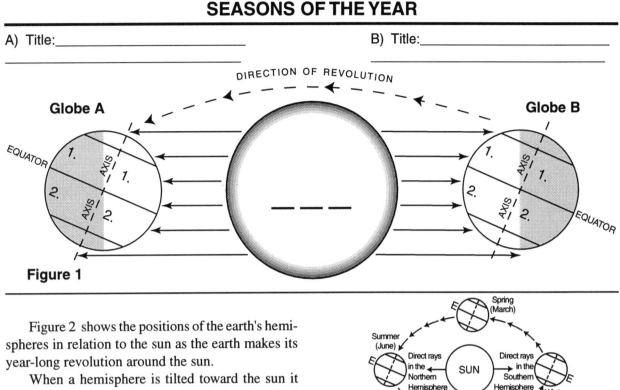

Figure 1

Figure 2 shows the positions of the earth's hemispheres in relation to the sun as the earth makes its year-long revolution around the sun.

When a hemisphere is tilted toward the sun it experiences summer; when a hemisphere is tilted away from the sun it experiences winter.

Figure 2

To the Instructor

It is suggested that students receive photocopies of the upper part of this page. They can annotate their diagrams as you explain and annotate a transparency.

1.   Print SUN in the circle in the center of Figure 1. Print SUN RAYS on all the lines extending from the sun.

2.   On globe A print NH for northern hemisphere at number 1. On globe B print SH for southern hemisphere at number 2.

3.   On both globes label the north pole as NP and the south pole as SP.

4.   Title Globe A: Summer in the Northern Hemisphere

5.   Title Globe B: Summer in the Southern Hemisphere

Explanation

The axis in each globe is tilted at 23½°. As the earth revolves around the sun the tilt of its axis remains the same.

In Globe A the northern hemisphere is experiencing summer because the sun's rays are striking it directly. However, the southern hemisphere is experiencing winter because the sun's rays are striking it indirectly, that is, at a slant.

In Globe B the globe has revolved halfway around the sun. Notice, however, that the tilt of the axis has remained the same. Thus, the northern hemisphere is not receiving the direct rays of the sun; it is winter. On the other hand, direct sun rays are striking the southern hemisphere; it is summer.

Also, as the diagram reveals, when it is winter in the northern hemisphere, the polar regions do not see the sun for six months. Of course, the same is true of the southern hemisphere's polar regions in the winter.

Figure 2 shows a more complete revolution of our globe around the sun. Again, notice the constant tilt of the globe's axis as it revolves. In the spring and fall of the year in both hemispheres the sun's rays are neither direct nor indirect; these are times of transition.

In summary, the tilt of the earth in relation to the sun causes the seasons of the year. If there were no tilt, there would be no seasons.

NOTES

Section 5: Reading and Study Skills

Reading and Study Skills (RSS)

RSS–1   **Guidelines for Outlining I (Instructor)**

RSS–2   **Guidelines for Outlining II (Instructor)**

RSS–3   **Completing a Topical Outline I**

RSS–4   **Completing a Topical Outline II**

RSS–5   **Sentence Outlines (Instructor)**

RSS–6   **Completing a Sentence Outline**

RSS–7   **Classifying Information (Instructor)**

RSS–8   **Gathering and Classifying Information**

RSS–9   **The Main Idea/Detail Study Method I (Instructor)**

RSS–10   **The Main Idea/Detail Study Method II (Instructor)**

RSS–11   **Practice in the Main Idea/Detail Study Method**

RSS–12   **Studying with a Partner (Instructor)**

RSS–13   **Bookmarking As a Study Technique (Instructor)**

RSS–14   **The Sun—Earth's Greatest Friend (Instructor)**

RSS–15   **Marking a Short Essay**

RSS–16   **Composing Questions As a Study Technique I (Instructor)**

RSS–17   **Composing Questions As a Study Technique II**

RSS–18   **Composing Questions As a Study Technique III**

RSS–19   **Ways to Improve Memory I (Instructor)**

RSS–20   **Ways to Improve Memory II**

GUIDELINES FOR OUTLINING I

1.   Outlining is a useful skill because it enables one to take a mass of information, given by spoken word or print, and condense it into main and subordinate ideas. Thus, when information has to be reviewed, as for a test, the outline aids recall of the entirety. Also, when students are delivering a speech or other oral presentation, outlines are useful as guides. As one speaks, one "fills-in" the "spaces" in the outline with words that connect and clarify the pre-sequenced and determined elements of the presentation.

2.   The very act of making an outline can help students understand and retain information. One cannot make an outline from printed material, for example, without responding to and thinking about what has been printed. One has to make conscious decisions as to whether elements are major ideas or supporting details. Likewise, making an outline as another person speaks "forces" concentration and eliminates daydreaming. When the speech is over the listener has a record that may be referred to again and again. (See number 4 below.)

3.   Students may construct outlines before writing papers of any length. Authors of books often make outlines of chapters and subtopics before they do actual writing. In such cases an outline is similar to a map that tells how to get to where one wants to go. Someone once compared an outline to a blueprint for a house; they both contain bare essentials that have to be fleshed out. As preparation for a talk about how to build a house, an outline can be developed that sequences the steps that should be followed: planning, excavating, constructing, plumbing, heating, siding, roofing, painting, and so on. Details for these main topics can be filled in through research and/or experience.

4.   Outlines may be constructed while a speech or talk is being delivered, but this presumes that the speaker is well organized, that what is being said is sequentially and topically organized. As is often the case, the offering may not lend itself to outlining because it has not been meticulously preordered. The speaker may jump ahead, retreat, or give extraneous information not really related to the main topic. In such cases, listeners should not attempt to outline; they should record as much as possible using abbreviations, phrases, and other stenographic shortcuts. Then, later, they can reorganize the information into outline form. The act of reorganizing can be most beneficial as a form of study because the outliner has to think, react, and otherwise manipulate what was recorded during the presentation. Greater understanding and retention will be the result.

5.   Some things to keep in mind when making an outline follow:

a.   The outline should have a title.

b.   The closer an outline entry is to the left margin, the greater its value.

c.   Roman numerals are used for major topics, capital letters for the next most important entry, Arabic numerals for the next most important entry, and lowercase letters for examples and details.

d.   Numbers and letters of the same kind are to be in vertical alignment.

e.   The first word of any topic, major or minor, should begin with a capital letter.

f.   No topic, major or minor, should have fewer than two items below it.

g.   Outlines utilizing letters and numbers may be developed in two ways:

   (1) Topical—All entries are single words or phrases

   (2) Sentence—All entries are complete sentences

   (3) An outline should be either the topical type or the sentence type; outlines should not be part topical and part sentence.

h.   In a topical outline entries should be parallel; that is, if entry A, for example, begins with a verb, then entry B should begin with a verb.

6.   While developing an outline from a chapter in a textbook, the outliner should take advantage of the study aids contained in most textbooks. For example, the title of the chapter becomes the title of the outline. Topics within the chapter, usually printed in bold print or italics, are major topics (Roman numerals). The main ideas of paragraphs become subtopics (capital letters), and information in the paragraphs such as facts and examples are topics of lesser importance (Arabic numerals and lower-case letters).

GUIDELINES FOR OUTLINING II

The following are suggestions for using the instructional material on this page and the previous page:

1. Distribute photocopies of the two pages.

2. Make a transparency of this page, project it, and help students understand how the topical outline suggestions were implemented.

3. Instruct students that they are to follow suggested procedures in outlining the articles on pages RSS–3 and 4.

Note: The outline on page RSS–5 illustrates how the topical outline below would be made if it were a sentence outline.

TROPICAL RAIN FORESTS

A tropical rain forest is a thickly wooded area located near the equator that experiences heavy rainfall, high temperatures, and a long growing season. Leaves are on the trees all year because there is no fall, winter, or spring; it is "summer" all year. All these things help explain why vegetation is so heavy in a tropical rain forest.

Think of a rain forest as being "layered." At ground level you find small, leafy plants. Vines are on the trunks of the trees and climb upward toward the sunlight. The level above the ground layer is called the "understory." Vines continue their climb up the straight tree trunks. In this middle layer the branches on the trees point upward as they reach toward the sun. Some of the branches intrude into the next layer called the "canopy." The canopy acts as a kind of awning. The branches grow horizontally and are densely leafed; they provide shade for the lower levels of the forest.

Estimates about the amount of animal life in tropical forests vary, but it is probable that 50% of the world's animal life make their homes in them. This figure is all the more remarkable because rain forests occupy only about 5% of the earth's surface. Each layer of the forest provides food for the animals that live there. At the ground level snakes, insects, crocodiles, and lizards abound. At the middle level you find predatory animals such as ocelots and harmless animals such as tapirs. Finally, in the upper level many birds such as toucans and parrots make their homes; monkeys swing from branch to branch, and snakes slither along the branches looking for birds' eggs to eat and, perhaps, the birds themselves.

TROPICAL RAIN FORESTS

I.   Description
   A. Thickly wooded
   B. Heavy rainfall
   C. High temperatures
   D. Long growing season

II. Structure
   A. Ground level
      1. Small, leafy plants
      2. Climbing vines
   B. Understory, or middle level
      1. Tree trunks
         a. Straight
         b. Vertical branches
         c. Encircling vines
   C. Canopy, or upper level
      1. Horizontal branches
      2. Densely leafed

III. Animal life
   A. 50% of world's animals in 5% of world's surface
   B. Ground level animals
      1. Snakes
      2. Lizards
      3. Crocodiles
   C. Understory animals
      1. Ocelots
      2. Tapirs
   D. Canopy, animals
      1. Birds
         a. Toucans
         b. Parrots
      2. Monkeys
      3. Snakes

COMPLETING A TOPICAL OUTLINE I

To Do:

1. Read the article below, "Water Pollution from Spilled Oil."

2. Your task is to complete the outline by filling in all of the blank lines. Notice that some of the items in the outline have been completed; this was done to help you get started. Also notice that, below Roman numeral I, you should list three causes of tanker oil spills as mentioned in the story, then, continue on in like manner until all the blank spaces are filled.

WATER POLLUTION FROM SPILLED OIL

Petroleum—oil— is a major polluter of water. Sometimes, oil leaks from tank ships when they collide with other ships or when they run aground. Often, large amounts of oil are released into waters when tankers take on or discharge oil in ports. Sometimes tankers are illegally cleaned out at sea—the oil is flushed into the ocean.

Landside oil spills also contribute to water pollution. A pipe in a refinery might burst and spew thousands of gallons of oil on the ground, oil that is carried to the sea by rains or streams. Or perhaps an oil transportation truck might be involved in an accident when loading oil at a seaside dock. There have been occasions when railroad tank cars have overturned and spilled oil into rivers, which eventually carried the oil to the sea.

Oil spills are disastrous. They cause millions of dollars of damage because of the loss of the oil itself and the costs of cleanup. Oil on the beaches can spoil vacations for families who have been working and waiting all year for a week or two at the seashore. Pleasure boats may have their bottoms and sides fouled and their motors and propeller blades damaged by floating oil. And, perhaps most disastrous of all, after a great oil spill, fish, sea birds, sea otters, and seals are found dead, floating in the water or washed up on the beach. Oil slicks have been known to catch on fire and then burn everything they touch.

© 1998 by John Wiley & Sons, Inc.

WATER POLLUTION FROM SPILLED OIL

I.   Causes of tanker spills at sea

    A. _____

    B. _____

    C. _____

II. Causes of oil spills on land

    A. _____

    B. _____

    C. _____

III. Results of oil spills

    A. Expenses

       1. _____

       2. _____

B. Spoiled seaside vacations

C. Oil slicks

    1. _____

    2. _____

    3. _____

D. Damage to animal life

    1. _____

    2. _____

    3. _____

    4. _____

COMPLETING A TOPICAL OUTLINE II

To Do:

In the second column, outline the article "Volcanoes and Air Pollution." To help you get started the two major topics of the article are shown by Roman numerals I and II. Be sure to use appropriate letters, numbers, and indentations.

VOLCANOES AND AIR POLLUTION

There are more than 500 active volcanoes in the world. On any given day ten or more of them are erupting. Their eruptions add substantially to the pollution of the atmosphere. Unlike pollution brought about by human activities (transportation, manufacturing, etc.), which can be controlled, it is impossible to control pollution from volcanoes. Pollution caused by volcanoes is part of nature's way of bringing about balance among plant and animal life and other elements of the earth such as land and water. It is human contributions to pollution that upset the balance.

The most notable recent volcanic eruption occurred in June 1991 in the Philippine Islands at Mt. Pinatubo. Vast amounts of sulfuric acid gas were blown into the atmosphere. The immediate effect was a measurable cooling of the earth so great that the warming of the earth from the Greenhouse Effect was slowed down. It is predicted that the sulfuric dioxide gas will dissipate in a few years; then, the carbon dioxide gas also spewed out by Pinatubo (and other volcanoes) coupled with industrial and transportation carbon dioxide emissions will accelerate earth's warming.

Along with the enormous impact on the atmosphere, what were some of the other results of the Pinatubo eruptions?

☐ The *National Geographic* (December 1992) reported that two cubic miles of ash were blown out of the volcano, enough to bury the District of Columbia up to 150 feet.

☐ Clark Air Base, a United States Air Force location only ten miles from Pinatubo, was covered with ash and has since been abandoned.

☐ Subic Naval Base, another United States installation, was also covered with ash; this forced the evacuation of United States personnel and dependents.

☐ 200,000 Filipinos were evacuated from their homes, whole villages were covered with ash, and thousands of acres of vegetation were destroyed.

☐ More than 900 people were killed.

☐ Rocks the size of grapefruit fell from the sky, and punched holes in roofs, cars, etc.

☐ A plus: Over a period of years the volcanic ash will significantly fertilize hundreds of square miles in the vicinity of the volcano.

I.   Volcano facts

_____

_____

_____

_____

_____

_____

_____

_____

_____

II.   Pinatubo eruption

_____

_____

_____

_____

_____

_____

_____

_____

_____

_____

_____

_____

_____

_____

SENTENCE OUTLINES

Sentence outlines have certain advantages over topical outlines. One advantage is that sentences express complete thoughts; topics do not. Also, there will be greater detail in sentence outlines than in topical outlines. A person who doesn't know much about the subject of an outline will probably gain a better understanding from reading a sentence outline. To put it in another context, as it is easier to converse with a person who speaks full sentences, so it is easier to understand written sentences rather than phrases.

Something to keep in mind when outlining is that once an outline is started, topical or sentence, there should be consistency in form; that is, the outline should be all sentences or all topics.

Following is a sentence outline of the short essay "Tropical Rain Forests." It would be helpful for students to compare it with the topical outline of the same essay on page RSS–2.

TROPICAL RAIN FORESTS

I. Tropical rain forests have several distinguishing characteristics.

    A. Most rain forests are located near the equator; this results in year-long summers.

    B. They are thickly wooded and allow only a little sunlight to reach ground level.

    C. Rainfall is heavy.

    D. Temperatures are always high.

II. Rain forests are structured so that there are three layers of vegetation.

    A. At ground level, small, leafy plants grow.

    B. At the middle level the straight tree trunks have branches that grow upward and protrude into the upper level. Vines encircle the tree trunks; they are climbing toward the sun.

    C. The top level, or canopy, acts as an awning for the two lower levels.

        1. Branches grow horizontally out of the tree trunks.

        2. Branches are densely leafed.

III. Many animals of different kinds live in rain forests.

    A. Rain forests occupy only 5% of the earth's land but contain about 50% of the world's animals.

    B. Each level of a rain forest is the habitat of different kinds of animals.

        1. Snakes, lizards, crocodiles, and other animals live at the ground level.

        2. Tree-climbing predatory animals such as the ocelot live in the middle level. Nonpredatory animals such as tapirs also live in the middle level.

        3. Birds such as toucans and parrots, monkeys, and snakes make the upper level their home.

        4. Although most animals stay in one level, they do sometimes climb up or down levels. For example, snakes are found in all levels.

COMPLETING A SENTENCE OUTLINE

THE EFFECTS OF TOPSOIL LOSS

Much of the farmland topsoil that washes away during heavy rains settles on the bottoms of river channels as sediment. Thus, over a period of years the depth of the water in channels decreases. This means that large boats may not be able to navigate the stream; their bottoms would scrape the channel bed. It also means that during periods of heavy rains the rivers will not be able to hold as much water. The rivers then rise over their banks and cause great property damage. Often in such situations, lives are lost through drowning.

Sediment settles on the bottoms of lakes and reservoirs, particularly near dam sites. This reduces the capacity of the reservoir to hold water. There are two bad results of the buildup of soil. One, in times of heavy rains reservoirs cannot hold as much water and floods can occur because of the spillover. Two, in times of little rain there may not be enough water for homes, factories, and farms downstream.

Sediment that eventually reaches the sea is deposited at the mouths of rivers. The sediment clogs bays, harbors, channels, and canals. This can affect the flow of ocean currents. The force and direction of waves can be changed. Finally, sediment can cover and pollute clam and oyster beds, and this, in turn, can put people who are employed on fishing boats and fisheries out of work.

To Do:

Carefully read the article above; then, make a sentence outline of the article on the lines below. To help you get started, the first line is already printed.

THE EFFECTS OF TOPSOIL LOSS

I.   River channels are affected by sedimentation deposits.

    A. _____

_____   _____

_____   _____

_____   _____

_____   _____

_____   _____

_____   _____

_____   _____

_____   _____

_____   _____

_____   _____

_____   _____

_____   _____

_____   _____

_____   _____

CLASSIFYING INFORMATION

To classify is to take objects, ideas, or facts and group them according to certain common characteristics. For example, animals may be classified as meat eaters (carnivores), plant eaters (herbivores), or both meat and plant eaters (omnivores). Lions and wolves would be classified as carnivores, deer and rabbits as herbivores, and bears as omnivores.

It is difficult to imagine a library that does not have a means of classifying books or a secretary's file that doesn't have folders with identifying labels filed, probably, in alphabetical order. Colleges have several kinds of classifying systems; for example, students may be classified as freshmen, sophomores, juniors, and seniors. They could be further classified within that system according to their main course of study such as science, history, education, and so on.

Classification helps us keep things in order. For students, classification skills help them organize information so that it can be readily recalled or found.

To Do:

1. Make a transparency and photocopies of the United States Facts listed below.

2. Help students understand the headings under which the facts should be placed. The classified facts can be listed by the number in front of each.

UNITED STATES FACTS

1. The first permanent English settlement in the New World was Jamestown, 1607.

2. Congress is made up of two parts: the House of Representatives and the Senate.

3. Alaska is the largest state in the United States.

4. The United States gained most of its southwest in a war with Mexico, 1846–1848.

5. Two of the great rivers that join the Mississippi River are the Missouri River and the Ohio River.

6. The world's greatest exporter of wheat is the United States.

7. The first ten amendments to the United States Constitution guarantee certain rights and freedoms to all Americans.

8. The highest peak in the Appalachian Mountains is Mt. Mitchell (6,684'), in North Carolina.

9. The population of the United States is approaching 270 million people.

10. The state with the greatest American Indian population is Oklahoma.

11. The highest recorded temperature in the United States was 134°F in Death Valley, California.

12. The tallest building in the United States is the Sears Tower in Chicago, Illinois, at 1,454'.

13. The strongest surface wind every measured in the United States occurred at Mt. Washington, New Hampshire, in 1934: 231 mph.

14. World War I ended on November 11, 1918.

15. In a recent year, Iowa produced more corn than any other state: 1,930,400,000 bushels.

16. The Secretary of State is responsible for conducting the foreign affairs of the United States.

17. A recent survey showed that 98% of homes in the United States had at least one television set.

Agriculture	
Climate	
Geography	
Government	
History	
Population	
Miscellaneous	

GATHERING AND CLASSIFYING INFORMATION

Kristin's assignment was to write a report on the life of Abraham Lincoln. So, she went to the school library and the town library to gather information. When she found an interesting fact she wrote it on a 3" by 5" card. On the same card she noted the title, author, publisher, date of publication, and the page number of the book in which the fact was found.

When she thought she had enough information about Lincoln she classified the cards according to topics. The next step was to use the facts to write a paragraph about each topic. At the end of the written report she used the information on the cards to make a bibliography (book listing).

Her teacher complimented her on her report. He wrote on her paper that the paragraphs were well written; that is, the main idea of each paragraph was very evident, and she had details to support each main idea.

To Do:

Place the number of each fact that Kristin noted next to the appropriate classification in the table below.

1. In 1846, Lincoln was elected to the Congressional House of Representatives.
2. He married Mary Todd when he was 33 years old; four children were born to them, but only one, Robert Todd Lincoln, lived past the age of 18.
3. He was first elected president in 1860; he was reelected in 1864.
4. In 1832, at age 23, he volunteered for service in the Black Hawk War.
5. Abraham Lincoln was born on February 12, 1809, in Kentucky.
6. In 1823, 19 years old, he was an oarsman on a flatboat that floated down the Ohio River and the Mississippi River to New Orleans, Louisiana.
7. In 1834, Lincoln was elected to the Illinois General Assembly; he was reelected four times for a total of eight years.
8. His total schooling amounted to about one year; he studied by himself, read the family Bible, and borrowed books whenever he could.
9. After moving from Kentucky to Indiana, the family moved to Illinois in 1830, when he was 21 years old.
10. Lincoln's father, Thomas Lincoln, was a farmer; sometimes he worked as a carpenter.
11. By age 21 Lincoln had worked at many jobs, including splitting rails for fences, plowing, planting, and harvesting.
12. At age 22, Lincoln felt free to leave his family; he took a job in New Salem, Illinois, as a clerk in a store.
13. At the early age of 8, Lincoln worked with his father on the farm; he was very good with an axe, for he was strong even as a young boy.

14. He was shot by John Wilkes Booth in April, 1865; the assassination took place while he was attending a play in a theatre.
15. In 1834 he began the study of law; he taught himself; he was very good as a lawyer and even tried cases in the state supreme court.
16. His mother was Nancy Hanks from Virginia; she died when he was only 9 years old.
17. At 21 years of age Lincoln was 6'4" tall, thin and wiry, dark-skinned, and very strong.
18. As President he issued the Proclamation of 1863; this freed the slaves in the Confederate states.
19. Lincoln had a sister named Sarah, who kept house for the family after their mother died.
20. After the two Union victories at Gettysburg, President Lincoln gave his famous Gettysburg Address, in which he said, "Government of the people, by the people, for the people shall not perish from this earth."
21. Lincoln was president when the Civil War began in 1861 and when it ended in 1865.
22. Lincoln was buried in Oak Ridge Cemetery, Springfield, Illinois.

Birth	
Family Life As a Child	
Education As a Youth	
Experiences Through Age 21	
Experiences: Age 22 to Presidency	
As President	
Death	

THE MAIN IDEA/DETAIL STUDY METHOD I

There are numerous study methods described in educational literature, and all of them have particular approaches and advantages. However, one thing they all have in common is that learners must be mentally and physically active while studying. And, the most effective way to ensure mental and physical activity is for the learner to write, within prearranged categories rather than randomly, the essential elements of what he or she has read. Then, the follow-up to the reading, thinking, and writing is for the learner to attempt to recall that which he or she has read.

Following is a description of the Main Idea/ Detail (MI/D) study approach, which implements the suggestions made above and which results in the organization of reading selections into manageable units.

This suggested method of studying is especially useful to students who are not permitted to mark books by underlining or making notations in margins. Any blank sheet of paper can be ruled in columns and headed to suit the MI/D method.

The following practice page can be a helpful start toward the development of the habit and skills of active study. However, instructors should also have their students apply this study method to portions of textbooks being used in the classroom.

Once students realize the efficacy of systematic study, perhaps through improved test scores, they may habitually and of their own free will utilize this method or other methods described elsewhere in this book. It is almost a certainty that students will make adaptations to any study method taught to them. And, this, of course, is a positive indication of maturity and competence.

Main Idea/Detail Method Sequences

1. Skim read the selection. One effective way to do this is to read the lead sentences of the paragraphs; the lead sentences usually tell the main ideas or topics of paragraphs. While skimming, the reader should note special aids in the selection such as maps, diagrams, charts, pictures, and tables. This activity develops an overview, a kind of "foreshadowing," of what the selection is about.

2. Return to the beginning of the selection, and in terse language list, under the Main Ideas header, items discussed in the text. Either at the same time or during the second reading, "flesh out" the ideas with details, and record them under the Details header.

3. Prior to a test, review that which has been noted, especially emphasizing repetition and rehearsal.

Suggestions for Teaching

1. Make a transparency of the following page for yourself and photocopies for your students.

2. Explain the model note-taking sample that is based on the story of Sequoia on the following page.

The two-column arrangement is purposefully simple. It clearly separates main ideas and supporting detail. Point out that main ideas should be simply expressed in short sentences and that abbreviations should be utilized. There is no good reason, for example, that Sequoia's name has to be completely written, except, perhaps, in the first mentioning of it.

Also call attention to the kinds of items that can be considered as details. The three dots (. . .) between items are aids to clarity and help distinguish between details.

3. Provide an opportunity for students to practice this study method on the selection printed on page RSS–11. Supply a blank replica of the arrangement of the columns and headings as shown in the MI/D model, RSS–10.

© 1998 by John Wiley & Sons, Inc.

THE MAIN IDEA/DETAIL STUDY METHOD II

SEQUOIA, INDIAN SCHOLAR

Sequoia was a Cherokee Indian born in Tennessee about 1770. He never saw a book until he was about 30 years old. When he finally did see books, he realized that they were tools for learning that his people needed. Up to that time, none of the Indian tribes in our country had developed a written language. Sequoia made up his mind to find a way to put the spoken words of the Cherokee people on paper.

His own people didn't understand what he was trying to do. Once, his wife burned work that Sequoia had taken years to develop. He left his tribe to live alone in the woods where he could work. This, too, was misunderstood by the other Indians. They thought he was practicing witchcraft and that he would bring great trouble to the tribe. One day a group of Indians burned Sequoia's cabin to the ground. Sequoia's work was once more destroyed. So, he started all over again.

At first Sequoia set out to make a separate symbol for every Cherokee word. He gave up this method because he realized that a person would have to remember thousands of symbols. This would be too difficult. Even he could not remember all the symbols he had made. Then he came up with the idea of making a symbol for each of the 86 sounds in the Cherokee language. Every Cherokee word is made up of one or more of these sounds. After twelve years of hard work, Sequoia developed an alphabet. He was able to put every Cherokee word into written form.

The chiefs saw that he had done a wonderful thing. They encouraged their people to learn to read. Cherokee of all ages learned Sequoia's alphabet. Soon newspapers and books were printed in the Cherokee language.

Sequoia went on to become a great leader. He ably represented, in Washington, Cherokee claims in Oklahoma and Arkansas, to which the Cherokees had been moved from their traditional lands in the East. Later, he helped other Cherokee tribes move to Oklahoma.

It was while looking for some Cherokee rumored to be in northern Mexico that Sequoia died at the age of about 73. This great American Indian's statue represents Oklahoma in Statuary Hall in the Capitol Building in Washington, DC. Another honor given to Sequoia was the naming of Sequoia National Park, the home of the giant Sequoia trees, after him.

Main Ideas	Details (Names, Dates, Places, Events, New Terms, Vocabulary)
Sequoia (S) wants to develop a written language.	S born about 1770, Tenn. . . . Cherokee (C) Indian . . . Realized books needed for his people . . . No written C language
S's work is misunderstood.	Wife burned work . . . Lived in woods . . . Suspected of witchcraft . . . Indians burned cabin
S invents written lang.	Tried symbols for each word — too many . . . Developed symbols for the 86 C spoken sounds . . . Took 12 years
S's work accepted.	Chiefs encouraged people to read . . . Newspapers, books published in C language
S is a leader.	Represented C in Washington . . . Helped develop C claims to Oklahoma and Arkansas
S is honored.	Statue in Capitol Bldg., Washington . . . Sequoia National Park named for him . . . Died at 73, 1843

PRACTICE IN THE MAIN IDEA/DETAIL STUDY METHOD

The story below tells about an important part of the American Revolution. Use the Main Idea/Detail (MI/D) method of studying it. First, skim read the entire selection. Then, return to the beginning of the selection to read more thoroughly. As you read, determine each paragraph's main idea and the details that support it and write them briefly in the blank outline below the story.

THE SWAMP FOX AND HIS MEN

1 Some of the most important fighting in the Revolution took place between small groups of British and American soldiers rather than between large armies. The battles were fought on lonely stretches of roads or trails, in dismal swamps, or in thick forests. Sometimes an engagement would last only a few minutes, sometimes an hour or more. Usually it was the Americans who were attackers and the British who were defenders. The British never knew when one of their posts, a detachment of their troops, or wagon trains carrying their supplies would be attacked. The Americans would suddenly appear, fight furiously, and then disappear.

2 To follow the attackers was hopeless. In the South the Americans used the swamps as hideouts. British troops who were foolish enough to attempt pursuit often became lost. Sometimes they were pulled under by quicksand. Many were killed by snakes and alligators. If they survived all these dangers, they risked capture by the Americans.

3 The Americans who made up these forces are hard to describe because of their great variety. Some were African Americans who were fighting side-by-side with men of Scottish, Irish, English, French, and German backgrounds. Sometimes the group members would all have the same uniform, but more often no two would be dressed alike. However, the men all had certain common characteristics. They were bold, brave, hardy, resourceful, and skillful.

4 The leaders of these fierce patriots were everything that their men were and more. Perhaps the greatest was Francis Marion, the "Swamp Fox," of South Carolina. He gained the "Swamp" part of his nickname because he attacked the enemy from the deep, dark swamps. He gained the "Fox" part of his name because of his cleverness. He was brave, but never foolish. He carefully planned every mission. He would not move his men during the day if he could help it. He preferred the cover of darkness. He seldom used known trails that would make it too easy for the enemy to ambush (surprise) his men. His men were taught to whistle in such a way that they could communicate with each other even at night. No one, not even his most trusted officers, knew Marion's complete plans. "Captured men," he said, "can be made to talk."

© 1998 by John Wiley & Sons, Inc.

Main Ideas	Details (Names, Dates, Places, Events, New Terms, Vocabulary)
1.	
2.	
3.	
4.	

182

STUDYING WITH A PARTNER

Studying with another person can be very productive. The old saying "Two heads are better than one" contains a significant truth. The reasoning behind the saying is based on the idea that working with another person requires active responses, and active responding is the key to learning and retaining information. Also, another person may have taken notes that are not within your notes. No two persons attending the same class and listening to the same words will react to what is being taught in the same way.

A way of studying with others is suggested below.

1. One student assumes the role of teacher. This student formulates and presents questions from personal notes and/or the textbook being used.

2. The other student* attempts to answer the questions.

3. If an answer is complete, the "teacher" says something like, "You got it." Or, even more effective for both persons concerned, repeats the answer.

Note: At this point consider what has happened in the first three steps as related to learning. The person formulating the questions had to read and think about what to ask. The person responding had to supply answers. Both the questioner and the responder were actively engaged, and this is the key to retention.

4. If the respondent's answers are incomplete or incorrect, the questioner can supply missing elements and/or make corrections. Or, in the case of an incomplete answer, the questioner can ask for further clarification. If further clarification is not forthcoming, the questioner can resort to prompting. Prompting is the asking of minor questions that help the responder to recall. Or, the prompter may offer a bit of information that could trigger associations in the mind of the responder.

The following dialogue will provide an example of how a two-party study session might be carried out.

Questioner: Why was the St. Lawrence River Valley an ideal place for French colonies?

Responder: Farms along the river had a natural road that could be used for transportation of their prod-

ucts . . . The Great Lakes were nearby, and this was very helpful to the fur trade.

Questioner: Good, but there are other reasons.

Responder: I can't think of anything else.

Questioner: What about Europe?

Responder: Oh, I know! The river, combined with the Atlantic Ocean, provided an all-water route to Europe.

Questioner: Anything else?

Responder: You're kidding! There's another reason?

Questioner: Yes, in fact there are two more reasons. One, the river supplied fish for food. Two, recreation such as boating, swimming in summer. . . . Okay. Now, tell me all the advantages.

(Responder repeats the five advantages)

Questioner: What were two disadvantages of having colonies on the river?

Responder: Easy! Warships could bombard the settlements from the river, and enemy troops could cross the river on the ice if the river froze over.

Questioner: You're sharp. Here's another question: Tell me three facts about the St. Lawrence Seaway.

Responder: Most of Canada's major cities are on or near the Seaway . . . It's about 2,400 miles long, from the Gulf of St. Lawrence to Duluth, Minnesota, on the western end of Lake Superior . . . Because the Great Lakes have different elevations, canals with locks were constructed to take ships from one lake to another.

Questioner: Okay! You mentioned major Canadian cities on or near the Seaway. Name five.

Responder: Boy, you never let up, do you? Anyway, five cities? Let me think. Okay. I know: Quebec, Montreal, Toronto, Hamilton, and . . . and, oh, yeah, Windsor.

Questioner: Not bad, not bad, Now, you can ask me questions.

---

*This technique will also be effective if there are three or four persons in the study group.

BOOKMARKING AS A STUDY TECHNIQUE

One of the limitations public school students encounter on the road to learning is that they are not allowed to mark textbooks they are using. The reason for this restriction is that textbooks are expensive; public schools cannot afford to furnish new books for students each year. Private school students do not have this problem; students usually buy their own books and can, therefore, mark them.

Students who are prohibited from marking their books cannot engage in certain study approaches such as underlining key ideas or details as they read. Nevertheless, all students should be aware of the benefits of bookmarking in learning and retaining information and should have some practice with the method. Hopefully, opportunities will come, perhaps in college or in other circumstances, when they will be able to fully utilize the method.

Benefits of Bookmarking

Following are some reasons why bookmarking as a study technique has proven to be beneficial.

1. Students are actively engaged in reacting and thinking about what they are reading. They must make conscious decisions as to what is essential and significant. In doing this students are not passive; they are purposefully engaged with the printed words. Their reading is directed; i.e., they have definite purposes for reading that they constantly apply.

2. The physical act of bookmarking brings another sensory application to the reading process. The more senses that are utilized when learning, the more effective the learning experience.

3. Bookmarking facilitates reviewing the printed material, as for a test or some other kind of application. It is not necessary for the student to reread, word for word, the entire printed material; the student rereads only that which is marked. If it took two hours to read and mark a 15-page chapter, it may take only a half hour to complete a review. Such a review is effective and efficient because the student's concentration is directed toward essentials that have been "set aside" in the bookmarking process.

Suggested Procedure for Using Bookmarking As a Study Technique

1. Quickly survey the entire selection to gain an overview of the subject.

2. Return to the beginning of the selection to start a more careful reading. During the reading do the following:

   a. Double line ===== main ideas as they are encountered.

   b. Single line ——— details that support the main ideas.

   c. Circle or bracket ( ) special vocabulary and definitions, special names, events, and numbers.

   d. Enumerate (1, 2, 3, etc.) special sequences and processes.

3. After marking an item in the selection, look away from it and try to recite what you have marked. The effort to recall is probably the most significant element in retention. In bookmarking, what is significant is *noted*; in recall, what is significant is *remembered*.

4. When reviewing, as for an examination, repeat step 3: at each marking recite from memory, and then read the marking to determine whether the recollection was correct. If the recollection was correct, reinforcement takes place; if it was not correct, the error can be rectified.

Suggestions for Teaching

1. Make a transparency and photocopies of the selection that is printed on the following page. Explain each marking as it is encountered.

2. Caution students about underlining indiscriminately or underlining too profusely. Impress them with the fact that it is the conscious choice of what to mark that is significant to the learning process. They must be selective; otherwise the marking is an exercise in futility.

3. After reviewing the following page, students should practice the approach on the selection that is printed on the second page following this one.

THE SUN—EARTH'S GREATEST FRIEND

Humans have been dependent upon the sun since the beginning of life on the planet Earth. The sun is Earth's primary source of energy. The sun gave Earth's earliest people light and heat, as it continues to do for today's people. The sun's uneven heating of Earth's surfaces causes winds to blow. Humans discovered that winds could move boats over water by blowing against hoisted sails. There was a gradual development from very small boats to great three-masted ships powered by the wind. Without the winds caused by the sun it is unlikely that early explorers such as Columbus could have crossed the oceans and discovered unknown lands.

There are many other ways that the sun helps us. The sun's heat causes evaporation, which is the changing of water into a mist-like gas called vapor. As the vapor, which is very light, rises high into the atmosphere, the band of air that surrounds Earth, it cools and forms into tiny droplets of water—a process known as condensation. Thousands of droplets combine and form large droplets of water, which, because of their weight, fall back to Earth as precipitation in the form of rain, snow, or sleet. This process— evaporation, condensation, precipitation—is called the hydrologic cycle, also commonly known as the water cycle.

Precipitation causes many other beneficial things to happen. Precipitation replen-①ishes Earth's lakes, rivers, and oceans. Water is used for transportation②, for drinking③, for power④ that comes from falling water, and water causes plants⑤ to grow. In turn, plants are eaten by animals, and the animals provide us with many things including meat①, eggs②, milk③, skins④, and wool⑤. Of course, animals also are used for work in farm⑥ing and for transportation of people and products. None of these many things would be possible if it were not for our friend, the sun.

© 1998 by John Wiley & Sons, Inc.

MARKING A SHORT ESSAY

PROBLEMS CAUSED BY POLLUTED AIR

Some costs of pollution cannot be accurately measured. It is impossible to determine the decrease in value of a great statue through corrosion caused by polluted air. How much of the value of crops is lost due to heavily polluted air? What is the price of sneezing, coughing, eye irritation, or even cancer, caused by dirty air?

Scientists, business people, and insurance companies have been able to estimate some the costs of air pollution. But notice the use of the word estimate, which is only a guess. Nevertheless, following are some examples of situations and costs.

In California damage to crops from air pollutants is at least $100 million yearly. Damage to crops on a nationwide basis is thought to be about five times that much. Also, it should be realized that the millions of gallons of spray used to kill crop-damaging insects is also an air pollutant.

Pollution from factories is especially bad—in spite of the efforts to reduce the poison they spew into the air. Not all of the fuel—coal and oil—used in power plants and factories is completely burned. The unburned and partially burned fuel goes up the chimneys and into the atmosphere. Some $300 million of fuel is wasted each year in this way. But the costs don't stop there. Damage to the environment costs millions of additional dollars.

Here is an interesting example: In Syracuse, New York, the furnace in an institution broke down. The result was that about 725 pounds of soot were blown out of the chimney and deposited in the surrounding area. Damage to automobiles, clothing loss, and cleaning costs came to about $38,000. Another example has to do with automobiles. It has been estimated that $3 billion of gasoline evaporates from American automobiles each year. This would average about $30 for each automobile in the country.

All in all, it is estimated that damage due to air pollution costs about $12 billion each year to the United States alone. This averages out to about $65 per person each year.

COMPOSING QUESTIONS AS A STUDY TECHNIQUE I

It is not likely that any two people will underline or otherwise mark the same reading material in the same way. Differences in background, purposes for reading, and what one considers important all help determine what will be marked.

As a study aid some students write in the margin of pages. In brief and concise language, using abbreviations that are meaningful to them, they write main ideas and some details. The act of writing is, in itself, a powerful tool. This is because one must decide what to write, and that decision can be made only if one thinks about what is being read. Also, the act of writing brings about an additional sensory application that contributes to a greater retention of information.

One of the most effective marking operations is to write brief questions that can be answered by what is being read. This approach puts students in the position of the instructor, who may compose a test based on the assigned material. The questions may be written in margins or on separate sheets of paper.

The questions written by students should be brief, yet comprehensive in the coverage of the material. If students read carefully, there probably will be close similarities between student questions and instructor questions. Prior to a test, students may review by reading their questions and then answering them. In cases of doubt or faulty recollection the text is there for help.

One of the reasons writing questions may be more helpful than underlining is that underlining can become perfunctory. That is, underlining can become an automatic action that is unaccompanied by serious thought. It is not likely that the writing of questions will become perfunctory. The act of composing questions disallows an approach that lacks thought.

Suggestions for Teaching

1. Make a transparency and student photocopies of the article on the following page.

2. Read the text and questions aloud. Emphasize the brevity of the questions. Do not be concerned that most of the questions involve facts. Knowing facts facilitates fluent responses to more comprehensive questions.

3. Provide the second page following this one for student opportunities to compose their own questions.

Note: Some students use underlining for one occasion and margin annotations for another. Other students will combine the two approaches when studying. It is a given that through time and opportunity students will appropriately amend any study method to which they have been exposed. The most important consideration is that students apply some kind of active approach beyond mere reading and rereading.

COMPOSING QUESTIONS AS A STUDY TECHNIQUE II

WATER AND THE LOSS OF SOIL THROUGH EROSION

Water that is not controlled can cause environmental damage that will have serious negative effects on humans, wildlife, and land. The following examples are only a few of the kinds of problems that result.

Farmer Jones is careless about the way that he takes care of his land. After he harvests his crops he fails to plant a cover crop—such as clover or spring wheat—that will protect the soil from the hard winds and rains of winter. As a result, tons of soil are blown or washed into ditches, brooks, and rivers. With the soil go minerals, such as nitrates, that are important to the growth of plants. Farmer Jones' topsoil losses bring about reductions in the size of his crops. Each year his lands yield less and less; this means less income for him and his family.

Multiply Farmer Jones' soil loss by the losses from thousands of other farms. Add to this the loss of soil from excavations for new homes and bulldozing for new highways. Include soil from unplanted ditches, overgrazed pastures, and strip-mining operations. The total yearly loss of topsoil to the United States? Enough topsoil to fill a convoy of dump trucks stretching far out in space.

Sediment—small particles of soil that has run off the land—settles on the bottoms of lakes and reservoirs, particularly near dam sites. As sediment builds up, the capacity of the reservoir to hold water is reduced. This, in turn, reduces the amount of water that goes over the dam to turn the turbines that produce electricity for homes and industries. Also, in times of heavy rains, the reservoir will not be able to hold as much water, and flooding will occur on the surrounding low lands. The opposite occurs in times of little rain; that is, there may not be enough water for fish, homes, industries, and irrigation of crops.

Sediment that reaches the sea via rivers is deposited at the mouths of the rivers. The sediment clogs the entrances to bays, channels, harbors, and canals. Also, sediment can cover and pollute clam and oyster beds, thus depriving many people of the means of making a living.

An impressive example of just how much soil can be washed from the land is the delta of the Mississippi River. Each year more than 300 million cubic yards of topsoil are deposited at its mouth. These yearly deposits that come from the Great Plains of the United States have created a delta that is larger than the state of New Jersey. And, the Mississippi delta is only one of hundreds throughout the United States and the world.

What is a cover crop?

Why is a cc necessary?

Why does FJ get poorer each year?

Name 5 contributors to soil loss.

- *Excavations*
- *Bulldozing*
- *Unplanted ditches*
- *Over-grazed pastures*
- *Strip mining*

What is sediment?

What are 3 bad effects of sediment buildup in reservoirs/dams?

- *Less water for power*
- *Increases chance of floods*
- *Reduces water for irrigation*

What are 2 bad results of sediment deposits at mouths of rivers?

How did the Mississippi delta come about?

How many cubic yards of soil are deposited in the delta each year?

COMPOSING QUESTIONS AS A STUDY TECHNIQUE III

To Do:

Read the article thoroughly; then, return to the beginning and compose brief questions about the information in each paragraph. Write your questions in the margin under the heading "Questions." Keep your writing as small as possible, and abbreviate when you can.

SOIL EROSION IN THE GREAT PLAINS

Questions

Weather sometimes occurs in what is called weather cycles. There may be a period of several years when the rainfall in a region is sufficient for crops to grow. This may be followed by a year or more of exceptionally light rainfall.

Weather cycles cause problems no matter where they occur, but they have been especially harmful in the Great Plains of the United States. Soon after the Civil War, about 1865, settlers in the Great Plains felt encouraged to plow and plant crops where Nature intended tall grass with deep roots to grow. They cut the thick sod with plows that exposed the soil to the weather. All went well in those years when rainfall was plentiful. Crops, mostly wheat and corn, were abundant, and farmers prospered. Other pioneers, hearing the good news, flocked to the region.

The "good years" for the early Great Plains farmers ended when periods of drought, or little rain, began. Because crops had been harvested and the land was uncovered, land was exposed to the weather. Added to the problem were the almost constant winds that blew over the land month after month. The winter winds were especially fierce. The absence of rain, the drying action of the winds, and the hot sun of summer made the region as dry as a desert.

The ever-blowing winds picked up soil and filled the air with dust. People placed handkerchiefs or masks over their mouths and noses to prevent dust from filling their lungs. Grains of soil piled up along fence rows, houses, and barns. Through keyholes, cracks in windows, and chimneys, winds below dust into houses.

During periods of prolonged drought, farms are abandoned and people move away. When people move away, many stores and services are forced to close their doors. Few people can make a decent living in such towns and places.

In recent years, much has been learned about farming in drier areas of our country. Soil erosion is gradually being brought under control, although much remains to be done. Some of the land that should never have been plowed in the first place has been replaced with grass. Some land is planted with specially developed grains that require less water. In some years land is left to "rest" with a cover crop such as clover, which, because of its extensive root structure, holds water for a long time. Also, trees have been planted in long rows that help to break the force of the winds as they blow over the land.

WAYS TO IMPROVE MEMORY I

It is important for students to realize that most things that they read, hear, or see, and that they understand immediately may quickly leave their minds, especially details. Studies have shown that as much as 50 percent of what is understood and "learned" will not be recalled 24 hours later. One week after a learning experience most students will have retained only 25–30 percent of the information. Fortunately, however, there are techniques that will slow down/decrease memory loss and help recall take place.

1. Much has already been printed in this book about repetition and rehearsal as important elements in retention. Rehearsal is hard work but ultimately rewarding. Also, rehearsals can become briefer and more effective through the application of various techniques. The mnemonics activities on the following page represent one of many approaches to better memories. Students should be aware that there are many different mnemonic devices including letter, word, and sentence schemes; rhymes, as at the bottom of the second column on the following page; and mental pictures. There is little doubt that students who understand mnemonic rationale and approaches will develop their own unique schemes for remembering.

2. "Card Stacking" is another relatively simple study technique that can yield positive results. Following are the steps of this approach.

Imagine that it is necessary to learn a significant number of facts related to a subject, for example World War I.

a. Select a number of key names, events, places, etc., from the textbook and/or class notes.

b. Make a number of cards approximately 2"× 2".

c. On the faces of the cards print selected key words and phrases—one key word or phrase per card.

d. On the reverse sides of the cards print a fact or facts related to the key word. Keep them brief.

e. Test by picking up a card, reading the key word, and trying to relate the associated fact(s).

f. If memory fails, turn the card over and read the associated fact(s).

g. If possible, play a "game" with a fellow student who has made a card stack that may contain the same and additional key words and facts.

h. If the test given is based on facts, it is probable that the card-stacking students will "ace" it. If the test requires short written answers or essays, students can incorporate the learned facts in their answers.

Examples

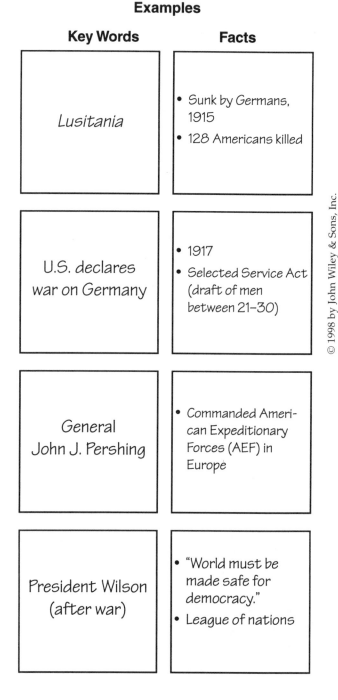

Key Words	Facts
Lusitania	• Sunk by Germans, 1915 • 128 Americans killed
U.S. declares war on Germany	• 1917 • Selected Service Act (draft of men between 21–30)
General John J. Pershing	• Commanded American Expeditionary Forces (AEF) in Europe
President Wilson (after war)	• "World must be made safe for democracy." • League of nations

WAYS TO IMPROVE MEMORY II

There are some "tricks" to remembering certain kinds of information, especially lists of things—the names of people and places and sequences in processes. The name given to such approaches is mnemonics, pronounced nih-mon-ics. Mnemonics is defined in *Webster's Intercollegiate Dictionary* as techniques for improving the memory.

One form of mnemonics is to remember the first letter of each of a series of things. Then, when you study or take a test, remembering the letters will remind you of the whole set of things. Here is an example: You need to remember the names of the Great Lakes. So, you think of the word HOMES. Each letter is the beginning letter of one of the Great Lakes, as follows:

H – Lake Huron
O – Lake Ontario
M – Lake Michigan
E – Lake Erie
S – Lake Superior

A way to remember the geographical west-to-east position of the lakes would be through the use of the letters SMHEO, Lake Superior is the farthest west, Lake Michigan is next, then Lake Huron, then Lake Erie, and, finally, Lake Ontario, the most eastern lake. SMHEO can be remembered by the following sentence: Sue Made Her Egg Omelet.

To Do:

1.a. Make up a sentence mnemonic that will help you remember the names of five rivers that contribute water to the Mississippi River. The rivers are Missouri, Red, Arkansas, Ohio, and Tennessee. The letters in your mnemonic may be in any order.

_____

_____

_____

b. If the letters cannot be combined to form a real word, you can combine them into a word you make up, for example, ROTMA or MATOR. Think of another made-up word that combines all five rivers.

2. Here is another opportunity to practice making sentence mnemonics.

You feel sure that your instructor is going to ask questions on a test that require you to know the names of generals in the Union army during the Civil War.

The generals are Grant, Meade, Sherman, Burnside, Hooker, and Rosecrans. Using the letters G, M, S, B, H, R, compose a sentence the words of which begin with the first letters of the six names.

_____

_____

_____

3. You're studying the geography of the United States Southwest. Your instructor has spent lots of class time helping students gain a mental picture of the area, especially place names. Here is the kind of question that might be asked on the examination: What states border Nevada?

Going in a clockwise direction from the north, write the first letters of all the states: O (Oregon), I (Idaho), U (Utah), A (Arizona), C (California). (OIUAC)

Think of a mnemonic sentence that will help you remember the states in the correct order, that is OIUAC.

_____

_____

_____

4. Imagine that it is necessary to remember the five largest states in order of size (Alaska, Texas, California, Montana, New Mexico). You could use first letters and syllables to make a sentence: After Tea, Calliope Modeled New Moccasins.

Try this approach on the five states that are on the Gulf of Mexico: Florida, Alabama, Mississippi, Louisiana, Texas.

_____

_____

_____

5. Here is a mnemonic poem that will help you remember the number of days in each month.

Thirty days in September,
April, June, and November.
All the rest have thirty-one
Except February which has twenty-eight.
But! Keep in mind!
Each fourth year February has twenty-nine.

NOTES

Section 6: Reading and Its Writing Connection

Reading and Its Writing Connection (RW)

GUIDELINES FOR CAPITALIZATION

Capitalization is one of the more complex elements that make up the language arts. In general, all proper nouns and the adjectives derived from them are capitalized; however, there are numerous situations that require special attention. This page is concerned with some of the most common instances when capitals, as compared to lower-case letters, should be used.

1. **The first word of sentences and sentence fragments**
   - An apple a day keeps the doctor away.
   - "Are you happy?"
   - "Of course!" (fragment)

2. **The first word in the greeting or closing of a letter**
   - Dear Susan,
   - Sincerely yours,

3. **The first word in a direct quotation**
   - He asked, "Will you promise me that you will come to the game?"

4. **The first word in each line of many poems**
   - *I want to travel the common road*
     With the great crowd surging by,
     Where there's many a laugh and many a load,
     And many a smile and a sigh. (Silas Perkins)

5. **Words in titles***
   - *On Becoming a Teacher: Tales of Tears and Laughter*

6. **Names of continents, countries, states, cities**
   - Africa, Bolivia, Utah, Los Angeles

7. **Organizations***
   - Boy Scouts of America, Parent Teachers Association

8. **Ships, airplanes, spacecraft, etc.***
   - Queen Mary, Spirit of St. Louis, Apollo

9. **Automobiles, trucks, motor vehicles**
   - Chevrolet, Dodge Dakota, Harley-Davidson

10. **Events, historic periods, holidays**
    - Olympic Games, the Middle Ages, Fourth of July

11. **Adjectives derived from proper nouns**
    - Egyptian (Egypt)
    - the Scottish clans (Scotland)

12. **Family relationships when used as a name or part of a name**
    - Uncle Bill, Cousin Sally

13. **Titles of personages***
    - General Douglas MacArthur, Mayor Jones

14. **Days of the week, months**
    - Monday, February

15. **Names of streets***
    - Broad Street, Avenue of the Americas

16. **Names of buildings, parks, schools, bridges, etc.**
    - Empire State Building, Central Park, Lafayette Elementary School, Brooklyn Bridge

17. **Specific physical features***
    - Cape Cod, Mount Kilimanjaro, Strait of Gibraltar

18. **Elements of the universe****
    - Jupiter, Big Dipper, Haley's Comet

19. **Treaties***
    - Treaty of Paris, North Atlantic Treaty Organization

20. **Deities and references to deities**
    - God is in His heaven; Buddha

21. **Abbreviations of organizations**
    - FTA (Future Teachers of America)
    - CIO (Congress of Industrial Organizations)

22. **Personal pronoun "I" when alone and in a contraction**
    - She told me I was lucky.
    - Perhaps I'm too quick to anger.

23. **School subjects that are languages**
    - This year I have one English, one mathematics, and one history class.

Note: As it is important to capitalize letters when required, it is equally important not to over-capitalize. Here is an example of over-capitalization: My neighbor, Jack Armstrong, is the Mayor of our town. *Mayor* should *not* be capitalized because it follows Jack's name; it is a common noun in this case. However, in the following sentence the capitalization is correct because Mayor is used as Jack's title: My neighbor is Mayor Jack Armstrong.

---

*   Except for articles, prepositions, conjunctions (Prepositions of five or more letter are capitalized: about, through, between, etc.)

**   Do not capitalize sun and moon, as they are not proper nouns. Capitalize earth only when it is referred to as a proper noun.

CAPITALIZATION PRACTICE

Draw a circle around the one letter in each item that is incorrectly capitalized or that should be capitalized.

1. I like my spanish class and my history class.

2. We saw governor Wilson at the place where the ceremonies for Memorial Day were held.

3. The headquarters of the Daughters Of the American Revolution is in Washington, D.C.

4. The abbreviation for the Toy Manufacturers of America is TmA.

5. Numerous british people settled in Australia after it was discovered.

6. The little girl said, "My names is Penelope." Her Aunt Mary said, "pretty name!"

7. I visited Uncle Don in Pittsburgh. While I was there a Cousin stopped by.

8. There were several Captains at the meeting called by General Carter.

9. The capital of chile is Santiago, but the country's main port is Valparaiso.

10. One of the most interesting countries in Europe is the Kingdom Of Norway, which is part of Scandinavia. Sweden and Finland are also parts of Scandinavia.

11. Dear President Clinton,
    May I please have your autograph?
    Yours Truly,

12. The straits of Magellan connect the Atlantic Ocean and the Pacific Ocean.

13. Poems are made by fools like me,
    But only god can make a tree.
                              J. Kilmer

14. My birthday is September 22. Last year it fell on friday.

15.
    | Robert Smith |
    | 24 Martin Luther King boulevard |
    | Trenton, NJ 08560 |

16. He said to me, "if you need help, don't be afraid to ask."

17.   *Maine the Beautiful*
    I want to go where the wind blows free,
    where I'm able to see the sea,
    And sit in the shade of the old oak tree;
    While I'm there I'll write some poetry.

18. One of the best books I've ever read is *Life On the Mississippi*, by Mark Twain.

19. The Plymouth sunbird is a really sporty automobile.

20. The Sun is millions of miles away.

21. In the following paragraph no words are capitalized. Put a check (✓) in the space directly over the letters that *should* be capitalized.

the american red cross is an organization that has its headquarters in washington, d.c. in the united states there are millions of people who volunteer their help. clara barton started the organization after the civil war. if you want to find out more about the arc, its address follows:

    811 gatehouse road

    falls church

    virginia

TEST YOUR CAPITALIZATION ABILITY

The following story has numerous capitalization errors. When you find an error, cross out the entire word or words. Then write your correction above what is crossed out. Note that extra spacing has been provided to allow room for writing.

Jonathan and Mike were students in mrs. Bonnelli's Fifth-Grade Class in Valley elementary school. All the students had been told by the Principal, Mr. Grey, not to walk home through Timberland park because it could be dangerous. In the Summer the main danger is Snakes. In the Fall hunters roam the woods in search of Deer. In the winter the trail through the Park is likely to be slippery. Once, in December 1966 several children tried to cross Lake Of The Woods. Two boys fell through the ice, but they were able to make it back to solid ground. They were frozen stiff. The Paramedics from Woodsville came and took them to the Hospital.

One day in the middle of february when there was a half day of School because it was Lincoln's Birthday, Jonathan and Mike disobeyed Principal Grey. They decided to walk home through the Park.

Mike said to Jonathan, "you aren't scared, are you?"

"a little," answered Jonathan. "We have to be careful."

Soon, they reached Big Bass river and began to walk along the Downstream bank. Suddenly, Jonathan stumbled and screamed, "help! i'm trapped!" He was caught in a Spring Trap meant to catch Beaver and muskrats. Neither Jonathan nor Mike was strong enough to release the spring. To make things worse, the trap was chained to a Spruce tree so that captured animals could not drag it away.

There was only one thing to do. Mike ran to a Texaco Gas Station that was about half a mile away. The people there called the Park police, who came and released Jonathan and took him to Overlook hospital.

The boys were not punished, but, as Mike said, "we both learned a lesson."

GUIDELINES FOR PERIODS, QUESTION MARKS, EXCLAMATION MARKS, AND COMMAS

1. *Periods*

a. At the end of declarative sentences or sentence fragments
   - He took a seat in the back of the room.
   - She said, "Nice dress."

b. At the end of abbreviations of certain common nouns
   - abbr. (abbreviation), mi. (miles), yds. (yards), rd. (road)

c. At the end of abbreviated personal or professional titles
   - Mrs. (married woman), Mr. (adult male), Dr. (doctor), Prof. (professor)

d. At the end of numerals or letters as in a list or outline
   - South America's largest countries:
     1. Brazil
     2. Argentina
   - I. American Revolution
        A. Causes
             1. Unfair taxes
             2. Appointed governors

2. *Questions Marks*

a. At the end of a question
   - How old are you?
   - She asked, "May I be excused from class?" He asked, "Why?"

3. *Exclamation Points*

a. At the end of an emphatic statement
   - You should not do that!
   - We won the game! Hurrah! Hurrah!

4. *Commas*

a. At the end of the salutation and the closing of a letter
   - Dear Kelly Lou,
   - With many thanks,

b. To separate cities and states and to separate day of the month from year. If a city and state or full date occur in a sentence, then a comma also follows the state and the year.
   - He was born on September 22, 1962, in Hoboken, New Jersey, in a hospital.
   - Sam Spam
     126 Mine Rd.
     Belvidere, New Hampshire 09754

c. To separate initials in an inverted name
   - Elliot, L. J.

d. To separate words, clauses, or phrases in a series
   - Please be sure to bring cheese, mustard, ketchup, and pickles to the picnic.
   - I was asked to congratulate the winners, to commend the losers, and to thank the sponsors.

e. To separate interruptive words or phrases that facilitate transition and to set off introductory transitional expressions and conjunctive adverbs. A comma is also required to follow a conjunctive adverb when the conjunctive adverb is preceded by a semicolon.
   - Your excuse, nevertheless, is unacceptable.
   - Therefore, having suffered all day, she went home and went to sleep.
   - The speaker was ill; consequently, the lecture was cancelled.

f. To set off independent clauses joined by a coordinating conjunction—and, but, for, nor, or, so, and yet
   - He drove down the street, and he didn't look to the right or left.
   - I want to go, yet I'm reluctant to leave the dog in a kennel.

g. To separate a series of short clauses
   - He played a great game. He ran, he passed, he kicked, he did it all.

h. To separate dependent clauses and phrases from main clauses when the dependent clause or phrase is at the beginning of a sentence
   - If you try hard, you may be able to pass the entrance examination.
   - When in doubt, the best thing to do is to proceed cautiously.

i. To set off an introductory yes or no
   - Yes, I will remember to use commas.

j. To set off nonrestrictive sentence elements
   - My best friend, who has infinite patience, waited.
   - Pennington, which is a lovely town, is near Princeton.

COMMAS AFFECT THE SENSE OF A SENTENCE

In a sentence the same words written in the same order can give two different messages if the punctuation is changed. Here is an example:

a. "Bobby," shouted Sue, "come back here!"

b. Bobby shouted, "Sue, come back here!"

Explanation

* In sentence *a* Sue is doing the shouting.
* In sentence *b* Bobby is doing the shouting.
* In sentence *a* Sue wants Bobby to come back.
* In sentence *b* Bobby wants Sue to come back.

To Do:

1. In the following activity rewrite each sentence. Use the same words in the same order, but change the punctuation. If you do this correctly, the rewritten sentence will be very different in meaning from the original sentence. Remember from the example above that the "trick" is to reposition the quotation marks.

a. "The coach," said the quarterback, "knows his football."

_____

b. "I won't make that mistake again," Eileen promised Jean.

_____

c. "Will you give me another chance?" Bob asked Bill.

_____

d. "Tom," asked Jim, "how long should it take me to fly my Cessna 172 from Trenton to Rochester?"

_____

_____

e. "If you go," Marie cautioned Gina, "don't take the shortcut."

_____

2. The meanings of the sentences that follow can be changed by repositioning the commas, by adding commas, by removing commas, and/or by repositioning the quotation marks. The sentence you write should use the same words and in the same order as the given sentence.

a. "If you help, Dan, we will be grateful."

_____

b. "Don't forget to cook Mary so we can eat."

_____

c. "Frank, the carpenter cautioned us to wear safety goggles."

_____

d. "Tommy said my brother is always playing jokes."

_____

e. "Angela, the attractive blonde, surely will win the beauty contest."

_____

PRACTICE IN CAPITALIZATION AND PUNCTUATION

The items that follow contain errors in the use of capitals, periods, exclamation points, question marks, and commas. Find the errors and then rewrite the item correctly in the second column.

1. I live at 60 Parsons Road Parlin New Jersey

2. Mary asked "how many people live in Ohio!"

3. "No I can't talk to you now," Anne replied.

4. Smiling broadly Bob accepted the certificate

5. Tommy asked in a quiet voice "How much does it cost!"

6. Mary heard the news. She asked, "now what?"

7. Pete Thompson teaches Biology a freshman course at Harvard

8. Here are the things I want for christmas:
   a Soccer ball
   b Nintendo game

9. This is my address: 99 Hill View road Dayton Ohio, 05723

10. Here is the winner of the contest: Bates, Susan A

11. "Pam please pass the paper" said the Teacher.

12. I think you are smart but, you shouldn't brag about it.

13. She shouted, "Great News. Our youngest son Tim made the team!"

14. Dear dr Smith
    thanks for all of your help
    Yours Truly
    Pam S Botts

GUIDELINES FOR APOSTROPHES, SEMICOLONS, COLONS, AND DASHES

1. *Apostrophes (Possession)*

a. Indicate possession in singular nouns—add an apostrophe and s
- The girl's dress was pretty.
- Kindly clean the painter's brush.
- The bear's fur was covered with burrs.

b. Indicate possession in plural nouns not ending in s—add an apostrophe and s
- The women's clothing was colorful.
- We must protect children's rights.

c. Indicate possession in plural nouns ending in s—add only an apostrophe
- The boys' caps blew off their heads.
- All the babies' eyes were turned toward the barking puppy.

d. Indicate possession in impersonal pronouns—add an apostrophe and s
- It was everybody's choice as the best car.
- One's speech is an indicator of one's level of education.

Note: Apostrophes should not be used with personal possessive pronouns—his, its, hers, yours, theirs, ours.
- Golf is his favorite sport.
- The horse flicked its tail.

Apostrophes (Contractions)

a. Indicate omitted letters in combined words, numerals, or a single word
- I'll (I will) help you.
- You've (You have) disappointed me.
- It is three o'clock (of the clock).
- It's (It is) not a good idea to drive when you're (you are) sleepy.
- He graduated in '98 (1998).

Note: Contracted words are sometimes confused with words that sound the same and are spelled similarly.
- You're (Your)
- There's (Theirs)
- It's (Its)

2. *Semicolons*

a. Separate two independent clauses that have a close relationship, and where there is no coordinating conjunction
- It is fun to fly an airplane; it is also a good way to make a living.
- You're a great teacher; I can see that you derive satisfaction from helping people learn.

b. Connect independent clauses where a conjunctive adverb (furthermore, however, consequently, therefore, thus, etc.) is used
- You made a decision; consequently, you will have to live with it.
- You worked hard; thus, you deserve the rewards.

c. Separate words and phrases in a series that has commas within listings
- A complete tool chest should include wrenches; slot and phillips head screw drivers; measuring tools such as callipers, rulers, and micrometers; and crosscut, rip, and scroll saws.

3. *Colons*

a. Act as "signals" to introduce a series or illustration that will follow an independent clause
- The Endangered Animals Conference brought several groups together: scientists, animal rights advocates, state park rangers, and veterinarians.

b. End the salutation of a business letter
- Dear Senator Conover:

c. Separate book and chapter in biblical references, separate titles from subtitles, and separate hours from minutes
- I quote from Luke 5:12.
- *Canada: Emerging World Power*
- We will meet promptly at 12:45.

d. Act to introduce appositives
- There was only one reason for the attack: revenge.

4. *Dashes*

a. Act to enclose parenthetical remarks that intend to give special emphasis or a side thought (interchangeable with parentheses here)
- If you are going to do this—and I strongly disagree—remember that you are on your own.

b. Act to separate a series or illustration from a sentence (interchangeable with colon when the series <u>follows</u> the independent clause)
- Patience, understanding, compassion, and love of children—these are personal characteristics that a teacher should have.

PRACTICE IN APOSTROPHES, SEMICOLONS, COLONS, AND DASHES

1. *Apostrophes*

Following are four sentences in which apostrophes are needed. Insert an apostrophe in the spaced words printed in italics.

a. His *f a t h e r s* car was wrecked on the highway.

b. The *c h i l d r e n s* toys were scattered all over the basement.

c. The *p l a y e r s* uniforms were covered with mud.

d. It is *e v e r y b o d y s* responsibility to obey the laws.

2. *Semicolons*

In the following sentences insert commas and semicolons where needed.

a. I walked the beach looking for seashells however I found only two.

b. Education will help you in many ways it will help you earn a good living.

c. She separated her housewares into several groups: knives for carving meat spreading butter cutting cheese glasses for milk or juice and miscellaneous tools including peelers ladles and scrapers.

3. *Colons*

Rewrite the following items in such ways that you use a colon.

a. Five minutes after two o'clock _____

b. Chapter 2, verse 7, of the section of the Bible called "Acts" _____

c. All workers will attend the meeting carpenters, plumbers, and electricians. _____

_____

_____

d. *Viking Explorers First to the New World*

_____

_____

e. You are interested in only one thing pleasure.

_____

_____

4. *Dashes*

Insert dashes were they are needed in the following sentences.

a. I tried hard harder than ever before to run five miles.

b. Good grooming, clear speech, alertness all will help when you seek a job.

5. *More Practice*

All of the sentences that follow contain one or more errors in punctuation. Correctly rewrite the sentences.

a. "Let me show you how to do it, Bob said."

_____

_____

b. If you like that refrigerator; you can buy it at a reduced price. _____

_____

c. He bought a used 95 Chevrolet Blazer. _____

_____

d. It's color is a mixture of blue and green. ____

_____

_____

e. Youre more than welcome to use the lawn mower. _____

_____

f. Bobs bike has a flat tire._____

_____

g. Try it, you'll like it. _____

_____

h. You may go, however, be careful. _____

_____

i. The newspaper article had the following headline *Earthquake in Nicaragua*. _____

_____

_____

GUIDELINES AND PRACTICE IN SYLLABICATION

Notes on Dividing Words

1. It is considered proper writing practice—and printers follow the practice—to attach a single-letter syllable to the syllable following it or preceding it rather than to let it stand alone. Following are some examples.

*   eventually: even•tu•al•ly
*   abroad: abroad
*   isolate: iso•late
*   voluntary: vol•un•tary
*   portfolio: port•fo•lio

2. Sometimes there is more than one acceptable way to divide a word into syllables. *Webster's New Collegiate Dictionary* points this out in the "Explana-tory Note" section of the book. An example they offer is the word *austerity*, an attitude or atmosphere of severity or sternness. Austerity may be divided as aus•ter•i•ty or au•ster•i•ty. Webster's explains that, for reasons of space, all the possibilities of division are not printed. Also, it may very well be that a dictionary from another publisher might use an alternate syllabication.

Note: The activity below will provide an opportunity for students to practice using a dictionary to find acceptable ways to divide words. It is suggested that the bottom portion of this page be detached and photocopied, or the entire page may be photocopied and kept in students' folders after the activity has been completed.

Dividing Words Appropriately

Assume that you have been assigned to write a paper for your English class. Your problem is that you are not sure of acceptable ways to divide some of the words at the end of a line of print or cursive writing. In such situations a dictionary is your best guide.

The word *fascination* is shown in a dictionary as fas•ci•na•tion. The dots (centered periods) show the breakdown of the word's syllables and indicate that, if the word were at the end of a line, it could end with fas, fasci, or fascina, as shown here:

fas- fasci- fascina-
cination nation tion

Look in a dictionary to determine how the following words could be divided. Be sure to show the centered periods.

*   appetite: _____

*   arithmetic: _____

*   brilliant: _____

*   continuation: _____

*   explanatory: _____

*   fragmentation: _____

*   gymnasium: _____

*   justifiable: _____

*   misery: _____

*   odorless: _____

*   opera: _____

*   particular: _____

*   reorganization: _____

*   revolution: _____

*   souvenir: _____

*   spaghetti: _____

*   tremendous: _____

*   utility: _____

*   vocabulary: _____

*   whisper: _____

SENTENCES THAT MAKE SENSE

All good writers edit their writings before they make a final writing. They look for errors of fact, punctuation, usage, spelling, capitalization, and paragraphing.

One of the most frequent errors has to do with the placement of modifying words within a sentence. Readers may gain an entirely different meaning from what the author intended. Here is an example: *Peter ran down the street shouting "Stop."* The impression given by the arrangement of words is that the *street* was shouting "Stop." The sentence would be clearer and give the correct impression if written this way: *Peter, shouting "Stop," ran down the street.* Notice how "shouting 'Stop'" is placed closer to Peter.

Here is another example of a sentence that doesn't make sense: *The lady sat in the chair chewing gum.* Can *chairs* chew gum? A better way to write the sentence would be as follows: *The lady chewing gum sat in a chair.* Again, notice how "chewing gum" has been placed closer to that which it is modifying.

To Do:

All the sentences that follow are written in such ways that they could confuse readers. Carefully read each sentence, notice its fault, and correctly rewrite the sentence. *Note*: The question after each sentence will help you realize why the sentence doesn't make sense.

---

1. Sue sat at her desk looking unhappy. (Can a desk look unhappy?)

    _____

2. When Mary drove her car down the street wearing a bathing suit people turned and stared. (Do streets wear bathing suits?)

    _____

3. Bobby batted the ball out of the ballpark with a terrific swing. (Does the ballpark have a terrific swing?)

    _____

4. He picked up the scattered coins while everyone watched with greedy fingers. (Who had the greedy fingers?)

    _____

5. Mr. Smith painted the room that he and his father had built with brushes. (Are rooms built with brushes?)

    _____

6. My teacher read from a book about life in France sitting on a stool. (Does France sit on a stool?)

    _____

7. He sang the song that his mother had written with a soft voice. (Can soft voices write songs?)

    _____

8. Amy and Beth swam to the dock at the end of the lake talking constantly. (What did the lake talk about?)

    _____

9. She threw the ball to her teammate over her shoulder. (Was her teammate over her shoulder?)

    _____

10. The comic told the joke to the unimpressed audience laughing hysterically. (Who was laughing hysterically?)

    _____

FRIENDLY LETTERS

1.   Most often, writers of friendly, personal letters use what is commonly known as the *indented* style: The headings and the paragraphs are all indented, as shown in the sample letters below. Also note that the heading and closing are on the right side of the page.

2.   The heading of a friendly letter usually takes three lines. As may be seen in the samples, the first line tells the street address and/or box number of the writer. The second line tells the town, the state, and the zip code. (Notice that there is no mark of punctuation between the state and the zip code.) The third line tells the date the letter was written. Notice that there are no commas at the end of each line in the heading; however, a comma separates the city and the state. A comma also separates the day from the year.

3.   The salutation is on the left side of the page, one skipped space below the heading. Notice that the salutation begins with a capital letter and is followed by a comma. Following are some sample salutations:

- Dear Susan,
- My good buddy, Bob,
- Dear Mrs. Smith,
- Dear Cousin Joan,
- Dearest friend,
- Dear Professor Hill,

4.   The closing of a friendly letter should be in line with the heading and one skipped space below the body. The first word is capitalized; the following words are not. A comma follows the closing.

5.   The signature should begin directly below the first word of the closing. The signature is the writer's "trademark." It's perfectly appropriate to use a nickname in a friendly letter.

6.   Consistent left and right margins should be kept. On a full sheet of paper, three-quarters of an inch would be an appropriate margin.

1275 Spruce Avenue
Hopewell, Iowa 51207
March 10, 1998

Dear Tom,

You can't imagine how much snow has fallen in the past 24 hours. I measured it myself; it was 24" deep. In some places there were 5' drifts. The snow plows buried Dad's car. I shoveled snow for two hours just to make a path from the front door to the mail box.

The snow wasn't all bad, though. We had some fun with our new snowmobile. It was the best way to get around. We were lucky we had it because Mom had a prescription that needed to be filled. When we got to the pharmacy the pharmacist asked if we would deliver a prescription to Mrs. Gray's house, which was about two blocks from our place. So, we did. Mrs. Gray really appreciated it.

So, you're lucky you are vacationing in Florida. You are probably swimming in the ocean at the same time I am swimming in snow drifts.

Give my regards to your family, especially your sister Joan!

Take care,

Steve

916 North Palm Ave.
Ocala, Florida 32741
March 14, 1998

Dear Steve,

I love Florida, but in some ways I wish I could have been with you when all that snow came down. I would have enjoyed riding on your Dad's snowmobile. Maybe your Dad will give me a ride when I get back home. I hope so!

I wish you could have been with me when we visited Disney World. The roller coaster was out of this world. I had three rides in a row, but it still wasn't enough. But the attraction I liked best was "It's a Small World." They take you through a tunnel, and all kinds of scenes come into view as the tiny train moves along the track.

I've got to go now. We're going to Sea World. I'm going to sit in the front row. They say the whales flip their tails and everybody gets splashed.

Bye! Oh yes! Joan says, "Hello."

Best regards,

Tom

WRITING FRIENDLY LETTERS

1. Unscramble the headings below, and write them correctly.

a.	Ocean Grove Maine 14 Ocean Rd. 1998 July 12 01253	
b.	July 1 Ohio 1998 15 Stump St. 07658 Dayton	
c.	1998 Seattle 08631 May 1 10 Bay Rd. Washington	
d.	June 9 1998 23 Block St. Fort Worth 43657 Indiana	
e.	15 Elk Drive 54231 April 9 IA 1998 Elksville	

2. Write the following salutations as they should appear in a friendly letter.

a. dear bobby _____

b. dear aunt molly _____

c. my dear friend _____

d. dear dr. jones _____

3. Write the following closings as they should appear in a friendly letter.

a. yours forever _____

   mark _____

b. with love _____

   brenda _____

c. sincerely yours _____

   uncle tom _____

4. Here is an opportunity to write a friendly letter to a real or imaginary friend. In your letter write two brief paragraphs. It would be helpful to write your letter first on the reverse of this page. Write carefully.

_____

_____

_____

_____

_____

_____

_____

_____

_____

_____

_____

_____

_____

_____

_____

_____

_____

_____

_____

Name: _____ Date: _____

WRITING BUSINESS LETTERS

There are several ways to write business letters; however, if you follow the suggestions and example of the *modified block* style on this page you will be using a proper form.

1.a. Your address and date should be placed in the upper right corner. Notice that there is no indentation.

b. The address of the organization to which you are writing should be on the left side of the page with no indentation. This name and address should be one skipped space below your heading.

c. The body of the letter should be one skipped space below the organization's heading. New paragraphs are not indented, and there should be an extra space between paragraphs.

d. The closing should be directly in line with your heading, and it should be placed one skipped space below the last line of the body of the letter.

Your signature should be written directly below the closing. Then, your name should be typed or printed below your signature.

2. In the next column write a letter in which you are applying for a job as a counselor in a summer camp. In the first paragraph tell what you want. In the second paragraph tell your experience and qualifications.

Your letter is going to John C. Cabot, Camp Mohican, Plattsburg, NY 12903

Note: Since this is an imaginary letter, don't hesitate to "invent" your experiences and qualifications.

12 Spring Street
Paradise, IA 52109
May 15, 1998

Mr. John Smith, President
Acme Trophy Company
16 Commerce Road
Des Moines, IA 52109

Dear Mr. Smith:

I am writing as president of the Paradise County Girls' Basketball League.

At the end of our season we give awards to outstanding players. Awards are given for "Best Fielder," "Best Batter," and "Best Sport." We also have an award for "Coach of the Year."

We would appreciate having a catalog that describes the awards your company makes. We would also like to know the costs of the awards, including lettering.

Yours truly,

Janet Johnson

Janet Johnson

ONE PARAGRAPH—ONE MAIN IDEA

Suggestions for Teaching

1. Make a transparency of the activity in the second column.

2. Present and elaborate on the information that immediately follows these suggestions.

3. Lead students through the **To Do** activity.

4. Assign the following application page for students to complete independently.

1. A paragraph may be defined as a group of related sentences containing information that supports one main idea. The supporting sentences supply detail, sequences, and/or explanation.

2. Sometimes information is included in paragraphs that is not really related to the main idea; the information is irrelevant. Writers should be careful not to include such material. The result of including irrelevant material is negative. Readers become confused, and the main idea may not emerge clearly.

3. Most often, main ideas of paragraphs appear in the opening sentence. However, in some paragraphs the main idea sentence is elsewhere, frequently in the last sentence. Finally, in some paragraphs the main idea is not directly stated but is implicit because the sentences are all related to a particular theme.

To Do:

1. In the next column there are some sentences that are essential to supporting the stated main idea. Also, there are sentences that are not relevant to the main idea and should not be included in the paragraph.

2. Cross out all the sentences that are not related to the main idea.

3. Number the related sentences in the order in which they should appear in the paragraph. The context (meaning) of the sentences will help you decide the order.

Main Idea: To understand how bagpipes are played, one must understand their construction.

_____ a. Finally, attached to a bag, is a blowstick through which the piper blows air into the bag.

_____ b. There are four main parts to a bagpipe.

_____ c. When people think about bagpipes they think of Scotland; however, bagpipes are played all over the world.

_____ d. First, is the bag itself, which is usually made of leather.

_____ e. Bagpipes are played for entertainment, but they were also used in battles to keep the spirit of Scottish soldiers high and to frighten the enemy.

_____ f. Second, attached to the bag are three pipes, called drones; two of the drones are tenor drones and the third one is a bass.

_____ g. A third part of a bagpipe is the chanter, which has eight holes; the note played depends on which holes are covered by the piper's fingers.

_____ h. When pipers pipe, they blow air into the bag through the blowstick; then they squeeze the bag so that air flows through the drones and the chanter.

Main Ideas and Supporting Details in Science

Students can be helped to realize the importance of the main idea/supporting detail organization of paragraphs by relating it to scientific research. For example, research biologists might formulate this hypothesis: Runoff from roads that have been salted during and after a snowstorm has negative effects on animal life in streams and rivers. The biologists would then gather information about stream and river animal life before and after salting: quantity, weight, growth, diseases, spawning, life span. After examining the evidence, they might determine that the salt runoff has negative effects and then report their findings. The approach to the report? The hypothesis is the main idea; the findings are the supporting details. No extraneous details are included.

Name: _____ Date: _____

SUPPORTING MAIN IDEAS OF PARAGRAPHS I

To Do:

Following is a list of main ideas for paragraphs. Select two, or with the permission of your teacher make up two of your own, and write at least five sentences that are *directly* related to the main idea. Do not include any sentences that are not directly related to the main idea.

It would be good procedure to write your paragraphs first on other paper. When you are satisfied with what you have written, copy it on this page.

Be sure your sentences are in logical order.

Some Main Ideas

- There are some good reasons why it is harmful to yourself and others if you are late for class.
- I want to tell you why I think Mr./Mrs./Ms. _____ is an excellent teacher.
- The best friend I ever had was _____, and I will tell you about one event that makes me feel this way.
- If you want to know how to make a supersandwich, here is what you do.
- Everybody tells me that I won't make much money as a teacher, but there are other things that are more important than money.

Paragraph 1	Paragraph 2

SUPPORTING MAIN IDEAS OF PARAGRAPHS II

1. Following are two short paragraphs. Each one has a sentence that doesn't belong in the paragraph because it is not directly related to the main idea. Your task is to read the paragraph and then cross out the irrelevant sentence.

Paragraph 1

There is nothing I enjoy more than a hike on the Appalachian Trail in the autumn. The leaves on the trees are turning from green to brilliant red, orange, and yellow. Views are more easily seen because many of the trees have lost their foliage, and it is possible to look through them to distant hills. The trail runs from northern Georgia to Maine. Also, because of the thinner foliage, it's easier to spy animals such as deer and fox. Another thing I like about fall hiking is that the weather is cooler than summer weather, and I don't perspire as much or get tired as quickly; the air is invigorating. For all these reasons, and more, I recommend fall hiking to all my friends.

Paragraph 2

Why are the waters off the coast of Cape Hatteras, North Carolina, called the "Graveyard of the Atlantic"? Hundreds of ships, mostly the old-time sailing ships, have been wrecked there, and many sailors have lost their lives. Tourists come by the thousands to Cape Hatteras. The cause of the wrecks is a combination of strong winds, currents, and the Diamond Shoals—an area of shallow water in otherwise deep water. When a ship strikes the shoals it becomes stranded. Then, crashing waves break up the ship. Ships with bright warning lights are now anchored beyond the shoals to warn vessels that they are sailing too close to the "Graveyard."

2. Reread paragraphs 1 and 2; then, decide what the *topic* is for each.

Note: Usually topics are not expressed in sentences; they are expressed as titles. Main ideas, however, are expressed in sentences.

Paragraph 1
Topic: _____

_____

Paragraph 2
Topic: _____

_____

3. Following is an opportunity to practice your paragraph writing skills.

Write a paragraph on the topic *What is a Friend?* or, if you prefer, *How to Be a Friend*. Start your paragraph with a sentence that expresses the main idea of the paragraph. Then, follow with four or more sentences that supply details, reasons, or examples that support the main idea.

USING DESCRIPTIVE VERBS

1.   Verbs such as *to walk* and *to run* are much over-used. We use them so frequently that they become boring; they fail to convey interest, anticipation, and the deeper meaning of action. "She walked to the car," does not convey the same feeling of anxiety as, for example, "She scurried to the car." And, "The cat scrambled across the kitchen floor," is much more descriptive of a frightened cat than, "The cat ran across the kitchen floor."

   Sometimes we use unimaginative verbs because we can't think of alternatives. If this is so, a thesaurus will provide synonyms. The positive results of using that reference will be not only improved writing, but also a widened vocabulary and an increased understanding of words encountered during reading and listening.

2.   To stimulate an awareness of alternate words for commonplace actions, read the following list of verbs closely related to the verb *to irritate*.

• pester	• roil
• torment	• harry
• baffle	• harass
• beleaguer	• anguish
• disquiet	• provoke
• badger	• unbalance
• belabor	• scathe
• ruffle	• vex
• hound	• annoy
• aggravate	• irk
• nettle	• rattle
• hassle	• distress
• addle	• trouble
• agitate	• worry
• perturb	• exasperate
• provoke	• needle
• anger	• upset

3.   Present, verbally and/or by transparency, the following pairs of sentences. Discuss the verb choices and the subtle differences between them. Following discussion ask what other action verbs could be used in the sentences. ***Note***: The word in parentheses after each of the items is an additional suggestion.

a.   The fullback *ran* through the opposing line.
        or
The fullback *battled* through the opposing line. (crashed)

b.   The freight train *traveled* down the railroad track.
        or
The freight train *rattled* down the railroad track. (click-clacked)

c.   The young girl trapped in the stalled elevator *called* for help.
        or
The young girl trapped in the stalled elevator *screamed* for help. (shrieked)

d.   You *wrote* an imaginative story about an invasion from outer space.
        or
You *created* an imaginative story about an invasion from outer space. (invented)

e.   The snake *moved* thorough the grass toward the unaware mouse.
        or
The snake *slithered* through the grass toward the unaware mouse. (glided)

f.   The dog *barked* when the veterinarian gave it a shot.
        or
The dog *yelped* when the veterinarian gave it a shot. (yapped)

g.   The window glass *broke* when the baseball hit it.
        or
The window glass *shattered* when the baseball hit it. (fragmented)

h.   She said, "Please, don't *bother* me when I'm working."
        or
She said, "Please, don't *distract* me when I'm working." (annoy)

i.   "Please don't *argue* with me about the incident."
        or
"Please don't *wrangle* with me about the incident." (debate)

USING A VARIETY OF VERBS AND ADJECTIVES

Descriptive Verbs

The following activity will help you to use verbs that are descriptive. Such verbs help those who read what you write better understand and visualize what you are trying to tell them.

1. In each item that follows complete the sentence with an appropriate verb listed in the box at the bottom of the column.

a. It was fun to watch people stop and listen as the baby robins _____ in the bird house.

b. The wild horses _____ across the plain; they were _____ by the helicopter flying overhead.

c. The water _____ over the paddles in the wheel that turned the mill's grindstone.

d. What was it that made Jane a great gymnast? She _____ all movements with confidence, control, and grace.

e. The bully _____ across the playground looking for someone smaller than himself to hassle.

f. The hawk high in the tree _____ its beady eyes over the field.

g. The kilts of the bagpipers _____ around their legs as they played "Scotland the Brave."

h. The audience was _____ by the Irish dancers, whose arms hardly moved while their feet tapped in perfect time.

2. Make up two sentences in which you use an unusual and descriptive verb to describe an action.

a. _____

_____

b. _____

_____

terrified	twittered	swirled
executed	swaggered	tumbled
stampeded	swept	entranced

© 1998 by John Wiley & Sons, Inc.

Meaningful Adjectives

What is true of verbs is also true of adjectives; that is, well chosen adjectives can make your writing more colorful and informative.

1. Each of the words that follow is a noun, which, you will remember, is the name of a person, place, or thing.

Think of four adjectives to describe each noun in the list that follows. Write your adjectives on the blank lines. Be as imaginative as possible. Following is an example:

a. skate boards: _bone-breaking, dangerous, exciting, challenging_

b. the horse: _____

_____

c. Rocky Mountains: _____

_____

d. girl: _____

_____

e. sharks: _____

_____

f. George Washington: _____

_____

g. teachers: _____

_____

2. With your teacher's permission, choose a partner. The two of you are to think of as many words as possible to describe a *line*—any kind of line. Write your adjectives below and on the reverse side of this paper if necessary. Which pair in the class lists the most adjectives? *Note*: only *one* color counts!

_____, _____, _____

_____, _____, _____

_____, _____, _____

_____, _____, _____

_____, _____, _____

REPORTING A STORY—NEWSPAPER STYLE I

1. The writing approach described on this page should prove helpful in organizing not only newspaper-type stories but also other kinds of reports. The fundamental approach of newspaper reporting is to report basic information in the opening paragraph and then, in the subsequent paragraphs, to supply interesting and informative details and/or background information.

2. The basic information and examples that follow may be shown via a transparency or photocopies.

3. The following student application page places students in the positions of (1) analyzing paragraphs for the 5W facts, and (2) writing a paragraph in which they utilize the 5W approach. (The 5W approach is explained below.)

Many newspaper readers may be interested in only the basic or most recent facts of a story. Other readers may want additional details that make the story more meaningful. So, when journalists write their stories they try to give the most important factual information in the first paragraph. Then, in the following paragraphs they supply detail that "rounds out" the story. They write the story in such a way that the least important details are reported at the end of the story. This technique serves the additional purpose of allowing editors to reduce the story's length merely by deleting the ending paragraphs if necessary.

To be sure that all the basic facts are reported in the first paragraph, the writer keeps the following questions, known as the 5W's, in mind: Who? What? When? Where? Why? Following is an example of a 5W paragraph.

> On Wednesday, July 30, at approximately 8:20 p.m., James Forester of 397 Canal Street, Riverdale, fell into the Tennessee River near Block Island and, presumably, drowned. He was thrown overboard, as told by a witness who requested anonymity, when a large, fast-moving powerboat passed his rowboat and swamped it.

An analysis of the paragraph reveals how the 5W reporting technique was used:

- WHO? James Forester

- WHAT? His boat capsized; Forester is presumed drowned

- WHEN? Wednesday, July 30, 8:20 p.m.

- WHERE? Tennessee River near Block Island

- WHY? Forester's rowboat swamped by a larger powerboat

Paragraphs following the first paragraph would offer more detail. For example:

> A search for Forester's body was carried out by the Riverdale Marine Rescue Squad. Two divers searched the river bottom where the accident occurred. Although several articles believed to be the victim's were discovered, the body was not. The divers reported that the search was difficult because the current was very strong, there was very little light, and the river bottom was covered with debris—sunken logs, ruptured metal tanks, and, surprisingly, a wrecked boat with the name *Flying Fish* still readable on the bow. Diver George Matthew said that the boat appeared to have been there "several years." The search will continue tomorrow.

© 1998 by John Wiley & Sons, Inc.

REPORTING A STORY—NEWSPAPER STYLE II

1.   Newspaper reporters write their stories with the 5W formula in mind. The 5W's are Who? What? When? Where? Why?

2.   Read the following account written in the style of the first paragraph of a newspaper article. Then, complete the 5W's following the story.

> On Saturday, August 13, Marianne Dorcas and a companion, Thomas Duncan, were hiking the Appalachian Trail on the Pennsylvania side of the Delaware Water Gap. Suddenly, a brown bear protective of her two cubs trailing behind confronted them. The two experienced hikers stopped in their tracks, kept their bodies perfectly still, and stared the bear down. After a tense wait of about 30 seconds, the bear and cubs turned and lumbered away. The hikers continued on and, upon meeting a forest ranger, reported the incident.

WHO? _____

WHAT? _____

WHEN? _____

WHERE? _____

WHY? _____

3.   Following the first paragraph the reporter could expand the story with more detail. The paragraph below is an example of what could have been written.

> Bears are becoming more and more common in the Appalachian Mountains of northern New Jersey and eastern Pennsylvania. This is because hunting laws protect them, and they have no natural enemies. The reported confrontation of the two hikers is only one of such incidents. Female bears have a strong protective instinct for their cubs. Since the bear sensed no hostility on the part of the hikers, she was willing to leave the scene. In an interview, Marianne Dorcas said that any movement on their part could have brought about a "disastrous encounter, with the bear probably winning."

4.   Write the first paragraph of a newspaper article in which you apply the 5W's formula. Refer to the example in the first column for guidance.

After you've written the paragraph, analyze it and state the 5W's.

Finally, write a second paragraph in which you supply detail relative to the first paragraph. The event you choose to report should be the product of your own imagination. Write rough drafts of your articles before writing in the spaces in this column.

_____

_____

_____

_____

_____

_____

_____

_____

_____

_____

WHO? _____

WHAT? _____

WHEN? _____

WHERE? _____

WHY? _____

The spaces below are to be used to write the second paragraph.

_____

_____

_____

_____

_____

_____

_____

_____

_____

_____

MAKING YOUR WRITING MORE INTERESTING I

Writing can be made more interesting in various ways. Perhaps the most obvious way is to use adjectives, adverbs, and verbs that vividly describe the events and people about which you are writing. The use of such words helps keep your writing from being monotonous.

Following are some additional suggestions relative to enlivening your writing.

Inverted Sentences

An inverted sentence is one that doesn't follow the usual order in which most sentences are written. Changing the position of phrases and clauses is one way to invert sentences. Here are two examples:

Ordinary: The boy frantically ran down the steps.
Inverted: Down the steps the boy frantically ran.

Ordinary: The wolf pack was hot on the trail of the deer.
Inverted: Hot on the trail of the deer was the wolf pack.

1. Invert the following sentences in the manner described and illustrated above.

a. The test was given in the last period on Friday.

_____

_____

b. I will try to do my best in the future.

_____

_____

c. Olivia took the train home, torn by her decision.

_____

_____

d. If you would pick up a newspaper on your way home from school, I'd appreciate it.

_____

_____

_____

e. The plane left the landing strip in a sharp climb.

_____

_____

Combining Short Sentences

The inclusion of a short sentence in a piece of writing can be very useful; short sentences can make a strong impact on the reader. However, too many short sentences can be boring and slow down the reading and understanding process. Often, one complex sentence can express what two, three, and even four short sentences can express. Following is an example of how four short sentences may be combined in one "flowing" sentence.

Jim carried his skateboard up the steps.
He mounted his skateboard.
He clattered down the steps.
He didn't fall.

Jim carried his skateboard up the steps, mounted the board, and clattered down the steps without falling.

1. Combine the following short sentences into one sentence.

We went to a football game.
It was exciting.
The game ended in a tie.

_____

_____

Challenge: Combine the three sentences in a different way.

_____

_____

_____

2. The airplane's propeller stopped spinning.
The airplane lost altitude.
It landed safely on a deserted stretch of highway.
Suggestion: Start your combined sentences with "Although" or "Even though."

_____

_____

_____

_____

_____

MAKING YOUR WRITING MORE INTERESTING II

Combining Sentences

There are several ways to make smooth sentence combinations. One such way is through the use of subordinate clauses. Another way, which can be used in conjunction with subordinate clauses, is to join two sentences with a coordinating conjunction—and, but, or, nor, for, yet, so. Here is an example of the techniques used together:

John ordered a hamburger.
Pete ordered a hot dog.
John asked for ketchup.
Pete asked for mustard.

Combined sentences: John, who ordered a hamburger, asked for ketchup, and Pete ordered a hot dog with mustard.

Notice in the example that the clause *who ordered a hamburger* is set off from the rest of the sentence by commas because it is nonrestrictive in nature. Notice also that the two independent clauses are joined by a comma and the coordinating conjunction "and."

To Do:

1. Combine the four short sentences that follow by using a clause that starts with who and a coordinating conjunction.

Mary's part in the play was to be a fairy.
Sue's part was to be a witch.
Mary carried a wand.
Sue rode on a broom.

_____

_____

_____

_____

2. Here is another opportunity to use a clause that starts with who and a coordinating conjunction to join short sentences.

John didn't know how to add fractions.
He was getting discouraged.
Mary noticed his struggles.
She showed him how to do them.

_____

_____

_____

_____

Quoting What People Say

If you were writing a story, one of your sentences might be something like this: *The farmer said that he hoped that he would have a good crop of corn*. This is a perfectly good sentence. However, the farmer's exact words are not quoted. Another way to write the sentence could be as follows: *The farmer said, "I hope that I will have a good crop of corn."*

The thing to realize is that it is helpful to vary how you write what people say. Sometimes you should quote exactly, and sometimes it is not necessary. If you do quote exactly what has been said, there are some punctuation rules you should remember.

1. If the sentence begins with a phrase such as *She said*, place a comma and a space before the first quotation marks.

2. Capitalize the first word of the quotation.

3. If the sentence ends with a quotation, put a period, a question mark, or an exclamation point before the closing quotation marks.

Here is another example of how to punctuate a sentence with a quotation: Sue asked, "What time will the dance begin?" Notice the question mark at the end of the quoted words is placed before the final quotation marks because it applies to the quoted material.

To Do:

On the blank lines that follow write sentences that end with quotations.

Example 1: A quotation that ends with a period.

_____

_____

_____

_____

Example 2: A quotation that ends with a question mark or exclamation point.

_____

_____

_____

_____

MAKING YOUR WRITING MORE INTERESTING III

Quotations at the Beginning of Sentences

Sometimes you may want to write a complete quotation at the beginning of a sentence and then tell who the speaker is at the end of the sentence. Here is an example: "I didn't like the movie; there was too much violence," she complained.

You can see that the quotation is still set off by a comma and quotation marks.

However, if the quotation is a question, a comma isn't placed at the end of the quotation. Rather, a question mark is used. The same would be true if the quotation ended with an exclamation point. Here is an example: "May I go with you?" asked the little boy.

Notice in the first example above that the ordinary *she said* is not used. A more descriptive phrase was used: *she complained*. As much as possible write descriptive phrases; they help the reader better understand what is happening. Here is a short list of alternate phrases:

Tom shouted, " . . ."
She screamed, " . . ."
Pam whispered, " . . ."
Frank mumbled, " . . ."
Lorna blurted out, " . . ."
Father warned, " . . ."

To Do:

On the blank lines that follow, write sentences that begin with a quotation and end with the identification of the person speaking. Also, try to use some of the phrases listed above, or some of your own invention, that better express the feeling of the speaker.

Example 1: Quotation ending with a period.

_____

_____

_____

_____

Example 2: Quotation ending with a question mark.

_____

_____

_____

_____

Interrupted Quotations

Sometimes quotations that are interrupted have greater impact on the reader than straightforward quotations. In any case, interrupted quotations can add variety and interest to your writing. Here is an example of an interrupted quotation: "Children," mother said, "please take off your shoes when you enter the house."

Notice that the punctuation is different in an interrupted quotation.

1.   The sentence opens with quotation marks.

2.   The quotation begins with a capital letter, just as the beginning of any sentence would.

3.   At the point of interruption there is a comma followed by quotation marks.

4.   After the interruption there is a comma, and a new set of quotation marks is opened so the sentence of the interrupted quotation can continue.

5.   At the end of the quotation there should be a period, question mark, or exclamation point.

6.   Quotation marks close the sentence.

To Do:

Revise each of the following sentences so that the quotation is interrupted and then continues.

1.   The teacher explained, "If you want to get good grades you have to study."

_____

_____

_____

2.   Dad said, "You'll feel better tomorrow, when the exam is over."

_____

_____

_____

3.   He warned, "Riding a motorcycle is fun, but you have to be careful."

_____

_____

_____

USING WORDS THAT HELP READERS VISUALIZE

In the list that follows what do you notice about the words that are used to group the animals?

- a *labor* of moles
- a *skulk* of foxes
- an *army* of ants
- a *business* of ferrets
- a *clash* of rhinoceroses

If you said that the group names reflect particular characteristics and actions, you are correct. Moles are constantly digging tunnels. To dig a tunnel requires labor (work). So, we have a *labor* of moles. Foxes are thought to be sly and devious; they slink or *skulk* while searching for prey. Ants are known to move from place to place in large numbers, much as a real army would; so, we have an *army* of ants. Ferrets are small animals that give the impression of being very quick and businesslike in their movements and habits. It is fit to call a group of them a *business* of ferrets. Rhinoceroses are so big and clumsy that they *clash* into each other and the things around them.

What does this have to do with writing? Good writing requires the writer to observe and imagine and, sometimes, to use language in exciting and unconventional ways. A person who wants to write effectively must continually try not only to describe things and events accurately, but also to make the writing engaging. If done often and consciously enough, using one's imagination and a variety of words becomes a habit of the writer.

To Do:

Following is a list that includes animals, people, and things. Your task is to try to think of a group name that characterizes what the group does or what it represents. Here are sample names for a grouping of automobiles:

- a *rolling* of automobiles
- a *motoring* of automobiles
- a *wheeling* of automobiles
- an *exhaust* of automobiles

Here is another example that has to do with *geese*. Ask yourself this: What is characteristic of geese? If you have observed geese you know that they "honk." So, why not a *honking* of geese? You have probably also observed that they fly in V-formation; so, why not call a group a *wedge* of geese?

Here is your list for which you are to make group names?

1. skateboarders:

_____

2. hockey players:

_____

3. teachers:

_____

4. bicycles:

_____

5. sailors:

_____

6. snow skiers:

_____

7. glue bottles:

_____

8. cheerleaders:

_____

9. gliders:

_____

10. police:

_____

11. piano players:

_____

12. cats:

_____

13. hot air balloons:

_____

SIMILES AND METAPHORS STIMULATE IMAGINATIONS

Soup can be nourishing, yet uninteresting to the diner. However, if a few spices are mixed into the soup the result can be delightful eating. Likewise, writing—fiction or nonfiction—can be informative but dull and boring. Without colorful words and expressions there is the possibility that the reader will doze off in the middle of a page.

Comparisons made by similes and metaphors are as helpful to writing as spices are to soup. An apt comparison can bring smiles to the faces of readers or, perhaps, contribute an insight that might otherwise not come. "She was as nervous as a mouse nibbling the cat's food," does more to stimulate one's imagination than a simple, "She was nervous."

Some similes and metaphors, however, have become overworked to the point where they have lost their power to stimulate the imagination. "As smooth as glass" and "He was as clumsy as an elephant" are but two examples.

Suggestions for Teaching

1. Be sure that students know what similes and metaphors are. Both are comparisons. A simile employs *as* or *like* to link the things being compared. A metaphor, on the other hand, makes a comparison by stating that something *is* something else familiar to the reader or listener. A metaphor is much more direct than a simile: *as* and *like* are not used.

Example of a simile: "She was as methodical in her typing as a woodpecker tapping a tree trunk."

Example of a metaphor (same two objects compared): In her typing she was a woodpecker methodically tapping a tree trunk.

2. Write the adjective "strong" on the chalkboard. Then, encourage students to "brain storm" by offering suggestions as to how the adjective may be used in comparisons.

Suggestions:
- oxen
- bulls
- Atlas
- Hercules
- iron rods
- concrete
- gravity

- oak tree
- steel cable
- team of horses
- vine
- hurricane
- ocean tides
- linked chain

3.a. Write the word *fast* on the board.

b. Tell students to think of words related to *fast* that could be used in similes and metaphors.

c. List contributions on the board.

d. After a list has been compiled tell students that they are to compose one simile or metaphor in which one of the listed words is used.

e. After a short work period have students read their creations.

Suggested list of words related to *fast*:
- racing cars
- cheetahs
- race horses
- light
- shooting stars
- computers
- satellites
- rockets
- house flies
- lightning
- sound
- electricity
- blinking eye

4. It may be that students who are talented in art can draw cartoon-like representations of their similes and metaphors. The results could make an interesting and attractive bulletin board.

Here is a description of a cartoon metaphor in which a man's arms are likened to "linked chains." He is holding on to another worker who has fallen off the scaffold. The arms of the worker who is holding his coworker are shown as chains with fingers on their ends. Beneath the cartoon is a caption, "His arms were linked chains holding his friend who had slipped off the scaffold."

ABBREVIATIONS IN WRITING

Abbreviations of Organizations

In writing it is frequently necessary to mention the names of business, government, social, fraternal, and other kinds of organizations. Sometimes the organization's name may have to be referred to several times. Repeating a long name such as the Daughters of the American Revolution can be tedious to the writer and boring to the reader. Here is an acceptable way of avoiding such repetition:

1. After the first time the organization's name has been given, write its abbreviation in parentheses. Example: Daughters of the American Revolution (DAR). Then, in the remainder of the writing refer to the organization by its abbreviation.

2. Notice in the DAR example that the preposition "of" and the article "the" are not included. Prepositions and articles are omitted in almost all abbreviations of organization names.

3. Another thing to remember about organization abbreviations is that a period is rarely placed at the end of the abbreviation.

Here are the abbreviations for some well known organizations:
AAA: *American Automobile Association*
AFL: *American Federation of Labor*
AMA: *American Medical Association*
IRS: *Internal Revenue Service*
NAACP: *National Association for the Advancement of Colored People*
NATO: *North Atlantic Treaty Organization*
NFL: *National Football League*
SPCA: *Society for the Prevention of Cruelty to Animals*
VFW: *Veterans of Foreign Wars*

Nonorganization Abbreviations

There are occasions in writing when common abbreviations are used. ASAP is an example. If a quick reply to a letter is needed, it is requested As Soon As Possible (ASAP).

Below are some other frequently used abbreviations:

BA: *Bachelor of Arts* (college degree)
BC: *Before Christ* (before Christ was born)
CEO: *Chief Executive Officer*
bu.: *bushel*

e.g.: *for example*
ft.: *foot*
hr.: *hour*
i.e.: *that is*
IQ: *Intelligence Quotient*
RN: *Registered Nurse*
SASE: *Self-Addressed Stamped Envelope*
SRO: *Standing Room Only*
UFO: *Unidentified Flying Object*
VCR: *Video Cassette Recorder*

To Do:

Read the following sentences carefully; then fill in the blanks with appropriate abbreviations from the lists on this page.

1. If you became a doctor you'll probably join the _____.

2. When you send for our catalog please enclose a _____.

3. The AFL and the _____ have playoffs in the fall to decide which teams will play in the Super Bowl.

4. After you receive your _____, you can work toward your Master of Arts (MA).

5. The claim that a _____ had been sighted over Kansas proved to be false.

6. If you observe someone being cruel to an animal you can call the _____.

7. The _____ investigates if they suspect someone is cheating on his or her income tax.

8. Large companies have a _____, who is in charge of the entire company.

9. Fortunately, an _____ was present when the accident occurred.

10. When we saw the _____ sign posted at the ticket box, we knew we wouldn't get seats.

11. Those who have served in the United States armed forces are eligible to become members of the _____.

12. If you are a member of the _____ you may have ancestors who were part of George Washington's army.

NOTES

Section 7: Reading and Research

GUIDELINES FOR ALPHABETIZATION

Alphabetization may be the first and most essential of all research skills. It is probably the most common arrangement for listing information. Indexes, dictionaries, glossaries, encyclopedias, telephone books, library file cards, and other items are all alphabetically arranged. Volumes within an encyclopedia set are, for example, alphabetically ordered, and each volume in a set has alphabetically arranged entries.

Understanding and using alphabetization goes far beyond the recitation of the alphabet letters in sequence, although, of course, memorization of the alphabet is the first step. Following are some elements of alphabetization that students should know and develop.

1. *Determining the letter that comes before or after a particular letter in the alphabet*. Students should be so familiar with the alphabet that they are able to make an immediate response to questions such as "What letter follows G? or What letter precedes L?"

2. *Knowing the approximate position of a letter in the alphabet*. When searching for a word in a dictionary, for example, it is more efficient to know approximately where in the book the section is for words beginning with the first letter of the word in question. Suppose the word begins with *m*. To what part of the dictionary would one open? (Middle) To what part would one open the book if the first letter of the word was *f*? (First quarter) Once the approximate placement of the word is found, there should be a minimum amount of turning the pages backward or forward to find the needed word.

3. *Knowing that it is often necessary to go beyond the first letter of a word to find the word in a listing.* It will probably be necessary to look at the second, third, fourth, or even fifth letters of the listed words to find the desired word. For example, if one was searching for the word *martial* in an index, it might be preceded or followed by several words beginning with *mar*: marry, Mars, marsh, mart, martial, martyr, marvel, marvelous.

4. *Knowing that proper nouns beginning with such words as Saint, Mount, and Point may be listed in one of two ways depending upon the particular reference*. Some references use abbreviations instead of the full words—for example, Saint Ambrose or St. Ambrose, Point Pleasant or Pt. Pleasant, Mount Hood or Mt. Hood, and so on. The *World Book Encyclopedia* and *Webster's New Collegiate Dictionary* use full words for such entries as mentioned above; however, the *World Almanac and Book of Facts* uses abbreviations: St. for Saint, Mt. for Mount, and so on.

Another special situation exists in the case of *Mac* as in *MacBeth*. In searching for MacBeth in a listing, students should treat the name as being a succession of continuous letters, that is, *Macbeth*.

In the case of *Mc* as in *McCarthy*, the approach is to find the end of the list of words that end with *ma*. The *Mc* words will then begin. After all the words with *Mc* have been listed, the next word in the listing will resume alphabetical order. For example, in the *World Book Encyclopedia* the last *Mc* listing is *McPherson*. Immediately following *McPherson* is *Mead*.

The following page will offer your students opportunities to practice the skills described above. However, as much as possible, alphabetical skills should be practiced within the context of the subject matter of the curriculum. For example, in studying a chapter on the American Revolution, students might be asked to list the names of the American patriots in alphabetical order, each name to be accompanied by a brief description.

PRACTICE IN ALPHABETIZING

Level 1: Alphabetizing Groups of Words

Put a check before the word in each grouping that should be first in an alphabetical listing.

1. ____ class
   ____ pocket
   ____ airplane
   ____ dog

2. ____ hat
   ____ flag
   ____ cot
   ____ park

3. ____ also
   ____ hit
   ____ chop
   ____ punch

4. ____ yellow
   ____ brown
   ____ green
   ____ red

5. ____ car
   ____ truck
   ____ bus
   ____ motorcycle

6. ____ Young, Tim
   ____ Jones, Andy
   ____ Miller, Mary
   ____ Owens, Susan

7. ____ June
   ____ March
   ____ August
   ____ November

8. ____ Mars
   ____ Jupiter
   ____ Saturn
   ____ Pluto

9. ____ Buick
   ____ Dodge
   ____ Chevrolet
   ____ Ford

10. ____ turnip
    ____ spinach
    ____ peas
    ____ lettuce

Level 2: Alphabetizing Groups of Words

In each grouping, number the words in the order in which they would be alphabetized.

1. ____ cut
   ____ cap
   ____ cape
   ____ caper

2. ____ run
   ____ runner
   ____ rung
   ____ runt

3. ____ Honduras
   ____ Honolulu
   ____ hogs
   ____ hockey

4. ____ Madagascar
   ____ Magellan
   ____ Madeira Islands
   ____ Magna Carta

5. ____ cancer
   ____ canals
   ____ Canada
   ____ canoe

6. ____ Hispanic
   ____ Himalaya Mountains
   ____ Hindus
   ____ Hibernians

7. ____ preliminary
   ____ pressure
   ____ presume
   ____ prediction

8. ____ conform
   ____ continuous
   ____ conifer
   ____ conference

9. ____ fortunate
   ____ Fort Knox
   ____ forfeit
   ____ fortuitous

10. ____ probable
    ____ probably
    ____ prohibit
    ____ productive

Level 3: Alphabetizing Groups of Words

In each grouping, number the words in the order in which they would be alphabetized.

1. ____ Parsons, John
   ____ parson
   ____ Parsons, James
   ____ Parsony, June

2. ____ Grand Canyon
   ____ Great Basin
   ____ Grand Teton
   ____ Great Smoky

3. ____ pneumonia
   ____ pseudonym
   ____ psychology
   ____ psychiatric

4. ____ knowledge
   ____ knowing
   ____ knot
   ____ knob

5. ____ Westwood
   ____ West Windsor
   ____ western
   ____ westward

6. ____ science
   ____ scientific
   ____ scimitar
   ____ scissor

7. ____ Patterson
   ____ pattern
   ____ patriot
   ____ pathetic

8. ____ predict
   ____ predicate
   ____ predatory
   ____ predictable

9. ____ MacArthur
   ____ machine
   ____ MacAdoo
   ____ match

10. ____ May
    ____ McNab
    ____ maze
    ____ Mazda

USING THE TABLE OF CONTENTS

UNITED STATES HISTORY BEFORE THE CIVIL WAR

TABLE OF CONTENTS

In which chapter of the Table of Contents above would you first look to find information about each of the following topics? Write the number of the chapter on the line before each topic.

_____ The war between the French and the English

_____ The failed English settlements on Roanoke Island

_____ Recreation in the English colonies

_____ The French settlement of Quebec on the St. Lawrence River

_____ The first people to enter North America from Asia

_____ Viking settlements in North America

_____ Problems in creating the United States constitution

_____ Spanish explorations in what is now Southeast United States

_____ Americans object to English laws forbidding settlement in former possessions of France

_____ Relations between Indians and William Penn, the founder of Pennsylvania

_____ Freedom of religion in the English colonies of Rhode Island and Maryland

_____ The struggles of the first successful English colony at Jamestown

_____ Indian reactions to the landing of Columbus in the New World

_____ What it was like to be a slave or an indentured servant in the English colonies

_____ The British plan for defeating the rebelling American colonies

GUIDELINES FOR USING INDEXES

Following are aspects—other than alphabetization—of using an index that should be brought to your students' understanding and then practiced.

1. *Understanding the punctuation marks that are used in indexes*. The four main punctuation marks used in indexes are the comma, semicolon, dash, and parentheses.

Commas are used in index entries to separate items that are related, as, for example, the first and last names of a person. In example *A* also note that the numeral does not have *page* or *p* before it; this is a convention of indexing.

> **A   Washington, George, 15**

In example *B*, commas tell the searcher that coffee is mentioned on page 27 and page 36. However, there is an extended discussion of coffee—indicated by the dash—starting on page 55 and ending on page 59.

> **B   Coffee, 27, 36, 55–59**

Sometimes items related to a major category are listed alphabetically on separate lines under the main heading, as in Example *C*.

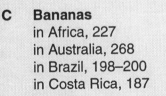

> **C   Bananas**
> in Africa, 227
> in Australia, 268
> in Brazil, 198–200
> in Costa Rica, 187

Example *C* could be arranged in another book as exemplified in *D*. Note that in such instances a semicolon is used to separate major items and that the items are still listed alphabetically. Note also that the second line of the listing is indented and that there is no period at the end of the listing.

> **D   Bananas:** in Africa, 227; in Australia, 268; in Brazil, 198–200; in Costa Rica, 187

Example *E* utilizes parentheses to indicate that there is a map on page 39, and a picture of a ski resort on page 172. An index may also use paren-

theses to indicate the page location of other graphics such as charts, tables, graphs, and diagrams.

> **E   Appalachian Mountains:** barriers to settlement of, 42; coal mining in, 107; location of, 39 (map); as source of lumber, 98; national parks in, 199–201; ski resorts in, 172 (picture); trees of, 206–210

2. *Cross-referencing*. Index searchers should not be discouraged if the listing for which they are searching does not appear in an index. An index may list a particular item in a variety of ways. Searchers should think of elements that are associated with or related to the item they have in mind and then search for them. For example, if they are seeking information on *Open-pit mining* and don't find such a listing, they might look for *Mining*, *Mines*, or *Industries*.

A searcher might be interested in knowing more about a particular kind of tree, such as *Hemlock*. Suppose *Hemlock* is not listed, what are some alternate listings? *Forests*, *Conifers*, *Trees* are three possibilities.

Indexes often suggest alternatives and/or additional sources of information. The example that follows shows how such help may be given.

> **Flying as a hobby,** 21–23. *See also*
> Planes, single engine

Suggestions for teaching

1. The examples in boxes on this page could be xeroxed and cut out, made into a transparency for an overhead projector, and projected as the instructor explains the elements of indexes.

2. The exercises on the facing page offer opportunities for students to practice using indexes.

It would also be helpful to devise similar activities on subjects being currently taught, perhaps history or science. For example, in their basic history textbook students could search for all the references to a prominent person such as Abraham Lincoln. Next, they could locate the references in the pages of their textbook and compile a "List of Facts About Abraham Lincoln."

Name: _____ Date: _____

USING INDEXES

The questions below can all be answered from information printed in the Index in the opposite column.

1. Which page would probably tell you the names of the southern colonies?　　　Page _____

2. On which page would you probably find information about colonial "dame schools"?
　　　　　　　　　　　　　Page _____

3. On which page would you find information on the Franklin stove, an invention of Benjamin Franklin?
　　　　　　　　　　　　　Page _____

4. Which page would probably tell you the date that Harvard College was started in the Massachusetts colony?　　　Page _____

5. Which pages probably describe or display a flag of Texas when it was an independent country?
　　　　　　　　　　　　　Pages _____

6. On which page would you be most likely to find the name of the tribe of Indians to which Sacajawea, an Indian guide, belonged?
　　　　　　　　　　　　　Page _____

7. Imagine that you want to find the width of the Bering Strait. Which page would be most likely to help you?　　　Page _____

8. On which pages would you look to find the names of the inventions of Cyrus McCormick?
　　　　　　　　　　　　　Pages _____

9. In which section of pages would you look first to find general information about the Algonquin Indians?　　　Pages _____

10. On which page would you probably find information about the discovery of gold at Sutter's Mill in California?　　　Page _____

11. What is the total number of pages on which there is information about Texas? _____ pages

12. Within which major entry would you place the following reference: *Square dancing*, 77?

_____

13. Are there any references in the Index that might give you information about the Spanish-American War of 1898? _____ Yes _____ No

DICTIONARY GUIDE WORDS AND MULTIPLE DEFINITIONS

Guide Words in Dictionaries

Dictionaries, telephone books, encyclopedias, and other reference books use *guide words* or phrases to help readers find words, names, or topics. Guide words are useful because they increase a searcher's efficiency by decreasing page-turning. In some dictionaries, for example, there may be as many as 75 words on a single page, and a section containing all of the words beginning with *a*, for example, may be 50 to 100 pages long.

1. In dictionaries, guide words are printed in the top margin of a page. Page numbers are also printed in the top margin. Here is an example top margin:

fresh–frill	**60**

The example tells you that *fresh* is the first word on the page and *frill* is the last word on the page. So, if a searcher is looking for a definition of *frigate* and reads the guide words, the searcher will know that frigate is somewhere on page 60. *Frigate*, alphabetically speaking, lies somewhere between *fresh* and *frill*.

2. Which of the following words would *not* be listed on page 60?

_____ fret	_____ frisk	_____ friar
_____ frigid	_____ frost	_____ fragile
_____ friction	_____ frieze	_____ fright
_____ front	_____ frolic	_____ freight

3. Imagine that you are an editor arranging words in a dictionary. You are devising guide words for the list of words that follow. The words are not in alphabetical order. Put a check (✓) in front of the two guide words you would have printed in the top margin.

_____ pudgy	_____ pug	_____ pulley
_____ puffer	_____ pugnacious	_____ pull
_____ puddle	_____ puck	_____ pueblo
_____ publish	_____ pudding	

Multiple Definitions of One Word

The meaning of a word often depends on how it is used in a sentence. This is because some words have multiple meanings. One dictionary, *Webster's New Collegiate Dictionary*, has more than 50 definitions for the three-letter word *set*. Set can be used as a verb, a noun, or an adjective.

Following are a few of the meanings for *set*:

- ■ **"set" as a verb**
  - To set a trap for catching animals, criminals, etc.
  - To set a time for visiting friends, for an appointment, etc.
  - To set a nail below the surface of wood, placing a picture on the wall, etc.
  - To become solid or to thicken as, for example, Jello sets, paint sets, etc.

- ■ **"set" as a noun**
  - Several things that have a close relationship such as a set of dishes, tools, etc.
  - A part of a game such as a set of tennis
  - An arrangement on a stage for a play, for example, a set made to look like a schoolroom

- ■ **"set" as an adjective**
  - Having a fixed and unchangeable opinion as, for example, a set way of thinking
  - Having a fixed and unchangeable habit as, for example, a set way of driving

Activity

Circle the letter at the end of each sentence that tells how *set* is used in each sentence. Circle *N* if *set* is used as a noun, *V* if it is used as a verb, and *A* if it is used as an adjective.

a. The children drew a diagram of the set for the first act of their play.   V   N   A

b. She was a stubborn person; she had a set mind that nobody could change.   V   N   A

c. The screws on the deck were set one-quarter of an inch below the surface. V   N   A

d. The drill bits were arranged in a set from the smallest to the largest.   V   N   A

e. The door was set so that an alarm rang if the door was opened.   V   N   A

f. The club set the time for the meeting as Friday at 2:00 p.m.   V   N   A

g. The concrete set in about three hours.
                                                        V   N   A

USING THE LIBRARY CARD CATALOG

1. Some libraries have card catalogs to help you locate books. This page will help you learn how to use the card catalog.

2. Below is a diagram of a card catalog with ten drawers. Some large libraries may have a card catalog with 100 or more drawers. Regardless of size, all card catalogs are used the same way.

Card Catalog

A-CZ	G-GY	K-MY	S-SZ	U-VRI
1	3	5	7	9
D-FYL	H-JU	N-RY	T-TY	W-ZWC
2	4	6	8	10

3. Filed in the card catalog are three cards for every book, as follows: *Author* card, *Title* card, and *Subject* card. The three kinds of cards are shown below. Notice that the basic information about the book is the same on all three cards.*

```
C       Miller, Alfred G.
599         The story of a whale.
M       Illustrated by Helen Damson.
        New York. Action Press (1964)
            114 p. illus.

    1. whale.          I. Title
                                (Author Card)
```

```
C       The story of a whale.
599
M       Miller, Alfred G.
            The story of a whale.
        Illustrated by Helen Damson.
        New York. Action Press (1964)
            114 p. illus.

                                (Title Card)
```

```
C       WHALE.
599
M       Miller, Alfred G.
            The story of a whale.
        Illustrated by Helen Damson.
        New York. Action Press (1964)
            114 p. illus.
        1. whale.
                                (Subject Card)
```

4. The name of the *author* of the book on the sample cards will be found on a card in drawer 5 because, as you can see, his name begins with *M*.

The *title* of the book can be found on a card in drawer 7 because the title begins with *S*.**

The *subject* of the book, which is a whale, will be found on a card in drawer 10 because the subject begins with the letter *W*.

To Do:

1. On the blank line following each item below write the number of the drawer where you would find cards for the following authors.

a. Walker, John _____   b. Botts, Gary _____

2. Write the number of the drawer where you would find cards for the following titles.

a. *All About Planets* _____

b. *The Last of the Mohicans* _____

3. Write the number of the drawer where you would find a card for each of the following subjects:

Caves_____   Oceans_____   Zebras_____

4. The catalog cards contain important information about books. Study the sample cards; then, answer the following questions.

a. What is the full title of the book?

_____

b. What is the full name of the author?

_____

c. How many pages are in the book? _____

d. What company is the publisher of the book?

_____

e. When was the book first published? _____

f. Who is the illustrator (one who draws pictures) for the book?

_____

g. Where in the library is the book shelved, that is, what is its *call number*? _____

* The cards have been reduced in size; original cards are larger.

** If a book's title begins with *The*, use the second word in the title to locate its card.

© 1998 by John Wiley & Sons, Inc.

USING ENCYCLOPEDIAS I

Information About Encyclopedias

Sets of young people's encyclopedias have much in common; however, there are significant differences among sets. Time and energy, not to mention frustration, can be saved if students are made aware of how the various sets of encyclopedias at their disposal are organized. Generally, the first volume of a set contains specific information about the set and how to use it. A class period devoted to explanations and specific encyclopedia exercises can pay great dividends over a lifetime.

Following is some general information about encyclopedias.

• Encyclopedias are organized in volumes, each of which is identified alphabetically and numerically. For example, the *A* volume will also be numbered as *1*; the *B* volume as *2*, and so on. Some volumes contain topics that span two, three, or even four letters. For example, *World Book* has one volume for *N* and *O*, one volume for *U* and V, and one volume for *W, X, Y* and *Z*.

• Within a particular volume, topics are arranged alphabetically. In the number 1 volume of *World Book*, the first topic treated is the letter *A* and its historical development; the last topic in the volume is *Aztec*.

At the end of major encyclopedia articles, a list of related articles or cross-references may be found. For example, in a treatment of Alaska some aspects of the state may be given slight attention. However, a list of related articles will include topics found in the same volume or another volume of the encyclopedia. Four Alaska-related articles listed may be Gold Rush, Alaskan Highway, Caribou, and Yukon River.

Indexes are another useful research resource found in all encyclopedias. The index may be contained in a single volume that indexes the entire set, or there may be an index at the end of each volume. Some encyclopedias, such as *The New Book of Knowledge*, contain an index at the end of each volume and a single-volume index as the last book in the set. The indexes are studded with cross-references. For example, the entry for *mining* would list every article in the entire set that sheds light on the subject.

Research Questions

The purpose of the following activity is to help students develop knowledge and skill in the use of encyclopedias. The answers to the questions that follow can be found in almost any young people's encyclopedia. The questions can be photocopied and used as a learning center activity, or the questions can be answered by students—perhaps in groups of two—during a library period.

It is suggested that this activity be completed after the activity on the following page.

1. Animals may be classified as *carnivorous* (meat eaters), *herbivorous* (vegetation eaters), or _____ _____ (eaters of both meat and vegetation).

2. The New Jersey signers of the Declaration of Independence were _____, _____, _____, _____, and _____.

3. What three oceans touch upon the shores of Antarctica? _____, _____, and _____.

4. What is the state bird of Nevada?

_____

5. What United States President is pictured on the $20 bill? _____

6. How long is the Panama Canal from end to end? _____ miles

7. Who was president of the United States after William H. Taft and before Warren G. Harding?

_____

8. Anthony Wayne was a famous patriot general during the Revolutionary War. What was his nickname? _____

9. The city of Pittsburgh, Pennsylvania, is at the confluence (junction) of two rivers, the _____ _____ and the _____.

10. In what state is Susquehanna University?

_____

Name: _____ Date: _____

USING ENCYCLOPEDIAS II

1. Imagine that the books shown above represent a typical set of encyclopedias as displayed on a book shelf. Notice that the books have letters and numbers. What is the *number* of the volume (book) you would first search to find information on the topics that follow?

a. Forests: _____

b. George Washington: _____

c. Famous dams: _____

d. Topeka (a state capital): _____

e. The Empire State Building: _____

f. Automobiles: _____

g. Virginia: _____

h. Yellowstone National Park: _____

i. The Ural Mountains: _____

j. The Bering Sea: _____

k. Methods of mining: _____

2. Imagine that you are looking for information on the topics listed below. What two volumes would most likely supply you with the information you need?

a. Mount Everest in the Himalaya Mountains

Volume#_____ and Volume#_____

b. President Ulysses S. Grant

Volume#_____ and Volume#_____

c. The planet Jupiter

Volume#_____ and Volume#_____

d. Fishing in the Grand Banks

Volume#_____ and Volume#_____

e. The Holland Tunnel in New York City

Volume#_____ and Volume#_____

f. Duke University, North Carolina

Volume#_____ and Volume#_____

g. Mining bauxite in Arkansas

Volume#_____ and Volume#_____

h. The discovery of gold in California

Volume#_____ and Volume#_____

i. Origination of Mothers Day as a holiday

Volume#_____ and Volume#_____

j. The liberation of Argentina by San Martin

Volume#_____ and Volume#_____

k. How heated air makes a balloon rise

Volume#_____ and Volume#_____

3. In what volume would you look *first* to find answers to the following questions?

a. What professional baseball player has hit the most home runs in a season? _____

b. What was the name of the first nuclear submarine? _____

c. In what city is the Liberty Bell displayed?

_____

d. In what year did Oklahoma become a state?

_____

GUIDELINES FOR USING ALMANACS

1. How are almanacs useful sources of information?

• Facts related to events that occurred during the year or years previous to the publication date have been gathered and organized in one volume.

• Information is offered on a great variety of subjects, the scope of which is so wide that a page of this size filled with small print could not include a complete list.

• Information is printed clearly and precisely with no attempt to influence the reader with opinion, figurative language, flowery adjectives, or unbalanced presentations.

• Tables and charts are used copiously to present information. A typical almanac contains hundreds of tables on such diverse topics as *Hazardous Waste Sites in the U.S.* and *World Track and Field Records*.

• The information presented is from reliable sources such as the United States Bureau of the Census, the United States Department of Energy, and the International Amateur Athletic Organization.

• The indexes are exceptionally inclusive, organized into main topics, and profusely cross-referenced. One entry, *Nebraska*, in the *World Almanac and Book of Facts*, serves as a typical example with 25 subtopics. Nebraska, however, is no exception; each state has a comparable number of subtopics—California has 31.

Suggestions for Helping Students Understand Indexes

1. Obtain at least one copy each of the most popular almanacs. The list would include *The World Almanac and Book of Facts*, *Information Please Almanac*, and *The Universal Almanac*.

2. Photocopy and distribute a page from the index of one of the almanacs. Then, make a transparency of the page.

3. Project the transparency, and then ask questions that will cause your students to respond actively.

Following are examples of the kinds of questions to ask. They are based on page 25 of the *Index* for *The World Almanac and Book of Facts, 1996*.

a. On what pages can we find biographies of the presidents? (530–531)

b. On what page are the zip codes for Puerto Rico listed? (445)

c. On what page can we find information about the major reservoirs in the U.S.? (707)

d. Suppose that we wanted to find information about the Revolutionary War. When we look for such an entry, we find that the index refers us to another entry. What is the reference? (*see American Revolution*)

e. We are interested in locating information about rainfall in the United States. What does the almanac tell us to do? (*see Precipitation*) Under *Precipitation* four page numbers are listed. At the end of the listing the searcher is told to "*see also Blizzards.*"

As may be seen from the one entry, *Rainfall*, we are led to several different locations in the almanac. Thus, we see that the almanac is "user friendly."

2. Suggestions for a learning center activity based on the *World Almanac and Book of Facts*:

a. Assume the class is studying about the environment. Find "Environment" in the almanac index. Scan the pages referred to in the listing.

b. Make 15 to 20 questions on aspects of the environment that you know are specifically answered. Typical questions:

• Which state has the most hazardous waste sites?

• What is the total number of hazardous waste sites in the United States?

• How many endangered species are there in the United States?

• How much money was allocated to the Environmental Protection Agency in the latest year listed?

BASIC REFERENCE BOOKS

Following is a brief list of kinds of reference books and specific reference books that can be helpful when it is necessary to research for specific facts.

1. *Atlas: A book of maps*. The index lists all the places located and shown on the maps. The page number and the quadrant where the place is located is usually given. Example: Las Vegas, p. 99, E-2 (E-2 means that Las Vegas is somewhere in that quadrant.)

2. *Dictionary: A book of words alphabetically arranged*. Following each word are pronunciations, derivations (where the word originated, and the base word), its part of speech (noun, verb, adjective), and the various meanings of the word depending on how it is used. Often, synonyms of the word are given.

3. *Thesaurus: A listing of words and their synonyms*. Thesauruses are useful to writers; they help them to make their writing more interesting. For example, in *Soule's Dictionary of English Synonyms,* the word *beg* is followed by more than 30 synonyms, each carrying a slight difference in meaning from the original listing.

4. *Bartlett's Dictionary of Quotations: Quotations from the writings of well known authors*. The quotations are alphabetized by author. Some authors have only one quote, while others are quoted much more extensively. For example, there are 2,422 quotes from the writings of William Shakespeare. Quotes range from ancient times to modern times.

5. *Statistical Abstract of the United States: A book of tables with statistical information*. The tables in the *Abstract* reveal thousands of facts about the United States, including population, elections, manufacturing, energy, and others. If information about egg production is needed, for example, the *Abstract* will tell you about it in the table titled "Egg Production Supply and Use." The *Abstract* contains more than 1,400 tables.

6. *Encyclopedia: A series of volumes or a single book that contains information on hundreds of topics*. Most sets of encyclopedias, such as *World Book* and *Encyclopedia Americana,* contain 15 or more volumes with topics listed in alphabetical order. Subjects covered range from "Alaska," to "Mexican War," to "Zoo."

7. *Reader's Guide to Periodical Literature: A listing of articles published in magazines such as* Time *and journals such as* Earth Journal. Listings are arranged alphabetically by topic. A typical topic is *Terrorism*; a typical title is "Terror at the Olympics." The *Guide*, as it is commonly called, is published monthly; issues for a particular year are collected and bound in one volume.

8. *World Almanac: A book of facts that is published yearly*. A typical world almanac will contain 900 or more pages. Tables and many brief accounts of events are included. Every country in the world is listed, and numerous facts such as population, economy, history, and form of government accompany each listing. Does someone want to know which college was national football champion in a particular year? The *World Almanac* will tell you.

At the end of each question circle the number of the reference book you would *first* use to find the answer.

1. In the most recent year how much corn was produced in Iowa?   1 2 3 4 5 6 7 8

2. In which state is the city of Dubuque located?   1 2 3 4 5 6 7 8

3. What is the last word in this quote from Lincoln, "The ballot is stronger than the _____"?   1 2 3 4 5 6 7 8

4. What team won the American League pennant in 1946?   1 2 3 4 5 6 7 8

5. What are five words that have almost the same meaning as malicious?   1 2 3 4 5 6 7 8

6. Where can I find a recent article that is concerned about drug abuse in schools?   1 2 3 4 5 6 7 8

7. What is the correct pronunciation of *theatre*?   1 2 3 4 5 6 7 8

8. Where can I find information on the causes, fighting, and results of the American Revolution?   1 2 3 4 5 6 7 8

9. Where can I locate a chronological listing of the major world events of the past year?   1 2 3 4 5 6 7 8

10. From what language did the English word *school* come?   1 2 3 4 5 6 7 8

11. In the past year has *National Geographic* printed an article about the shrinking tropical forests?   1 2 3 4 5 6 7 8

12. Was it Joyce Kilmer or Henry Longfellow who wrote, "I think that I shall never see a poem lovely as a tree"?   1 2 3 4 5 6 7 8

13. Are there more than ten communities in the United States that have the name Springfield?   1 2 3 4 5 6 7 8

14. Since there has been so much concern about the ill effects of smoking, has the United States' production of tobacco declined in the past ten years?   1 2 3 4 5 6 7 8

USING VARIOUS REFERENCE BOOKS

The game show "JEOPARDY!" is one of the most popular programs on television. The contestants, always three in number, are presented with facts on a wide variety of subjects, including history, geography, books, presidents, and so on. The contestants have to ask a question that is answered by the fact presented. For example, a fact might be "After President Lincoln was assassinated, this vice-president (?) took over the presidency." The winning question would be, "Who was Andrew Johnson?"

To Do:

Use encyclopedias, almanacs, and other reference books such as textbooks to make questions that are answered by the facts presented below. Write your questions on the blank lines that follow the facts.

Note: The question mark in parentheses (?) after a word or words, indicates what your question should be directed toward.

1. In North Carolina, this city (?) was named after the person who was the organizer of the first attempt to start an English colony in the New World.

_____ ?

2. Alaska is the largest state; the second largest is Texas; the third largest is California; and the fourth largest is this state (?), whose capital is Helena.

_____ ?

3. When the Scots on the island of Great Britain were in battle, these musical instruments (?) were often played to encourage the soldiers to fight harder.

_____ ?

4. The small, mountainous country of Andorra lies between these two (?) much larger countries.

_____ and

_____ ?

5. This object (?) is missing from this Mother Goose rhyme:

"Jack be nimble, Jack be quick,
Jack jump over the __?__ .

_____ ?

6. John Adams was the first president of the United States who was a graduate of this first college (?) established in what is now Massachusetts.

_____ ?

7. Lake Champlain, the largest lake in Northeast United States, lies between New York and this much smaller state (?) to New York's east.

_____ ?

8. Earth, the third planet from the sun, is next to this planet (?), which is named after the Roman god of war.

_____ ?

9. In our national anthem, "The Star Spangled Banner," the author tells about the British bombardment of this fort (?) located on Chesapeake Bay and just south of the city of Baltimore.

_____ ?

10. At a baseball game, fans see the bat hitting the ball before they hear the sound of the bat, especially if they are sitting far out in the bleachers. This is because light travels through air at about 186,000 feet per second; this is very fast compared to this speed (?), which is about 1,100 feet per second.

_____ ?

11. One of the causes of the Spanish-American War was that in February 1898 this American battleship (?) was blown up as it lay at anchor in the harbor of Havana, Cuba.

_____ ?

12. This large island (?) south of Australia is the home of some animals not found any place else.

_____ ?

13. Zoology is the study of animals, and this (?) is the study of handwriting.

_____ ?

LOCATING INTERESTING UNITED STATES FACTS

This activity will involve students in research that should result in a table of facts.

Suggested Procedure

1. Suggest books that will be helpful in finding data:
- *World Almanac and Book of Facts*
- *Information Please Almanac*
- *Guiness Book of Records*

- Encyclopedias (*World Book, Colliers, Americana, Britannica, The New Book of Knowledge, Compton's,* etc.)

2. Students may work cooperatively in groups of two.

3. Set a time limit of, perhaps, two weeks for completion of the table.

4. Facts are to be listed in the table below.*

INTERESTING UNITED STATES FACTS			
Item	**Name**	**Location**	**Detail**
Largest state		-----------------	Square miles:
Smallest state		-----------------	Square miles:
Highest mountain			Height:
Lowest point			Feet below sea level:
Last state to enter the U.S.A.		-----------------	Date:
First state to enter Union		-----------------	Date:
Tallest building			Height:
Largest indoor stadium			Seating for conventions:
Longest river (not combined)		-----------------	Length in miles:
State with most counties		-----------------	Number of counties:
State with least counties		-----------------	Number of counties:
Roller coaster, tallest			Height:
Largest lake totally in U.S.			Square miles:
Deepest lake			Depth:
Northernmost city			Latitude:
Highest waterfall drop			Drop:

* Spaces under Location that have dashed (-----) lines do not have to be completed.

© 1998 by John Wiley & Sons, Inc.

INTERVIEWING A PERSON FOR A NEWS STORY

One kind of research newspaper reporters often do is to interview people. When doing so they may use a form that guides them in their questioning. After the interview they take the information and write a story.

Your task: Interview a person who is somewhere near the age of 40 or beyond. Take brief notes on the form below. Clip the form to a hard board for easier writing. Bring extra paper for more detailed notes.

PERSONAL INTERVIEW

1. What is your name?_____ What do your friends call you?_____

2. When were you born? _____ What town? _____ What country? _____

3. What are one or two of your very earliest memories before you started school?

    _____

    _____

    _____

4.a. What was the name(s) of your elementary school(s)? _____

   b. How did you get to school from your home? _____

    _____

   c. What was your favorite subject? _____ Least favorite? _____

   d. Please use five adjectives to describe the best teacher you ever had.

   _____, _____, _____, _____, _____

   e. What was one amusing/humorous incident that happened to you or your classmates while you were in

   elementary school? _____

    _____

    _____

5. What is, or was, your main occupation? Please explain. _____

    _____

6. What is your favorite food? _____

7. What two books have you recently read that you enjoyed the most and that you would recommend?

    _____ and _____

8. What is the name of the best movie you have ever seen? _____

9. What person in history do you most admire? Why? _____

    _____

    _____

10. Do you have any hobbies or things that you especially like to do?_____

    _____

11. If you were asked to give two special bits of advice to young people growing up in today's world, what

   would they be?

   a.   _____

   b.   _____

A PRIMARY RESEARCH PROJECT ABOUT AIR AND AIR POLLUTION

Title: Survey of Knowledge About Air and Air Pollution

Background: Solutions to environmental problems can only be developed if there is awareness and concern of individuals; community, political, and social groups; commercial and industrial organizations; and government at all levels. A classroom is composed of individuals. As a group they can help other students and adults be aware of our pollution problems.

An effective way to bring about pollution awareness is to circulate an air/air pollution questionnaire, collect it, collate the results, and then distribute the results with correct answers. In addition to raising the consciousness of respondents, such a project will afford your own students an experience in conducting primary research.

Procedure: 1.   Photocopy the survey on the following page.
2.   Have your own students respond to the questionnaire.
3.   Distribute the questionnaire to other teachers who are willing to have their students participate.
4.   Collect the questionnaires.
5.   After all the questionnaires have been collected, have your students score them and then collate the results. The tally form below will help in this effort. You and your students should offer the survey results to cooperating teachers so that they and their students can also benefit from it.

RESULTS OF AIR/AIR POLLUTION SURVEY					
Questions	**A***	**B***	**C***	**D***	**Correct Answers**
1					
2					
3					
4					
5					
6					
7					
8					
9					
10					

*   The numbers under columns A, B, C, and D tell how many respondents made that answer choice in each of the questions.

© 1998 by John Wiley & Sons, Inc.

SURVEY OF KNOWLEDGE ABOUT AIR AND AIR POLLUTION

Explanation: Our class is learning about the environment. As one of our activities we decided to conduct a survey to find out what other students know about air. We hope that by responding to the questions students will become more interested in air. We also hope to learn what students do and do not understand about air and air pollution so that environmental education can improve.

After we have collected all of the surveys and tallied the answers to the questions we will tell you the answers and results.

Please understand that this is not a "test." Neither your name nor your teacher's name is on the questionnaire.

Directions: Circle the letter of the correct answer.

1. Which one of the following adds the most oxygen to air?
   A: Oceans   C: The sun
   B: Trees   D: The atmosphere

2. Circle the one way that nature does not pollute air.
   A: Volcano eruptions   C: Dust storms
   B: Forest fires   D: Tidal waves

3. Circle the one way that acid rain does not harm the environment.
   A: Damages metal statues   C: Pollutes outer space
   B: Destroys trees   D: Kills fish

4. Circle the one statement about air that is not true.
   A: It has weight.   C: It expands when heated.
   B: It contains some solids.   D: There is less nitrogen than oxygen in air.

5. Circle the one statement about air that is not true.
   A: The higher one goes up into the atmosphere, the more air there is.
   B: It is possible to crush a can with air.
   C: A balloon filled with air is heavier than a balloon of the same size with no air.
   D: Air rises when it is heated.

6. Circle the one statement that is not true about temperature inversions.
   A: Hot air is trapped below a layer of cold air.
   B: They can only occur above oceans.
   C: People may get sick and even die during a temperature inversion.
   D: Pollutants cannot escape into the upper atmosphere.

7. Circle the one statement that is true about radon gas.
   A: It is created when trash is burned.   C: It kills people instantly if breathed.
   B: It is dropped on the earth by jet planes. D: It is present in many homes.

8. Which one of the following adds the most pollution to air each year in the United States?
   A: Smoking cigarettes, cigars
   B: Transportation vehicles such as cars and trucks
   C: Factories
   D: Spraying crops

9. About how many tons of all pollutants are poured into the air each year in the United States?
   A: 50 million tons   C: 150 million tons
   B: 90 million tons   D: 220 million tons

10. Which one of the energy sources listed below pollutes air the most?
    A: Solar energy   C: Hydroelectric energy
    B: Nuclear energy   D: Fossil fuel energy (gas, oil, coal)

© 1998 by John Wiley & Sons, Inc.

INFORMATION GAINED THROUGH EXPERIMENTATION I

Conducting research in books is, perhaps, the most frequent research task students will experience. But, as was seen in the survey of knowledge about air and air pollution (RR–15,16) there are other ways to obtain information, especially information of a primary nature, that is, information generated by the researcher.

Still another way to conduct research is by the approach known as the *scientific method*. It is a classic approach used by scientists of every level of experience. There are variations, but the basic approach is as follows.

1. *A question is asked*. There is something the researcher wants to find out. Here is a sample question: Will frozen lima beans sprout into plants?

2. *A hypothesis is stated in declarative sentence form*. A hypothesis is a suggested answer. It is only an opinion, an opinion that has to be proved true or false. Here is an example hypothesis for the question asked above: Lima beans that have been frozen will not become plants.

3. *The hypothesis is tested in a controlled experiment*. In the lima bean experiment the design could be laid out as follows.

a. *A general experimental scheme is designed*. Obtain a bag of lima beans. Freeze 2 beans, and select 2 other beans not to be frozen. Plant the seeds in four pots. Observe for ten school days.

b. *Operational definitions of words and terms are stated*. An operational definition is one that defines by an action. For example: When does a seed become a *plant*? *A seed becomes a plant when it has emerged at least two inches above ground*. A second example: When is a seed considered *frozen*? *A seed is considered frozen when it has been in the freezing compartment of a refrigerator for 24 hours and water that was placed in the freezing compartment at the same time is completely frozen*.

c. *Controls are arranged*.
   (1) All soil from same source
   (2) All pots to receive equal water simultaneously
   (3) All pots to receive equal sun
   (4) All seeds planted same depth
   (5) All seeds planted in same kind of pot

d. *Daily procedures are identified, organized, and distributed*.
   (1) Watering: one-half cup to each pot, 8 a.m., daily
   (2) Pots to be turned 180° at noon each day

4. *Daily observations are made and recorded*. Some form of graphic and/or recording form is nec-

Day	Seed 1: Frozen	Seed 2: Frozen	Seed 3: Unfrozen	Seed 4: Unfrozen
1	no	no	no	no
2				
3				
4				
5				1/2 inch
6			1/2 inch	
7				
8	ETC.	ETC.	ETC.	ETC.
9				
10				

5. *Data is studied for growth, relationship, predictions, patterns, etc.*

6. *Conclusions are drawn*.

a. *Primary conclusion*: The data shows the original hypothesis is _____

b. *Secondary conclusion*: (if any) _____

_____

_____

_____

7. *The experiment is reported*. A laboratory report is written that includes all pertinent information: Dates, participants, hypothesis, conclusions, drawings and diagrams, etc.

Suggestions for Teaching

1. Distribute the blank form shown on the following page.

2. Explain the experiment as outlined above. Students should take notes.

3. Actually perform the experiment in the manner described. After ten days arrive at a conclusion relative to the truth or falseness of the hypothesis.

INFORMATION GAINED THROUGH EXPERIMENTATION II

1. *A question is asked.*

_____

_____

2. *A hypothesis is stated in declarative sentence form.*

_____

_____

3. *The hypothesis is tested in a controlled experiment.*

a.   General experimental scheme: _____

_____

_____

_____

_____

b.   Operational definitions:

(1) _____

_____

_____

_____

(2) _____

_____

_____

_____

c.   Controls:

(1) _____

_____

(2) _____

_____

(3) _____

_____

(4) _____

_____

(5) _____

_____

d.   Daily procedures:

(1) _____

_____

(2) _____

_____

4. *Daily observations are made and recorded.*

Day	Seed 1: Frozen	Seed 2: Frozen	Seed 3: Unfrozen	Seed 4: Unfrozen
1				
2				
3				
4				
5				
6				
7				
8				
9				
10				

5. *Data is studied for growth, relationships, predictions, patterns, etc.*

6. *Conclusions are drawn.*

a.   Primary conclusion: _____

_____

a.   Secondary conclusion(s): _____

_____

7. *The experiment is reported.*

Title: _____

Dates: _____

Participants: _____

_____

Hypothesis: _____

_____

Conclusions: _____

_____

_____

_____

Drawings and Diagrams:

GUIDED RESEARCH IN MULTIPLE BOOKS I

1. Multiple reading and resources should be used in teaching social studies, science, and other subjects when there is a need for the learner to find the answers to a variety of questions.

2. Some rationale for the method:
   - All children do not have the same reading ability.
   - Students should be comfortable using more than one source to obtain information.
   - Learners should become increasingly responsible for their own learning.
   - Learners should develop independent work-study skills such as reading, researching, organizing, and preparing information.
   - Whenever possible the methodology used by the teacher should utilize the principles of individualization: Learners proceeding at their own pace on their own levels of ability, interest, and need.
   - Teachers are free to work with the slower children because they are not instructing the entire class.

3. A suggested method of organizing and implementing a multi-resource approach:
   a. Decide on the topic (Clothing, for example).
   b. Research the topic yourself in a good encyclopedia, various children's texts, filmstrips, etc.
   c. Divide the main topic into a number of subtopics. In the case of clothing some subtopics might be as follows:

   | - Cotton | - Skins | - Clothing and occupations (Firemen, cowboys, etc.) |
   | - Wool | - Synthetics | - Clothing and climate |

   d. Obtain source materials including books, pictures, filmstrips, realia, etc. Be sure they are actually available for the children's use in your classroom and/or the library.
   e. Compose specific questions under each topic that you know are answerable from the resources you have gathered.
   - Ask a variety of questions that will require a variety of response methodologies:

   | - listing | - diagramming | - true-false | - complete sentences |
   | - sketches | - outlining | - multiple choice | - fill-ins |

   - For some questions give very specific clues as to where the answers can be found; for other questions give limited clues.
   f. Explain the procedure to the children. (Read the questions; reach agreement on standards of behavior; give instruction on using indexes; etc.)
   g. Periodically call the class together and discuss progress.

Notes:

A. The work can be completed in one period or may go for as long as 10 to 15 periods.

B. It is sometimes desirable for the children to work in pairs.

C. If you use pictures, it is helpful to number them for easy reference.

D. Eventually, the need for highly structured questions decreases. Then, more general questions may be posed along with some subquestions. For example:

Major: What part did the French play in developing North America?

Sub: Who was Cabot and where did he explore?

Sub: In 1763 what parts of North America were claimed by the French?

GUIDED RESEARCH IN MULTIPLE BOOKS II

The following is an <u>abbreviated</u> example of how research experiences may be arranged for learners who have not had much prior experience.

Unit: Clothing

Cotton

1. Make a list of the states in the United States where cotton is grown. Write the names of the states in order from the highest producer to the lowest. See the map on page 77 of *Your Country and Mine*.

(1) _____

(2) _____

(Allow room)

2. Make a list of the steps a farmer takes when he grows cotton. See *Workers at Home and Away*, Chapter 2.

(1) _____

(2) _____

(Allow room)

Note: There would be other questions relative to cotton as a fiber for making cloth. Try to arrange the questions in developmental fashion. Notice that in the two questions above there is a sequence from where cotton is grown to how it is grown.

Wool

1. In the following list, all of the animals produce wool except three. Look in the *World Book* under "Wool" for more information. Check all those that are wool producers.

_____	rabbits	_____	raccoons
_____	camels	_____	deer
_____	cows	_____	sheep
_____	lambs	_____	alpacas
_____	llamas	_____	goats

2. After wool fibers are washed and combed, a _____ machine twists the wool into yarn.

3. With a magnifying glass examine some of the raw wool on the display table. What do you notice about the ends of the fibers?

_____

_____

Make a sketch that shows what the fibers look like.

(Allow room)

Describe what the raw wool feels like when you touch it.

_____

_____

Clothing and the Kind of Work People Do

1. *Workers Near and Far* shows a picture of a cowboy with his working clothes. Tell how he uses each item of clothing listed below:

Chaps _____

Bandanna _____

Hat _____

2. Look on page 7 of *Learning About Latin America*. Are most of the people dressed in light colored clothing or dark colored clothing? _____

Explain why the clothing is colored as it is from what you read in your science book, *Science at Work*. Find the page numbers under *insulation* in the index of the book.

_____

_____

3. The Sahara Desert in North Africa is very warm during the day. Yet, the picture on page 175 of *Living in Africa* shows people with long robes and head coverings. What is the explanation for such warm-looking clothing? The caption to the picture will tell you.

_____

_____

_____

(Allow room)

NOTES

ANSWER KEY

Section 1: Reading for Deeper Meanings

<u>**Reading for Deeper Meanings (R)**</u>

R–4   **Practice in Scanning II**

1. 52 mph
2. 60 miles
3. Carbon monoxide

4. Nancy Wittenberg
5. Lacks fast getaway

R–6   **Determining Paragraph Topics**

1. a. Mike's Personal and Physical Qualities
   b. A Repaired Guitar for Mitzi

2. a. Tom's Tool Box (Suggested)
   b. Pam's Basketball Practice (Suggested)
   c. Why Luke Wants a Job (Suggested)

R–8   **Determining Main Ideas**

2. Topic: Early Homes in the Great Plains (Suggested)
   Main idea: Early Great Plains homes were built with sod.

3. Main idea: Many (other) kinds of horses are used for different purposes.
   Topic: The Many Uses of Horses (Suggested)

4. Main Idea: Taking minerals such as iron or copper ore from the surface of the earth is called strip mining. (1st paragraph)
   Topic: The Strip-Mining Process (1st paragraph)

   Main idea: Strip-Mining is a great contributor to soil erosion. (2nd paragraph)
   Topic: Strip-mining and Soil Erosion (2nd paragraph)

R–9   **Combining Details to Reach Conclusions**

Wind Energy (1st paragraph)

1. a. Do as one thinks is right or as one chooses
   b. Come and go as one pleases
   c. Choose one's life's work
   d. Choose one's companions

2. a. Clean
   b. No cost
   c. No one deprived of property
   d. Supply never diminishes

3. Wind energy has many advantages. (Suggested)

Wind Energy (2nd paragraph)

1. Nearly six times more

2. a. Need for energy will increase.
   b. Oil will become increasingly expensive.

3. Wind is the energy source of the future.

© 1998 by John Wiley & Sons, Inc.

R–10 Comparing Accounts of the Same Event

Details in Agreement

- Man runs out of bank
- Man wore blue denim trousers
- Man had revolver in right hand
- Black and red jacket
- Cherry-red car
- Redheaded driver
- Car turned on to Harding Drive
- First letters of license plate: "AWE"
- Security guard shouted
- Security guard fired one shot
- Car almost hit old lady

Details in Disagreement

- Height of man: 5'9" or 6'2"?
- Hair: Blond or red?
- Hat: Yes or no?
- Left hand: Bundle or bandage?
- Jacket: Striped or checked?
- Shoes: Tennis or hiking?
- Age: 25 or 50?
- Car: Chevrolet Blazer or Ford Explorer?
- Driver: Woolen hat or bareheaded?
- Car turn: Left or right onto Harding Drive?

R–11 Recognizing Cause-and-Effect Relationships I

1. Cause: Discouragement and disappointment about not going to West Point

2. Cause: Overheated engine
   Effect: Madeline is stranded and cries.

3. Effects:
   - On the outcome of the game: Playoff elimination for losing team
   - On the fan who caught the ball: Admiration on the part of some fans; television appearance
   - On the players on the losing team: Loss of thousands of dollars
   - On the center fielder who didn't catch the ball: Disagreement with the umpire and ejection from the game
   - On one of the losing player's plans to help his mother and father: The plans could not be carried out.
   - On the mother and father: Continued to live in rough part of the city and were robbed

R–12 Recognizing Cause-and-Effect Relationships II

1. Effect Column (from top to bottom): g, e, a, c, b, h, d, f

2. a. . . . the boy jumped out of the way of the car.
   b. . . . he was late for his appointment.
   c. . . . she had to withdraw from the tennis tournament.
   d. . . . Joan being late for class.
   e. . . . he was recognized at the town's "Heroes Banquet."
   f. . . . flooding in every street in town.

   Note: All the above answers are suggestions; answers will differ.

3. a. The brush fire got out of control, so . . .
   b. The enemy had twice as many soldiers, so . . .
   c. When Tom made a basket from midcourt in the final second of the game, . . .
   d. The pond became filled with algae, which consumed the oxygen, so . . .
   e. She realized she didn't have enough money for gas, so . . .
   f. After he read that tobacco can cause cancer, . . .

   Note: All the above answers are suggestions; answers will differ.

R–14 Words That Signal Opinions

Words to be Circled

1. Apparently	8. surmised	15. don't think; probably
2. guess	9. belief	16. alleged
3. prediction	10. Perchance	17. chance
4. possibility	11. seems	18. point-of-view
5. supposition	12. conjectured	19. inference
6. speculated	13. likely	
7. hypothesis	14. theory	

R–15 Determining If a Statement Is Provable

1. a. NP	f. P	k. P
b. P	g. NP	l. NP
c. P	h. NP	m. P
d. NP	i. NP	
e. P	j. NP	

2. Note: The number in ( ) indicates the line(s) where the opinion is expressed.
   - Nobody was ever more frightened . . . (1)
   - I'd say that it was . . .(3)
   - To me, it looked like . . . (4)
   - I'll bet that . . . (9)
   - I probably broke . . . (13)
   - . . . and not too soon, either. (17)
   - I don't think . . . (19)
   - You'll probably . . . (23)

R–16 Fact and Opinion in History

1. • Report, magazine, letter, newspaper, book, diary, proclamation
   • A person might be bribed to lie. (Suggested)

2. a. Number 5 was in front and could not see what happened.
   b. Number 2 shot LaSalle and might lie to protect himself.
   c. Number 4 was too far in front to witness the shooting.
   d. The Indian, number 6, could see everything that happened. Also, he would most likely be "neutral." Number 1 was in a good position to see, but he might not tell the truth, especially if the murderer was his friend or if he was afraid.

3. Suppose, imaginary

R–17 Justifying Inferences I

3. a. Tom was able to make a complicated device that required knowledge and skills rarely held by young children.
   b. There was a garage; this increases the likelihood that there was a car.
   c. A regular wood saw would not cut metal very well.
   d. Tom must have used a wood saw to cut a piece from the plank.
   e. Tom cut nylon string.
   f. Tom measured the lengths of the pipes before he cut them.
   g. Tom drilled holes in the pipes.
   h. The family had fishing string, so someone probably fished.
   i. The pipes were different lengths, and they produced different notes.
   j. Tom's mother smiled when she heard the tinkling pipes.

R–18   Justifying Inferences II

1. a. Inference: It is a short race over hurdles.

    Explanation: "Over the first, the second; and then the last barrier . . ." indicates hurdles.

   b. Inference: Mary Jane is a senior.

    Explanation: Mary Jane is anticipating going to college.

   c. Inference: Mary Jane's family is not wealthy.

    Explanation: "There was no way her family could pay . . ."

   d. Inference: Mary Jane is younger than her brother and sister.

    Explanation: Mary Jane's brother and sister were or are in college.

   e. Inference: Mary Jane won the race.

    Explanation: The streamer would not have streamed behind her if she had not been the first to reach it.

   f. Inference: Mary Jane won the scholarship.

    Explanation: The university athletic director would not have told her to report for spring training if he wasn't sure she would get the scholarship.

2. Inference: The pilot had radioed that he was in trouble; otherwise the fire truck, the ambulance, and the Civil Air Patrol wouldn't have been standing by.

    Inference: The CAP official waved the plane off because he could see something wrong with the plane or because the rescue team was not yet ready.

    Inference: The pilot ignored the CAP signal because he felt the dangers of another go-round were greater than the dangers of an attempted landing.

    Note: All the above are suggestions; answers will differ.

R–20   Recognizing Propaganda

2. a. Plain Folks
   b. Band Wagon
   c. Card Stacking
   d. Testimonial
   e. Name Calling (isolationists)
   f. Name Calling (do-gooders)
   g. Transfer
   h. Glittering Generalities
   i. Band Wagon
   j. Card Stacking

R–21   Recognizing the Author's Purpose I

- What two things is Dad trying to persuade Jan to do?
  1. Prepare for a profession
  2. Become a certified teacher

- The author's purpose in writing this article is to alert the reader to the dangers of hiking the Appalachian Trail and, possibly, to discourage someone from hiking the trail without thinking it through first.

- Mr. Tomasino wrote this letter in an attempt to convince readers that all-year-round school would be advantageous for children, especially those children who live in inner city environments.

R–22   Recognizing the Author's Purpose II

1. Modest, not forward or aggressive, graciously, cheerful, ready smile, generous, often helped, willingly spent

2. a. Tobacco smoke on breath and clothing
   b. Nicotine stains on fingers
   c. Lungs covered with soot that may lead to cancer or emphysema
   d. Yellow stains on smoker's teeth
   e. Source of pollution for nonsmokers
   f. Harmful to children living with smokers
   g. Pregnant woman's smoke harmful to her unborn child

3. a. Knowledgeable
   b. Considerate
   c. Fair
   d. Humorous
   e. Supportive
   f. Experienced
   g. Patient

   Note: All items are suggestions; answers will differ.

R–23   Recognizing the Author's Purpose in Poetry I

1. "Would you want that to happen to a friend—or even you?"

2. "Pacing up and down, removed from friends and home . . ."

3. "Forced to swim in circles inside a glass bowl
   Or run around a treadmill and never reach a goal."

4. Contrast: frigid north and tropic zoo

5. Turtle, snake, etc.—eagle, hawk, etc.

R–24   Recognizing the Author's Purpose in Poetry II

1. Earth: Take care of Earth because, even though it is strong, it is old and can be easily damaged.
   Redwood Tree: These oldest living things should be protected from lumber interests.
   Eagle: Eagles are endangered; they have to be cautious in order to survive.

2. Animals have as much right to live on Earth as humans, so be considerate of them.

3. Students' haikus will vary.

Note: All of the above are suggestions.

R–26   Reading for Thorough Comprehension II

Details and Facts

1. Friday
2. It was a shortcut home.
3. To test the ice
4. (1) Be careful.
   (2) Don't let go of the branch.
5. Yes. Mike went in the water "over his head."
6. Mike's hands became stiff with cold.
7. Jonathan couldn't run that far. or—Jonathan was afraid Mike would disappear under the ice.
8. Sentences to be underlined: final two sentences, paragraph 9
9. The bottom of the lake began to slant upward.
10. Mike used his coat to drag Jonathan over the snow.
11. The house was one-quarter mile away.
12. The woman called the emergency squad and had warm blankets ready.

Main Ideas
From top to bottom: 2, 5, 8, 11, 13

Vocabulary
a. with great effort
b. carefully
c. extraordinary

Figurative Speech
Mike covered the distance to the house in <u>Olympic-record time</u>.

Inferences
1. Mike was daring.
2. Mike and Jonathan had a close relationship.
3. She was capable of handling emergencies.

Note: All of the above inferences are suggestions.

Section 2: Reading and Vocabulary

Reading and Vocabulary (RV)

RV–3   Practice in Prefixes and Suffixes II

Prefixes

1. ex
2. dis
3. sub
4. inter
5. mono

6. mis
7. super
8. post
9. pre

10. un
11. bi
12. non
13. anti
14. poly

Suffixes

1. ity
2. ize
3. ic
4. graph
5. less

6. ity
7. ory
8. able
9. ate

10. ous
11. ible
12. ism
13. ion

Prefixes–Suffixes

Students' answers will vary.

RV–5   Practice in Root Words

1. a. fear
   b. oil
   c. people-ruled
   d. study of the earth
   e. one who fears or dislikes books
   f. writing about his life
   g. by hand
   h. ancient study
   i. beyond the present
   j. turns
   k. each year
   l. leader
   m. able to be heard
   n. the study of god (religion)

2. a. He or she believes in more than one god.
   b. He or she loves wisdom.
   c. He or she fears high places.
   d. He or she studies ancient things.

3. communism, individualism, cannibalism, capitalism, catechism, monotheism, despotism, etc.

4. a. umbrella
   b. medical, medicine
   c. medium
   d. population
   e. scribble
   f. audition, audio
   g. incredible, credulous

   Note: Students' answers will vary.

5. a. monologue, monotone
   b. geography
   c. polygon, polygamy
   d. communism
   e. biology, biography
   f. metropolis, metropolitan, politics

   Note: Students' answers will vary.

RV–7 Determining Word Meanings from Glossaries

1st Column	2nd Column
3	1
2	12
6	5
8	11
7	10
9	
4	

RV–8 Grouping Words with Similar Meanings

leading	riot	announce	bold	honest
most important	uproar	advertise	fearless	reliable
first	quarrel	publish	daring	honorable
main	outbreak	declare	valiant	truthful
chief	commotion	broadcast	heroic	sincere
foremost	mutiny	proclaim	unafraid	fair
principal	disturbance	circulate	courageous	free from trickery
head	brawl	make known	dauntless	trustworthy
major	strife	give notice of	brave	decent

RV–10 Determining the Meanings of Unknown Words

1. separate
2. native people
3. group of islands
4. an even pile of stones
5. trees with needles
6. oval hill shaped like a half egg with its flat side on the ground
7. a deep crack in the surface of ice
8. a scientist who studies how wind, water . . .
9. flows around curves
10. lightly rain within a cloud

RV–11 Using Context Clues to Determine Meanings of Words

1. Synonym: techniques (methodology)
   Definition: The way or manner by which one does something, for example, teach

2. Synonym: mixed, diverse (heterogeneous)
   Definition: A mixture of students who have different backgrounds and abilities

   Synonym: unvaried (homogeneous)
   Definition: A mixture of students who have similar backgrounds and abilities

3. Synonym: peacefully (amicably)
   Definition: Differences, disputes, quarrels, etc., are settled in peaceful, friendly ways

   Synonym: negotiators, consultants (ombudsmen)
   Definition: Those who bring people together to settle differences

4. Synonym: walk, traverse (perambulate)
   Definition: To walk around the boundaries of a property, etc., for the purpose of inspecting, observing

5. Synonym: small, tiny (minuscule)
   Definition: Something that is very small as, for example, a bit of saw dust

6. Synonym: highest praise, distinction, honor (summa cum laude)
   Definition: A phrase indicating the recipient is one of the very best students upon graduation from college

Note: Answers are suggested. Accept all reasonable responses.

RV–12   Synonym Crossword Puzzle

1 A	B	2 D	I	C	3 A	T	4 E			5 M		
B		E		B		N			6 G	O	R	7 E
8 D	E	L	E	T	E		L		O			N
U		U			9 T	R	A	V	E	R	S	E
C		G			R		R		10 M			M
11 T	H	E	12 O	R	Y		G		I			Y
			C				13 E	X	T	O	L	
14 T		15 A	C	M	16 E							17 P
E			U		N							L
18 P	R	E	L	U	D	E		19 M	O	20 D		O
I		T	U					A		I		D
D			21 R	E	P	R	O	V	E			
	22 P	R	I	M	E			T		E		

RV–13   Antonym Crossword Puzzle

1 U	N	S	2 C	R	U	3 P	U	L	O	U	S	
			O			A						4 P
	5 P	R	O	F	E	S	S	I	O	6 N	A	L
7 R			P			S				A		A
8 O	U	T	E	R		I		9 B		Y		I
B			R			10 V	A	R	Y			N
U		11 A	B	L	E			A			12 F	
13 S	E	N	T					V			R	
T		14 I	N	15 H	A	16 L	E			17 B	A	N
	18 R		V		E		A		19 V		N	
20 G	O		21 E	F	F	I	C	I	E	N	T	
	A				T		K		T		I	
22 O	R	A	L		Y			23 F	O	R	C	E

RV–15 Practice in Figurative Language

1. a. Personification
   b. Oxymoron
   c. Metaphor
   d. Personification
   e. Simile
   f. Hyperbole
   g. Hyperbole
   h. Oxymoron
   i. Hyperbole
   j. Unnecessary words (Redundancy)
   k. Metaphor
   l. Simile

2. Students' answers will vary.

3. Students' answers will vary.

RV–17 Creating Similes and Metaphors

1. a. slow: turtle, glacier
   b. quiet: whisper, falling snow
   c. noisy: jackhammer, bulldozer
   d. blue: ocean, sky
   e. beautiful: rainbow, sunset
   f. big: mountain, hippopotamus
   g. small: period, needle's eye
   h. smooth: velvet, baby's skin

2–3. Student's choices

Note: Answers are suggested. Accept all reasonable responses.

RV–19 Completing Analogies I

1. road
2. peninsula
3. equator
4. temperature
5. plateau
6. glacier
7. zoology
8. rock
9. river
10. sending out
11. leaves
12. bumps
13. table
14. France
15. west
16. southeast
17. night/day
18. Florida
19. maps
20. Student's choice
21. Student's choice

Note: Some answers may vary in numbers 13–19. Accept all reasonable answers.

RV–20 Completing Analogies II

1. couch
2. teacher
3. fish
4. 42
5. stingy
6. airplane
7. crow
8. Greece
9. car
10. division
11. tree
12. stale
13. Savannah River
14. cotton gin
15. incomplete
16. telescope
17. automobile, truck
18. North Carolina
19. Student's choice
20. Student's choice
21. Student's choice

RV–21 A "Synonymous Titles" Puzzle

1. Star-Spangled Banner
2. America the Beautiful
3. Home Sweet Home
4. You Are My Sunshine
5. Raindrops Keep Falling on My Head
6. Three Blind Mice
7. Row, Row, Row Your Boat
8. God Bless America
9. I've Been Working on the Railroad
10. Down by the Old Mill Stream
11. Old MacDonald Had a Farm
12. Twinkle, Twinkle Little Star
13. Somewhere over the Rainbow

RV–22 Understanding Compound Words

1. a. dish and washer
   b. cross and bow
   c. neck and tie
   d. blue and berry
   e. blow and torch
   f. cook and ware
   g. entry and way

2. a. cake
   b. way
   c. glass
   d. soil
   e. blazer
   f. door
   g. point
   h. house
   i. maid
   j. night
   k. fly
   l. master

3. a. rowboat
   b. paperwork
   c. low-level
   d. doorknob
   e. crossroad
   f. dry-clean

4. a. A wind that strikes an airplane on a side rather than head-on
   b. A person who doesn't talk very much
   c. A person who makes a fuss when things go wrong
   d. A person who has difficulty making choices or decisions

RV–23 Recognizing Homophones

1. a. stake
   b. foul
   c. too
   d. grate
   e. coarse
   f. wrap
   g. peers
   h. brake
   i. rite
   j. site
   k. fir
   l. dear
   m. peek
   n. hoarse
   o. ring

2. a. A plain is a flat area with some hills here and there, but the hills are not very high.
   b. When you are at the beach in the summer, be careful that you do not get too much sun.
   c. We made a wrong turn on the road, so we were one hour late and missed the plane.

RV–24 Homophone Crossword Puzzle

1 S	O	2 N		3 W	4 A	5 Y
E		E	6 K	7 D	O	E
E		8 W	O	N		U
			O	9 F		
	10 T		11 W	H	O	L	12 E
13 P	O	U	14 R			U		I
I			A		R		G
E			P				H
R		15 S	C	E	16 N	T
	17 P		O		U	
	E		M		N	
18 S	T	A	K	E		19 T
I		K		20 N		E
T		21 H	O	R	22 S	E
E				T		O

RV–25   Understanding and Using Homographs

1. He <u>dove</u> into the swimming pool.
2. Please try not to <u>tear</u> your dress.
3. I was <u>present</u> when the awards were given.
4. The clock was <u>wound</u> so tight the spring broke.
5. He was a person who would never <u>desert</u> a friend in need.
6. Please <u>read</u> the last paragraph.
7. He had <u>perfect</u> attendance for five years.
8. The Indian's <u>bow</u> was useless because he had no more arrows.
9. I wonder what it would be like to <u>live</u> in a cave.
10. If you wait a <u>minute</u>, I will go with you.
11. It is important that your <u>conduct</u> be without fault.

Note: Students' answers will vary.

RV–26   Some Experiences with Foreign Expressions

1. Rest in peace.
2. Do it immediately!
3. Good day. . . . How are things going?
4. Time goes quickly by (Time flies).
5. Until I see you again. . . . Until we meet again
6. Good day.
7. Always faithful
8. Please respond.
9. French is spoken here.
10. Out of many—one
11. For one's country

Section 3: Reading Diagrams/Charts, Tables and Graphs

Reading Diagrams/Charts (RD/C)

RD/C–2   Polluted Air

1. Polluted air could cause lung disease because smoke or dangerous particles could become deposited in a person's lungs.
2. One side: $6,000; four sides: $24,000
3. a. . . . kills trees and plants . . .
   b. . . . destroys wire insulation . . .
   c. . . . turns paper brittle . . .
   d. . . . corrodes train rails . . .
   e. . . . ruins car paint . . .

RD/C–3   Solar Water Heaters

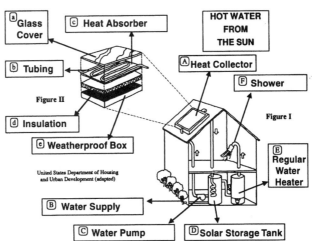

RD/C–4 Annotating a Cross Section

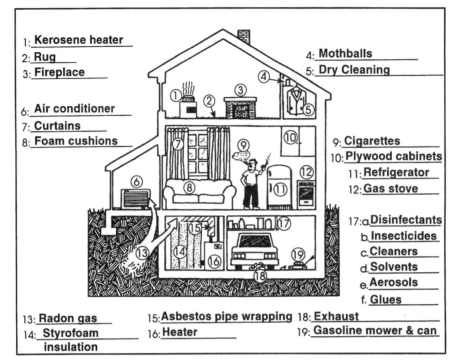

1: **Kerosene heater**
2: **Rug**
3: **Fireplace**

6: **Air conditioner**
7: **Curtains**
8: **Foam cushions**

4: **Mothballs**
5: **Dry Cleaning**

9: **Cigarettes**
10: **Plywood cabinets**
11: **Refrigerator**
12: **Gas stove**

17: a **Disinfectants**
b **Insecticides**
c **Cleaners**
d **Solvents**
e **Aerosols**
f **Glues**

13: **Radon gas**
14: **Styrofoam insulation**
15: **Asbestos pipe wrapping**
16: **Heater**
18: **Exhaust**
19: **Gasoline mower & can**

RD/C–6 Sequences in the Water Cycle II

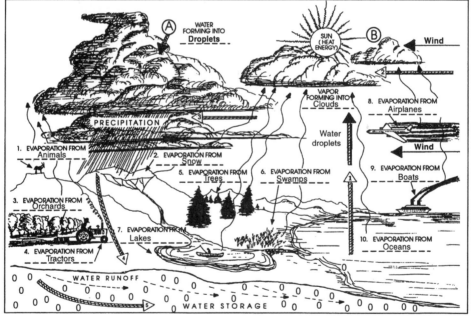

RD/C–7 Air Has Weight

1.a. Air weight on towel: 9,000 lbs.
  b. Air weight on napkin: 1,200 lbs.
2. Air weight on cube: 450 lbs.
3. Check diagram for gradually decreasing particulate symbols (dots) as the top of the diagram is approached.

Note: Remind students that air presses on all surfaces equally and, therefore, is not noticed.

RD/C–8   Understanding Whales

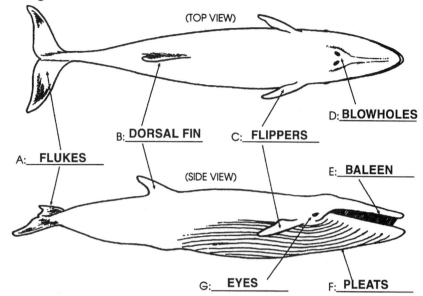

(TOP VIEW)

D: <u>BLOWHOLES</u>

B: <u>DORSAL FIN</u>   C: <u>FLIPPERS</u>

A: <u>FLUKES</u>

E: <u>BALEEN</u>

(SIDE VIEW)

G: <u>EYES</u>   F: <u>PLEATS</u>

RD/C–9   The Earth's Atmosphere

Air Is Mixture of Gases

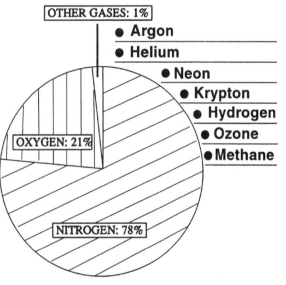

OTHER GASES: 1%
- Argon
- Helium
- Neon
- Krypton
- Hydrogen
- Ozone
- Methane

OXYGEN: 21%

NITROGEN: 78%

Title: <u>Air Is Composed of Several Different Gases</u>

Note: Student titles may vary.

The Atmosphere of Earth

1.a. Troposphere
  b. Exosphere
  c. Exosphere
  d. Troposphere

  e. Mesosphere
  f. Exosphere
  g. Troposphere
  h. Ionosphere

2. about 5.5 miles
3. about 6.5 miles

RD/C–10   Sources of Water

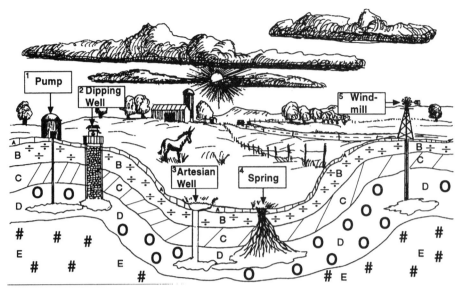

RD/C–12   Protecting Soil II

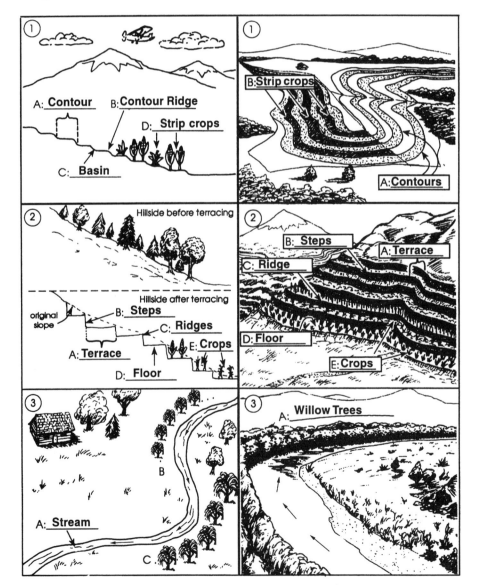

RD/C–13 Understanding Windbreaks

1.a. To be underlined: "Blowing soil may even create highway driving hazards by limiting vision."

  b. To be underlined: "Windbreaks are simply rows of trees that are positioned to break the force of winds."

2. Crops become so poor that farmers cannot make a living.

3. 30 m.p.h.; 15 m.p.h.; 21 m.p.h.; 10 m.p.h.

4. See students' figures.

RD/C–14 Dangers Birds Face

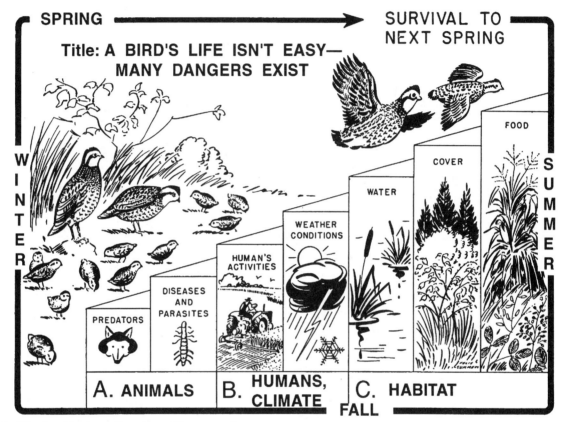

3. Hawks, Snakes, Fox, Cats (Suggested)

4. Hunting; Destroying bird habitats for farming, lumbering, housing developments, roads, etc. (Suggested)

5. Severe: droughts, cold, snow, storms (Suggested)

6. Lack of: food, water, cover (Suggested)

7. Food loss; Lack of protection from predators (Suggested)

8. Humans can help nonmigrating birds to survive by providing feeding stations and cover areas for protection from weather elements. (Suggested)

9. Students' choices

1, 3, and 6

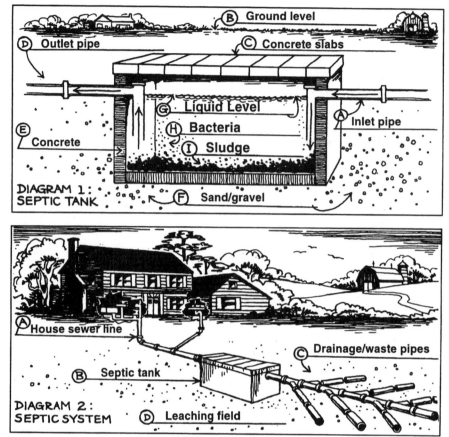

2.a. The well should be at least 100' from a septic system.

b. The septic system should not drain toward the well.

5.a. Some waste is reduced to liquids.

b. Wastes that cannot be liquefied settle as sludge.

7. Sentences to be circled: The sentence that begins with "The liquids drain . . ." and the following sentence.

8.a. Some liquid evaporates.

b. Some liquid is purified by filtration.

9. The waste liquid could contaminate a stream.

RD/C–17   Understanding Watersheds and River Flow I

Activities

3. Tributaries: Indian River, Otter River, Roaring River, Wolf River, Snake River, Goose Creek

Note: Goose Creek is a tributary to Snake River and, in that sense, is a tributary to Big Elk River.

Questions

1. Tunnel

2. All the rivers and streams start in the highlands.

3. Snake River: Southeast

Wolf River: Southeast

Goose Creek: Northwest

Indian River: South

Otter River: South

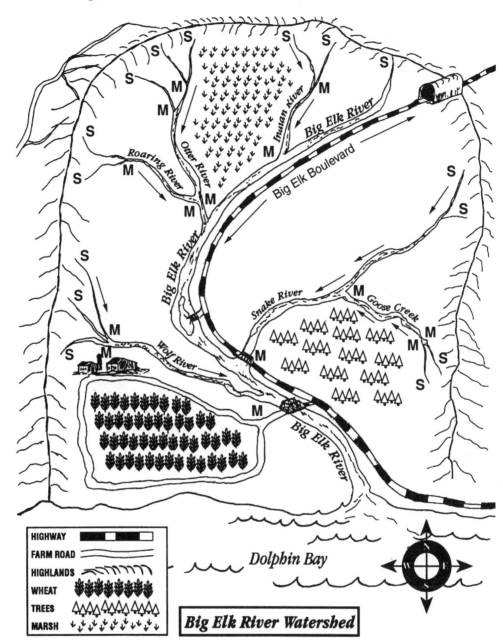

HIGHWAY
FARM ROAD
HIGHLANDS
WHEAT
TREES
MARSH

Big Elk River Watershed

Dolphin Bay

RD/C–19   Using a Form to Record a Demonstration

Notes:

1. The face of the form on the following page does not have room for the diagrams shown in Figure 2. Students should draw the figure 2 diagrams on the reverse side of the form.

2. Additional extension questions:

   • Would the demonstration succeed without water? (Yes. The water is placed in the can because the water, when heated, gives off a visible vapor thus indicating escaping air.)

   • What are some ways air pressure is useful? (Air pressure is used to inflate tires and balloons. Also, air pressure is used in tools, in steam engines, etc.)

RD/C–20 Science Demonstration Observation Form

1. Topic: Air Pressure
2. Title: Air Pressure Has the Ability to Crush Objects*
* Do not reveal or ask for a title before the experiment/demonstration ends. The title implies the conclusion that will be developed.
3. Problem: How does the weight of air affect surface areas?
4. Equipment and Materials:
   • 1 gal. can w/screw-on cap
   • 1 tsp.of water
   • Paper towels
   • Hot plate
5. Steps in Demonstration:
   a. Pour water into can.
   b. Connect hot plate.
   c. Place uncapped can on hot plate.
   d. Heat can until all vapor has escaped.
   e. Remove can and quickly replace screw-on cap.
   f. Allow can to cool.

6. Observations:
   a. Vapor (air) escaping (sight)
   b. Burning odor (smell)
   c. Crunching of sides of can (sight & sound)
7. Explanation:
   The heat forced the air in the can to rise and escape. When the cap was replaced, no more air could enter the can. The weight of the air outside the can crushed the can.
8. Notes and Questions:

Note: Students use this space to record the answers to questions asked by the teacher.

Sample questions:

Would the demonstration work on top of Mt. Everest? (Probably not—as altitude increases, air pressure decreases.)

Note: Project and explain the Mt. Everest diagram shown in Figure 1 of preceding page. Note that air weighs only 1 lb. per square inch at 29,028'.

9. Drawings & Diagrams (See reverse side of students' SDOFs.)

RD/C–21 Your Environmental Beliefs

Students' choices

Reading Tables (RT)

RT–2 Reading a Year Calendar

1. 7, 14, 21, 28
2. June
3. Jan. 21
   Feb. 18
   March 18
   April 15
   May 20
   June 17
   July 15
   Aug. 19
   Sept. 16
   Oct. 21
   Nov. 18
   Dec. 16
4. Check students' calendars.
5.a. July 24
  b. Aug. 29
  c. Oct. 30
6. 4 months have only 30 days
7. 7 months have 31 days

RT–3 Reading a Membership/Unit Table

1.a. 4,165,000
  b. 2,613,000
2. 1980
3. 1970
4. 1,190,000
5. 827,000
6. 28,000
7. Yes
8. 32.3
9. 11.8
10. Irving, Texas
11. New York, New York

RT–4   Two Ways to List the Same Information

FIFTEEN LEADING OIL PRODUCERS–1993*			
Country	**Barrels of Oil (000's)**	**Country**	**Barrels of Oil (000's)**
Saudi Arabia	8,198	Nigeria	2,050
U.S.S.R. (former)	7,297	United Kingdom	1,909
United States	6,847	Kuwait	1,872
Iran	3,650	Canada	1,678
China	2,911	Indonesia	1,507
Mexico	2,671	Libya	1,377
Venezuela	2,377	Algeria	1,190
United Arab Emirates	2,241	Total	11,583
Total	36,192	Total of two columns	47,775

RT–5   Reading a Bus Schedule

2.a. 5:40 p.m., 8:10 p.m., 2 hrs. and 30 min.
  b. 7:50 p.m.; 20 minutes
  c. 10; 60 minutes

d. No. The 3:40 bus from Neptune does not travel beyond the N. Cape station.

RT–6   Reading a Road Mileage Table

1.a. 1,037 miles
  b. 996 miles
  c. 2,976 miles
  d. 796 miles
  e. 674 miles
  f. 1,242 miles
2.a. 2,821 miles
  b. 1,517 miles
  c. 3,006 miles

3. Dallas to Boston
4. $30.00
5. Road distances between cities:
   - Washington, DC, to New Orleans: 1,078 miles
   - New Orleans to San Francisco: 2,246 miles
   - San Francisco to Seattle: 808 miles
   - Seattle to Chicago: 2,013 miles
   - Chicago to Washington, DC: 671 miles

RT–7   Transferring Information from a Table to a Map

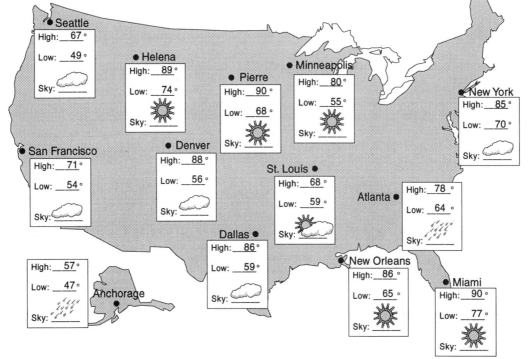

RT–7   Transferring Information from a Table to a Map (continued)

2. Miami

3. Denver, Colorado; 32

RT–8   Completing a Table of "Animal Workers"

Number	Animal or Natural Feature	Work	Number	Animal or Natural Feature	Work
1	Sun	Produces heat energy	8	Rotating Vegetation	Enriches soil
2	Cloud	Collects and dispenses moisture	9	Bee	Collects honey, distributes pollen
3	Bird (Swallow)	Catches and eats insects	10	Beaver	Builds dams
4	Bird (Woodpecker)	Catches and eats insects	11	Squirrel	Plants acorns (oak trees)
5	Owl	Catches and eats rodents	12	Nutrients, Microbes	Enrich soil
6	Racoon	Catches and eats fish	13	Mole	Digs tunnels
7	Cow	Supplies manure (fertilizer)	14	Worm	"Turns over" soil

RT–11   Reading a Windchill Table

1. "Windchill" column from top to bottom: 16°F, -24°F, -68°F, 28°F, -40°F, -116°F

2. "Wind Speed" column from top to bottom: 10 m.p.h., 15 m.p.h., 30 m.p.h., 25 m.p.h.

RT–12   Working with Large Population Numbers

1.a. 3,800,000,000

  b. • 500,000,000
  • 700,000,000
  • 700,000,000
  • 900,000,000

2.a. China, India, United States, Indonesia, Brazil, Russia, Japan

  b. 939,000,000

  c. No

  d. 114,000,000

  e. 3,045,000,000

RT–13   How Much Water Goes Down the Drain?

1. $1 \times 6 \times 5 \times 4 \times 7 = 840$ gallons

2. $4 \times 5 \times 4 \times 7 = 560$ gallons

3. $1 \times 15 \times 7 = 105$ gallons

4. $1 \times 30 \times 7 = 210$ gallons

5. $1 \times 4 \times 4 \times 7 = 112$ gallons

6. 1,827 gallons

7. 95,004 gallons

RT–14 Space-Shuttle Flights

1. 4/12/81
2. 1985
3. April, 11 flights
4. Atlantis: 13; Challenger: 10; Columbia: 17; Discovery: 18; Endeavor: 7

RT–15 Counting Calories

Breakfast	Measure	Calories
Orange	1	60
Milk, whole	1 cup	150
Oatmeal	1 cup	145
	Total calories	355
Lunch	**Measure**	**Calories**
Swiss cheese	2 oz.	190
Bread, white	2 slices	130
Mayonnaise	1 tbsp.	100
Potato chips	20	210
Cola	12 oz.	160
Brownie	1	100
	Total calories	890
Supper	**Measure**	**Calories**
Beef, ground	6 oz.	490
Broccoli	3 spears	150
Milk, whole	1 cup	150
Bread, white	2 slices	130
Butter, salted	2 tbsp.	200
Pie, pecan	1 piece	575
	Total calories	1,695
	Total calories for the day	2,940

Breakfast	Measure	Calories
Orange	1	60
Milk, skim	1 cup	85
Corn flakes/sugar	2 oz.	220
	Total calories	365
Lunch	**Measure**	**Calories**
Tuna, canned in oil	3 oz.	165
Bread, white	2 slices	130
Potato chips	10	105
Milk, skim	1 cup	85
Crackers, graham	2	60
	Total calories	545
Supper	**Measure**	**Calories**
Turkey, roasted	1 cup	240
Carrot, raw	2	60
Tomatoes	2	50
Soup, chicken noodle	2 cups	150
Ice cream, hardened	1 cup	270
	Total calories	770
	Total calories for the day	1,680

How many fewer calories did she consume on the second day? 1,260

RT–16 An Array of Cattle Brands

1. Top row: E, H, B, L
   2nd row: K, I, G, C
   3rd row: M, A, J, O
   4th row: D, N, P, F
2. See students' drawings.

RT–17   Completing a Map and Table of Sea Distances

From New York to:	Sea Distance in Miles	Hours of Sea Travel at an Average Speed of 30 Miles Per Hour
1. Helsinki, Finland	4,257	141.9
2. Oslo, Norway	3,644	121.4
3. Glasgow, Scotland	3,210	107.0
4. Southampton, England	3,169	105.6
5. Cherbourgh, France	3,134	104.4
6. Barcelona, Spain	3,714	123.8
7. Athens*, Greece *Actual port is Piraeus	4,688	156.2

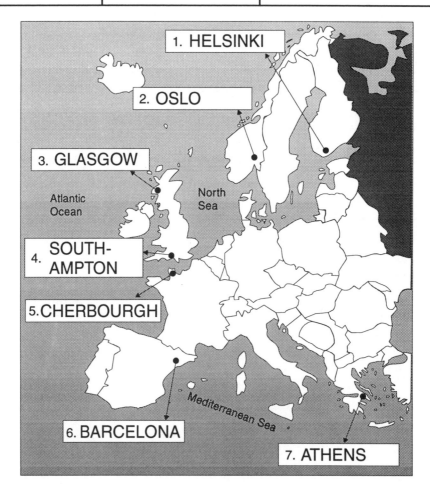

RT–18   A "Time" Table of Various United States Cities

1. **Time Column**
   Albany, NY: 12:00 Noon
   Atlanta, GA: 12:00 Noon
   Austin, TX: 11:00 a.m.
   Bismarck, ND: 10:00 a.m.
   Boise, ID: 10:00 a.m.
   Cheyenne, WY: 10:00 a.m.
   Columbus, OH: 12:00 Noon
   Frankfort, KY: 12:00 Noon

   Lincoln, NE: 11:00 a.m.
   Sacramento, CA: 9:00 a.m.
   Salem, OR: 9:00 a.m.
   Santa Fe, NM: 10:00 a.m.
2. Boise, ID: 6:00 a.m.
   Austin, TX: 7:00 a.m.
   Salem, OR: 5:00 a.m.
3. Columbus, OH: 2:00 p.m.
   Lincoln, NE: 1:00 p.m.

RT–19   Comparing the Yearly Salaries of Men and Women

1.a. $10,620
  b. $40,547
2.a. $8,034
  b. $25,922
3. $9,698
4. $21,737
5.a. less
  b. 45–54

RT–20   Designing a Table

STUDENTS IN THE NORTHEASTERN UNITED STATES
WHO ENTERED HIGH SCHOOL IN 1990 AND GRADUATED IN 1994

STATE	PERCENT OF STUDENTS
Connecticut	78.9%
Delaware	66.5%
Maine	74.0%
Maryland	74.7%
Massachusetts	78.0%
New Hampshire	78.3%
New Jersey	85.3%
New York	64.5%
Pennsylvania	78.9%
Rhode Island	73.4%
Vermont	84.6%
Virginia	72.4%
West Virginia	78.0%

Reading Graphs (RG)

RG–2 Reading Picture Graphs

1. a. 20
   b. 2
   c. 108
   d. In order of the number caught

2. a. 15
   b. 6
   c. Yes
   d. Boys, 24; Girls, 24

3. a. May, 6
   b. 23
   c. 53
   d. $26.50

RG–3 Making Picture Graphs

Title: THE GROWTH OF STEVE'S ABILITY TO

MAKE FREE THROWS

DATES	FREE THROWS
JUNE 20	●●●●●
JULY 4	●●●●●●
JULY 18	●●●●●●●
AUG. 1	●●●●●●●
AUG. 15	●●●●●●●◗
AUG. 29	●●●●●●●●

Each symbol (●) equals **2** baskets

Title: OLYMPIC MEDALS WON IN 1994

BY EIGHT LEADING COUNTRIES

COUNTRIES	MEDALS
NORWAY	⊕⊕⊕⊕⊕⊕◗
GERMANY	⊕⊕⊕⊕⊕⊕
RUSSIA	⊕⊕⊕⊕⊕◗
ITALY	⊕⊕⊕⊕⊕
CANADA	⊕⊕⊕◗
UNITED STATES	⊕⊕⊕◗
AUSTRIA	⊕⊕◗
SWITZER-LAND	⊕⊕◗

Each symbol (⊕) equals 4 medals

266

RG–5 Reading Bar Graphs

1. 1993: 28"; 1996: 26"
2. 1994
3. 110"
4. 2"
5. 1993

6. 32 million
7. 14 million
8. 4 million
9. Less
10. 107 million (approximate)

RG–6 Making a Bar Graph

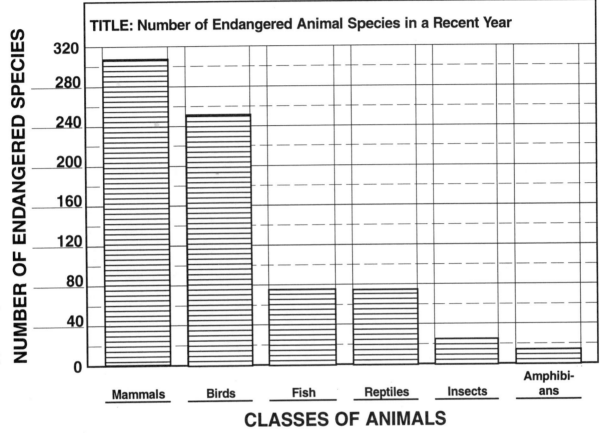

TITLE: Number of Endangered Animal Species in a Recent Year

NUMBER OF ENDANGERED SPECIES

CLASSES OF ANIMALS

Mammals   Birds   Fish   Reptiles   Insects   Amphibi-ans

6. Check students' questions and answers.

RG–8 Interpreting a Single-Bar Graph

1. Canada: 45%
   United States: 44%
   Mexico: 9%
   Central America: 2%
2. a. 22 times
   b. 4 times

Challenge Question

$$\begin{array}{r} 8{,}487{,}000 \\ \times \quad\quad .45 \\ \hline 42435000 \\ 33948000 \\ \hline 3{,}819{,}150.00 \text{ square miles} \end{array}$$

RG–10   Completing a "Time Line" Bar Graph

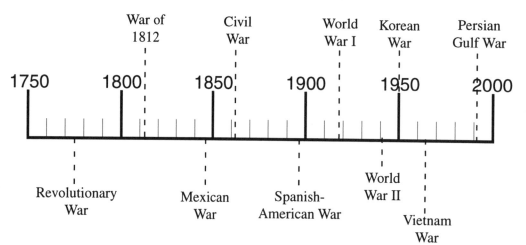

UNITED STATES WARS

War of 1812 · Civil War · World War I · Korean War · Persian Gulf War

1750   1800   1850   1900   1950   2000

Revolutionary War · Mexican War · Spanish-American War · World War II · Vietnam War

RG–11   Interpreting and Completing Line Graphs

<u>Temperature Graph</u>
1. Miami
2. 62°F (+ or - 2°)
3. July and August
4. 9°F (+ or - 2°)
5. 55°F (+ or - 2°)
6. January, February, March, November, December

<u>Susan's Saving Graph</u>
1–5

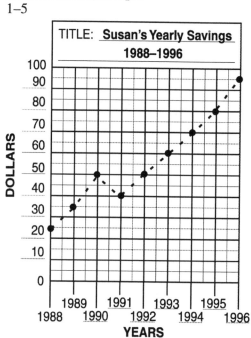

6. Check students' questions and answers.

RG–13   Interpreting Circle and Square Graphs

<u>Circle Graph</u>
2. a. Tank ships, tank barges
   b. Freighters, passenger ships, etc.
   c. Land spills

<u>Square Graph</u>
1. Africa: 20%
   Antarctica: 9%
   Asia: 30%
   Australia: 6%
   Europe: 7%
   North America: 16%
   South America: 12%
2. 5
3. 3

<u>Challenge Question</u>
• Asia occupies 17,370,000 square miles.
• North America occupies 9,264,000 square miles.

RG–14   A Circle Graph Showing Immigration

3. 800,000 (804,000 including Australia and New Zealand)

4. a. False   d. False
   b. True   e. False
   c. True   f. False

RG–16   Volcanoes—Natural Sources of Pollution II

Title: Notable Volcanic Eruptions

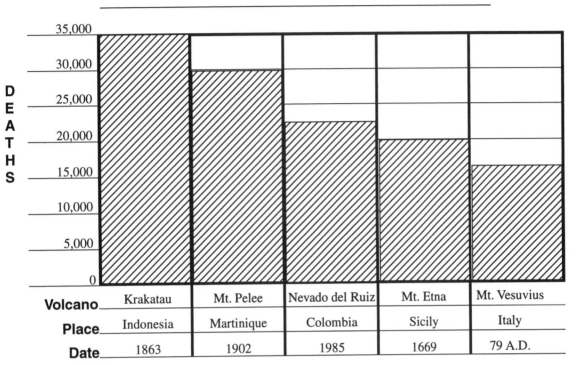

	Krakatau	Mt. Pelee	Nevado del Ruiz	Mt. Etna	Mt. Vesuvius
Volcano	Krakatau	Mt. Pelee	Nevado del Ruiz	Mt. Etna	Mt. Vesuvius
Place	Indonesia	Martinique	Colombia	Sicily	Italy
Date	1863	1902	1985	1669	79 A.D.

Place and Year of Eruption

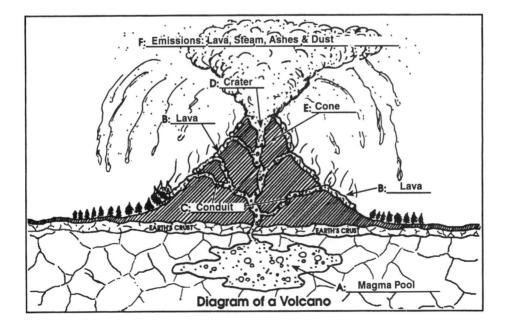

Diagram of a Volcano

RG–17   Bar Graph of Recreational Activities

Participation in 10 Most Popular Activities*

1. Exercise walking
   Male: 19%; Female: 37%
   Swimming
   Male: 25%; Female: 28%
   Bicycle Riding
   Male: 22%; Female: 19%
   Camping
   Male: 21%; Female: 16%
   Bowling
   Male: 18%; Female: 17%
   Fishing
   Male: 27%; Female: 13%
   Exercising with equipment
   Male: 15%; Female: 15%
   Basketball
   Male: 19%; Female: 7%
   Aerobics
   Male: 3%; Female: 18%
   Golf
   Male: 15%; Female: 4%
2. Exercise walking
3. Exercise walking, swimming, aerobics

Attendance and Participation in Various Activities*

1. 18 years and older
2. Movies: 59%
   Sports events: 38%
   Amusement parks: 50%
   Exercise: 60%
   Playing sports: 39%
   Outdoor activities: 33%
   Home improvement: 48%
   Gardening: 55%
3. Movies
4. Most popular: Exercise
   Least popular: Outdoor activities

* Accept + or - 1 in percent estimates

RG–18   Line Graph of Motor Vehicle Production

1. 30 years
2. 1990
3. 1980 and 1990
4. United States
5. 22 million
6. 24%

RG–20   Making a Circle Graph

1. 94,450 square miles
3. Superior: 121°
   Huron: 87°
   Michigan: 85°
   Erie: 38°
   Ontario: 29°

Title: Areas of the Five Great Lakes
in Square Miles

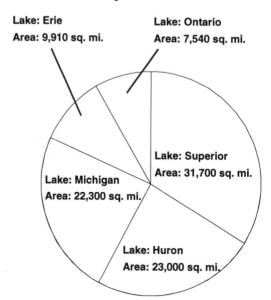

Lake: Erie
Area: 9,910 sq. mi.

Lake: Ontario
Area: 7,540 sq. mi.

Lake: Superior
Area: 31,700 sq. mi.

Lake: Michigan
Area: 22,300 sq. mi.

Lake: Huron
Area: 23,000 sq. mi.

Section 4: Reading Pictures/Cartoons and Maps

Reading Pictures/Cartoons (RP/C)

RP/C–4   Jamestown, 1607: Pictorial Facts and Inferences

1. ① Minding a baby
   ② Carrying water
   ③ Cooking
   ④ Bringing game home
   ⑤ Cutting wood
   ⑥ Chasing (herding) pigs
   ⑦ Bringing fish home
   ⑧ Removing trees
   ⑨ Harvesting vegetables
   ⑩ Thatching a roof
   ⑪ Hanging clothes to dry
   ⑫ Spinning yarn

2. a. In the event of an attack, the pointed logs would be difficult for the enemy to climb over. Also, it was safer for defenders to look for the enemy without exposing their heads.
   b. Straw is being laid on boards.
   c. cannon
   d. well
   e. It is a crossbow used to defend against invaders or for hunting.

RP/C–5   A Colonial Home: Pictorial Facts and Inferences

1. Reading from top left in a clockwise direction: f, j, e, n, g, d, l, o, m, c, p, k, a, i, b, h

2. a. The boy is probably climbing the ladder to go to bed in the loft.
   b. The pan is placed between the covers of a bed and moved from side-to-side and, thus, warms the bed on cold nights.
   c. The stick in the churn is moved up and down and in circles. The movement thickens the cream, which becomes butter.
   d. When the bellows is squeezed, air blows out of its spout, thus increasing the amount of oxygen available to the fire.

RP/C–6   An Abandoned Farm: Pictorial Facts and Inferences

1. Colorado, Kansas, New Mexico, Oklahoma, Texas
2. To be circled: "Dust piled up along fence rows, houses, and barns."
3. No signs of human or animal life; no farm machinery; no crops; sand and dust covering the ground
4. Students' titles will vary.
5. Students' paragraphs will vary.

RP/C–7   Sources of Air Pollution: Pictures with a Specific Main Idea

Picture 1
1. Truck, automobile, and airplane emissions
2. Motorcycles, buses, tractors, trains
3. States have passed laws that require vehicles to have pollution-reduction devices.

Picture 2
2. coal and oil
3. b. Waste could kill plant and animal life.

(continued next page)

Picture 3

1. to kill insects, to paint, to kill mosquito larvae
2. Fruit could become contaminated and, when eaten, be harmful to humans. The men could become sick as a result of inhaling fumes.
3. The tractor emissions

Picture 4

1. quarries, building roads, plowing
2. Spray the rock with water; this will decrease dust.

RP/C–8 Four Pictures, Each with a Special Meaning

Picture 2

Facts: Tractor and driver . . . worker planting . . . worker on tractor dispensing plants . . . plants, not seeds, being planted . . .

Inference: This must be a large farm because three workers are working, and special farm machinery is being used. (Suggested)

Picture 3

Facts: Two boys, one with fishing pole . . . "No Swimming" sign . . . debris in pond (sticks, bottles, boards) . . . tire hanging from tree . . . uncovered excavation on side of pond . . .

Inferences: The pond has become contaminated and is no longer safe for swimming. There are probably no fish in the pond. (Suggested)

Picture 4

Facts: Various objects made of wood are shown: log, board, newspaper, gunstock, pencil, baseball bat, rocking horse, house, chair, turpentine, box, telephone pole, railroad ties . . . axe imbedded in stump . . . conifer tree and deciduous tree . . .

Inference: Wood is an important element in our lives and is used in many different ways.

RP/C–9 A Frontier Home and Store: Pictorial Facts and Inferences

Picture, Col. 1

1.a. One story with loft . . . logs of cabin laid horizontally . . . no window visible . . . wooden door . . . chimney with smoke coming from it . . .

   b. Appears to be hoeing . . . appears to be 16 to 18 years old . . .

   c. Appears to be 10 to 12 years old . . . fishing pole is a tree branch . . . fish on end of line . . . patched trousers . . .

   d. Carrying two pails (water?) . . . apron . . . skirt to ankles . . .

   e. Dog . . . corn . . . cabbage (?) . . . chopping block with axe . . . tree stumps . . . gun against tree . . . powder horn . . .

2. In colonial times families were dependent upon the environment and worked to provide the necessities for living.

Picture, Col. 2

1. Household Equipment: clocks, brooms, pots, pans, baskets, scissors
   Farm Tools: rake, hoes, axe, shovel, horse/mule harness
   Food, Clothing, etc.: cloth, boots, flour, candy, guns, powder horn
2. **Merchant**: "I wish he would make up his mind to buy the axe."
   Shopper: "He is asking a high price for this axe. I wonder if it will hold an edge very long."
   Child: "If I keep looking at this candy long enough maybe Dad will buy me a piece."
   Note: All the above are suggestions.

RP/C–10 A Pictorial Representation of Life in Spain's Latin American Colonies

1. plowing, hoeing, carting, reaping
2. Possibilities: seeds, water for workers and animals
4. oxen, horses
5. The supervisor is armed with a sword and mounted on a horse. His jacket is probably made of metal.
6. Supervisor's appearance: hat with plume, high boots, bandolier, sword; he appears very watchful
7. Students' choice. (*Note*: It is likely that they are talking resentfully about the work they are forced to do under the supervision of an armed guard on a horse.)

RP/C–11 A Picture Story of Magellan's Voyage

1. Picture captions: 4 3 6 8 7 1 5 9 2
2. Students' choice
   Note: Magellan took sides in one of the islanders' wars. He and some of his men were killed in one of the battles.

RP/C–12 A Picture Comparison of Two Indian Tribes

Column 1
1. PNW
2. SW
3. PNW
4. SW
5. PNW
6. SW
7. PNW
8. SW
9. SW

Column 2
1. It was used as a ladder.
2. She is weaving.
3. Perhaps the boat is being built.
4. The person might be carrying fish.
5. In an attack they could (1) pull up the ladders and (2) throw objects and/or shoot arrows from the roofs.

RP/C–16 Air Pollution Situations in Cartoons

Cartoon 1
1. The face indicates bewilderment and/or puzzlement—a kind of "Why are you allowing this to happen?"
2. The American flag
3. Students' choice

Cartoon 2
1. Factories are often associated with low-income neighborhoods. The woman may not have a clothes dryer.
2. Students' choice

Cartoon 3
1. The person is complaining about air pollution when, at the same time, he is contributing to air pollution.

Cartoon 4
1. The children are telling the man that he should not be burning leaves or rubbish.
2. Students' choice

RP/C–17 Interpreting and Creating Cartoons

Students' captions and cartoons will vary.

RP/C–19 A Water Pollution Cartoon

1. The pond became polluted because careless people threw old oil cans into the water. The oil killed the fish and other natural life.
2. Students' choice (Suggested: The children's faces show disappointment and sadness.)
3. Students' choice (Suggested: You might not have meant to kill us, but your carelessness and neglect killed us anyway.)

RP/C–20   A Cartoon That Delivers a Message

1. America (North), California, Alaska, Normandy (France), Texas Panhandle
2. Comic books (or possibly some other book not related to school).
   Small detail: Geography book not on desk; scattered papers
3. All the headlines are historical events taking place in specific geographical settings.
4. The television is showing an event that is currently occurring in a geographical setting.
5. The student is ignoring the displays, which contradict what he is thinking/saying.
6. Students' choice

Reading Maps (RM)

RM–2   Cardinal and Intermediate Directions I

5.a. Washington: Northwest
  b. Minnesota: North Central
  c. Georgia: Southeast
  d. Arizona: Southwest
  e. Louisiana: South Central
  f. Maine: Northeast
  g. Kansas: Central

6.a. Cheyenne: Southeast
  b. Jefferson City: Central
  c. Pierre: Central
  d. Juneau: Southeast
  e. Albany: East Central
  f. Madison: South Central
  g. Salem: Northwest
  h. Topeka: Northeast

RM–3   Cardinal and Intermediate Directions II

1.a. Southeast
  b. North
  c. West
  d. Southwest
  e. Northeast
  f. East

2.a. Austin, TX, to Santa Fe, NM
  b. Sacramento, CA, to Salem, OR
  c. Raleigh, NC, to Richmond, VA;
     Richmond, VA, to Charleston, WV
3. Lake Superior
4. a. True   b. True   c. False

RM–5   Routes of Travel

1. NJ, PA, OH, IN, IL, IA, NE, WY, UT, NV, CA
2. IA: Des Moines
   NE: Lincoln
   WY: Cheyenne
   UT: Salt Lake City
   CA: Sacramento

3. Arizona
4. Jacksonville, Los Angeles
5. Tallahassee, FL, and Baton Rouge, LA
6. 8
7. Rio Grande
8. Mississippi River
9. Arkansas

RM–6   Pattern Maps I

4. (See table at top of first column.)
5.a. Texas; 6,000
  b. Eight states lost farms; 72,000 farms
7. Minnesota, Wisconsin, Iowa, Missouri, Oklahoma, Texas, Tennessee, Kentucky, Ohio
8. Central

RM–7   Pattern Maps II

1. a (copper), c (granite)
2. b (Ken)
3. a (petroleum)
4. b ($3,000,000)
5. a (fish), c (lumber)
6. a (Tatt)

7. a (mountains), b (river), d (a lake)
8. c ($5,600) (80 x 700 x $.10)
9. c (Bess)
10. b and c
11. b (forests)

RM–9   Latitude and Distance

Loocating Places on Lines of Latitude

1. B: 50°N
   C: 40°N
   D: 30°N
   E: 0° (Equator)
   F: 20°S
   G: 40°S

2. H: 65°N
   I: 45°N
   J: 25°N
   K: 12°N
   L: 2°S
   M: 25°S

Determining Distance on Lines of Latitude

1. 2,700 miles (C to D)
2. 3,105 miles (E to F)
3. 5,175 miles (G to H)

RM–11   Longitude and Distance

Locations on Lines of Longitude

C: 45°W
D: 15°E
E: 60°W
F: 52°E or 53°E
G: 45°W
I: 90°W
J: 45°W
K: 67°E or 68°E

Distances on Lines of Longitude

1,400 miles (P to Q)
700 miles (R to S)
2,100 miles (T to U)
2,800 miles (V to W)
3,500 miles (X to Y)

RM–12   Mapping a Hurricane

SOUTHEAST UNITED STATES AND THE WEST INDIES

4. Puerto Rico
5. Miami

RM–13   Locations and Time on a Mercator Map I

Combining Latitude and Longitude

1. B: 50°N–45°W
   C: 40°N–45°E
   D: 30°N–150°E
   E: 3°S (approximately)–135°W
   F: 30°S–75°W
   G: 30°S–45°E
2. Check student maps.

Determining Distance on Mercator Maps

1. 4,900 miles
2. 7,200 miles

Telling Time on the Mercator Map

30°W: 10:00 A.M.
45°E: 3:00 P.M.
150°W: 2:00 A.M.

RM–16   Map Indexes and Road Distances II

1. – Calypso; C4, 2,500–10,000
   – Cape Hope; D7, Under 1,000
   – Coppertown; D2, 2,500–10,000
   – Mountain View; B6, Under 1,000
   – Pine City; C5, 2,500–10,00
   – Point City; B2, 2,500–10,000
   – Pokeville; B4, 1000–2,500
   – Seaside; D5, 2,500–10,000
   – Silverton; C3, 2,500–10,000
   – Wolfville; A7, 2,500–10,000

2.a. 22 miles
   b. 33 miles
   c. 30 miles
   d. 42 miles
3. Dirt road
4. 1,357'
5. U.S. highway 20 and state highway 42

RM–18   Measuring Altitude II

1.a. 5,000' (approx.)
   b. 9,000' (approx.)
   c. -4,000'
   d. 3,000'–3,200' (approx.)
2.a. 6,000'
   b. 12,000'

3. 1,000' (approx.)
4. 3,000' (approx.)
5. See students' papers.
6. 2,000'–4,000'
7. See students' papers.

RM–19   Elevations Shown by Numerals and Color

1. Cutt: 0'–2,000'
   Butt: 0'–2,000'
   Putt: 2,000'–4,000'
   Rutt: 0'–2,000'
2. Deer River: 2,000'–4,000'
   Moose River: 6,000'–8,000'
   Bear River: 4,000'–6,000'
   Fox River: 6,000'–8,000'
3. Narrow coastline with high elevation; no bays or inlets
4. Fox River's source is higher than Deer River's, and Fox River has a shorter, steeper run to the ocean.
5. (The X should be drawn on the shore directly above the L in Little.)

RM–21   United States Government Topographical Maps

1.a. True
   b. True
   c. False
   d. False
   e. False
   f. False
   g. False

2. 1¾ miles
3. It's a road under construction, which makes it difficult for a large truck to traverse.

RM–22   Reading a Topographical Map

1. See students' maps.
2. – Pine tree: 150'
   – Snake: 250'
   – Water tank: 250'
   – Bird: 150'
   – Cabin: 100'
   – Shelter: 200'

3. A–B (Contours close together indicate steepness.)
4. Between 17 and 18 miles
5. Between 11 and 12 miles
6. Between 300' and 349'
7. Between 200' and 249'
8. Yes. The cabin is at a lower elevation than X is.

RM–24   Reading Polar Maps II

3. Airplane Directions
   1: West
   2: North
   3: North
   4: East
   5: North
   6: South
   7: East
   8: North
   9: South
   10: East

4. Greenland, Iceland
6. U: 50°W
   V: 80°E
   W: 130°E
   X: 170°W
   Y: 150°W
   Z: 80°W
7. 3,850 miles

RM–25   Understanding Globe Maps

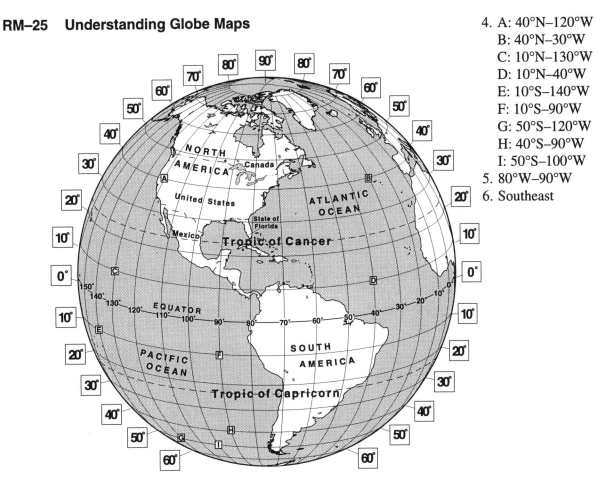

4. A: 40°N–120°W
   B: 40°N–30°W
   C: 10°N–130°W
   D: 10°N–40°W
   E: 10°S–140°W
   F: 10°S–90°W
   G: 50°S–120°W
   H: 40°S–90°W
   I: 50°S–100°W
5. 80°W–90°W
6. Southeast

Section 5: Reading and Study Skills

Reading and Study Skills (RSS)

RSS–3   Completing a Topical Outline I

WATER POLLUTION FROM SPILLED OIL

I. Causes of oil spills in oceans
  A. Leaks from ship collisions
  B. Leaks from loading/unloading
    operations
  C. Illegal clean-outs at sea
II. Causes of oil spills on land
  A. Burst oil refinery pipes
  B. Accidents at seaside docks
  C. Overturned railroad tank cars
III. Results of oil spills
  A. Expenses
    1. Lost oil
    2. Cleanup costs

  B. Spoiled seaside vacations
  C. Oil slicks
    1. Fires
    2. Boat bottoms, sides fouled
    3. Boat motors, propellers damaged
  D. Damage to animal life
    1. Fish
    2. Sea birds
    3. Otters
    4. Seals

RSS–4   Completing a Topical Outline II

VOLCANOES AND AIR POLLUTION

I. Volcano facts
  A. 500+ volcanoes worldwide
    1. Ten or more daily eruptions
    2. Eruptions pollute atmosphere
      a. Cannot be controlled, unlike
        human pollution
      b. Nature's way of creating balance
II. Philippine Islands eruption at Pinatubo
  A. June 1991
  B. Gaseous emissions
    1. Sulfuric acid gas: an earth cooler
    2. Carbon dioxide: an earth warmer

  C. Negative impact
    1. Clark Air Base ash covered
    2. Subic Naval Base evacuated
    3. 200,000 Filipinos evacuated
    4. Villages covered with ash
    5. Thousands of acres of vegetation
      destroyed
    6. More than 900 people killed
    7. Rocks destroyed property
  D. Positive result: ash fertilizer

Note: Student outlines may vary. Accept reasonably correct work.

RSS–6   Completing a Sentence Outline

THE EFFECTS OF TOPSOIL LOSS

I. River channels are affected by sedimentation deposits.
  A. The depth of water in channels decreases.
  B. Decreased water levels cause problems.
    1. Large boats cannot use channels.
    2. Flooding occurs in times of heavy rains.
    3. Property is damaged.
    4. People are drowned.
II. Sediment settles on the bottoms of lakes and reservoirs.
  A. Reservoirs' capacity is reduced.
    1. Floods can occur due to spillover.

    2. During droughts, the reservoirs may not contain enough water to prove helpful.
III. Rivers deposit soil in river mouths.
  A. Numerous negative results occur.
    1. Bays, harbors, channels, and canals become clogged.
    2. The flow of ocean currents can be altered.
    3. The force and direction of waves can be altered.
    4. Oyster beds can be covered and polluted, putting fishermen out of work.

278   *Note*: Student outlines may vary. Accept reasonably correct work.

© 1998 by John Wiley & Sons, Inc.

RSS–7   Classifying Information

Agriculture	6, 15
Climate	11, 13
Geography	3, 5, 8 (possibly 4)
Government	2, 7, 16
History	1, 4, 14
Population	9, 10
Miscellaneous	12, 17

RSS–8   Gathering and Classifying Information

Birth: 5
Family Life As a Child: 9*, 10, 13, 16, 19
Education As a Youth: 8
Experiences Through Age 21: 6, 11, 17
Experiences Age 22 to Presidency: 1, 2, 4, 7, 12, 15
As President: 3, 18, 20, 21
Death: 14, 22

---

* Could be classified as Experiences Through Age 21

RSS–11   Practice in the Main Idea/Detail Study Method

Main Ideas	Details (Names, Dates, Places, Events, New Terms, Vocabulary)
1. Americans in the RW attack British troops.	Small groups . . . Lonely places . . . "Hit and run" . . . Surprise
2. British rarely successful in pursuing Americans.	Swamp hideouts . . . British troops lost, killed, captured
3. American troops made up of many backgrounds.	Scottish, Irish, English, French, Germans, African Americans . . . Bold, brave
4. Francis Marion was an especially able leader.	Brave . . . Careful planner . . . Nickname Swamp Fox . . . Secretive

Note: "Main Ideas" and "Details" are suggested. Accept reasonably correct work.

PROBLEMS CAUSED BY POLLUTED AIR

Some costs of pollution cannot be accurately measured. It is impossible to determine the decrease in value of a great statue through corrosion caused by polluted air. How much of the value of crops is lost due to heavily polluted air? What is the price of sneezing, coughing, eye irritation, or even cancer, caused by dirty air?

Scientists, business people, and insurance companies have been able to estimate some the costs of air pollution. But notice the use of the word estimate which is only a guess. Nevertheless, following are some examples of situations and costs.

In California damage to crops from air pollutants is at least $100 million yearly. Damage to crops on a nationwide basis is thought to be about five times that much. Also, it should be realized that the millions of gallons of spray used to kill crop-damaging insects is also an air pollutant.

Pollution from factories is especially bad—in spite of the efforts to reduce the poison they spew into the air. Not all of the fuel—coal and oil—used in power plants and factories is completely burned. The unburned and partially burned fuel goes up the chimneys and into the atmosphere. Some $300 million of fuel is wasted each year in this way. But the costs don't stop there. Damage to the environment costs millions of additional dollars.

Here is an interesting example: In Syracuse, New York, the furnace in an institution broke down. The result was that about 725 pounds of soot were blown out of the chimney and deposited in the surrounding area. Damage to automobiles, clothing loss, and cleaning costs came to about $38,000. Another example has to do with automobiles. It has been estimated that $3 billion of gasoline evaporates from American automobiles each year. This would average about $30 for each automobile in the country.

All in all, it is estimated that damage due to air pollution costs about $12 billion each year to the United States alone. This averages out to about $65 per person each year.

Note: Students' underlinings, markings, etc., will vary. Accept reasonably correct work.

© 1998 by John Wiley & Sons, Inc.

RSS–18 Composing Questions As a Study Technique III

SOIL EROSION IN THE GREAT PLAINS

Questions

Weather sometimes occurs in what is called weather cycles. There may be a period of several years when the rainfall in a region is sufficient for crops to grow. This may be followed by a year or more of exceptionally light rainfall.

Weather cycles cause problems no matter where they occur, but they have been especially harmful in the Great Plains of the United States. Soon after the Civil War, about 1865, settlers in the Great Plains felt encouraged to plow and plant crops where Nature intended tall grass with deep roots to grow. They cut thick sod with plows that exposed the soil to the weather. All went well in those years when rainfall was plentiful. Crops, mostly wheat and corn, were abundant and farmers prospered. Other pioneers, hearing the good news, flocked to the region.

The "good years" for the early Great Plains farmers ended when periods of drought, or little rain, began. Because crops had been harvested and the land was uncovered, land was exposed to the weather. Added to the problem were the almost constant winds that blew over the land month after month. The winter winds were especially fierce. The absence of rain, the drying action of the winds, and the hot sun of summer made the region as dry as a desert.

The ever-blowing winds picked up soil and filled the air with dust. People placed handkerchiefs or masks over their mouths and noses to prevent dust from filling their lungs. Grains of soil piled up along fence rows, houses, and barns. Through keyholes, cracks in windows, and chimneys, winds below dust into houses.

During periods of prolonged drought farms are abandoned and people move away. When people move away, many stores and services are forced to close their doors. Few people can make a decent living in such towns and places.

In recent years, much has been learned about farming in drier areas of our country. Soil erosion is gradually being brought under control, although much remains to be done. Some of the land that should never have been plowed in the first place has been replaced with grass. Some land is planted with specially developed grains that require less water. In some years land is left to "rest" with a cover crop such as clover, which, because of its extensive root structure, holds water for a long time. Also, trees have been planted in long rows that help to break the force of the winds as they blow over the land.

Note: Students' marginal questions and notes will vary.

Questions

What is a weather cycle?
- *Periods of heavy rain followed by periods of little rain*

Where in the U.S. have weather cycles been especially harmful?

What happened to the natural grass in the G.P.?

What three things happened in the G.P. that caused soil erosion?
- *Absence of rain*
- *Winter winds*
- *Uncovered soil*

What were some of the effects of the blowing winds?

How are farms and businesses affected by droughts in the G.P.?

What four things have been done to decrease the effects of droughts?
- *Land replaced with grass*
- *Grains requiring less water*
- *Land left to "rest"*
- *Windbreaks planted*

RSS–20 Ways to Improve Memory II

1.a. <u>M</u>om <u>O</u>ven <u>R</u>oasted <u>A</u>nother <u>T</u>urkey
1.b. TORMA
2. <u>G</u>osh, <u>M</u>y <u>S</u>ister <u>B</u>roke <u>H</u>er <u>R</u>ib!
3. <u>O</u>livia <u>I</u>s <u>U</u>sing <u>A</u>ir <u>C</u>onditioning
4. <u>F</u>rank <u>A</u>nd <u>M</u>ike <u>L</u>eft <u>T</u>own

Note: All the above are suggestions.

Section 6: Reading and Its Writing Connection

Reading and Its Writing Connection (RW)

RW–2   Capitalization Practice

	Incorrect	Correct		Incorrect	Correct
1.	spanish	Spanish	17.	where	Where
2.	governor	Governor	18.	*On*	*on*
3.	Of	of	19.	sunbird	Sunbird
4.	TmA	TMA	20.	Sun	sun
5.	british	British	21.	Should be capitalized:	
6.	pretty	Pretty		• The	
7.	Cousin	cousin		• American Red Cross	
8.	Captains	captains		• Washington, D.C.	
9.	chile	Chile		• In	
10.	Of	of		• United States	
11.	Truly	truly		• Clara Barton	
12.	straits	Straits		• Civil War	
13.	god	God		• If	
14.	friday	Friday		• ARC	
15.	boulevard	Boulevard		• Gatehouse Road	
16.	if	If		• Falls Church	
				• Virginia	

RW–3   Test Your Capitalization Ability

Note: The correct version of the story is printed below. In the original story the underlined words are in error with regard to capitalization.

Jonathan and Mike were students in <u>Mrs.</u> Bonnelli's <u>fifth-grade class</u> in Valley <u>Elementary School</u>. All the students had been told by the <u>principal</u>, Mr. Grey, not to walk home through Timberland <u>Park</u> because it could be dangerous. In the <u>summer</u> the main danger is <u>snakes</u>. In the <u>fall</u> hunters roam the woods in search of <u>deer</u>. In the winter the trail through the <u>park</u> is likely to be slippery. Once, in December 1966 several children tried to cross Lake <u>of the</u> Woods. Two boys fell through the ice, but they were able to make it back to solid ground. They were frozen stiff. The <u>paramedics</u> from Woodsville came and took them to the <u>hospital</u>.

One day in the middle of <u>February</u> when there was a half day of <u>school</u> because it was Lincoln's <u>birthday</u>, Jonathan and Mike disobeyed Principal Grey. They decided to walk home through the <u>park</u>.

Mike said to Jonathan, "<u>You</u> aren't scared, are you?"

"<u>A</u> little," answered Jonathan. "We have to be careful."

Soon, they reached Big Bass <u>River</u> and began to walk along the <u>downstream</u> bank. Suddenly, Jonathan stumbled and screamed, "<u>Help</u>! <u>I'm</u> trapped!" He was caught in a <u>spring trap</u> meant to catch <u>beaver</u> and muskrats. Neither Jonathan nor Mike was strong enough to release the spring. To make things worse, the trap was chained to a <u>spruce</u> tree so that captured animals could not drag it away.

There was only one thing to do. Mike ran to a Texaco <u>gas station</u> that was about half a mile away. The people there called the <u>park</u> police, who came and released Jonathan and took him to Overlook <u>Hospital</u>.

The boys were not punished, but, as Mike said, "<u>We</u> both learned a lesson."

RW–5   Commas Affect the Sense of a Sentence

Rewritten sentences

1.a. The coach said, "The quarterback knows his football."
   b. "I won't make that mistake again, Eileen," promised Jean.
   c. "Will you give me another chance, Bob?" asked Bill.
   d. Tom asked, "Jim, how long should it take me to fly my Cessna 172 from Trenton to Rochester?"
   e. "If you go, Marie," cautioned Gina, "don't take the shortcut."
2.a. "If you help Dan, we will be grateful."
   b. "Don't forget to cook, Mary, so we can eat."
   c. "Frank, the carpenter, cautioned us to wear safety goggles."
   d. "Tommy," said my brother, "is always playing jokes."
   e. "Angela, the attractive blonde surely will win the beauty contest."

RW–6   Practice in Capitalization and Punctuation

1. I live at 60 Parsons Road, Parlin, New Jersey.
2. Mary asked, "How many people live in Ohio?"
3. "No, I can't talk to you now," Anne replied.
4. Smiling broadly, Bob accepted the certificate.
5. Tommy asked in a quiet voice, "How much does it cost?"
6. Mary heard the news. She asked, "Now what?"
7. Pete Thompson teaches biology, a freshman course at Harvard.
8. Here are the things I want for Christmas:
   a. Soccer ball
   b. Nintendo game
9. This is my address: 99 Hillview Road, Dayton, Ohio 05723
10. Here is the winner of the contest: Bates, Susan A.
11. "Pam, please pass the paper," said the teacher.
12. I think you are smart, but you shouldn't brag about it.
13. She shouted, "Great news! Our youngest son, Tim, made the team."
14. Dear Dr. Smith,

      Thanks for all of your help.

                              Yours truly,

      Pam S. Botts

RW–8   Practice in Apostrophes, Semicolons, Colons, and Dashes

1.a. father's
   b. children's
   c. players'
   d. everybody's
2.a. seashells; however,
   b. ways; it
   c. . . . knives for carving meat, spreading butter, cutting cheese; glasses for milk or juice; and miscellaneous tools, including peelers, ladles, and scrapers.
3.a. 2:05
   b. Acts 2:7
   c. All workers will attend the meeting: carpenters, plumbers, and electricians.

d. *Viking Explorers: First to the New World*

e. You are interested in only one thing: Pleasure. (***Note***: Capital P in pleasure is optional.)

4.a. I tried hard—harder than ever before—to run five miles.

b. Good grooming, clear speech, alertness—all will help when you seek a job.

5.a. "Let me show you how to do it," Bob said.

b. If you like that refrigerator, you can buy it at a reduced price.

c. He bought a used '95 Chevrolet Blazer.

d. Its color is a mixture of blue and green.

e. You're more than welcome to use the lawn mower.

f. Bob's bike has a flat tire.

g. Try it; you'll like it.

h. You may go; however, be careful.

i. The newspaper article had the following headline: *Earthquake in Nicaragua.*

RW–9   Guidelines and Practice in Syllabication

Note: Syllabications from *Webster's New Collegiate Dictionary*

- appetite: ap•pe•tite
- arithmetic: arith•me•tic
- brilliant: bril•liant
- continuation: con•tin•u•a•tion
- explanatory: ex•plan•a•to•ry
- fragmentation: frag•men•ta•tion
- gymnasium: gym•na•si•um
- justifiable: jus•ti•fi•able
- mademoiselle: ma•de•moi•selle
- misery: mis•ery
- odorless: odor•less

- opera: op•era
- particular: par•tic•u•lar
- reorganization: re•or•ga•ni•za•tion
- revolution: rev•o•lu•tion
- souvenir: sou•ve•nir
- spaghetti: spa•ghet•ti
- tremendous: tre•men•dous
- utility: util•i•ty
- vocabulary: vo•cab•u•lary
- whisper: whis•per

RW–10   Sentences That Make Sense

1. Sue, looking unhappy, sat at her desk.
2. When Mary, wearing a bathing suit, drove her car down the street, people turned and stared.
3. With a terrific swing, Bobby batted the ball out of the ballpark.
4. With greedy fingers, he picked up the scattered coins while everyone watched.
5. With brushes, Mr. Smith painted the room that he and his father had built.
6. Sitting on a stool, my teacher read from a book about life in France.
7. With a soft voice, he sang the song that his mother had written.
8. Amy and Beth, talking constantly, swam to the dock at the end of the lake.
9. She threw the ball over her shoulder to her teammate.
10. The comic, laughing hysterically, told the joke to the unimpressed audience.

RW–12   Writing Friendly Letters

1.a. 14 Ocean Rd.
  Ocean Grove, Maine 01253
  July 12, 1998

b. 15 Stump St.
  Dayton, Ohio 07658
  July 1, 1998

c. 10 Bay Road
  Seattle, Washington 08631
  May 1, 1998

d. 23 Block St.
  Fort Worth, Indiana 43657
  June 9, 1998

e. 15 Elk Drive
  Elksville, IA 54231
  April 9, 1998

2.a. Dear Bobby,

b. Dear Aunt Molly,

c. My dear friend,

d. Dear Dr. Jones,

3.a. Yours forever,

b. With love,

c. Sincerely yours,

4. Students' letters will vary.

RW–13   Writing Business Letters

Students' letters will vary.

RW–14   One Paragraph—One Main Idea

2. c: a different topic that has to do with bagpipes around the world
   e: a different topic that has to do with the uses of bagpipes
3. b, d, f, g, a, h

RW–15   Supporting Main Ideas of Paragraphs I

Students' paragraphs will vary.

RW–16   Supporting Main Ideas of Paragraphs II

1. Paragraph 1: Irrelevant sentence: "The trail runs from northern Georgia to Maine."
   Paragraph 2: Irrelevant sentence: "Tourists come by the thousands to Cape Hatteras."
2. Paragraph 1: Suggested topic: Hiking the Appalachian Trail in Autumn
   Paragraph 2: Suggested topic: The Dangerous Waters of Cape Hatteras
3. Students' paragraphs will vary.

RW–18   Using a Variety of Verbs and Adjectives

<u>**Descriptive Verbs**</u>

1.a. twittered
  b. stampeded; terrified
  c. tumbled
  d. executed
  e. swaggered
  f. swept
  g. swirled
  h. entranced
2. Students' sentences will vary.

<u>**Meaningful Adjectives**</u> (Suggestions)

1.b. charging, bucking, skittish, stubborn
  c. snow-covered, craggy, awesome, forbidding
  d. vivacious, flirtatious, graceful, poised
  e. fearsome, fierce, menacing, frightening
  f. able, brave, determined, inspiring
  g. understanding, scowling, knowledgeable, brilliant
2. wavy, dotted, uneven, faint, broad, dark, dashed, dot-dashed, wandering, short, long, crooked, ascending, descending, narrow, arching, horizontal, vertical, diagonal, imaginary, intersecting, dividing, finish, beginning, sky, horizon, stop, interrupted, telephone, clothes, latitude, longitude, power, electric, guide, tree, snow, football, fishing, railroad, country, state, time

RW–20   Reporting a Story—Newspaper Style II

2. Who? Marianne Dorcas, Thomas Duncan
   What? Confronted by a bear
   When? Saturday, August 13
   Where? Appalachian Trail, Pennsylvania
   Why? Mother bear concerned about her cubs
4. Students' articles will vary.

RW–21 Making Your Writing More Interesting I

Inverted Sentences

1.a. In the last period on Friday the test was given.
 b. In the future I will try to do my best.
 c. Torn by her decision, Olivia took the train home.
 d. I'd appreciate it if, on your way home from school, you would pick up a newspaper.
 e. In a sharp climb, the plane left the landing strip.

Combining Short Sentences

1. We went to an exciting football game that ended in a tie.
   Challenge: The exciting football game that we went to ended in a tie.
2. Although we lost altitude when the airplane's propeller stopped turning, we landed safely on a deserted stretch of highway.

RW–22 Making Your Writing More Interesting II

Combining Sentences

1. Mary's part in the play was to be a fairy who carried a wand, and Sue, who was to be a witch, rode on a broom.
2. John, who didn't know how to add fractions, was getting discouraged, but Mary, who noticed his struggles, showed him how to do them.

Quoting What People Say

Students' sentences will vary.

RW–23 Making Your Writing More Interesting III

Quotations at the Beginning of Sentences

Students' sentences will vary.

Interrupted Quotations

1. "If you want to get good grades," the teacher explained, "you have to study."
2. "You'll feel better tomorrow," Dad said, "when the exam is over."
3. "Riding a motorcycle is fun," he warned, "but you have to be careful."

RW–24 Using Words That Help Readers Visualize

(Suggestions)
1. A clattering of . . .
2. An icing of . . .
3. A blackboarding of . . .
4. A pedaling of . . .
5. An ocean of . . .
6. A sliding of . . .
7. A sticking of. . .
8. A rah! rah! of . . .
9. A soaring of . . .
10. A badge of . . .
11. A tinkling of. . .
12. A clawing of . . .
13. A drifting of . . .

RW–26 Abbreviations in Writing

1. AMA
2. SASE
3. NFL
4. BA
5. UFO
6. SPCA
7. IRS
8. CEO
9. RN
10. SRO
11. VFW
12. DAR

Section 7: Reading and Research

Reading and Research (RR)

RR–2   Practice in Alphabetizing

	Level 1	Level 2	Level 3
1.	airplane	4, 1, 2, 3	3, 1, 2, 4
2.	cot	1, 3, 2, 4	1, 3, 2, 4
3.	also	3, 4, 2, 1	1, 2, 4, 3
4.	brown	1, 3, 2, 4	4, 3, 2, 1
5.	bus	3, 2, 1, 4	4, 3, 1, 2
6.	Jones, Andy	4, 2, 3, 1	1, 2, 3, 4
7.	August	2, 3, 4 ,1	4, 3, 2, 1
8.	Jupiter	2, 4, 3, 1	3, 2, 1, 4
9.	Buick	4, 2, 1, 3	2, 3, 1, 4
10.	lettuce	1, 2, 4, 3	1, 4, 3, 2

RR–3   Using the Table of Contents

9, 6, 8, 5, 1, 2, 12, 4, 10, 8, 8, 7, 3, 8, 11

RR–5   Using Indexes

1. p. 36
2. p. 45
3. p. 112
4. p. 45
5. pp. 173–175
6. p. 92
7. p. 2
8. p. 160, and/or p. 222, and/or p. 158
9. pp. 3–19
10. p. 188
11. 6 pages
12. Recreation
13. No

RR–6   Dictionary Guide Words and Multiple Definitions

Guidewords in Dictionaries

2. front, frisk, frost, frolic, fragile, freight
3. publish–pulley

Activity

a. N
b. A
c. V
d. N
e. V
f. V
g. V

RR–7   Using the Library Card Catalog

1.a. Walker, John (10)
  b. Botts, Gary (1)
2. *All About Planets* (1), *The Last of the Mohicans* (5)
3. Caves (1), Oceans (6), Zebras (10)
4.a. The Story of a Whale
  b. Miller, Alfred G.
  c. 114 pages
  d. Action Press
  e. 1964
  f. Helen Damson
  g. C599M

RR–8 Using Encyclopedias I (Instructor)

1. omnivorous
2. Richard Stockton, John Hart, Abraham Clark, John Witherspoon, Francis Hopkinson
3. Indian, Pacific, Atlantic
4. Mountain bluebird
5. Andrew Jackson
6. 50.72 miles
7. Woodrow Wilson
8. Mad Anthony Wayne
9. Monongahela, Allegheny
10. Pennsylvania

RR–9 Using Encyclopedias II

1.
a. 5
b. 16
c. 4
d. 15
e. 4
f. 1
g. 16
h. 17
i. 16
j. 2
k. 10

2.
a. 4, 7 (*Note*: 10 is also a possibility)
b. 12, 6
c. 12, 8
d. 5, 6
e. 7, 11
f. 4, 11 (*Note*: 3 is also a possibility)
g. 2, 1 (*Note*: 10 is also a possibility)
h. 6, 3
i. 10, 7
j. 1, 14
k. 1, 2

3.
a. 2
b. 14
c. 10
d. 11

RR–11 Basic Reference Books

1. 5
2. 1
3. 4
4. 8
5. 3
6. 7
7. 2
8. 6
9. 8
10. 2
11. 7
12. 4
13. 1
14. 5

RR–12 Using Various Reference Books

1. Who was Sir Walter Raleigh?
2. What is Montana?
3. What are bagpipes?
4. What are Spain and France?
5. What is a candlestick?
6. What is Harvard?
7. What is Vermont?
8. What is Mars?
9. What is Fort McHenry?
10. What is the speed of sound?
11. What is the *Maine*?
12. What is Tasmania?
13. What is graphology?

RR–13   Locating Interesting United States Facts (Instructor)

INTERESTING UNITED STATES FACTS			
Item	**Name**	**Location**	**Detail**
Largest state	Texas	--------------------	Square miles: 656,424
Smallest state	Rhode Island	--------------------	Square miles: 1,545
Highest mountain	Mt. McKinley	Alaska	Height: 20,320'
Lowest point	Death Valley	California	Feet below sea level: -282'
Last state to enter the U.S.A.	Hawaii	--------------------	Date: August 21, 1959
First state to enter Union	Delaware	--------------------	Date: December 7, 1787
Tallest building	Sears Tower	Chicago, IL	Height: 1,454'
Largest indoor stadium	Superdome	New Orleans, LA	Seating for conventions: 97,365
Longest river (not combined)	Mississippi	--------------------	Length in miles: 2,348 (+ or - 10)
State with most counties	Texas	--------------------	Number of counties: 254
State with least counties	Delaware	--------------------	Number of counties: 3
Roller coaster, tallest	Superman: The Escape	Valencia, CA	Height: 415'
Largest lake totally in U.S.	Lake Michigan	--------------------	Square miles: 22,300
Deepest lake	Crater Lake	Oregon	Depth: 1,932' (+ or - 20')
Northernmost city	Point Barrow	Alaska	Latitude: 71°N
Highest waterfall drop	Feather Falls	California	Drop: 640'

RR–14   Interviewing a Person for a News Story

Students' choices

RR–16   Survey of Knowledge About Air and Air Pollution

Answers: B, D, C, D, A, B, D, B, C, D

NOTES